UNMARRIED COUPLES
WITH CHILDREN

UNMARRIED COUPLES WITH CHILDREN

PAULA ENGLAND AND KATHRYN EDIN

EDITORS

Russell Sage Foundation • New York

The Russell Sage Foundation

Library of Congress Cataloging-in-Publication Data

Unmarried couples with children / edited by Paula England and Kathryn Edin.
    p. cm.
    Includes bibliographical references and index.
    ISBN 978-0-87154-285-4 (alk. paper)
    1. Unmarried couples—United States. 2. Unmarried mothers—United States. 3. Unmarried fathers—United States. 4.
Single-parents—United States. I. England, Paula. II. Edin, Kathryn, 1962– III. Title.

    HQ803.5.U66 2007
    306.84'1—dc22

2007009607

Text design by Suzanne Nichols.

RUSSELL SAGE FOUNDATION
112 East 64th Street, New York, New York 10021
10 9 8 7 6 5 4 3 2 1

Contents

About the Authors

Kathryn Edin is Professor of Public Policy and Management at the John F. Kennedy School of Government at Harvard University and Faculty Associate at the Population Studies Center at the University of Pennsylvania.

Paula England is professor of sociology at Stanford University.

Amy Claessens is a Ph.D. candidate in human development and social policy at Northwestern University.

Mimi Engel is a Ph.D. candidate at Northwestern University's program in human development and social policy.

Christina M. Gibson-Davis is an assistant professor at the Terry Sanford Institute of Public Policy, Duke University.

Heather D. Hill will receive her Ph.D. in human development and social policy from Northwestern University, and is a visiting scholar at the Taubman Center for Public Policy at Brown University.

Kathryn D. Linnenberg is an assistant professor of sociology at Beloit College.

Katherine A. Magnuson is an assistant professor of social work and a research affiliate of the Institute for Policy Research at the University of Wisconsin, Madison.

Lindsay M. Monte is a doctoral candidate in Northwestern University's program in human development and social policy.

Joanna Reed is a Ph.D. candidate in sociology at Northwestern University.

Emily Fitzgibbons Shafer is a Ph.D. candidate in the Department of Sociology at Stanford University.

PART I

INTRODUCTION

Chapter 1

Unmarried Couples with Children: Hoping for Love and the White Picket Fence

PAULA ENGLAND AND KATHRYN EDIN

ONE IN three babies born in the United States today have unmarried parents (Carlson, McLanahan, and England 2004), up from about one in twenty (5 percent) in 1960 (Moore 1995; McLanahan 2004; Wu and Wolfe 2001). The lower couples are on most dimensions of socioeconomic advantage, the more likely they are to be unmarried when their children are born (Ellwood and Jencks 2004; Moore 1995). Thus, if we are to understand today's low-income couples and families, we need to study the relationships of couples who have children outside marriage. This volume reports on such a study, devised to provide rich qualitative detail about the relationships of poor and near-poor couples who share nonmarital births, focusing on their circumstances, behavior, and beliefs. The chapters address a variety of questions. What were the circumstances surrounding the pregnancy? What are couples' relationships like in terms of affection, companionship, and conflicts before, around, and in the several years after the birth? What do the parents think about cohabitation and marriage? What breaks up their relationships? How involved are fathers with economic provision and direct care of their children while they are living with the baby's mother and, in cases of breakup, after they break up?

Few of these questions would be relevant if most unmarried fathers were long gone from the mothers' lives by the time of the birth. Nothing, however, could be further from the truth. A national survey of nonmarital births in twenty large urban areas, the Fragile Families and Child Wellbeing Study, found that 82 percent of unmarried parents were romantically involved with the other parent when their baby was born, 48 percent were living together at the time of the birth, and 76 percent of fathers visited the hospital to see the baby. Of mothers romantically involved with the father at the birth, 78 percent of the cohabitors and 49 percent of those not living together said they saw at least a good or almost certain chance that the two would marry sometime in the future (all of these are mothers' reports, from Carlson and McLanahan 2002). Fathers are even more likely than mothers to predict that they will marry their partner eventually (Shafer 2006).

With the vast majority still romantically involved and about half cohabiting at their child's birth, most of these couples thus form a two-parent family of sorts despite being unmarried. Yet the precarious situation of these families, economically and relationally, led Ron Mincy (1994) to coin the term *fragile families* for what was clearly a growing population.[1] Although hopes of marrying and raising the child together are typically high at the time of birth, that is not what usually unfolds. Among the approximately half of nonmarital births in which parents are cohabiting at the birth, Fragile Families data show that 46 percent have broken up and only 27 percent are married to each other five years after the baby is born. Among the approximately 30 percent of unmarried parents who are romantically involved but not cohabiting when the baby is born, 77 percent have broken up and only 7 percent are married to each other five years later.[2]

Our qualitative study of 48 unmarried couples who shared a nonmarital birth in 2000 is embedded in the Fragile Families study, which sampled births in hospitals in 20 cities, interviewing both parents where possible.[3] We drew the couples for our study from among the couples in the larger survey in three of the 20 cities. We conducted a series of in-depth qualitative interviews with these parents over a period of about four years after the birth. The papers in this volume reflect analysis of the rich qualitative interview data, supplemented by quantitative assessments from the Fragile Families data. In this chapter we first describe how the data were collected. We then highlight a few key findings of each chapter. Finally, we overview themes that emerge from the papers taken as a whole, noting commonalities between findings in this volume and those in earlier qualitative studies of low income families throughout the century.

The TLC3 Study

Our Time, Love, and Cash among Couples with Children project (TLC3) is a four-year, in-depth qualitative study embedded within the Fragile Families and Child Wellbeing Study (Fragile Families), a nationally representative birth cohort study of approximately 3,700 unmarried couples who had a baby near the turn of the century and a comparison sample of 1,200 married couples. Births were sampled from seventy-five hospitals in twenty large cities throughout the United States. Both mothers and fathers were interviewed shortly after the child's birth and reinterviewed when the child was one, three, and five years old. When weighted, the Fragile Families sample is representative of all births to parents in cities with populations greater than 200,000.

A group of researchers, including Kathryn Edin (as principal investigator) and Paula England, devised the TLC3 as a qualitative study embedded in the Fragile Families study.[4] When choosing sites for its sample, we chose three of the Fragile Families cities that varied in size, economic conditions, and social policy climates. Graduate students from Northwestern and Columbia universities were dispatched to the maternity wards of one hospital in each of these cities—New York, Milwaukee, and Chicago—to await the birth of babies. In the spring and early summer of 2000, these TLC3 interviewers worked side by side with the Fragile Families researchers in these hospitals, recruiting new mothers and fathers for the Fragile Families Survey, conducting the baseline Fragile Families Survey, and offering those mothers and fathers still involved in romantic relationships the opportunity to participate in the TLC3 study as well.

For the Fragile Families survey, interviewers recruited all mothers who gave birth in sampled hospitals when participants were being recruited. In the three hospitals from which we drew the TLC3 sample, interviewers recruited a stratified random sample limited to couples romantically involved at the birth (and a few other ways that Emily Shafer describes in the final chapter of this volume). Like the survey, we oversampled unmarried births and created targets to ensure representation of whites, African Americans, and Latinos.

The most important sampling decision was that couples had to be romantically involved at the birth to be included, which, as the Fragile Families study indicates, more than 80 percent of parents sharing a nonmarital birth are. Because our focus was on couple dynamics and what happened to father involvement if the couple broke up later, we wanted to start from an intact couple. Married couples were included to provide a basis for comparison, but we recruited approximately twice as many unmarried couples because they were our target of interest. We ended up with twenty-seven married and forty-eight unmarried couples in the sample. Among the unmarried couples, thirty-seven were cohabiting and eleven were romantically involved but not living together when the baby was born.

The TLC3 sample was also restricted to couples who had reported household incomes of less than $75,000 in the previous year. However, very few came even close to the ceiling. The average household income of cohabiting couples was $22,500. The average earnings of the unmarried cohabiting fathers in our sample in the year before the birth was $17,500, and those of unmarried fathers who were not cohabiting even lower, $12,500. Twenty-nine percent of fathers and 26 percent of mothers had neither a GED nor a high school degree, and few had any college. Thus, like unmarried parents nationwide, this is a very disadvantaged group (see chapter 12 for this and other descriptive statistics on our sample, in comparison to the larger Fragile Families sample). Throughout the volume, we will refer to TLC3 couples and unmarried parents in general as typically low income. One way to see the extent of this socioeconomic disadvantage is to compare TLC3 couples to all couples, married and cohabiting, who had had a baby the year before the 2000 census, the same year our TLC3 couples had their baby. Taking all census couples with a new baby in the last year, average household income was $51,650, more than twice that of TLC3 couples. The personal earnings of the fathers in the census households was $32,000, much more than the $22,500 earned by the cohabiting TLC3 fathers. Only 16 percent of mothers and 17 percent of fathers in these census households had less than a high school degree, much lower than the 26 and 29 percent of TLC3 parents.[5]

Interviews with the seventy-five couples recruited into the TLC3 sample began two to three months after the child was born, when the euphoria of birth had faded somewhat, but couples' hopes were still high. We followed the mother, father, and child through the child's fourth birthday. We engaged parents, both as a couple and individually, in a series of focused, in-depth, qualitative interviews, regardless of whether they stayed together or broke up. If couples were not willing to be interviewed together after breakup, we still interviewed each parent individually. Interviews were conducted shortly after the birth, in 2000, and when the baby was approximately one, two, and four years old. When parents took on new romantic partners, we interviewed the new couple as well, with both individual and couple interviews. In waves three and four, when the baby was two and four years old, we videotaped the entire couple interview, and ended the interview with a couple discussion, in which couples were asked to discuss two issues they disagreed on after the interviewer left the room.

In all, the study produced roughly 1,200 pages of transcript for each of the families of the seventy-five focal children, in addition to several hours of videotape. Each chapter in this volume makes use of the longitudinal nature of the rich qualitative TLC3 data; one also draws from the videotaped discussions. Several also draw from Fragile Families survey data. Although the chapters vary in terms of which subsample of TLC3 couples was appropriate to the question asked, most focus on all or a subset of the unmarried parents, though some include married parents as well.[6] To preserve confidentiality, each respondent was given a pseudonym used across chapters so that readers can easily follow a specific respondent by name.

The Chapters

In wave four, TLC3 collected detailed fertility histories for all of the parents surveyed at baseline and any new social parents living in the household of the focal child. In chapter 2, Kathryn Edin and her colleagues analyze each nonmarital pregnancy that our original sample of unmarried parents ever had—whether it was the focal TLC3 child, a previous conception with the same or a different partner, or a conception occurring after the birth that brought them into our study. Pregnancies ending in miscarriage and abortion were included. Although a small number of the conceptions are planned (12 percent), and roughly a fifth occur due to what parents report as technical contraceptive failure, most pregnancies are in neither of these categories. Those that were planned were almost universally to couples in serious relationships. Roughly a quarter were the result of inconsistent contraception, most of these to couples in serious relationships as well. These couples often use contraception consistently when their relationship is new, but let their vigilance lapse when the relationship becomes more serious. Roughly another 18 percent are described as neither planned nor unplanned. These couples are almost always in a serious relationship and want children, or more children, together eventually. Unsure that their current circumstances are ideal, their ambivalence leads them to leave conception to chance. The remaining pregnancies, approximately a quarter, are those that were unplanned, but occurred when couples were not contracepting. Many of these are in the context of casual relationships and high-risk lifestyles. These are the couples for whom children are often genuinely unwanted both before and after the fact as well as the category for which abortion is most often considered and pursued.

This analysis identifies two underlying dimensions affecting nonmarital fertility. First is a continuum of intentionality and highlights the reality that many couples are somewhere in between a strong positive or negative desire to have a child now. The clearest predictor of how much couples want children is the seriousness of their relationships—even within the nonmarital context. A second dimension is efficacy. About a quarter of the conceptions occur to those who really didn't want a child at the time but somehow didn't align their contraceptive behavior with their goals. A majority of these were couples with high-risk lifestyles who are in casual relationships.

In chapter 3, Paula England and Emily Shafer use data from the couple conflict discussion administered in waves three and four. Interviewers began by asking the pair to identify the two most important issues they didn't see eye to eye on and to articulate each side of the issue. After this, the interviewer asked the couple to talk about the issue and try to come to a resolution they could each be at least somewhat happy with. The video camera continued to run when the interviewer left the room for ten minutes. Based on their analysis of the videotaped discussion, England and Shafer identified four major issues that came up most often in these intact couples—emotional attention and companionship, child discipline, housework, and money issues. The chapter focuses on the two that occur most frequently: women wanting more emotional attention and men wanting stricter child discipline. Earlier literature suggested that only in the middle class do women expect emotional intimacy and shared activities with men. This, however, has clearly changed. The women in our poor and near-poor sample complained bitterly that their partners didn't listen to them or talk to them enough, and didn't spend quality time with them. Women also complained about men spending time on the street or with male friends or kin rather than with them. Child discipline was another hot and gendered issue. Men generally wanted a stricter regime than women. Either the father wanted the mother to run a tighter ship while doing the child minding that they both agreed was her job or the father wanted to discipline children (especially sons) more harshly than the mother thought was appropriate.

Christina Gibson-Davis considers aspirations for marriage among those who have nonmarital births in chapter 4. Starting with the first wave of interviews, we asked couples, both alone and together, whether they saw themselves getting married at some point, and what it would take for them to decide to marry. To put this chapter in context, recall that more than 80 percent of couples in the Fragile Families sample who had a nonmarital birth were still romantically involved at the time of the birth. Most of these talked about aspirations to marry the partner. Although some problems with the relationship were mentioned as holding couples back, the almost universal response by men and women to our questions about what it would take for them to decide to marry was that they were waiting to meet certain economic standards. Gibson-Davis focused on the economic bar because 83 percent of couples named it in the interview slightly after the birth. The idea that couples need to be able to afford to set up a household and support a child before getting married has of course long been traditional. What is interesting about today's unmarried couples who have had a child together is that they articulate this standard, even when, like most of our TLC3 respondents, they have already started living together. Indeed, couples who had not married by four years after their baby's birth, but had not broken up either, still clung to this bar as a major reason they had not yet married. Gibson-Davis operationalizes getting above the bar as meeting the following criteria: household income increased at least 10 percent by four years after the birth, both members are working or going to school (or if one was at home, it was voluntary homemaking rather than unemployment), neither received any public assistance, they did not need a loan from family or friends to make ends meet, they were able to pay their bills each month, and they did not describe their economic situation as unstable or shaky. Although those who married did not usually cite economics as the reason they wed, 78 percent of those who met the bar did marry and only 19 percent of those who did not meet it had married four years after the birth. The largest group neither met the bar nor married. Gibson-Davis started the project thinking that perhaps articulating the economic bar to marriage was simply a convenient excuse for those who didn't want to marry for other reasons. However, the huge differential convinced her that finances are a real constraint to marriage among low-income unmarried parents.

American couples in committed romantic relationships overwhelmingly expect sexual exclusivity regardless of their marital status, research shows, though infidelity is higher among unmarried than married couples. Studies also show that women cheat far less than men (Laumann et al. 1994). In chapter 5, Heather Hill examines the events leading up to and following each incidence of infidelity among unmarried TLC couples. More than half (58 percent) experienced at least one instance over the course of their relationship. Most of the time it was only men who cheated, but in a third of the instances in which the man did, the woman cheated as well. Only rarely was the woman the sole culprit. Incidents of infidelity often occurred around events that brought the future of the relationship into question, such as the incarceration of one partner or a major argument. Chronic infidelity often broke couples up, whereas isolated incidents did not, though relationship quality in the aftermath of the incident was sometimes low. Sexual jealousy and sexual mistrust are even more pervasive than reports of actual infidelity. Approximately 75 percent of couples reported these problems. Indeed, sexual jealousy, whether based on a real incident of infidelity or not, is sometimes a trigger for violence.

In chapter 6, Joanna Reed looks at how and why TLC3 couples broke up, by chronicling the process of breakups in qualitative detail and by comparing those unmarried couples who broke up to those who stayed together (whether married at the end of the study or not). Respondents report infidelity, arguing, verbal and physical abuse, lack of love and attention, and substance abuse as primary reasons for their breakups; often those who broke up had multiple problems. Relationship quality is central, and men's bad behavior is key. Indeed, it is almost always women who initiate the breakup and the men who move out. Interestingly, economic problems are never central to these stories. Economics may be a reason to hold off on marriage, but no one discussed it as a reason for breakup. The one economic factor that differentiates those who broke up is that they didn't pool their money initially, but retained some separation between his and her money. Not surprisingly, couples who broke up had much worse relationships at the outset, when their baby was born. Indeed, it appears that the bad relationships were usually bad from the beginning. Over half the breakups that occurred within four years actually happened in the baby's first year.

We take an in-depth look at fathering in chapter 7. Limiting herself to couples who lived together (some married, the others as cohabitors), Kathryn Linnenberg examines the range of father involvement and how it varies with relationship quality. Psychologists studying married couples have proposed that the quality of parents' relationship spills over into men's parenting—that if the father's relationship with the mother is angry or distant, he often withdraws emotionally from the children. Linnenberg concludes that relationship quality affects father involvement, but not in the straightforward way suggested by spillover theory. Consistent with spillover, the worst couple relationships have least and lowest quality father involvement. However, the most involved fathers—the ones who split the care work 50–50 with their partners—are the unemployed, cohabiting fathers in the intermediate category of relationship quality, which Linnenberg dubs "happy with some problems." The care work done by these fathers is appreciated by the mother, but the men have economic and behavioral problems that strain their relationships. Their high involvement in parenting results in large part from unemployment. The happiest and most stable relationships had some men who rivaled women in their care work (the "family-first fathers"), but the general pattern was a one in which the care work was seen as the mother's responsibility and the fathers specialized in play and helping the mother. It appears that men's unemployment coupled with women's employment is as important a determinant of father's care work as relationship quality.

Linnenberg also offers a portrait of what fathers do when they interact with their children. In most cases, the father's primary role is to serve as a playmate. When fathers do other types of care work, they often view themselves as helpers, and mothers view them this way as well. Mothers therefore often carefully scrutinize and closely supervise their work. The higher the quality of the relationship, however, the less fathers are scrutinized and supervised.

In chapter 8, Lindsay Monte looks at a special kind of parenting—nonmarital stepparenting. She profiles those unmarried cohabiting couples where at least one had a child by a previous partner, a common scenario today. Monte found that parents legitimated the stepfather role by talking about how it takes more than blood to make a father—that time, love, and money count more. This leads to the distinction between a biological father and the man who takes responsibility for the functions of being a father, an earned status. The problems that seem to emanate from the stepparent situation are largely jealous tensions. When the father goes to see his other children, his new partner is jealous of the time away from her and her children. Both men and women are sometimes suspicious that dealing with an ex with whom one has had children will lead to romantic or sexual reengagement. Perhaps the most significant finding is which couples got married—it was those in which the woman's previous partner was no longer an active father to her children and the man was no longer involved with any of his children who lived with their mother. This poses a dilemma. It appears that a good way to encourage marriage among these couples is to encourage fathers to be deadbeat dads to their former children, hardly a compelling policy recommendation.

The Fragile Families survey shows that at the time of a child's birth, most unmarried fathers are dedicated to staying involved with their child, and most of their children's mothers are committed to that goal as well (Carlson and McLanahan 2002). Yet surveys have consistently shown that as children whose parents are separated grow older, most fathers disconnect, particularly those who were never married to the mother. In chapter 9, Amy Claessens considers two sides of the story of how fathers become uninvolved, offering a rare "he said, she said" account. Fathers blame mothers and charge them with gatekeeping, and mothers say they have good reasons to limit fathers' access to the children. Claessens investigates both claims. Among couples unmarried at the birth and separated by the time of our interview when the child was four, 72 percent report at least some gatekeeping. Gatekeeping does not always preclude father involvement, however, because nearly six in ten fathers still saw their child in the last two months. In cases where no gatekeeping is evident, mothers say they value the role the father plays in the child's life and they are more reliant on the fathers for childcare.

Mothers offer three main justifications for their gatekeeping: previous inconsistency in visitation, safety concerns about the dangers associated with the father's lifestyle (usually his drug or alcohol use), and the inability of the parents to get along after the breakup. Although one might assume that safety concerns would prompt mothers to completely shut fathers out, this was not so. In fact, fathers whose contact was limited for these reasons alone often had some degree of contact, though mothers controlled when the contact occurred. These mothers usually arranged for the fathers to visit in the mother's home. Fathers on house arrest, however, could entertain the children in their own homes because the mother felt confident that the father couldn't get into trouble. It was when the two parents just couldn't get along that fathers were most likely to be shut out completely, sometimes by a restraining order. Some fathers claimed that these had been obtained fraudulently. Most interesting, however, is that most mothers who gatekeep their children's fathers out have repartnered, which strains an already tenuous co-parenting relationship. This suggests that maternal repartnering, as well as poor couple dynamics and paternal behavior, may well play a significant role in declining father involvement over time.

In chapter 10, Katherine Magnuson and Christina Gibson-Davis examine whether fathers support children from previous relationships, and if so, how. They consider formal and informal child support arrangements and compare the life circumstances of fathers who are contributing to fathers who are not. They find little evidence of deadbeat dads—fathers who could support their children but choose to not do so. However, this is partly because child support systems are now stringent enough that those who are employed have support automatically garnished from their wages; we don't know how many of these fathers would have paid in a less stringent regime. For those not paying, mothers and fathers point to incarceration, unemployment, and a lack of resources as reasons for the low levels of support. However, fathers often portray their contributions in a much more positive light than their female ex-partners do. Although the causal order is unclear, most mothers without support from fathers are relying on a new partner to help provide for their families by the study's end.

One of the unique aspects of TLC3 is that it is that it is embedded in a larger survey. Because the qualitative interviews address many of the same topics the Fragile Families survey does, but more in depth, the two sources of data can be used to assess the consistency of information gathered two ways. In chapter 11, Mimi Engel compares responses in six areas of overlap, including the degree to which respondents believe their partners express affection or love, the level of understanding and encouragement between partners, conflict over finances, physical conflicts, conflicts relating to drinking and drug use, and an overall assessment of relationship quality. Obviously, all of these items are somewhat sensitive, so one might expect inconsistent reporting. Some are arguably more sensitive than others. In general, Engel found a relatively high level of consistency regardless of topic. Bivariate analyses show that women and those with more education are more consistent in their reports across the two studies, though these differences often escape statistical significance.

Today's Fragile Families and Yesterday's Low-Income Families

How do the findings of this volume compare with qualitative research on low-income families from past decades? Take first the nonmarital pregnancies that Edin and her colleagues examine. In earlier decades, it was common for unmarried low-income couples to find the woman pregnant out of wedlock, just as our unmarried sample members did, though rates have probably gone up. Intercourse, however, typically would not have started until relationships were more serious (Hollingshead 1949), and on discovering a pregnancy, white couples at least were far more likely to have a shotgun marriage (Rubin 1976). Among blacks in some parts of the old South, it might have occasioned a common-law marriage, because few black communities upheld the idea of forced legal marriage (Powdermaker 1939/1969). Within or outside of marriage, though, having children only when planned has long been more frequent in the middle class than in the working and lower classes (Rainwater 1960, 1965). As it was decades ago, it is common today for low-income couples to get pregnant without explicitly planning for it, and for pregnancy to escalate the seriousness of their relationship. Premarital sex undoubtedly increased with the sexual revolution of the 1960s and 1970s, but so did the use of contraception. One thing contributing to the increase in nonmarital births is the reduction in how often pregnancies prompt couples to move to marriage or to stable common-law arrangements (Moore 1995; Akerlof, Yellen, and Katz 1996). The extent to which the sexual revolution reduced shotgun marriages underscores the degree to which these marriages in earlier eras reflected the shame entailed in the revelation of premarital sex, a shame that was heaped particularly on the women.

Several papers in the volume point to change in the meaning of marriage over time (Cherlin 2004, Edin and Kefalas 2005). Gibson-Davis shows that, as long as they are still romantically involved, unmarried parents almost always see marriage to the coparent as something to aspire to, but they don't want to marry until a certain economic bar is met, even when they are already living together and have a child together. By contrast, in the older ethnographic studies it is clear that, among whites, one almost had to be married and have children to "count" as a social adult (Morland 1958). Today, marriage is seen as more optional, but its symbolic value has increased (Cherlin 2004; Edin and Kefalas 2005). People feel that marriage is not culturally appropriate unless the couple's relational and economic status are above a certain threshold (Edin and Kefalas 2005; Gibson-Davis, Edin, and McLanahan 2006). Rising emotional standards for marriage are a continuation of a long-term trend; Stephanie Coontz (2005) argues that the trend dates all the way back to the love revolution of the eighteenth century. In the early twentieth century, Robert and Helen Lynd (1929) saw the idea that marriage should be based only on romantic love to be "new." Although this may have been the ideal, ethnographies of the 1950s and 1960s pointed out how little companionship and shared leisure there was between spouses (Bott 1957; Gans 1962), and how, after early marriages (that couples were often catapulted into by pregnancy), women often resigned themselves to little mutuality and considered themselves lucky if their men brought home most of their paycheck and didn't beat them (Komarovsky and Phillips 1962; Rubin 1976). Today's low-income women, black, white, and Hispanic, clearly have much higher relationship standards. In analyzing reported couple conflicts in this volume, England and Shafer found that women's top complaint was that men didn't talk to them enough, show enough affection, and spend enough quality time with them.

The rising emotional and economic standards for marriage have left many low-income couples in the situation where neither their relationships nor their budgets meet their own standards for marriage. It is probably not that today's relationships among low-income couples are worse than those of earlier decades, though the advent of mass incarceration and crack cocaine may be taking more of a toll. Part of the problem is that the earnings of men in the bottom half of the class hierarchy have fallen in relative and absolute terms since the 1970s (Bernhardt et al. 2001). But this explains only a small fraction of the retreat from or delay of marriage (Ellwood and Jencks 2004). Poor men, particularly poor black men, have always been unable to support a family in the normatively approved style. As modest as the standards of the couples we study here seem, they are undoubtedly much higher than those held by their counterparts decades back (Edin and Kefalas 2005). In the past, at least among whites, it was other strong forces that pulled couples into and kept them in marriages even when relationships were awful and conditions poor—the need to be married to be a "regular" adult, the moral crisis of reputation that nonmarital pregnancies caused for women, and women's economic dependence on men. These patterns were less true for blacks; there was a tradition of durable common-law marriages in some areas (Drake and Cayton 1945/1962; Du Bois 1967; Powdermaker 1939/1969), and the extreme precariousness of black men's earning power made black women less economically dependent on their men than white women were (Drake and Cayton 1945/1962; Powdermaker 1939/1969).

Older qualitative portraits of low-income families, black and white, paint relationships as riddled with conflict, often violent, and prone to breakup (Du Bois 1899/1967; Frazier 1939/1966; Howell 1973). There have long been class and race differences in divorce rates and in rates of less formal consensual unions over marriage, and these differences clearly remain and have even increased (Raley and Bumpass 2003; McLanahan 2004). In the older literature, several explanations are offered, somewhat speculatively, for why relationships among the lower classes seemed less happy and more prone to break up. One thesis, implicit in many studies, is simply that economic deprivation puts strain on marriages and the individuals in them. Housing is crowded, dreams are unfulfilled, debates over how to spend money are more difficult when there isn't enough, and women may feel that men have failed in their role as provider (Frazier 1939/1966; Drake and Cayton 1945/1962; Leibow 1967).

Other authors focus less on the level of family income and more on the lack of men's economic dominance over women as a problem for relationship stability, especially among blacks (among whites, men's incomes are often enough to keep women at home). One version of this argument is Gary Becker's (1991) view that specialization is what makes marriage rational. Some of the older qualitative studies seem to take this view. They also take the view that it violates strongly held norms for men not to be the economic heads of the family, and this is somehow bad for marriages (Lewis 1965; Hannerz 1969; Drake and Cayton 1945/1962; Powdermaker 1939/1969). Indeed, reading these old pre-feminist studies, it is striking that the notion that egalitarian marriages might be more satisfying for women, and that lack of mutuality might be the problem, seems not to have occurred to the authors.

Another possible explanation for lower quality and less stable relationships among low-income individuals posits that, compared to growing up middle class, growing up disadvantaged is less conducive to developing efficacy. Efficacy, as Edin and her colleagues use the term in chapter 2, refers to the ability to organize one's behavior into sequences of action that further one's goal, even when this requires doing things that are onerous in the short term. Growing up in chaotic or dangerous conditions may make it hard to believe that future-oriented behaviors will succeed, and hard or even futile to engage in long-term planning. Edin et al. argue that about a quarter of the unplanned pregnancies they observed might reflect a lack of efficacy—there was no clear intention to conceive, even ambivalently, yet no contraception was used. Efficacy probably affects earnings and relationship stability as well.

Another view of why informal unions, breakups, and divorces are more common among the disadvantaged involves men—both black and white—"doing gender" in compensation for their low earning power, either relative to their wives or to other men. In this view, when men can't provide much money, they feel a heightened need to display some socially defined marker of masculinity. They then enact masculinity through violence (sometimes toward women), through sexual conquest (which involves infidelity to partners), or by hanging out and posturing with the guys (Drake and Cayton 1945/1962; Leibow 1967; Anderson 1989, 1990; Edin and Kefalas 2005). It is as if there are two ways to "be a man," being the legitimated economic provider and being the less legitimated tough guy nonetheless culturally coded as masculine. Being seen as masculine trumps legitimacy when the two can't be combined, a situation faced by poor but not by middle-class men. These arguments anticipate the later intersectionality perspective on race, class, and gender (Collins 1990), which sees gender enacted differently in social locations that differ because of race and class. The papers in this volume support this view in some ways, and not in others. Infidelity by married and cohabiting men is discussed in many of the older studies of low-income families (Powdermaker 1939/1969; Lewis 1965; Drake and Cayton 1945/1962; Morland 1958; Hannerz 1969; Rainwater 1970; Howell 1973; Kurz 1995), and Hill's analysis in chapter 5 finds men's cheating and women's and men's jealousy a big issue in low-income couples. Whereas some of the old studies suggest that infidelity by men was accepted if it remained discreet (Powdermaker 1939/1969; Hannerz 1969; Rainwater 1970), in our study, women were not found to be willing to stay with men who were chronically unfaithful, even outside of marriage. This is an example of the rising expectations for relationships. Stories of the breakups that Joanna Reed analyzes in chapter 6 are full of reports of men's violence and infidelity, with women eventually putting the men out. Amy Claessens's account in chapter 9 of mothers who are gatekeeping men out of seeing their children depicts many of them as claiming to do so because of the men's involvement in crime, drugs, or the street. Several chapters in this volume find that women resent men spending time on the street with their buddies rather than at home with them, a theme in earlier ethnographies (Gans 1962; Hannerz 1969; LeMasters 1975; Halle 1984). All this seems consistent with the compensatory gender display argument.

However, some of our findings are not consistent with this compensatory gender display perspective. Applying the argument to housework, Julie Brines (1994) offered survey evidence that men whose earnings are much lower than those of their wives do less housework than those who earn about the same as their wives.[7] Rather than thinking they need to do more housework if they aren't contributing money, as some other theories would predict, men whose masculinity is threatened on one front shore it up on another by eschewing housework (Brines 1994). This is not, however, what Linnenberg finds in her analysis of father involvement in the intact relationships (chapter 7, this volume). The highest involvement in child care was among fathers who were unemployed, because they had the time available to provide it.

Parallel to increasing expectations for relationships and marriage are increasing notions of appropriate father involvement. Married fathers in all social classes spend more time with their children than previously (McLanahan 2004). This new norm is in a tension with the increase in nonmarital childbearing and the high rate of breakup of unmarried couples who have a child together. As mentioned, in the Fragile Families study, among unmarried parents cohabiting at the birth, 46 percent have broken up five years later, and 77 percent of those romantically involved but not living together when their baby was born have done so. Given the prevalence of nonmarital births among the poor and the high rate of breakup among unmarried parents, as well as the high divorce rate among low-income couples, an important determinant of low-income children's connection to their fathers is how much fathers stay involved after parents break up.

Although father involvement and child support payment after a breakup were not prominent themes in qualitative studies reporting on periods before the 1970s, Leibow's (1967) black male informants observed that the new man often pushes the "old daddy" out, and LeMasters (1975) similarly found that divorced working-class white men felt pushed out when their wives repartnered. Claessens's analysis (chapter 9, this volume) shows mothers gatekeeping men out either because the father's involvement causes jealousy or other problems with their new partners, or because of the fathers' high-risk lifestyles. Older studies allude to the role of the new boyfriend in helping provide for women's children from past partnerships (Rainwater 1970; Drake and Cayton 1945/1962; Lewis 1965); consistent with this, many unmarried fathers in our study are living with and contributing money to their female partners' children from prior relationships. But Monte (chapter 8, this volume) finds that the blended family couples who married were those where the "outside" father of the woman's children was not visiting, and the man was not visiting his children from former partners. Clearly, there are tensions inherent in maintaining biological father involvement simultaneous with cohesive blended families in new partnerships. What has changed is that we are now at much higher levels of multiple-partner fertility because of the increased instability of unions, both marital and nonmarital (Raley and Bumpass 2003). Thus, many more families are experiencing these dynamics.

Overall, our study is consistent with the older literature on low-income couples in finding many troubled relationships and much behavior by men that women find unacceptable. How much such behavior is simply a response to economic strain, a lack of efficacy, or is motivated by a need for a compensatory enactment of gender, is an important question for future research. Low-income families have long had higher breakup rates than the middle class, but huge increases occurred in the 1960s and 1970s in all classes, and class differences have intensified (Raley and Bumpass 2003). Authors of older studies expressed horror at levels of nonmarital births, breakups, and single motherhood in the poor and minority population that were often no higher than what now prevails in the white middle class, and were certainly much lower than what prevails in low-income communities today. To contribute to our understanding these couple relationships in an era of persistent inequality coupled with higher standards for relationships, we turn now to the individual papers.

Notes

1.   Ron Mincy was the program officer at the Ford Foundation responsible for the initial funding of the Fragile Families and Child Wellbeing Study, the larger survey in which TLC3 is embedded. Later, the Fragile Families study also received substantial funding from National Institute for Child Health and Development at NIH.

2. We thank Jean Knab for these calculations from the Fragile Families survey. They use weights to make the estimates representative of births in U.S. cities with populations of over 200,000.

3. Ours is one of two qualitative studies embedded in Fragile Families. The other was a qualitative interview study of a different subset of Fragile Family respondents by Maureen Waller (1999; 2002).

4. Two of the principal investigators of the Fragile Families Study, Sara McLanahan and Jeanne Brooks-Gunn, were members of the MacArthur Network on the Family and the Economy, a research group funded by the MacArthur Foundation. In 1999, with data in from the first seven of the Fragile Families Survey cities, this network decided to launch a qualitative addition to the Fragile Families study, the TLC3 study. The network members who originated ideas for the TLC3 study included McLanahan and Brooks-Gunn, along with Nancy Folbre, Lindsay Chase-Lansdale, Greg Duncan, Paula England, Shelley Lundberg, and Robert Pollak. They then recruited Kathryn Edin to join the network and serve as principal investigator of the qualitative TLC3 study. Later, Cecilia Conrad, Irwin Garfinkel, Ronald Mincy, and Robert Willis also joined the network and helped lend guidance to TLC3. The MacArthur Foundation provided the major funding for the TLC3 study. Additional funding was provided by the National Science Foundation (in a grant from the sociology program to Edin and England) and the William T. Grant Foundation (in a grant to Edin).

5. Mean household income for black census (cohabiting and married) couple households who had had a baby in the last year was $44,000, with fathers' earnings averaging $24,300, and 16 percent of both mothers and fathers without a high school degree. For Hispanics of any race, the comparable figures are household income of $36,500, with fathers earning $20,000 last year and 46 percent of women and 49 percent of men without a high school degree.

6. Three couples participated sporadically or not at all after the first wave, so, as all our papers are longitudinal, they were never included. Other than this, subsamples were chosen by topic. Six papers restrict their focus to couples who were unmarried at the time of the birth of the focal child. Gibson-Davis, who looked at the economic bar for marriage in chapter 4, includes all unmarried couples who participated in two or more waves of the study (forty-six couples). Edin and her colleagues, who look at pregnancy intentions in chapter 2, and Hill, who analyzes infidelity in chapter 5, use all unmarried parents who participated in an individual interview at wave four (forty couples). Magnuson and Gibson-Davis's chapter 10, on child support, includes all unmarried couples in which at least one partner also had children by other partners, thus rendering them subject to either payment or receipt of child support. In addition, they include those who broke up during the course of the study, thus making the focal child potentially eligible for support, whether they married someone else or not, and whether or not they had children by other partners. These two groups add to thirty-two couples. Monte's paper on twenty-seven unmarried blended families, chapter 8, is limited to couples who entered the TLC3 study unmarried with at least one child from another

partnership, and who participated in at least two waves of interviews. Reed's chapter 6, on breakups, uses only unmarried couples who broke up at least once over the course of the study (twenty-two), though a few subsequently reunited. Four of the papers are not restricted to unmarried couples. England and Shafer rely in chapter 3 on data from a videotaped couple discussion that was only collected in the third and fourth waves. All sixty-one couples who were still intact and participated in this task in either wave are included, because preliminary analysis did not find different types of conflicts for the unmarried and married. Linnenberg's paper on father involvement in intact couples (chapter 7) includes all couples, married or not, who were cohabiting at both the wave one interview and the wave two interview for whom there was enough information on father involvement and relationship quality (fifty-seven couples out of the sixty cohabiting at both waves). Claessens's paper (chapter 9) on whether fathers who had broken up with the mother continued to see their children includes the eighteen couples who had broken up during the study and had at least one parent interviewed by wave four. Engel's paper, chapter 11, which matches survey questions on sensitive issues to comparable TLC3 data on the same topics, uses a unique sample for each question considered, including all respondents for whom there were data. Five of the chapters (England and Shafer, Linnenberg, Gibson-Davis, Edin et al., and Hill) include a core sample of twenty-two couples. These couples were all unmarried at the birth, still in the study by the fourth wave, and still in a romantic relationship. Seven of the chapters (those just mentioned plus Magnuson and Gibson-Davis and Monte) include a subset of this core, fourteen couples, who also included at least one parent with a child by another partner.

7. The relationship was curvilinear, with men earning much more or much less than their wives doing the least housework and those with equal earnings doing the most (Brines 1994; see also Bittman et al. 2003, Gupta 2007 on this theme).

References

Akerlof, George A., Janet L. Yellen, and Michael L. Katz. 1996. "An Analysis of Out-of-wedlock Childbearing in the United States." *Quarterly Journal of Economics* 111(2): 277–317.

Anderson, Elijah. 1989. "Sex Codes and Family Life Among Poor Inner-City Youths." *Annals of the American Academy of Political and Social Science* 501(1): 59–78.

———. 1990. *Streetwise: Race, Class, and Change in an Urban Community.* Chicago, Ill.: University of Chicago Press.

Becker, Gary. 1991. *A Treatise on the Family*, enlarged ed. Cambridge, Mass.: Harvard University Press.

Bernhardt, Annette, Martina Morris, Mark S. Handcock, and Marc A. Scott. 2001. *Divergent Paths: Economic Mobility in the New American Labor Market.* New York: Russell Sage Foundation.

Bittman, Michael, Paula England, Liana Sayer, Nancy Folbre, and George Matheson. 2003. "When Does Gender Trump Money? Bargaining and Time in Household Work." *American Journal of Sociology* 109(1):186–214.

Bott, Elizabeth. 1957. *Family and Social Network: Roles, Norms, and External Relationships in Ordinary Urban Families*. London: Tavistock.

Brines, Julie. 1994. "Economic Dependency, Gender and the Division of Labor at Home." *American Journal of Sociology* 100(4): 652–88.

Carlson, Marcy, and Sara McLanahan. 2002. "Fragile Families, Father Involvement and Public Policy." In *Handbook of Father Involvement: Multidisciplinary Perspectives*, edited by Catherine S. Tamis-LeMonda and Natasha Cabrera. Mahwah, N.J.: Lawrence Erlbaum Associates.

Carlson, Marcia, Sara S. McLanahan, and Paula England. 2004. "Union Formation in Fragile Families." *Demography* 41(2): 237–61.

Cherlin, Andrew J. 2004. "The Deinstitutionalization of American Marriage." *Journal of Marriage and Family* 66(4): 848–61.

Collins, Patricia Hill. 1990. *Black Feminist Thought: Knowledge, Consciousness, and the Politics of Empowerment*. New York: Routledge.

Coontz, Stephanie. 2005. *Marriage, A History: From Obedience to Intimacy, or How Love Conquered Marriage*. New York: Viking.

Drake, St. Claire, and Horace R. Cayton. 1945/1962. *Black Metropolis: A Study of Negro Life in a Northern City*. New York: Harper and Row.

Du Bois, W. E. B. 1899/1967. *The Philadelphia Negro: A Social Study*. New York: Schocken.

Edin, Kathryn, and Maria Kefalas. 2005. *Promises I Can Keep: Why Poor Women Put Motherhood Before Marriage*. Berkeley, Calif.: University of California Press.

Ellwood, David and Christopher Jencks. 2004. "The Spread of Single-Parent Families in the United States Since 1960." In *The Future of the Family*, edited by Daniel P. Moynihan, T. Smeeding, and Lee Rainwater. New York: Russell Sage Foundation.

Frazier, E. Franklin. 1939/1966. *The Negro Family in the United States*. Chicago, Ill.: University of Chicago Press.

Gans, Herbert J. 1962. *The Urban Villagers*. Glencoe, Ill.: The Free Press.

Gibson-Davis, Christina, Kathryn Edin, and Sara McLanahan. 2006. "High Hopes but Even Higher Expectations: A Qualitative and Quantitative Analysis of the Marriage Plans of Unmarried Couples Who are New Parents." *Journal of Marriage and Family* 67(5): 1301–12.

Gupta, Sanjiv. 2007. "Autonomy, Dependence, or Display? The Relationship Between Married Women's Earnings and Housework." *Journal of Marriage and Family* 69(2): 399–417.

Halle, David. 1984. *America's Working Man: Work, Home, and Politics Among Blue-Collar Property Owners*. Chicago, Ill.: University of Chicago Press.

Hannerz, Ulf. 1969. *Soulside: Inquiries into Ghetto Culture and Community*. New York: Columbia University Press.

Hollingshead, August B. 1949. *Elmtown's Youth*. New York: John Wiley & Sons.

Howell, Joseph T. 1973. *Hard Living on Clay Street*. Garden City, N.Y.: Anchor Books.

Komarovsky, Mirra, and Jane H. Phillips. 1962. *Blue Collar Marriage*. New Haven, Conn.: Yale University Press.

Kurz, Demie. 1995. *For Richer, For Poorer: Mothers Confront Divorce.* New York: Routledge.

Laumann, Edward O., John H. Gagnon, Robert T. Michael, and Stuart Michaels. 1994. *The Social Organization of Sexuality: Sexual Practices in the United States.* Chicago, Ill.: University of Chicago Press.

Leibow, Eliot. 1967. *Tally's Corner: A Study of Negro Streetcorner Men.* New York: Little, Brown.

LeMasters, E. E. 1975. *Blue Collar Aristocrats: Lifestyles at a Working Class Tavern.* Madison, Wisc.: University of Wisconsin Press.

Lewis, Oscar. 1965. *La Vida: A Puerto Rican Family in the Culture of Poverty—San Juan and New York.* New York: Random House.

Lynd, Robert S., and Helen Merrell Lynd. 1929. *Middletown: A Study in Modern American Culture.* New York: Harcourt Brace Jovanovich.

McLanahan, Sara. 2004. "Diverging Destinies: How Children Are Faring Under the Second Demographic Transition." *Demography* 41(4): 607–27.

Mincy, Ronald B. 1994. *Strengthening Fragile Families: A Proposed Strategy for the Ford Foundation Urban Poverty Program.* New York: Ford Foundation.

Morland, John Kenneth. 1958. *Millways of Kent.* Chapel Hill, N.C.: University of North Carolina Press.

Moore, Kristin A. 1995. "Executive Summary: Nonmarital Childbearing in the United States." In *Report to Congress on Out-of-Wedlock Childbearing.* DHHS Publication Number 95-1257. Washington: U.S. Government Printing Office.

Powdermaker, Hortense. 1939/1969. *After Freedom: A Cultural Study of the Deep South.* New York: Atheneum.

Rainwater, Lee. 1960. *And the Poor Get Children: Sex, Contraception, and Family Planning and the Working Class.* Chicago, Ill.: Quadrangle Publications.

———. 1965. *Family Design: Marital Sexuality, Family Size and Contraception.* Chicago, Ill.: Aldine de Gruyter.

———. 1970. *Behind Ghetto Walls: Black Family Life in a Federal Slum.* New York: Aldine de Gruyter.

Raley, R. Kelly, and Larry Bumpass. 2003. "The Topography of the Divorce Plateau: Levels and Trends in Union Stability in the United States after 1980." *Demographic Research* 8(8): 245–59.

Rubin, Lillian B. 1976. *Worlds of Pain: Life in a Working-Class Family.* New York: Basic Books.

Shafer, Emily Fitzgibbons. 2006. "Are Men or Women More Reluctant to Marry in Couples Sharing a Nonmarital Birth?" *Gender Issues* 23(2): 20–43.

Waller, Maureen R. 1999. "Meanings and Motives in New Family Stories: The Separation of Reproduction and Marriage Among Low-Income, Black and White Parents." In *The Cultural Territories of Race: Black and White Boundaries,* edited by Michèle Lamont. Chicago, Ill.: The University of Chicago Press.

———. 2002. *My Baby's Father: Unmarried Parents and Paternal Responsibility.* Ithaca, N.Y.: Cornell University Press.

Wu, Larry, and Barbara Wolfe, eds. 2001. *Out of Wedlock: Causes and Consequences of Nonmarital Fertility.* New York: Russell Sage Foundation.

PART II

COUPLE RELATIONSHIPS AMONG UNMARRIED PARENTS

Chapter 2

Forming Fragile Families: Was the Baby Planned, Unplanned, or In Between?

KATHRYN EDIN, PAULA ENGLAND,
EMILY FITZGIBBONS SHAFER, AND JOANNA REED

THE BIRTH control pill prevents pregnancy 95 to 99 percent of the time, Depo-Provera and the patch are 99 percent effective, the IUD works 98 percent of the time, and condoms are 86 to 98 percent successful if used correctly (Federal Drug Administration 2005). Yet more than one-third of all recent pregnancies in the United States are unintended (Chandra et al. 2005; Henshaw 1998).

Nonmarital conceptions are most likely to occur among those least able to bear the economic cost of children (Chandra et al. 2005). Why is this? Are some explicitly planned, or at least ambivalently desired in a way that quantitative studies are not capturing? Is it a lack of sex education? Are people just not thinking about the possibility of pregnancy when they have sex? Are the men indifferent, thinking they needn't be around if their sexual partner has a baby? Are contraceptives too hard to get or too expensive? Is birth control too much of a hassle?

Right after the birth of their child, interviewers for the Time, Love, and Cash among Couples with Children study asked both the mothers and fathers whether the baby was planned, unplanned, or in between. We asked similar questions for subsequent births. In the fourth wave of interviews, we asked parents in detail about the circumstances surrounding the conception of all their children, including those conceived with other partners. We also asked about miscarriages and abortions and the circumstances surrounding these conceptions.

Our analysis here is based on fertility histories of seventy-six parents who were unmarried when our study began and remained in the study across the four waves (78 percent of the baseline sample of ninety-six unmarried parents). We look at the 202 pregnancies of these seventy-six parents that had occurred outside of marriage. We conduct both qualitative and quantitative analyses of these data, and propose a reconceptualization of the propensity to conceive, involving two continua. At either end of the first continuum are strong negative intentionality and strong positive intentionality with regard to pregnancy. The second continuum is efficacy, the ability or inclination to organize the complex set of behaviors required to avoid pregnancy, such as making and keeping doctor's appointments to get the pill or patch, going to the drug store to fill a prescription or purchase over-the-counter contraceptives, and using the pill or condoms regularly.

We identify five primary types of conceptions: planned, between planned and unplanned, inconsistent contraception, unplanned conceptions to non-contraceptors, and contraceptive failures.[1] We identify a sixth category as well: pregnancies to those who believe they were sterile. Because the last category is very small, we do not discuss it, though we include it in our tables. Categories vary along both continua.

Intention and behavior are at least somewhat aligned in four of the five main types of pregnancy, and, in these, the stronger the intention (either to conceive or to avoid conception), the more behavior falls into line (Andrews and Kandel 1979). This is consistent with psychologists' theory of reasoned action (Fishbein and Ajzen 1975) as well as economic theory. A strong predictor of the strength of intention is the seriousness of the couple relationship. However, there is one category—capturing a quarter of the pregnancies—in which behavior and intentions are not aligned. In these cases, there was no expressed desire to conceive, yet no contraception was used, even inconsistently. Not surprisingly, those reporting pregnancies of this kind were the most unhappy when they learned of the pregnancy, and the most likely to consider abortion. It is for this group that the concept of efficacy seems especially relevant (Musick, England, and Edgington 2005; Rainwater 1960; Brown and Eisenberg 1995).

Background

The Role of Intentions

Demographers typically divide unintended pregnancies into two types, mistimed and unwanted. Pregnancies to women who say that they did not want to conceive when they did, but did want to have another child at some point, are considered mistimed; those to women who say they did not want any more children are described as unwanted. By these definitions, 22 percent of all pregnancies are mistimed and 14 percent are unwanted (Chandra et al. 2005, table 26; see also Kost and Forrest 1995). The very different reactions of pregnant women (or, when available, men) to the news of a mistimed versus an unwanted pregnancy suggests an underlying continuum of intention. More than nine in ten women with a planned conception were at least moderately happy about it, a characterization that fits only 60 percent of those with a mistimed pregnancy and only about 30 percent of those with unwanted births (Chandra et al. 2005; see also Williams, Abma, and Piccinino 1999).

The Role of Efficacy

We can partially infer an intention to avoid pregnancy from contraceptive behavior. More than half, 53 percent, of U.S. women who had a pregnancy they later said was unplanned were using some form of contraception during the month they became pregnant, and abortion is somewhat more common among those who were using contraception at the time than those who were not, 51 versus 43 percent (Henshaw 1998). Both of these facts suggest that motivation to avoid pregnancy leads to more contraceptive use or termination. Nonetheless, as anyone who has tried to stick to an exercise plan or a diet knows, we don't always do what we intend to do.

Low-income Americans are, on average, less regular and effective in contraception (Brown and Eisenberg 1995). Thus, it is not surprising that unintended pregnancies are more common among them. Unmarried women are more likely to characterize their conceptions as unintentional than married women are, and African American and Hispanic women are more likely than whites to do so. More educated women have fewer unintended pregnancies than the less educated (Chandra et al. 2005, table 20; see also Kost and Forrest 1995; Williams, Abma, and Piccinino 1999).

Class differences in the ability to postpone or avoid pregnancy are apparently long-standing. Analyzing qualitative interviews among working class and poor white married couples in the 1950s, Lee Rainwater (1960) found that such couples usually ended up with more children than they wanted. Operating in an era before the birth control pill, and before sterilization became common, the main forms of birth control were condoms and the diaphragm. The higher the husband's education and the more prestigious his occupation, the greater the consistency in contraceptive use.

Somewhat speculatively, Rainwater argues that the lower one's social class, the less life teaches that the future can be trusted and the less one develops the tendency to follow through on complex behaviors that will help realize one's goals. We call this efficacy, which is distinct from values or motivation. As Rainwater suggests, it involves learned skills and habits of organization, follow-through, consistency, and so forth. Those awash in disadvantages presumably have less opportunity to develop these skills and habits, and might well reap fewer rewards when they do so. Low efficacy presumably influences behaviors in a variety of domains other than contraceptive use, such as education, employment, and the quality of interpersonal relationships.

The Role of the Couple Relationship

Among teens and young adults, consistent contraceptive use is more common among those in more casual relationships than those whose relationships have become more serious. Among American teen males, condom use is highest at the beginning of relationships and declines as relationships mature (Ku, Sonenstein, and Pleck 1994). Dutch teens who use sex to express love and intimacy use condoms less, as do those in steady relationships. Fewer than 20 percent of those who have sex with a steady partner use condoms at each contact, whereas 50 percent of those in casual relationships do so (Gebhardt, Kuyper, and Greunsven 2003).[2] These studies fail to take into account other forms of contraception a couple may move to once their relationship becomes serious, but one study that does finds that consistent use of contraception becomes less likely the longer the couple is together (Manlove, Ryan, and Franzetta 2003).

Why does contraceptive use decline as relationships get more serious? It could be that the more serious the relationship, the more the unmarried couple wants to have a child. On the other hand, some forms of contraception, especially condoms, may be more associated with disease prevention than birth control, and continued use might signal mistrust (Edin and Kefalas 2005). Because the literature to date still leaves us somewhat in the dark on this question, we deploy our rich qualitative data to shed light on which is the case, or whether both are operative.

Present Study

Most studies have presumed that pregnancies are either intended or unintended, and fail to consider whether there is a continuum of intention with regard to pregnancy, including a middle ground of ambivalence. They also fail to consider that individuals may be happy about an unplanned pregnancy (for exceptions, see Trussell, Vaughan, and Stanford 1999; Bachrach and Newcomer 1999; Luker 1999; Sable 1999; Zabin et al. 2000; Fischer et al. 1999; Waller 1999; Edin and Kefalas 2005). This dichotomous conceptualization also does not fit well with evidence that the concept of planning a pregnancy may simply not be meaningful to some (Edin and Kefalas 2005; Fischer et al. 1999; Moos, Petersen, and Melvin 1997). Moreover, emphasizing the distinction between mistimed and unwanted pregnancy makes more sense for married than unmarried couples, who have higher rates of multiple partner fertility. For poor, unmarried individuals, the desirability of having another child may depend more on what partner one is with, how stable the relationship is, and other situational factors, than on abstract notions of ideal family size (Zabin et al. 2000; Speizer et al. 2004). Although past research has distinguished between conceptions of married, cohabiting, or noncohabiting couples, most has not looked directly at the level of relationship solidarity in nonmarital partnerships, which we will do. Finally, even when recognizing ambivalence, researchers have generally seen propensity to conceive as unidimensional, and have seldom considered the degree of intent and the degree of efficacy together.[3] This is important, because when efficacy is low, outcomes don't reflect intentions well. By offering more substantial qualitative grounding to the research on pregnancy intention for the subset of the U.S. population that is most likely to have unintended pregnancies—the unmarried—we hope to address some of these deficiencies.

Data and Methods

This analysis drew data from all four waves of interviews with all unmarried TLC3 couples, but relies largely on the wave four interviews. We started from the seventy-six parents still in the study at wave four who had been unmarried at baseline, these seventy-six individuals were from forty of the forty-eight unmarried couples, who entered the study in 2000, since we sometimes lost one parent but retained another.[4] We asked each individual about their entire fertility history, including abortions and miscarriages. Including only births, abortions, or miscarriages experienced while respondents were unmarried, those parents reported 202 pregnancies. Some of our unmarried-at-baseline sample were married either before or after, so we excluded any marital births, abortions, or miscarriages they experienced while married. We sorted all portions of transcripts that referenced these questions into text fields, along with any other transcript material that was relevant, working inductively to create a typology that would capture the salient dimensions of each pregnancy and the behavior surrounding it.[5] The resulting categories reflect both how strongly respondents wanted to avoid pregnancy or to become pregnant as well as their contraceptive behavior. We analyzed these narratives further to identify precursors and consequences for pregnancies in each category. We considered each parent's responses separately without taking into account any information gleaned from the other parent. This is because the vast majority of parents in our study shared at least one if not more pregnancies with partners outside of our sample, usually before, but sometimes after, the birth of the focal child.[6] Here we describe the decision rules we used to put cases into these types. Later in the chapter, we explore their properties and correlates.

> Planned. All pregnancies where respondents were not using any form of contraception, even inconsistently, and expressed a strong intention to have a child at the time, with no ambivalence.[7]

> In between planned and unplanned. Some ambivalence and some degree of positive intention about having a baby at the time were

Table 2.1   Proportion of Nonmarital Pregnancies in Six Categories

Planned	12%
In between planned and unplanned	18
Unplanned, inconsistent contraception	22
Unplanned, not contracepting	25
Unplanned, technical contraceptive failure	18
Unplanned, reason to believe infertile	5
N	202

Source: Authors' calculations.

expressed. Contraception may have been used inconsistently or not at all around the conception.[8]

Unplanned, inconsistent contraception. Those who expressed no desire to have a baby right then and who had been using contraception around the time of conception, but inconsistently.[9]

Unplanned, no contraception. Pregnancies to those who said they were using no contraception around the conception, but expressed no positive intention to get pregnant at the time they conceived.

Unplanned, technical contraceptive failure. Those who said they were consistently using condoms or a hormonal method of birth control, or who strictly adhered to the natural family planning method of birth control around the time of conception. Our attempt was to exclude "user failures" from this category.[10]

Table 2.1 shows the proportion of the pregnancies in each category. Twelve percent were planned, 18 percent were in between, 22 percent were the result of inconsistent contraception, 25 percent were unplanned, and 18 percent were contraceptive failures.

Quantitative Analysis

Because we wanted to examine various correlates of pregnancies in our six categories, we draw some additional variables from the qualitative narratives. We created a measure of the seriousness of the couple relationship at the time the conception occurred, separating relationships into three categories; serious, casual, and unstable (formerly serious but in the throes of a breakup). We noted whether the pregnancy ended in miscarriage, abortion, or live birth, and whether the respondent said she or he considered abortion at any time during the pregnancy.[11] We coded the responses to our question of whether they had ever been in a situation where they wanted to use birth control but couldn't afford it or get access to it. Reactions to the news of the pregnancy were sorted into happy, unhappy, or in between. However, reactions to the pregnancy were not used to code respondents into planning types, since it is possible to have a clear intent not to get pregnant yet be happy upon discovering the pregnancy.

In addition, because the larger study centered on the birth of a focal child—the one whose birth brought the couple into the study—we identified whether the conception was of the focal child and, if not, whether it occurred before or after the focal birth. We wanted to control for whether the conception was focal in case the attention our study (and the survey) gave to the focal birth might have biased respondents' reports in any way. We also coded whether the pregnancy was a first, second, or higher order pregnancy. We further noted whether the respondent was still with the partner with whom they had conceived when reporting on the pregnancy, thinking that current relationship status might affect reporting. Sex and race-ethnicity were taken from data gathered in the TLC3 baseline interviews.[12]

From the Fragile Families survey, we used the respondent's level of education (less than high school and no GED, high school or GED, more than high school) as reported at baseline. We also used an indicator, collected when the focal child was about three, of whether the respondent was clinically depressed (Filippone and Knab 2004). Respondents' substance abuse was measured by whether they reported that alcohol or drug use had interfered in their work or personal lives in the past year (collected just after the focal child's birth). Finally, we used a measure of whether the respondent had lived with both parents at age fifteen. Table 2.2 shows descriptive statistics for each of these variables, whether coded from our narratives or taken from the Fragile Families data.

Results

We begin with a narrative analysis of each of the categories in our typology. Then, to get some purchase on possible causes of variation in either intention or efficacy, we look at bivariate associations between other variables and pregnancy types (see tables 2.3 and 2.4) and present multivariate analyses to see which of these factors predict pregnancy type and a closely related outcome, how happy respondents were when they learned about the pregnancy. We use a multinomial logistic regression to predict pregnancy type by relationship seriousness and other sociodemographic controls. We use an ordered logistic regression to predict how happy respondents were upon learning of the pregnancy from these same background variables and, in a second model, the pregnancy type. Both regression analyses use robust standard errors, clustering cases by the individual who reported all their pregnancies. This takes account of the fact that multiple pregnancy observations from a single individual are not independent.[13]

Table 2.2   Means on Selected Variables for Sample of Nonmarital Pregnancies

	Female Mean	Male Mean	Overall Mean
Pregnancy type			
Planned	0.13	0.11	0.12
In between	0.17	0.20	0.18
Unplanned, inconsistent contraception	0.21	0.23	0.22
Unplanned, but not contracepting	0.24	0.26	0.25
Unplanned, technical contraceptive failure	0.17	0.18	0.18
Unplanned, reason to believe infertile	0.07	0.03	0.05
Wanted to get pregnant before conception			
Yes	0.19	0.10	0.15
In between	0.19	0.21	0.20
No	0.61	0.69	0.65
Considered abortion	0.38	0.57	0.46
Had abortion	0.06	0.14	0.10
Miscarried	0.11	0.09	0.10
Happiness when learned of pregnancy			
Happy	0.29	0.30	0.30
In between*	0.27	0.46	0.36
Unhappy*	0.44	0.24	0.34
Good age for your child to have first child	24.43	25.19	24.75
Ever wanted birth control but couldn't afford	0.02	0.00	0.01
Relationship at time of conception			
Casual*	0.20	0.34	0.27
Unstable	0.17	0.11	0.14
Stable romantic	0.64	0.55	0.60
This was TLC3 focal child	0.35	0.32	0.33
Pregnancy number for this parent	2.50	2.68	2.58
Birth number for this parent	2.41	2.39	2.40
Respondent's race			
Black	0.56	0.54	0.55
Hispanic	0.33	0.35	0.34
White	0.11	0.10	0.11
Respondent's education at birth of focal child (FF)			
High school dropout	0.42	0.46	0.44
High school diploma/GED	0.40	0.31	0.36
Post–high school education	0.18	0.23	0.20
Depression probability (FF)	0.14	0.14	0.14
Biological parents together at fifteen (FF)	0.28	0.38	0.33
Alcohol or drugs have interfered with work or personal relationships in the last year (FF)*	0.02	0.10	0.06
Not romantically involved w/this parent by wave four	0.57	0.57	0.57

Source: Authors' calculations.
Note: All variables coded from TLC3 data except where FF noted; these are from the FFCWBS.
*p < .05 for test of gender difference in mean.

Table 2.3 Relationship Between Nonmarital Pregnancy Type and Other Variables

	Planned	In Between Planned and Unplanned	Unplanned, Inconsistent Contraception	Unplanned, Not Contracepting	Unplanned, Technical Contraceptive Failure	Unplanned, Reason to Believe Infertile	N
Wanted to get pregnant before conception (used in coding planning status)							199
Yes	0.88*	0.22	0.00*	0.00*	0*	0.09	
In between	0.08	0.61*	0.19	0.06*	0.14	0.00	
No	0.04*	0.17*	0.81*	0.94*	0.86*	0.91	
Considered abortion**	0.04*	0.19	0.32	0.76*	0.42	0.17	124
Had abortion	0.04	0.05	0.07	0.18*	0.06	0.00	202
Miscarried	0.13	0.03	0.05	0.06	0.11	0.18	202
Happiness when learned of pregnancy							202
Happy	0.67*	0.49*	0.27	0.08*	0.22	0.27	
In between	0.33	0.43	0.30	0.34	0.33	0.36	
Unhappy	0.00*	0.08*	0.43	0.58*	0.44	0.36	
Good age for your child to have first child**	23.86	24.52	24.77	24.90	23.96	28.42*	119
Ever wanted birth control but couldn't afford	0.04	0.03	0.00	0.00	0.00	0.00	202

(continued)

Table 2.3 Relationship Between Nonmarital Pregnancy Type and Other Variables (Continued)

	Planned	In Between Planned and Unplanned	Unplanned, Inconsistent Contraception	Unplanned, Not Contracepting	Unplanned, Technical Contraceptive Failure	Unplanned, Reason to Believe Infertile	N
Relationship at time of conception							199
Casual	0.04*	0.14	0.23	0.41*	0.32	0.45	
Unstable	0.00*	0.08	0.09	0.16	0.26*	0.36*	
Stable romantic	0.96*	0.78*	0.68	0.43*	0.41*	0.18*	
This was TLC3 focal child	0.38	0.49*	0.36	0.18*	0.31	0.45	202
Pregnancy number for this parent	2.92	2.32	2.50	2.90	2.19	2.64	202
Birth order for this parent	2.70	2.17	2.24	2.88*	2.00	2.45	185
Respondent's race							202
Black	0.38	0.41*	0.50	0.70*	0.64	0.82	
Hispanic	0.38	0.54*	0.41	0.16*	0.31	0.09	
White	0.25*	0.05	0.09	0.14	0.06	0.09	
Respondent's education at birth of focal child							202
High school dropout	0.46	0.49	0.36	0.48	0.53	0.18	
High school diploma/GED	0.33	0.22	0.39	0.40	0.39	0.27	
Post–high school education	0.21	0.30	0.25	0.12	0.08*	0.55*	

Depression probability	0.11	0.15	0.08	0.16	0.18	0.24	193
Biological parents were together at fifteen	0.33	0.35	0.32	0.40	0.22	0.36	202
Alcohol or drugs have interfered with work or personal relationships in the last year	0.17*	0.08	0.07	0.00*	0.06	0.00	202
Not romantically involved w/this parent by wave four	0.42	0.38*	0.59	0.60	0.75*	0.64	202

Source: Authors' calculations.

Note: Numbers in pregnancy type columns are conditional means. In the case of categoric variables, these are column proportions (% of the column pregnancy type that were in that category of the row variable). * indicates significant t test of mean difference ($p < .05$), always taking this category of the row variable compared to all others combined. For example, the * for .88, the upper left-most cell, indicates that the proportion of all planned pregnancies where respondent said that s/he wanted a pregnancy before the conception is significantly different than the proportion of all pregnancies other than planned where respondent said she/he wanted a pregnancy before conception.

Numbers in the final column (N) are the total number of nonmissing cases for each row variable.

**Interviewers did not ask consistently about what would be a "good age for your child to have a child" or whether the respondent had considered terminating the pregnancy (considered abortion). Thus, the sample sizes are lower for these questions.

Table 2.4   Proportion of Nonmarital Pregnancies

	Planned	In Between	Unplanned, Inconsistent Contraception	Unplanned, but Not Contracepting	Unplanned, Technical Contraceptive Failure	Unplanned, Reason to Believe Infertile	Total
Relationship at time of conception							
Casual	0.02*	0.10	0.19	0.38*	0.21	0.10	1.00
Unstable	0.00*	0.11	0.14	0.29	0.32*	0.14*	1.00
Stable romantic	0.19*	0.24*	0.25	0.18*	0.12*	0.02*	1.00
Respondent's race							
Black	0.08	0.13*	0.19	0.31*	0.20	0.08	1.00
Hispanic	0.13	0.30*	0.27	0.12*	0.16	0.01	1.00
White	0.27*	0.09	0.18	0.32	0.09	0.05	1.00
Respondent's education at birth of focal child							
High school dropout	0.12	0.20	0.18	0.27	0.21	0.02	1.01
High school diploma/GED	0.11	0.11	0.24	0.29	0.20	0.04	1.00
Post-high school education	0.12	0.26	0.26	0.14	0.07*	0.14*	1.01

Source: Authors' calculations.

Note: Numbers are row proportions. Totals not equaling 1.00 are due to rounding. * indicates significant t test of mean difference ($p < .05$), always taking the particular pregnancy type (column variable) compared to all others combined. For example, the * for .02 in the upper leftmost cell indicates that the proportion of pregnancies that began in a casual relationship between mother and father has a significantly different proportion of pregnancies that were identified as planned compared to all other pregnancies types that began in a casual relationship.

A Qualitative Typology of Pregnancies

Although we recognize that these analyses do not tell us definitively what causes respondents to plan pregnancies or avoid unplanned pregnancies, we use the large number of pregnancies to provide some purchase on these causal questions.

Planned   Trevor, who is black and nineteen years old when he enters the study, had been with Tonya for about a year and a half when she became pregnant. It had not been an easy relationship because Trevor was incarcerated for part of the time. Nonetheless, this pregnancy was planned. "Before I got out of prison, we used to talk on the phone and write each other letters and stuff . . . and she always told me, you know, one day, hopefully soon—the Lord's will—you know, she'd have her own child. . . . That's something that we always talked about, you know, what would happen if we had kids, you know, [if] she'd get pregnant or what I'd do— if I'd be here for her and stuff like that, so when I got out, you know, we spent the whole day together, you know, and she actually sat down and said she was ready, so yeah, so that's how it came about. . . . She was very happy. Still is happy." Trevor also claims responsibility for three earlier pregnancies (not with Tonya), but does not describe them as planned. In this respect, Trevor is not unusual: the parents in our sample characterized only 12 percent of nonmarital conceptions in their fertility histories as planned.

Only 4 percent of parents reporting a planned pregnancy said they did not want a child at the time of conception (table 2.3). Not surprisingly, two-thirds said they were happy, none said they were unhappy when they found out about the pregnancy, and the remaining third were in between (table 2.3). Although women and men are about equally likely to report a planned pregnancy, whites are far more likely to say their pregnancies were planned, 27 percent, than either Hispanics, 13 percent, or African Americans, 8 percent (table 2.4).[14]

Planned pregnancies almost always occur among couples who are in serious stable relationships, 96 percent (table 2.3). In fact, almost all of these couples are cohabiting when the conception occurs.[15] Tabitha, who is white and thirty years old at the beginning of the study, confides, "I definitely thought that he was the one. It wasn't nothing casual about it. It was like really a planned thing. We're in love, [so] we want to have a baby." A few planned pregnancies, though, seem to be an attempt to hold a failing relationship together or to solidify a relatively new relationship. A twenty-two-year-old Puerto Rican father, Rafael, says of his first child, "It was planned. . . . We thought we weren't going to get separated if we had a baby."

In planning a pregnancy, couples usually discuss their desire to have a child with one another, agree together that the time is right, and decide to stop using contraception. What constitutes the right time for a particular couple depends on the strength of their commitment to one another, their ages or the ages of their other children, their financial situation, or health concerns.

Between Planned and Unplanned   Tyrone, a black father who is twenty-nine years old when the study begins, was in a stable relationship with Tiny when they conceived his first child. When asked whether he wanted a baby at the time, he replies, "You know what? No. I mean, that's just something that just happened—it wasn't planned or anything." When we ask whether the two had been using contraception, he said "We was at first, but then, you know, we wasn't afterwards . . . I guess because we was just used to each other, you know, it was just me and her." Although they had discontinued birth control, when Tyrone found out about the pregnancy he says he was "shocked—oh my God! And then I was . . . like, wow! But when I got the chance to go back home . . . I was kinda excited." Like Tyrone, those in this category at least ambivalently want a child now, even though the pregnancy is not explicitly planned.

Eighteen percent of the pregnancies our respondents described are neither fully planned nor unplanned, but fall somewhere between these categories (table 2.2). Men and women are about equally likely to characterize pregnancies this way. Thirty percent of Hispanic conceptions, but only 13 percent of African Americans and 9 percent of whites, are in this group (table 2.4). Seventy-eight percent are to those in stable romantic relationships (table 2.3). Many are cohabiting before the conception.

Despite the fact that these births are less than fully planned, only 8 percent are unhappy when they learn of the pregnancy, though 43 percent are ambivalent. Nineteen percent consider abortion but only 5 percent of the pregnancies are terminated. As reflected in the range of reactions, there is a range of intentionality as well.

The following exchange with Marquis, a twenty-three-year-old black father, shows the genuine ambivalence some parents report when describing how they felt around the time of conception. "We was [using condoms], but then we suddenly just stopped. . . . We had talked about it, but it wasn't a big thing. It wasn't no big talk about it." Later, he clarifies, "To be honest, if I'm with her [for the long term], there wasn't no need [to use contraception], [not] if we was gonna be together." For Marquis and others, condoms connote mistrust, and are typically used only before the couple deems themselves an exclusive pair. Their continued use may thus signal suspicion of the partner's infidelity or indicate unspoken doubts about the relationship's future (Edin and Kefalas 2005).

Like Marquis, the vast majority were in a serious relationship with their partner at the time of conception (table 2.3). Such couples often describe pregnancies that arise not just from the heat of passion, as some in this category clearly do, but from a deep sense of love and commitment. Twenty-year-old Freddie, who is Hispanic, says, ". . . we didn't use protection either because we were so serious. And I mean, I think for young people it's a matter of, if you really have feelings for that person, you're thinking backwards. You're thinking, 'Well I don't care if I get AIDS from this person, I don't care if we have a kid, because I love this person.' "

Some respondents in this group hoped they wouldn't conceive until personal circumstances made the timing more ideal. Few respondents in this group say they saw a great cost to bearing children at the time of conception, as the majority were in stable relationships and were planning on having children (or more children) together anyway. For example, NaKeisha, who is black and twenty-one years old, says her second pregnancy was not exactly planned "because I wasn't 100 percent decided that, 'Yeah, this is what I want to do,' because I was only 20 at the time. I thought about it, and I wasn't *against* it."

What NaKeisha says next suggests that some in this category just don't think it is normal to plan or time their conceptions precisely when in a serious, long-term, monogamous partnership. "I don't think we gave it much thought because we were in a monogamous relationship. [We] had lived together for the past two years, so it was alright if we *did* have a child. I mean we weren't like, 'Yeah, let's have a child [right now],' so . . . but it was OK."

Suzanne, who is white and twenty-two years old when the study begins, also offers this kind of narrative when describing the circumstances that led to her second pregnancy. "Well, we were planning on getting married, and planning to save for a house, so Myron and I are very committed to each other, so we just were—I don't know. If we were to get pregnant it wouldn't be a big deal. Or it wouldn't be something unwanted or unplanned. And if we didn't [get pregnant] it wasn't a big deal either."

Some very stable couples definitely desire children (or more children) together. In some cases, they talk about it beforehand and intentionally discontinue contraception. Twenty-six-year-old Alex, who is black, says he's been responsible for seven conceptions, but only three have resulted in live births, the last two with Rochelle. When asked about whether his youngest was planned, he replies, "Kinda sorta, but we just, you know, if it was going to happen just let it happen. . . . I wanted more kids. . . . I wanted to . . . have a couple of kids by Rochelle if I could afford it. . . . It wasn't a thing where like, you know, every time we [have sex] I'm going to try to [get her pregnant] you know. You know, out of love, just let it happen."

The most interesting theme that emerges from these cases is how respondents seem to be implicitly defining the term planned. Planning a pregnancy seems to connote a kind of striving, where calendars are kept, doctors consulted, and fertility drugs used. Such an approach seems stilted and unnatural to many respondents. In fact, Wanda, who is white and thirty-six years old when the study begins, describes her fifth conception as in-between because even though she wanted to get pregnant at the time, she wasn't keeping a calendar or taking fertility drugs as she had for her fourth pregnancy.

Unplanned, Inconsistent Contraception   Kenneth, who is black and thirty-four years old when the study begins, is the father of six children, three with his current partner Ciana, and three with a previous partner, Delores. Kenneth says his first conception with Delores was unplanned. They weren't living together but were in a serious relationship. In fact, Kenneth was already helping to care for her children when she worked as a bartender. When we ask him about their contraceptive practices around the time the pregnancy occurred, Kenneth claims Delores was on the pill, but confides, "that's not 100 percent." On learning she was pregnant, Kenneth reacted this way: "You know when you're not ready for a baby at the time [you're upset]. But after a while . . . it's okay." He concludes, "But the first news of pregnancy, that's not good."

Veronica, a twenty-one-year-old black mother, conceived her third child with Jason after being in a relationship with him for two years. "We had just moved in with each other . . . three months . . . before I found out that I was pregnant. We were in a serious relationship." When we ask her whether she wanted a baby at the time, she responds, "Um, actually no. he was a surprise. We hadn't really talked about kids. Jason, he already [had] two and I think I was like twenty-one. And I was . . . really not thinking about kids. I was having fun, traveling." The couple had been using condoms but stopped as she was transitioning to the birth control pill. After experiencing side effects with the first brand she was prescribed, she switched to another, but had side effects again so stopped taking them for a month. When Veronica learned she was pregnant, she was "a little disappointed because I wasn't in a position to have a child, [but] I love kids. I mean I always babysit for like all my best friends. . . . I'm very good with kids and I knew that I always wanted kids."

Later in the interview, Veronica confides to us. "I wanted to go back to school and I was talking to my uncle about it. . . . I was like, I don't know how I'm gonna tell [my boyfriend]." The uncle encouraged Veronica to terminate the pregnancy, but she "just couldn't do it. . . . I don't believe in abortion. . . . And I just had to stop and think, what reasons would I have not to have him, other than I can't travel anymore? I can't spend my money on myself anymore? That's not a valid reason not to have my baby."

More than a fifth (22 percent, table 2.1) of the nonmarital pregnancies our parents describe were similar to those reported here by Kenneth and Veronica. They and their partners aren't planning a child, but aren't using contraception consistently. Women and men are about equally likely to report a pregnancy in this category (table 2.2) and differences by race and ethnicity are not large (table 2.4). Sixty-eight percent were in stable romantic relationships (table 2.3). None say they wanted child at that time. Just over a quarter (27 percent) say they were happy when they learned of the pregnancy, and 32 percent were unhappy enough to consider abortion (table 2.3). In general, the strength of the motivation to avoid childbearing matches the vigilance in contraceptive practices; those in this category typically express a weaker negative intention in regard to pregnancy at the time of conception than those who using contraception consistently.[16]

Unplanned, No Contraception   Anton, a twenty-five-year-old black father, tells us about seven pregnancies and five births by three mothers. "All of 'em was unplanned," Anton says. At sixteen, he was "just messing with" the first girl who got pregnant. "It really wasn't supposed to happen. It just happened. Not being careful." Two subsequent partners became pregnant in a similar fashion, though he didn't find out until after the abortions. When we ask if any of these relationships were serious, Anton says, "I ain't never seen myself having no kids with them!"

Then Anton met Sherise, who was still in high school. Sherise, who is also black, says they weren't using any contraception either. "I wasn't smart then, so no. . . . It just happened." Anton says that when he learned of the pregnancy, "I just asked her what was she going to do, was she gonna have it, or what. . . ? I was thinking to myself, I don't want [a] child. . . . She didn't want . . . one neither. . . . But she had it anyway."

Meanwhile, Anton was surreptitiously seeing someone else. Sherise's daughter was born just weeks before the other woman gave birth to her son. This spelled the beginning of the end of the relationship. However, when Anton came back on the scene after a brief stint in jail, the two reunited just long enough to accidentally conceive another daughter, the child that brought them into our study. Another child by Anton is the last thing Sherise wanted, and she seriously considered adoption.

By the time their second daughter is born, twenty-five-year-old Anton has already claimed responsibility for six unplanned pregnancies. Four years later, he's just learned that he's responsible for a seventh. When asked if he's going to change his ways with regard to birth control, Anton responds, "Maybe. . . . I don't really like condoms." Sherise, only twenty when she has their second daughter, had already had an early miscarriage. Over the next four years, Sherise has a third child by a boyfriend named Hiram, this one planned. A second pregnancy with Hiram is terminated after Sherise learns Hiram has been unfaithful. In

2004, when we talk with her the final time, she is pregnant again by another partner, a pregnancy she intends to bring to term despite the fact that she doesn't want any more children. "I wasn't trying to get pregnant, but it just happened. . . . I had stopped using the pill. That's my problem."

Sherise and Anton are a somewhat extreme example of respondents with conceptions in this category, constituting a quarter of the total pregnancies (table 2.1). Although these respondents almost unanimously say they did not want a child at the time of the pregnancy, even ambivalently, they often admit, "I just wasn't thinking" when asked about contraception. Fully 94 percent of respondents with conceptions of this kind claim they did not want a child at that time, even a little (table 2.3). Only 8 percent say they were happy when they learned of the pregnancy, and 76 percent considered abortion (18 percent of the total were actually aborted) (table 2.3). Women and men are equally likely to report a pregnancy in the "unplanned but not contracepting" category (table 2.2). Such pregnancies are more common among whites (32 percent) and blacks (31 percent) than Hispanics (12 percent) (table 2.4).

Despite the very strong value low-income communities place on children (Edin and Kefalas 2005; Sayer, Wright, and Edin 2003), many mothers and fathers in this situation admit outright that the children that resulted from these pregnancies were definitely unwanted.[17] A twenty-seven-year-old black mother, LaShawnda, recalls, "When I got pregnant with [my first child], it was like [me and her father were already] drifting apart. . . . And then, 'Oh, God, I'm pregnant!' When asked if she wanted to have a baby at that time, LaShawnda replies, "Not at all. . . . Never. I never wanted kids."

This is the category where behavior is least aligned with intention. Though sometimes the intention not to have a child hadn't been clearly formulated, not much thought had been given to the risk. Yet the impediment does not seem to be lack of access to birth control, because no one admits to ever being in a situation where they wanted birth control but couldn't afford it (table 2.3).

Forty-one percent of these pregnancies were in the context of casual relationships (table 2.3). Several of the fathers questioned their paternity almost immediately when learning of the pregnancy.[18] Others say they didn't even know about the pregnancy until it had already been terminated or the child had been born. Another 16 percent were in unstable relationships at the time; these relationships, as well as the individuals in them, were typically very troubled. Over twice as many men as women with conceptions in this category say they were in a casual relationship when the pregnancy occurred (58 versus 24 percent, not shown in tables).

Despite the disproportionate number of casual or unstable relationships, nearly half of these conceptions are to couples in stable romantic relationships (43 percent, table 2.3). A somewhat extreme example is Ciana, whom we mentioned earlier. She has ten children with two fathers, all but one of them unplanned. The first seven were with Junior, but the pair became so severely addicted to crack the children were removed by child protection services and entrusted to the custody of Ciana's mother, where they remain. Her first child with Kenneth is also in her mother's custody, an indication that it took time to break her habit. At thirty-two, she gives birth to their second child and enters our study. Two years later, they add her tenth child. Like Ciana, even those who are in stable relationships but conceive accidentally while neglecting to use contraception are seldom stable in other domains and show unusually low efficacy in several domains.

Unplanned, Technical Contraceptive Failure   Contraceptive failure accounts for 18 percent of pregnancies (see table 2.1). Women and men are equally likely to report pregnancies in this category (see table 2.2). Most failures occur when the couple is using the pill, but condoms, the patch, the shot, the sponge, and a strict adherence to the natural family planning method of birth control are also named. African Americans and Hispanics are much more likely to report a contraceptive failure than whites—20 percent for blacks, 16 percent for Hispanics, and 9 percent for whites (table 2.4). Only a few respondents (14 percent) in this category say they were ambivalent about whether they wanted a child at the time (table 2.3). Only 22 percent are happy when they learn of the pregnancy (table 2.3), although men in this category are considerably less unhappy than women (not shown). Forty-two percent consider abortion, and 6 percent of all reported conceptions are terminated.

By our definition, contraceptive failures can only occur when the couple is consistently using some form of birth control, and there are some patterns to these practices. As noted earlier, many couples use contraception when the relationship is new, but let these practices lapse as their relationship becomes exclusive. Thus, 32 percent of contraceptive failures occur to couples in casual relationships (table 2.3). Rafael, the twenty-two-year-old Puerto Rican father mentioned earlier, describes his relationship with his fourth child's mother as "a one-night thing." Eugenia told him she was on the pill, and he knew nothing about the existence of the child until a court-ordered paternity test revealed him to be the father—almost three years after their only night together.

Just over 25 percent of contraceptive failures are to couples in an unstable relationship type (table 2.3). Couples who are in the process of breaking up often reinstate the careful birth control practices they used when the relationship was just beginning. Rochelle, introduced earlier, conceived her third child with a boyfriend she was about to break up with, despite having gone back on the shot. She says, "I didn't want another baby [with him] at all."

The third pattern concerns couples in serious relationships who use contraception because they have a strong motivation to delay pregnancy. Forty-one percent of contraceptive failures are to couples in stable romantic relationships. Samantha was a serious student and wanted to wait until she graduated to have children. She was on the shot (Depo-Provera), but still conceived and gave birth to her first child when she was in high school. This twenty-eight-year-old black mother's third pregnancy also occurred when she was using birth control—the pill this time—and at an even more inconvenient time. "I had just got on my feet with . . . a job. . . . I felt that I wasn't ready for . . . another baby, so I had got an abortion. . . . I didn't want another baby at the time. . . . I just, you know, didn't wanna have another child."

Sometimes, concerns about timing among serious couples are linked to notions of ideal spacing, for though parents usually don't want their children to be too far apart in age, they don't want them to be too close together either. Occasionally, the decision to wait is linked to financial considerations. Nubia, a twenty-six-year-old black mother, had been seeing her boyfriend for about a year before they conceived, despite conscientious condom use. Although their relationship was already quite serious and they even discussed marriage, she says they didn't want a child together so soon.

Some very stable couples also use contraception consistently because they have already reached their ideal family size. Roger and Alison, both white and in their late thirties, were planning a wedding when their second child was conceived despite their use of both the pill and a spermicide. Alison says, "I wasn't sure how I was gonna handle it, now we were getting married and everything but . . . it's rough with *one* child. [You] give up a lot for having kids, and then when you have two, you give up even more." They subsequently decided to have two additional children, and then agreed they were through. When Alison conceived their fifth child, again while on the pill and just returning to school, she greeted the news with dismay: "The more [children] we have the more it's gonna' cost us. You can't stretch yourself too far."

Comparing the Types

Tables 2.3 and 2.4 show bivariate relationships between our pregnancy types and all other variables. Table 2.5 presents results from a multinomial logistic regression predicting pregnancy type. Table 2.6 contains results from an ordinal logistic regression predicting the degree to which respondents were happy when they found out about the pregnancy, an outcome closely related to pregnancy type.

If all pregnancies were divided into the first four types (all but the unplanned, no contraception group and those who believed they were sterile), a clear story emerges. We rigorously refrained from using reports of happiness upon discovering the pregnancy or consideration of abortion to put cases in categories. Nonetheless, it is not at all surprising that we see a steady positive progression (more happiness) as we move toward more

Table 2.5 Odds Ratios from Multinomial Logistic Regression Predicting Pregnancy Type, Relative to Planned and In Between Planned and Unplanned (both are the Reference Category)

	Unplanned, Inconsistent Contraception	Unplanned, Not Contracepting	Unplanned, Technical Contraceptive Failure	Unplanned, Reason to Believe Sterile
Male	1.11	0.93	1.08	0.27
Race dummies (black = reference)				
White	0.96	0.83	0.71	0.57
Hispanic	0.93	0.22*	0.42+	0.06
Biological parents were together at age 15	1.12	2.76	0.96	3.16
Educational attainment dummies (H.S. dropout = reference)				
High school diploma/GED	1.56	1.99	1.08	2.96
Post-high school	1.22	0.44	0.07**	17.32+
Depression probability	0.43	1.29	1.22	2.26
Pregnancy number	1.17	0.13***	0.43	0.60
Pregnancy number squared	0.97	1.32***	1.04	1.09
Before focal pregnancy	1.35	4.81**	0.62	2.11
After focal pregnancy	1.44	3.93+	2.25	1.39
Relationship status at time of conception (stable, romantic = reference)				
Casual	2.41	9.34**	4.89*	57.78**
Unstable	2.13	10.45**	7.60**	72.63**
Mother and father romantically involved when reported	1.95	0.57	3.69*	0.45
N	190			

Source: Authors' calculations.
***p < .001, **p < .01, *p < .05, +p < .10

Table 2.6   How Happy Respondent Was When Nonmarital Pregnancy Discovered

	Model 1	Model 2
Male	0.68+	0.88*
	0.36	0.39
Race dummies (black = reference)		
White	0.12	0.08
	0.52	0.71
Hispanic	0.33	0.16
	0.37	0.40
Biological parents together at fifteen	−0.52	−0.37
	0.38	0.45
Educational attainment dummies (dropout = reference)		
High school diploma/GED	0.63	0.87+
	0.41	0.47
After high school	0.46	0.25
	0.45	0.54
Depression probability	0.50	0.55
	0.54	0.63
Pregnancy number	−0.04	−0.52+
	0.26	0.30
Pregnancy number squared	0.00	0.07+
	0.03	0.04
Birth before focal pregnancy	−0.97**	-0.84*
	0.33	0.35
Birth after focal pregnancy	−0.86*	−0.78+
	0.37	0.40
Relationship status at time of conception (serious romantic = reference)		
unstable	−1.51***	−1.15**
	0.34	0.42
casual	−0.81*	−0.35
	0.41	0.43
Mother and father not romantically involved when reported	−0.05	−0.02
	0.38	0.37
Pregnancy type dummies (planned = reference)		
Between planned and unplanned		−0.68
		0.63
Unplanned, inconsistent contraception		−2.19**
		0.77
Unplanned, not contracepting		−3.06***
		0.62
Unplanned, technical contraceptive failure		−2.18**
		0.78

(continued)

Table 2.6   How Happy Respondent Was When Nonmarital
            Pregnancy Discovered (*Continued*)

	Model 1	Model 2
Unplanned, reason to believe sterile		−1.47+
		0.75
cut 1	−1.24	−3.41
cut 2	0.44	−1.43
N		190

Source: Authors' calculations.
Notes: Ordered categories of happiness are happy, in-between and unhappy. Numbers in italics are standard errors.
***$p < .001$, **$p < .01$, *$p < .05$, + $p < .10$

planned pregnancies (table 2.3). The percentage considering abortion gets higher as conceptions are less planned. Table 2.6, which predicts happiness level, shows a similar pattern net of sociodemographic variables such as race, education, family background, pregnancy number, and so on.[19]

Staying with these four categories, the clear predictors are the characteristics of the relationship with the partner. Again here, the four categories—planned, in between, unplanned with inconsistent contraception, and unplanned with technical contraceptive failure—are clearly ordered with the former entailing more serious relationships. Table 2.3 shows that the more stable the romantic relationship, the higher the degree of intent. The same patterns are evident in table 2.5, net of other factors.

The unplanned, no contraception category does not fit these patterns. There is no evidence that those contraceptions were really revealed preferences that the couples even ambivalently wanted a child at the time (as is the case in the in-between category and perhaps for those who use contraception inconsistently). Hardly any were happy when they learned of the pregnancy and more than 75 percent considered an abortion. One key to why these pregnancies caused so much anguish is their relational context. Other than the small group of those who thought they were sterile, this category had the highest percentage of casual relationships. This is true even net of socioeconomic and other factors (see table 2.5). The multivariate analysis in table 2.6 shows that, net of other precursors, parents were the least happy to hear the news when the conception occurred under these circumstances. Both the men and the women report more unhappiness than in any other group, but this unhappiness is especially pronounced among the women—72 percent of women versus 36 percent of men, the largest gender difference within any category (results not shown).[20]

Some might wonder whether there is a learning curve, so that those with early pregnancies in the unplanned but no contraception category might be more likely to plan future births or use birth control when they have no desire for a baby. Table 2.5 presents some evidence of this: all else being equal, lower order births are more likely to fall in this category relative to the planned and the in between category than higher order births up to the third or fourth birth (the inflection point of the non-linear curve is 3.64).

We had thought that conceptions among this group—those who were not planning a pregnancy but were also not contracepting—might be especially disadvantaged in a number of ways—more caught up in a high-risk life style involving drugs, or more depressed. Unfortunately, we have survey measures of these problems only at one point in time, just after the birth of the focal child or, in the case of depression, two years later. Table 2.3 shows that our hypothesis is not substantiated. Does this mean that socioeconomic disadvantage, with all it entails, doesn't relate to efficacy with regard to contraception? Perhaps. We suspect, however, that it is because our measures of drug and alcohol use and depression were collected only at one point in time, and because our sample has a truncated income distribution. Moreover, our reading of their narratives strongly suggests that the individuals in this category are the most disadvantaged and have the most chaotic and troubled lives.

Was the barrier to contraception among those with no desire to get pregnant a matter of not having the money? We asked respondents whether they had ever been in a situation where they wanted to use birth control but could not afford it or find it. All said no. Many use neighborhood clinics with free or sliding scale services. Some laughed when we asked this question, pointing out how hard clinics and schools in their communities push contraceptives. One woman did say that once she had had to wait in between health insurance plans to get a new prescription for the pill. Table 2.3, however, shows that not one of the respondents reporting pregnancies in the unplanned but no contraception group claimed to have ever had this problem. Unfortunately, we did not ask about cost or access barriers to abortion.

Conclusion

Our analysis shows the importance of two distinct continua of pregnancy planning—the strength of intention to conceive and the level of efficacy in taking the necessary steps to avoid a pregnancy. Planned pregnancies were relatively rare, and were almost always in the context of serious, stable, cohabiting relationships, the most marriage-like in our sample. On the other end of the intentionality continuum, consistent contraceptive practices sometimes failed. Failures occurred in three very different relationship contexts. Some were in casual relationships. Some, however, were in serious relationships. These couples had usually already had children together and didn't want another child at the time.

For the rest, roughly 65 percent, the pregnancy was neither fully planned nor carefully avoided. Approximately 20 percent were between planned and unplanned. Almost all of these occurred within stable relationships. Here, the typical couple clearly wants children together, and may even want a child at the time, but given their circumstances, the timing is less than ideal. This produces ambivalence. Many such couples are operating in a normative context where children come naturally when a couple is in a serious, long-term, monogamous relationship (Rainwater 1960: 54; 1965: 282; Ladner 1971: 256). This is particularly true for Hispanics. For them, taking steps to avoid pregnancy might be viewed by others in their communities as unnatural, or a sign that the relationship is in trouble. Overall, it appears that the strong positive valuing of children and the normative assumption that children are the expected outcome of stable, committed, relationships overwhelms timing concerns.

Nearly 25 percent of all pregnancies were due to inconsistent contraception. Pregnancies among inconsistent users were much more likely to spring from serious relationships than technical contraceptive failures were. When couples' relationships move from casual to serious, they often let contraceptive practices lapse. The need to indicate trust is part of the reason. Weak negative intention to avoid pregnancy is another. Inconsistent users usually know, or have at least begun to believe, that they want a child or more children with their partner eventually. In this way, they are like the between group, whose pregnancies also usually occur within a serious relationship. The main difference is one of degree—their desire for a child is not as strong or as immediate. Thus, when we compare these pregnancies to planned pregnancies or to contraceptive failures, it seems that the intermediate level of intent produces some contraception, but not diligent contraception.

It is in the unplanned no contraception group, which includes 25 percent of the pregnancies, where behavior and intention do not seem aligned. Many, especially women, were unhappy to learn they were pregnant, and those with these pregnancies were by far the most likely to consider abortion or terminate the pregnancy. None claimed that the problem was being unable to afford birth control. More of these pregnancies occurred in the context of casual relationships than the other categories. Indeed, the fact that the relationship was new or casual was often the reason respondents said they were unhappy to learn of the pregnancy. These respondents did not seem to differ from the other groups in the value they placed on a stable relationship as the right context for having children.[21] They differed by whether they used contraception when they weren't in such a relationship.

We were surprised that the quantitative analyses did not show that those reporting pregnancies in this group had experienced more depression or substance abuse problems, though, as noted earlier, we drew these measures from the survey, they were collected at a single point in time, and significant underreporting might have occurred. We were also surprised that these respondents were not more likely to have grown up with a single parent, or to have less education. Despite this, our reading of their narratives strongly suggests that the individuals with the most chaotic and troubled lives have pregnancies in this category.[22]

In sum, leaving aside the planned pregnancies and the contraceptive failures, where do the rest fit? Do they reflect a high social value of children and a lack of perceived (and actual) opportunity costs associated with having them young? Or do they suggest a lack of efficacy with regard to contraception might be the cause? The answer is both. Pregnancies in the between group, as well as some portion of pregnancies following inconsistent contraception, provide the clearest fit for the former notion. The unplanned but no contraception group might well hold similar values, but their situation best fits the latter idea. Although these parents were often just not thinking, to use their words, before conception, their lack of thought did not denote a desire to have a child at that time.

Our analysis shows the importance of two distinct continua of pregnancy planning—the level of efficacy in taking the necessary steps to avoid a pregnancy and the strength of intention to conceive. The latter is strongly affected by how serious the relationship is at the time of conception. The causes of the former are fertile ground for further study.

Notes

1. Some of the between group were using some form of contraception on and off, but also expressed some level of positive intention with regard to pregnancy in the period just before conception. If they had not, we would have placed them in the inconsistent contraception category.

2. Stacey Plichta et al. (1992), Constance Pilkington, Whitney Kern, and David Indest (1994), Carol Reisen and Paul Poppen (1995), and Jonathan Ellen et al. (1996) report similar findings.

3. Exceptions to our claim that a wider array of dimensions determining pregnancy have not been considered include Kathryn Edin and Maria Kefalas (2005), Ilene Speizer et al. (2004), and Laurie Zabin et al. (2000).

4. In addition to these seventy-six parents from our baseline sample, our qualitative analysis also draws from wave four interviews with seven social fathers—new partners of original TLC3 mothers who had broken up with the focal father. Our quantitative analysis of the 202 pregnancies uses only the seventy-six parents, however, as we lacked survey measures for these cases.

5.   There are limitations in having respondents retrospectively recall their intention at the time. Other researchers have questioned the validity of retrospective reporting of pregnancy intention (Joyce, Kaestner, and Korenman 2002).

6.   In the case of the focal child, we have reports from both parents, each taken from individual interviews. The reports about planning status are generally concurrent, though the two often differ in how happy they are on the discovery of the pregnancy, with men less often unhappy.

7.   Two men said their pregnancy was explicitly planned, but that they had not initially wanted a child right then. In both cases, they said their partners talked them into trying to get pregnant. We coded these as planned.

8.   Some respondents in this category said the pregnancy was planned because they had not been taking steps to avoid conception at the time, but later admitted the pregnancy was not actually planned in advance. Others said their pregnancy was unplanned, but their narratives revealed that they were feeling ambivalent about whether they wanted a child and recognized they were taking a pregnancy risk by engaging in unprotected sex.

9.   Some respondents said the pregnancy was in between planned and unplanned because they recognized they had not been taking consistent steps to avoid pregnancy, even though they did not want a child at the time. We counted these cases as unplanned but inconsistent contraception, rather than in the in between category, because there was no other evidence that the respondent wanted a baby at the time, even ambivalently.

10.   Those who said they forgot to take the pill or buy condoms sometimes were put in the inconsistent contraception category.

11.   If the respondent never wanted abortion, but the partner did, we did not code the respondent as considering abortion.

12.   In the TLC3 data, all respondents were in one of these groups except one man who was part white and part Native American. He was coded as white here.

13.   We cannot simultaneously adjust for the nonindependence of multiple pregnancies within a person and the fact that we have two reports of most focal pregnancies (one by each parent).

14.   Elijah Anderson's (1989) ethnographic analysis of teen childbearing in poor black communities depicts women who stop using birth control in hopes that a pregnancy will nudge their boyfriends into marriage, and men who "game" the women for sex but don't want the responsibility of children. One would expect this scenario to produce more women than men reporting planned pregnancies, but we do not find this. Nor do we find a sex difference in the proportion of pregnancies that are in between planned and unplanned, as his analysis would predict (table 2.2).

15.   We did not instruct interviewers to ask if the couple was cohabiting at conception. However, for about half the pregnancies, we were able to code this information from spontaneous mentions in the narratives. Among planned pregnancies for which we had information on whether the couple was cohabiting at conception, 100 percent were doing so. The percent was substantially lower (less than 60 percent) for all other pregnancy types.

16. A subgroup of respondents who reported inconsistent contraception at the time of an unplanned pregnancy deserves special mention: those primarily using coitus interruptus, or pullout. Almost all (82 percent) of the sixteen pregnancies that resulted when pullout was practiced were in the context of a serious relationship.

17. This does not mean that these respondents had achieved their ideal family size, only that they were strongly opposed to having a child with a particular partner at a particular time.

18. Of parents reporting that a pregnancy was unplanned but used no contraception, over twice as many men as women called it a casual relationship. Some of those in this category may be similar to those in the low-income black neighborhood Anderson described (1989), where men who are not really interested in long-term romantic relationships or parenthood game young women into having sex with them by leading them to think the relationships have serious futures. However, whereas this motivation is ubiquitous among those Anderson interviewed, it does not characterize the large majority of male pregnancies described in this analysis.

19. In this analysis, we see some indication of a halo effect on reporting happiness as their reaction to the pregnancy, because, all else being equal, respondents were more likely to characterize their responses positively if they were reporting on the focal conception, as opposed to one of their earlier or subsequent pregnancies. However, all focal births were to couples still romantically involved when the baby was born, so this rather than reporting bias might explain the greater happiness.

20. Across all pregnancy types, women were less happy on discovering they were pregnant than men (tables 2.2 and 2.6).

21. Nor did they differ from those with more planned pregnancies in what age they thought would be ideal for their child to become a parent (table 2.3). Although many of them had their first pregnancy in their teens, they thought about twenty-five was an ideal age for a first birth.

22. Many other factors presumably shape both the strength of intention and efficacy with regard to pregnancy. These include childhood and adolescent socialization by parents, peers, neighbors, religion, and the media, and early adolescent relationship experiences. We did not have measures of many of these. Other analyses suggest that factors such as these have significant affects on adolescent's sense of self-efficacy with regard to contraception (Longmore et al, 2003; Manning, Longmore, and Giordano 2000).

References

Anderson, Elijah. 1989. "Sex Codes and Family Life Among Poor Inner-City Youths." *Annals of the American Academy of Political and Social Science* 501(1): 59–78.

Andrews, Kenneth H., and Denise B. Kandel. 1979. "Attitude and Behavior: Specification of the Contingent Consistency Hypothesis." *American Sociological Review* 44(2): 298–310.

Bachrach, Christine A. and Susan Newcomer. 1999. "Intended Pregnancies and Unintended Pregnancies: Distinct Categories or Opposite Ends of a Continuum?" *Family Planning Perspectives* 31(5): 251–2.

Brown, Sarah S., and Leon Eisenberg, eds. 1995. *The Best Intentions: Unintended Pregnancy and the Well-Being of Children and Families.* Washington: National Academy Press.

Chandra, Anjani, Gladys M. Martinez, William D. Mosher, Joyce C. Abma, and Jo Jones. 2005. *Fertility, Family Planning, and Reproductive Health of U.S. Women: Data from the 2002 National Survey of Family Growth.* Vital Health Statistics, series 23, number 25. Washington: U.S. Department of Health and Human Services, National Center for Health Statistics.

Edin, Kathryn, and Maria Kefalas. 2005. *Promises I Can Keep: Why Poor Women Put Motherhood Before Marriage.* Berkeley, Calif.: University of California Press.

Ellen, Jonathan M., Sarah Cahn, Stephen L. Eyre, and Cherrie B. Boyer. 1996. "Types of Adolescent Sexual Relationships and Associated Perceptions about Condom Use." *Journal of Adolescent Health* 18(6): 417–22.

Federal Drug Administration. 1997. "Pregnancy Rates for Birth Control Methods." http://www.fda.gov/fdac/features/1997/conceptbl.html.

Filippone, Melissa, and Jean Knab. 2004. Fragile Families Scales and Documentation and Question Sources for One-Year Questionnaires. http://www.fragilefamilies.princeton.edu/documentation.asp.

Fischer, Rachel C., Joseph B. Stanford, Penny Jameson, and M. Jann DeWitt. 1999. "Exploring the Concepts of Intended, Planned and Wanted Pregnancy." *Journal of Family Practice* 48(2): 117–22.

Fishbein, Martin, and Icek Ajzen. 1975. *Belief, Attitude, Intention, and Behavior: An Introduction to Theory and Research.* Reading, Mass.: Addison-Wesley.

Gebhardt, Winifred A., Lisette Kuyper, and Gwen Greunsven. 2003. "Need for Intimacy in Relationships and Motives for Sex as Determinants of Adolescent Condom Use." *Journal of Adolescent Health* 33(3): 154–64.

Henshaw, Stanley K. 1998. "Unintended Pregnancy in the United States." *Family Planning Perspectives* 30(1): 24–29.

Joyce, Ted, Robert Kaestner, and Sanders Korenman. 2002. "On the Validity of Retrospective Assessment of Pregnancy Intention." *Demography* 39(1): 199–213.

Kost, Kathryn, and Jacqueline Darroch Forrest. 1995. "Intention Status of U.S. Births in 1988: Difference by Mothers' Socioeconomic and Demographic Characteristics." *Family Planning Perspectives* 27(1): 11–17.

Ku, Leighton, Freya L. Sonenstein, and Joseph H. Pleck. 1994. "The Dynamics of Young Men's Condom Use During and Across Relationships." *Family Planning Perspectives* 26(6): 246–51.

Ladner, Joyce. 1971. *Tomorrow's Tomorrow: The Black Woman.* Garden City, N.Y.: Doubleday.

Longmore, Monica, Wendy Manning, Peggy Giordano, and Jennifer Rudolph. 2003. "Contraceptive Self-Efficacy: Does it Influence Adolescents' Contraceptive Use?" *Journal of Health and Social Behavior* 44(1): 45–60.

Luker, Kristin C. 1999. "A Reminder that Human Behavior Frequently Refuses to Conform to Models Created by Researchers." *Family Planning Perspectives* 31(5): 248–53.

Manlove, Jennifer, Suzanne Ryan, and Kerry Franzetta. 2003. "Patterns of Contraceptive Use Within Teenagers' First Sexual Relationships." *Perspectives on Sexual and Reproductive Health* 35(6): 246–55.

Manning, Wendy D., Monica A. Longmore, and Peggy C. Giordano. 2000. "The Relationship Context of Contraceptive Use at First Intercourse." *Family Planning Perspectives* 32(3): 104–10.

Moos, Merry-K., Ruth Petersen, and Cathy Melvin. 1997. "Pregnant Women's Perspectives on Intendedness of Pregnancy." *Women's Health Issues* 7(6): 385–92.

Musick, Kelly, Paula England, and Sarah Edgington. 2005. "Education and Class Differences in Intended and Unintended Fertility." Presented at the Seventieth Annual Meeting of the Population Association of America. Philadelphia, Pa., March 31–April 2, 2005.

Pilkington, Constance J., Whitney Kern, and David Indest. 1994. "Is Safer Sex Necessary with a 'Safe' Partner?: Condom Use and Romantic Feelings." *Journal of Sex Research* 31(3): 203–10.

Plichta, Stacey B., Carol S. Weisman, Constance A. Nathanson, Margaret E. Ensminger, and J. Courtland Robinson. 1992. "Partner Specific Condom Use Among Adolescent Women Clients of a Family Planning Clinic." *Journal of Adolescent Health* 12(7): 506–13.

Rainwater, Lee. 1960. *And the Poor Get Children: Sex, Contraception, and Family Planning in the Working Class*. Chicago, Ill.: Quadrangle.

———. 1965. *Family Design: Marital Sexuality, Family Size, and Conception*. Chicago, Ill.: Aldine Press.

Reisen, Carol A., and Paul J. Poppen. 1995. "College Women and Condom Use: Importance of Partner Relationship." *Journal of Applied Social Psychology*. 25(17): 1485–98.

Sable, Marjorie R. 1999. "Pregnancy Intentions May Not be a Useful Measure for Research on Maternal and Child Health Outcomes." *Family Planning Perspectives* 31(5): 249–50

Sayer, Liana C., Nathan Wright, and Kathryn Edin. 2003. "Class Differences in Family Attitudes." Presented at the Sixty-Eighth Annual Meeting of the Population Association of America. Minneapolis, Minn., May 1–3, 2003.

Spweizer, Ilene S., John S. Santelli, Aimee Afable-Munsuz, and Carl Kendall. 2004. "Measuring Factors Underlying Intendedness of Women's First and Later Pregnancies." *Perspectives on Sexual and Reproductive Health* 36(5): 198–205.

Trussell, James, Barbara Vaughan, and Joseph Stanford. 1999. "Are All Contraceptive Failures Unintended Pregnancies? Evidence from the 1995 National Survey of Family Growth." *Family Planning Perspectives* 31(3): 246–60.

Waller, Maureen R. 1999. "Meanings and Motives in New Family Stories: The Separation of Reproduction and Marriage Among Low-Income, Black and White Parents." In *The Cultural Territories of Race: Black and White Boundaries*, edited by Michèle Lamont. Chicago, Ill.: The University of Chicago Press.

Williams, Lindy, Joyce Abma, and Linda J. Piccinino. 1999. "The Correspondence Between Intention to Avoid Childbearing and Subsequent Fertility: A Prospective Analysis." *Family Planning Perspectives* 31(5): 220–7.

Zabin, Laurie Schwab, George R. Huggins, Mark R. Emerson, and Vanessa E. Cullins. 2000. "Partner Effects on a Woman's Intention to Conceive: 'Not with This Partner.' " *Family Planning Perspectives* 32(1): 39–45.

Chapter 3

Everyday Gender Conflicts in Low-Income Couples

PAULA ENGLAND AND EMILY FITZGIBBONS SHAFER

W HAT ARE the everyday bones of contention in couples' relationships? Research on middle-class couples emphasizes women's
longing for more emotional intimacy and the inequity of the
fact that employed women still do most of the housework, though it isn't
clear whether these are the issues that couples would say are most important. We know less about the issues of contention in lower-income couples, especially given that many studies of working-class couples have
been limited to white, married couples and are decades old. In this paper,
we explore the issues that low-income cohabiting or married couples with
children identify as their main conflicts.[1]

Low-income couples have the obvious problem of less money, making
disagreements about spending priorities more difficult to solve. Life-
course trajectories differ profoundly by class in ways that might affect
couple conflicts. At lower education and class levels, and among disadvantaged minority groups, women get pregnant earlier, often before
marriage, pregnancies are more often unplanned, and fertility is higher
(Ellwood and Jencks 2001; Edin and Kefalas 2005; Musick, England, and
Edgington 2005; chapter 2 this volume). Among the poor, children are
often the main source of meaning in women's lives (Edin and Kefalas
2005). Relationships break up at higher rates, so repartnering leads many
households to include the woman's children from a past as well as the
present partner (Carlson and Furstenberg 2006), which may lead to disagreements about how stepfathers should act (Cherlin 1978).

To explore couple relationships among low-income parents, we use the
Time, Love, and Cash among Couples with Children Study. As part of this
longitudinal, qualitative study of new parents, we employed a couple discussion at the end of the couple interviews two and four years after they

had a baby. In this discussion, the couple was asked to identify two important issues that they didn't see eye to eye on. The interviewer asked them to explain each side, and then left them alone to discuss the issue for ten minutes. Our analysis comes from a content analysis of the videos and transcripts from these sessions, supplemented by other data on the couples from the qualitative interviews and the quantitative survey data from the Fragile Family and Child Wellbeing study (Fragile Families). After coding all conflicts into nine categories, we focus our analysis on two issues, because they came up most often and had a clear pattern to which gender took what position. In about a third of the couples, one of the two issues selected concerned women wanting more attention from men. Women want men to spend more time with them, talk and listen to them more, and show more affection. Few men articulate this grievance. About a third of couples chose our second issue: how strict the child rearing regime should be, with fathers generally wanting things stricter than mothers.

We call the issues we examine here everyday conflicts. We know from what the couples in this study told us in individual interviews that many have had serious problems such as sexual infidelity (see chapters 5 and 6, this volume). Few parents chose this issue when couples were interviewed together, however. This is in part because sexual infidelity broke up some couples, and those who broke up, though interviewed individually, typically did not participate in the couple interviews two to four years into the study that we use here. Additionally, people may shy away from talking about infidelity in front of a partner because to do so is destabilizing. Thus, what we describe are the chronic conflicts that couples are willing to talk about, have a clear pattern to which gender takes what position, and are seen by couples as important. We make no claim that they are the issues that break up relationships, but they are the everyday stuff of gender conflicts in low-income couples with children. We also make no claim that they are the same or different than those of middle-class couples. To facilitate future comparisons, we think it important to document what coupled life looks like in the low-income population, where patterns of partnering and childbearing are very different.

Emotional Intimacy and Companionship

One way to identify important conflicts in ongoing relationships is to look at what causes divorce. Sexual infidelity, jealousy, drinking, spending money, moodiness, not communicating, and anger increase the odds of divorce (Amato and Rogers 1997). What, though, do divorced individuals say were the big issues that broke up their marriages, and how do they differ by class? Gay Kitson (1992) found that high-SES individuals often attributed divorces to lack of communication, changes in interests or values, incompatibility, or partners' self-centeredness. Low-SES individuals complained more about physical abuse, cheating, criminal activities, financial problems, and employment problems (for similar findings, see Bloom, Niles, and Tatcher 1985; Amato and Previti 2003; Levinger 1966). Dernie Kurz's (1995) mostly working-class female interviewees regaled her with tales of abuse, infidelity, and alcohol abuse before their divorces. Overall, the pattern is that lower-SES individuals complain more of overt abuse and misbehavior, and that those higher up the class structure offer more rarified reasons relating to emotional relationship quality.

Higher-SES individuals are somehow able to create better relationships (Voydanoff 1991; Conger et al. 1990) and have lower rates of divorce (Teachman 2002; McLanahan 2004). Their more emotional reasons for divorce, however, suggest that they have a higher sense of entitlement to relationships with love and companionship.

Several qualitative sociological studies of couples focus on the emotional issues that upper-middle-class women seem to consider the sine qua non of relationships.[2] Francesca Cancian (1987) argues that a feminized conception of love has evolved, where practical assistance or sex aren't seen to "count" as expressing love. Our culture discourages men from orally expressing tender emotions but defines love in terms of such expression, so men can't both follow gender norms and be the kind of intimate partners women want. Lillian Rubin's book, *Intimate Strangers*, based on qualitative interviews of mostly middle-class husbands and wives, painted a vivid portrait of this gender conflict:

> Women complain to each other all the time about not being able to talk to their men about the things that matter most to them—about what they themselves are thinking and feeling, about what goes on in the hearts and minds of the men they're relating to. And men, less able to expose themselves and their conflicts—those within themselves or those with the women in their lives—either turn silent or take cover by holding women up to derision. (1983, 66)

In his clinical practice and his research, the psychologist John Gottman (1994) noticed that women are more likely to want to talk about problems within their relationships than their male partners, a gender difference heightened in unhappy marriages. Married women are more likely than men to have a confrontational conflict style, whereas more men have a conflict-avoidant style (Mackey and O'Brien 1998; Gottman 1994). Not only do women want verbal sharing for emotional intimacy, they also want problems solved, and are often willing to be confrontational to achieve this.

Scholars differ in the causes to which they attribute women's desire for and skills at communication and intimacy. Gottman (1994) points to a greater physiological responses of men to conflict, and speculates that it may be innate. Nancy Chodorow's (1978) feminist revision of psychoanalytic theory suggests an environmental cause. Having a primary care-giver of the other sex than the child, as most boys do, means that gender identity encourages individuation from mother and vice versa. For girls, gender identity can be achieved without losing the bond to mother, thus does not encourage individuation. In this view, as long as women do most of the child rearing, so that girls are reared by same-sex and boys by other-sex caretakers, women will be predisposed to connection and men predisposed to emotional separation. Another sociological view posits socialization; girls and women are encouraged to be empathic and sensitive, but any sign of emotional sensitivity is discouraged in boys. Based in ethnomethodology, the doing gender perspective that gender is something we do—a display—more than who we are. In this view, we do gender to render ourselves accountable to norms of gender that others are presumed to hold, rather than to express our preferences, values, or iden-tities (West and Zimmerman 1987).

We examined several qualitative studies of low-income couples to see what they reveal about whether emotional intimacy is an issue. Lee Rainwater, Richard Coleman, and Gerald Handel (1959) found that, com-pared to middle-class women, wives of working-class men felt less secure about their husbands' affection, and saw their men as more controlling, insensitive, and inconsiderate. Yet they saw little hope of changing the sit-uation. Mirra Komarovsky (1964) interviewed wives of working-class men and found differences in wives' expectations depending on whether the wives had graduated from high school. The graduates believed more strongly in spouses talking and being friends than those who had not fin-ished high school. Those who hadn't graduated from high school some-times resented men's lack of mutuality, but felt lucky if men didn't drink too much, cheat, or beat them. Communication and companionship were impeded by separate leisure pastimes for men and women and men's reluctance to talk to their wives. Men's segregated activities were also described by the white unionized blue-collar workers that David Halle (1984) interviewed. These men were embedded in male friendship net-works that excluded women and involved drinking, watching sports on television, fishing, and hunting. Men often reported that their wives com-plained about how much they were out with the boys. However, if mar-riages survived, couples were often more companionate in middle and older age when children were grown and the men had more vacation. Rubin's (1976) book on blue-collar couples in the early 1970s, *Worlds of Pain*, showed women wanting men to attend more to their feelings, but having little sense that it was possible. Like the women Komarovsky interviewed, Rubin's respondents felt that if their men brought home their paycheck, didn't drink too much, and didn't hit them, they were fairly lucky. Twenty years later, Rubin (1994) reinterviewed thirty-six of the same white couples she had interviewed for *Worlds of Pain* as well as some additional couples. Comparing responses in the two studies, Rubin reports an increase in women's sense of entitlement to a relationship in which men attend to their emotional needs, share with housework, and regard them more as equals. Men in the later study often conceded that they should do these things more than they do. She sees this change as most pronounced in the working class; the norm was developed in the middle class earlier (75–91).

Overall, these studies suggest that women of all classes want emotional companionship, but middle-class women expect and get it more, and lower-income women are pessimistic that it is possible, so evaluate relationships more by whether men at least abstain from cheating, violence, irresponsibility with money, and substance abuse.

Children and Housework

A large body of research shows that the birth of children increases stress for couples, lowers their report of happiness with the relationship, but also makes it less likely that they will break up (Cowan and Cowan 1992; Amato et al. 2003). Part of the conflict arises because couples typically increase the gender division of labor when they have a child, and later women often chafe at how much of the child rearing and housework they have taken over (Cowan et al. 1985). Men lose some of women's emotional nurturance, as her energy is depleted by the child (Cowan et al. 1985; Rubin 1976).

Despite rising women's employment, women still do most of the housework even when employed (Hochschild 1989; Brines 1994). When women see their share of housework as unfair, they are less happy with their relationships, more conflict occurs, and the odds of divorce rise (Stohs 2000; Voydanoff and Donnelly 1999; Yogev and Brett 1985; Frisco and Williams 2003; Huber and Spitze 1980). What this research doesn't clarify is how important this issue is to women (or men) relative to other issues or whether it is as much an issue for low-income and high-income couples.

Child rearing might be a conflict just like housework—with each partner wanting the other to do more. Conflicts, however, could also be about how to raise children, not just who will do the work. Are there typical gender disagreements about how to treat children? We could find little literature on this. Some studies show that fathers, more than mothers, encourage gender-traditional behavior in children (Maccoby and Jacklin 1974; Maccoby 1998). Rubin's (1976) qualitative interviews suggest this may be more prevalent among working-class fathers compared to middle-class fathers, especially in regards to sons.

In 1978, Cherlin pointed out the problem for remarriages caused by the lack of clear norms about how much stepfathers should discipline children. Since he wrote, the prevalence of blended families has increased even more. Lower-income individuals are more likely to marry or cohabit with someone who has children from a previous union (Carlson and Furstenberg 2006). Some studies show that stepchildren from other partnerships are associated with lower quality relationships (Clingempeel 1981; White and Booth 1985) though others do not find this (MacDonald and DeMaris 1995; Furstenberg and Spanier, 1987). These studies, regardless, tell us little about what couples in these situations fight about.

One could hypothesize that the simple fact of higher fertility in lower-income families might lead more conflicts to center around child rearing. One could also hypothesize less conflict about child rearing because lower-income families have more relaxed notions of what constitutes adequate child rearing. Annette Lareau argues that the upper middle class engages in "concerted cultivation," and the working and lower class have a notion of the "natural growth" of children as long as they are kept safe and fed (2003).

We started without clear hypotheses about what conflicts would surface as important issues in our sample of low-income parents. The literature suggested that women are dissatisfied with emotional intimacy in all social classes, but that often lower-income women deal with grosser forms of misbehavior by men, so that this, combined with lower expectations of emotional intimacy might lead the issue to be deemphasized. We started without priors about whether conflicts regarding housework or child rearing would be salient. Finally, we imagined that arguments about money might be important in low-income couples. Thus, we set out with a fairly open, inductive approach to discover what the salient, everyday conflicts were in low-income couples with kids.

Data and Methods

The data from this study are from the TLC3, a longitudinal qualitative study of seventy-five couples who are a stratified probability sample from the Chicago, Milwaukee, and New York respondents to the larger Fragile Families study. In waves three and four, approximately two and four years after the birth of their child, the couple interview was immediately followed by a "couple discussion."[3] The primary data for this paper are transcripts of these discussions.[4]

Sample

Our analysis comes from the fifty-four intact couples at wave three and the forty-seven intact couples at wave four who did a couple interview and thus a couple discussion at these waves.[5] All couples who were still romantically involved by wave three or four were either married or

Table 3.1   Descriptive Statistics on Romantically Involved Couples
Who Participated in Couple Conflict Discussion

	Wave Three	Wave Four
Mother's race		
Black	43%	47%
Hispanic	35	32
White	22	21
Father's race		
Black	46	45
Hispanic	35	36
White	19	19
Mother and father do not identify as the same race	17	15
Mother's educational attainment at baseline		
Less than high school graduation	24	26
High school graduate	39	40
Post–high school education	37	34
Father's educational attainment at baseline		
Less than high school graduation	26	30
High school graduate	37	38
Post–high school education	37	32
Relationship status		
Couple married at birth	41	36
Couple cohabiting at birth	50	57
Couple married at discussion	56	60
Couple cohabiting at discussion	44	38
Discussion is with a new social father	6	13
Mother has children who are not biologically current partner's in the household	31	45
Father (non-social only) has children who are not biologically current partner's	33	39
N	54	47

Source: Authors' calculations.

cohabiting at the time of the discussion. Table 3.1 provides descriptive statistics.

The proportion of couples in our sample who were married at the birth of the child that got them into the study was 41 percent of the wave three and 36 percent of the wave four sample. Because some of the TLC3 unmarried couples married between wave one and the couple discussions two to four years later, however, and because a few of our couples dropped out of the study, more than half of our couple conflict discussions were with married couples—57 percent at wave three and 62 percent at wave four. To our surprise, the conflict areas couples identified as most important did not differ significantly by marital status at the time of the discussion or at wave one.[6] Thus, we included married and unmarried couples to provide a larger, richer data source.

Our analytic sample is largely low income. Selection for participation in the TLC3 study required that parents have a total household income of less than $75,000. Most couples were far below this. At wave three, the household income reported to the Fragile Families survey of those of our TLC3 couples who had a couple discussion at wave three or four had a median of $20,000.[7] As table 3.1 shows, mothers are 43 percent black and 35 percent Hispanic at wave three, and 47 percent black and 32 percent Hispanic at wave four. About 25 percent have not completed high school or a GED, and the ratio is even higher for fathers. About 65 percent of mothers and fathers have no more than a high school degree or GED. A large minority of households contain the mother's children from a previous partner, 31 percent at wave three and 45 percent at wave four. A similar fraction of fathers have children by other mothers, generally not living with the couple.[8]

The Couple Discussion: The Data Gathering Tool

In the Couple Discussion added to the end of the Wave Three and Wave Four interview, the interviewer helped the couple to identify the two most important conflicts in their relationship, and left them alone, being videotaped, while they discussed the issues.[9] After finishing the questions in the regular interview, the interviewer explained that we were interested in learning how couples talk about issues they "don't see eye-to-eye on." The interviewer then gave each a worksheet to complete. It asked "how often do you and your partner disagree about" and listed the following topics of disagreement: child's sleeping or eating, disciplining child, how much time one of us spends taking care of child, child's personality, housework, money matters, communication, one of our personalities, one of our personal habits, working or jobs, friends, other family members, drug or alcohol use, amount or quality time we spend together, need for time alone, sex, marriage, jealousy or infidelity, or other (respondents were asked to define other). Respondents were asked to circle, without the aid of their partner, one of four answers—neither, once or twice, sometimes, or often—for each disagreement topic. Interviewers kept the two from talking with each other as the sheet was filled out. The goal was to stimulate thinking across the broad range of issues that often come up among couples. After the worksheets were filled out, interviewers asked them to identify the most important conflict between them. Interviewers then asked each partner to explain his or her perspective on the issue, keeping the other party from interrupting. The interviewer then summed up each party's side and asked if the summary accurately represented their positions.[10] The interviewer then transcribed the two issues and left the paper with the couple as a reminder of the task.[11] The couple was asked to discuss the issues for ten minutes to try to come to a resolution that both would be at least somewhat happy with. The interviewer then left the room.

Analysis

Our analysis draws mainly from the videos and verbatim transcriptions of the couple discussions of wave three and wave four, just described. We employed emergent theme and narrative analysis (Strauss and Corbin 1990) in our effort to categorize and describe issues on which couples experienced conflict. As we watched videos and read each couple discussion transcript, we let a typology of topics emerge inductively. The topics that emerged are: the father wants child rearing stricter, the mother wants child rearing stricter, the mother wants more attention from the father, the father wants more attention from the mother, the mother wants the father to do more housework, the father wants the mother to do more housework, the father is irresponsible with money (in her view), the mother is irresponsible with money (in his view), and the mother and the father disagree on what to spend money on. All other topics were categorized as other; we do not discuss or present statistics on this residual category here. Table 3.2, discussed shortly, gives the distribution of couples across each theme for both waves.

After identifying the common categories, we used narrative analysis, a hallmark of qualitative research, to further investigate the top two conflict areas. We read the entire group of couple discussion transcripts, along with summaries of other interview transcripts about the couple's situation. Our focus was on understanding what men and women typically disagreed on, what behavior of each bothered the other, and how they saw issues differently. This paper is focused on the two most prevalent gendered themes— women wanting more attention from men, and men wanting a stricter parenting regime than women. We coded an issue into "mom wants more attention" if the woman articulated a desire for her man to spend more time with her, to give her more emotional or sexual attention, or for him to talk or listen to her more. In "dad wants child rearing stricter than mom," we coded only those conflicts about child rearing that could be construed as disagreements over how strict the rules or punishments should be, and in which the man wanted things stricter than the woman did.

We made use of the linked Fragile Families quantitative data to investigate whether social or demographic characteristics correlate with which issues they identified. None were significant except that white couples

Table 3.2   Romantically Involved Couples Identifying Selected Subjects as One of Two Main Conflicts

	Wave Three	Wave Four	Ever
Father wants stricter child discipline	28%	28%	34%
Mother wants stricter child discipline	9	15	15
Mother wants more attention from father	22	28	33
Father wants more attention from mother	2	9	8
Mother wants father to do more housework or child care	17	11	21
Father wants mother to do more housework or child care	4	4	5
Money issues (combines three categories below)	24	19	30
Mother irresponsible in father's view	6	9	10
Father irresponsible in mother's view	11	6	11
Spending priorities differ	7	4	10
Number of Couples	54	47	61

Source: Authors' calculations.
Note: Percents do not add up to 100% because each couple was asked to select two issues, and because the residual category, other conflicts, is not shown.

were more likely to identify the father as wanting a stricter parenting regime as an issue.[12]

Common Conflicts

Table 3.2 shows the percentage of couple discussions that identified each of the issues as one of the two important issues, for wave three, wave four, and either (a couple is counted here if they chose this as one of their two most important issue in either wave). By far the biggest issues were women wanting more attention from men and men wanting a stricter regime (and women a less strict regime) in child rearing. About 30 percent of couples identified each of these issues as one of the two important issues chosen for discussion.

The two biggest issues—strictness and attention—were clearly gendered. Whereas 34 percent of couples had an issue where the father wanted things stricter for children, only 15 percent had the opposite problem—that the mother thought things should be stricter. Similarly, where 33 percent of couples had an issue with the mother wanting more attention from the father (whether emotional, verbal, or sexual), only 8 percent reported the father as wanting more attention. Nor was it just that men complained about lack of sex and women complained about lack of emotional intimacy; if either partner complained about the other's willingness to have sex, we coded it here as a desire for more attention. Even with this decision rule, we still found few men with the complaint.[13]

The other predictable gender conflict was women wanting men to do more housework, which came up in 21 percent of couples. In 5 percent of cases, the man said the woman should do more housework. We did not analyze this extensively because it was less common than the two larger issues. We note, however, that the standard to which women were holding men was generally not equality. Many women complained that the man did not take out the trash regularly; they saw this as the man's job. Another common theme was women wanting men to clean up their own mess around the house more.

Money issues, in contrast, were not gendered, though money was identified by 30 percent of couples, almost as many as identified the other two main issues. Money conflicts typically involve one parent thinking the other spends too much or too irresponsibly. However, the culprit was equally likely to be the woman (10 percent) or the man (11 percent), and another 10 percent were matters of disagreement on spending priorities with no clear allegation by either party that the other was spending too much or irresponsibly.

Because our interest is in gender patterns, because parenting and attention were the more gendered areas of conflict and the most common conflicts, we focus our qualitative analysis on them.

She Wants More Attention

The biggest issue for women was their longing for more attention from their men. These mothers, many of them low-income and black or Hispanic, sounded strikingly like the upper middle-class white married women that Lillian Rubin (1983) interviewed in *Intimate Strangers*. Our reading of the past qualitative literature on working-class couples suggested that women may want more emotional mutuality, but be fairly resigned to not getting it. Instead, we found women very willing to complain about inadequate attention, and no evidence in our sample that higher-SES women had more of a focus on the issue. In fact, in our sample the issue was no more common among whites, married couples, or couples with higher education or income. If anything, this theme is more prevalent among the less advantaged parents in the sample. This was one of the conflict areas identified by 41 percent of black, 35 percent of Hispanic, but only 8 percent of white couples, and the difference between whites and the other two groups combined is statistically significant.[14] It was identified by 43 percent of the unmarried couples and 24 percent of the married, although this association does not rise to statistical significance. It is certainly not an issue limited to middle-class white married couples.

Among mothers wanting more attention, four subcategories emerged: complaints about men spending too little time with them; the quality of what happens in their time together—his lack of affection, talking, or listening; being sick of being alone with the kids; and wanting him to get off the streets and spend time with them.

Time Together

LaShawnda, twenty-nine, wants Tyrone, thirty-one, to spend more time with her. This African American couple was living together when their baby was born and has since married. LaShawnda complains that they don't do much together. Tyrone responds, "Sometimes . . . I be tired." He's a bus driver and says "she just don't know how much that take out of me," though he concedes that he should spend more "quality time" with her. LaShawnda doesn't buy the excuse that he is tired, pointing out that "he don't spend quality time with me . . . even on his days off. . . . He'll stay up really late at night to play video games, so that's time that we probably could spend together."

Calista has a similar grievance against Gavin. Four years after this black couple's daughter is born, they are each thirty-nine, unmarried, and living with kin. The interviewer summarizes the issue this way: "So, Calista, you feel like you want to spend more quality time together, and Gavin, you feel like it's perfectly fine as it is. . . . Is that right?" Gavin says "yes." Calista takes offense and retorts, "Well, we don't spend *no* time together. Oh yeah, things are just fine the way they are to you, huh? . . . You don't *want* to spend no time together."

His Verbal and Emotional Responsiveness

In some cases, the complaint is more about quality time. Sierra and Donte, both African American, were married when their daughter was born, and are now thirty-one and thirty-two. Sierra complains about how much verbal and emotional response she gets when she raises issues. She says "I felt that what was important to me wasn't important to him. . . . If I want to talk about something . . . sometimes he would like have no response. So I took that as it wasn't important what I had to say. . . . So after a while I decided to just talk about things less. . . . I couldn't sleep. . . . I wanted to talk about it."

Samantha, thirty-two, also complains about the lack of verbal response from her partner, Ali, who is twenty-nine. This couple, also black, have two children together. She says:

> He don't like to communicate. . . . He's always quiet. . . . I'm used to somebody else talking too and they give me . . . feedback, instead of sitting there looking at me like, "I wish she'd just shut up and go to sleep." . . . I feel that, if I'm . . . wanting to talk, that you should talk with me.

Lattice and Jerome, an African American couple, were married when their baby was born. We talk to them when their baby is two, and she is twenty-six and he is twenty-seven. She recounts that he recently "was trying to go over to my brother's house so he can drink . . . the Hennessey. . . . Why didn't he come over here and drink Hennessey?" When the interviewer asks "what bugs you most about it?" she notes that "he was more concerned about . . . drinking Hennessey than he was with her [the baby's] well-being and my well-being." We revisit this couple two years later (at wave four), and Jerome mentions that Lattice doesn't like how much time he spends at her brother's house, where he says he goes to work on cars or "sit around." The issue is thus apparently still alive, but he says it is a "small issue." In this interview Lattice also complains about sex: "It's like, when I want to have sex, he . . . says he's too tired, but if somebody calls him, he's gone, up and gone. . . . It seems like the only time we do have sex is when he wants to." Jerome concedes that she is right.

She'd Like Him Off the Streets

One place that the urban, poor environment of our sample shows is when women say that they want their men home rather than in the streets. Mothers talked about it as a desire for more attention, but beneath their complaint was sometimes worry about the dangers and temptations of the streets.

Dominique was twenty-one and not married when she had her baby with twenty-three-year-old Steven. This African American couple has since broken up, and Dominique now lives with Marquis, with whom she has a one-year-old baby. She laughs and says, "It's not like that I don't want him to go out or nothing, it's just . . . when he go out, he'll go out for a long time. So when he come in, I be expecting him . . . to spend a little more time but . . . he'll leave back out." Marquis defends himself saying, "I'm thinking we live together. We can't do nothing but spend a lot of time together." Later he says, "I be here before the street lights come on. That's enough. . . . I come in at eight o'clock, nine o'clock every day." In this case, the issue seems to be her desire for more attention, rather than any distrust or worry about what he is doing.

Janell is twenty-three and has had two daughters with Leonard, whom she married after the birth of the second child. Janell says, "I don't think it's enough time put into our relationship on Leonard's part. I feel he runs the streets too much. . . . That's okay, you know, but you still have to remember that you have to spend quality time. . . . Sometimes it does become an issue." She continues:

I'll say when he works, he doesn't come straight home from work. He'll . . . stop on Bishop and then he won't come in till like twelve or two. . . . And my thing is why can't you come home to your family first, and then if you want to go back out, that's okay. . . . You should want to come home to your family first . . . to see what we doing or you know how our day was.

Leonard concedes: "[I] should be here more than I am." But, in his defense, he mentions that Janell knew him for about eight years before they "started talking." He says "she knew that I was always the type of person—I like to hang out." He describes a recent episode in which he was about to go out and she said, "Where you going? . . . You need to spend more time with us." He says, "I saw her attitude . . . I heard it in her voice. I think she doesn't know that when she gets like that . . . that's really gonna make me keep going instead of . . . making me feel like . . . I should stay home." After the interviewer leaves them to discuss the issue themselves, he says, "And quality and quantity of time, you get me on that, but I tell you I don't like staying in the house." She says, "But you don't necessarily have to stay in the house." She goes on to suggest that they set a date when he knows he'll be off work and "say what time we be going out to eat and . . . to the show, whatever. . . . Unless you just don't wanna spend time with me or with us. That's something totally different." He retorts, "If I didn't want to spend time with you . . . I would have told you." He ends up saying, "I guess we can try what you said." It sounds like the issue is that Janell wants him to spend time with her and the children, not that she's worried about what he'll get into on the streets. Unfortunately, however, the streets did hold peril for this African American family. The next day, when the TLC3 interviewer called to say he was on his way for the individual interview with Leonard, Janell told him that Leonard had been killed by a bullet in a drive-by shooting at a convenience store.

In the case of Gabriella, twenty-six, a Puerto Rican mother, Travis's going out is a matter of trust as well as a complaint about emotional inattention. She's had two children with Travis, the twenty-nine-year-old African American man she lives with. She says:

We really don't spend much time together. He'll probably . . . leave around eleven in the daytime and he'll come back at nine at night or even at two in the morning. I'll be like, "Okay, I got a man, but he is not here." So what should I think? . . . Because, you know, you come in to sleep, get up in the morning, and by eleven or twelve, gone. So, that's my thing right there with the trust. You tell . . . you're going to be, at Mama's, but I don't know that. I'm here. You can tell me you're going there, but as you leave you might change your mind and go somewhere else. . . . You say you want to be with me. . . . When you want to be with a person, you put in the time. You know, go places together, talk about things. We don't do that. We don't go nowhere. . . . It's like . . . we're spending time now . . . because we're talking here.

When asked his side of the story, Travis says, "She knows everywhere I go. She calls, and you *do* call." Gabriella interjects, "Then he'll be like 'I'm outside.' So I feel like there's pressure. So I leave rather than just stay here, get angry . . ."

She's Tired of Being Alone with the Kids

In three cases where mothers complain about wanting more of the father's attention, they are also tired of being alone with the children. They want time with the father when a baby sitter is taking care of the children, freeing both of them from the responsibility. Or they want the father to help with child care while they do something fun as a family. If mothers said they were tired of taking care of children and wanted the fathers to do more of the child care, we did not code that into the "mother wants more attention" category but instead as "mom wants dad to do more housework or child care." A case was only coded here if the mother said that being sick of being with the children led her to want the father to spend more time with her.

The plea of Celeste, twenty-six, who has been married to Nathan, twenty-eight, since before their child was born, sounds desperate. This African American mother says, "I'm *serious*. We have to spend more time together. I mean, I be by myself all the time with kids. I'm tired of being with kids all the time."

Maria, a twenty-seven-year-old Puerto Rican mother, has lived with Matt since before their daughter was born. She wants them to go out alone more. He says, "I don't like leaving my kids with nobody" and suggests they go out as a family. Maria says, "It's just being with him alone. No one crying, no one screaming, but he doesn't want that."

Daisy, twenty-six, lives with Paulo, thirty-three. This Puerto Rican couple has had five children in a long-term marriage-like cohabitation. She says, "I think it is important that we get to have our quality time together away from the kids. I mean, I love to spend time with my kids but I think that we also need time for ourselves." She suggests that her father could take the children sometimes. Paulo agrees that time alone would be good, but thinks her father wouldn't take care of the children right. She sees time together away from the children as a more urgent priority than he does, though she concedes that there are problems with any of the baby sitting options they can afford.

He Wants Stricter Parenting

Issues about parenting were a frequent source of conflict among these young parents. All of them had at least one child (the child that led to their being included in the study) who was two to four years old at the time of the couple discussion.[15] Many had other children together, with other partners, or both. Thirty-one percent of couples having the discussion at wave three and forty-five percent at wave four have at least one child in the household who is hers but not his biological child (table 3.1). A similar proportion of the men have children by previous partners, but these children usually live with their mother. As we listened to the specifics, we saw a common dimension to most of the arguments about children. The two often disagreed about how much bad cop versus good cop is called for. They differed in their views of how much parents should set limits and enforce them, how much either should punish, how acceptable it was to let children cry, and so forth. The gender pattern is striking. More often, it was men who wanted a stricter regime, and women who found a stricter regime either too heartless or too difficult to hold to. We coded cases as "dad wants more strict child rearing" if she complained that he is too strict or harsh, or if he complained that she is too lax in some area of discipline.

Thirty-four percent of couples chose fathers wanting things stricter as one of their two most important conflicts. If fathers are more lenient toward their biological children than their stepchildren (perhaps because they have bonded less with the stepchildren), we would expect to find this issue more often when he is a stepfather rather than the biological father to some of the children. We do see such a tendency in the data: 39 percent of couples with one or more of her children from a previous partner in the household chose this as one of their two issues, whereas only 21 percent of other couples chose it, but the association is not statistically significant using either a bivariate chi square test nor a logistic regression with other controls. The father wanting things stricter was an issue for 39 percent of the married but only 28 percent of the unmarried couples, though this relationship did not reach statistical significance. Neither income nor education was significantly associated with identifying dad wanting things stricter as an issue (in either bivariate chi square tests or a logistic regression with controls). However, the issue was significantly more common among white couples. Half of white couples, versus only 25 percent of black and 15 percent of Hispanic couples, identified this as an issue.[16] (Whites were also significantly more likely to choose the issue when we used a logistic regression, and controlled for household income, whether mom has children from another partner in the household, education, marital status, and age.) When the father wants things stricter, there are two subtypes: he thinks she isn't strict enough, or she thinks he is too harsh.

He Wants Her to be Stricter

Monte, thirty-five, a black, married father wishes Angel would impose more structure on when their children get up and take naps when she is home with them during his work day. He says, "I think it's an important issue 'cause . . . if you let them get up late, let them take a nap late, then they gonna stay up . . . late and so it's gonna be harder to put them to bed." Angel says, "I just try to get them to sleep when they . . . feel tired or they fall asleep . . . as opposed to a schedule. . . . He'd prefer me to have some kind of the structure to the nap thing." She doesn't see the problem, and talks about how she orchestrates which types of housework she does according to whether they are asleep or not. Monte's preference for structure seems to be partly for his own convenience, so that they're tired enough to go to bed—and are thus out of his hair—by nine p.m., but he also says structured schedules are for their own good.

Roger, forty-one, a white, married father, wishes that Alison, forty-four, would follow through more on discipline. He says, "I keep telling her . . . the old guy, he kinda lip you and that's because she . . . never follow through with it so now they're just empty threats and they know it." If Alison threatens to discard some of the junk in their rooms if they don't clean them, he thinks she should follow through and throw the items out if the children don't clean up. Later in the conversation, Alison says, "Time outs don't work. That's punishment for the parent, that ain't punishment for the child. You take the toy away from them and all they do is sit there and scream." Roger retorts, "Let him scream."

Ted, a thirty-nine-year-old, unmarried father of white and Native American descent, wishes that Melissa wouldn't sleep in the children's room. He couches it as an issue of the children's well-being, saying, "They're never gonna learn independence or good sleeping habits while mom's in the same room with them." Ted then challenges the interviewer: "How long did you sleep with your mom?" Their oldest son, he says, "slept with mom until he was four." Melissa, a thirty-one-year-old white mother says, "Nah, he was not." Although he doesn't come right out and say it, watching him lift his eyebrows dramatically to the male interviewer, one senses that part of Ted's grievance is that he doesn't have much chance for sex with Melissa. "Me and Melissa do not sleep together. . . . She sleeps in a separate room with the children and I sleep in the bedroom by myself. . . . No, for the past three years we haven't shared that bed together." She says, "It has not been three years." He insists, saying, "Not once." She says, "that's not true." He persists, saying "not a single night." She says, "He's lying." He says, "Well, okay, in March it'll be three years." Getting to why she doesn't make the kids sleep in their own room without her, she says, "It's harder to break it after you started it. In the beginning I did it 'cause I just . . . worry about SIDS . . . so till they're a year I like to stay there. But it's harder to break away than I thought. . . . I'd like her to go into her own bed now." He says, "Just break away; cut the apron strings. They gotta grow up sometime." She concedes, "I know. It makes Mom sad."

Ramon and Flora, both Puerto Rican and twenty-two, live together with their two-year-old. Ramon wishes that Flora wouldn't give their daughter cookies at night. He says, "If it's late at night she shouldn't be eating no more candy or sweets." In a similar vein, Alejandro, thirty-one, from Mexico, wishes that his American-born Hispanic wife, Paz, wouldn't let their five-year-old stay up so late. He also doesn't want her to let him eat fast food instead of healthier home-made meals of meat and vegetables.

Phillip, a married, white forty-three-year-old father, thinks he and Kaitlyn, thirty-eight, should make their son clean his plate. He says, "I say, 'doggone it; he's going to eat everything on his plate that we feed him.' Not too much to ask." Kaitlyn wishes that "instead of making a big issue out of it" he would wait till the son learns to like more foods "naturally." But, she says, "Phillip now wants to enforce the law every night" and, as a result, "everybody doesn't enjoy their meal."

Melvin, a thirty-five-year-old white father, complains. "My lovely wife lets the kids . . . get away with . . . too much, doesn't let them know who's in charge. . . . She lets it build up. . . . She has . . . patience with them, lets them get away with murder, and then she gets very upset and she's ready to kill them." Explaining how he does a better job, he says that with him "they have to do what they're told. And if I yell at them or give them a little smack, I wait until they calm down and I explain to them why. They don't think I'm mean." Jocelyn, thirty-one, also white, concedes that "maybe I have too much patience" but complains that he doesn't have enough. She laments that "sometimes they don't really respect me" and that "I don't know what he wants me to do with the kids." Sometimes, she says, "I don't know what to do." It seems that she doesn't feel capable of getting the children to obey her, and doesn't think her husband understands how hard it would be to do what he is recommending.

Tony, thirty-five, a Puerto Rican who lives with Dahlia, thirty-three, wants her to be stricter. Speaking of their four-year-old son he says, "When he's with me, he's all right. . . . But you—he thinks you're a total joke. He'll be laughing in your face. . . . But you keep saying, 'That's my baby,' you hug him, you kiss him, even when he does something mean to you. You still do it. And . . . that's where you need to take him and put him in the corner." Dahlia concedes some of this, but says, "sometimes he's a little bit too rough on him. But then . . . he needs to be a little bit too rough because he's a boy."

Bob, thirty-nine, a black married father, complains:

She get mad when I spank them. I mean, they're boys. . . . They be arguing and fighting, and so when I go in there, I say one thing to them, and they continue doing what they're doing, and I go in there and pop them. She get angry. . . . She gets mad and then she'll say, "That's enough. Don't hit them twice." All they gotta do is holler and scream like they losing their mind and she falls for it.

He wants her to "quit making me look like the bad guy all the time." Cynthia, thirty-six, replies, "I'm the Mommy." She clarifies. "I would prefer if he would talk to them more. . . . Because the kids today . . . I don't think they can stand the whoopings that we got when we were kids." He chortles. "They getting off way easier than that." When they are left alone to discuss the issue, he says, "I think that you should do a little bit more of the disciplining than you do. . . . You are too soft. They are boys." She responds, "But they're my boys." He says, "They're my boys too. But you are too soft with them. You're like a cotton ball. . . . They figure if I say no they can come running to you." She concedes, "Yes they do. But what do you want? I'm their mother."

Like Bob, Victor, a twenty-eight-year-old Latino father, thinks that boys should be treated more roughly than girls. That causes conflict with Jacinta, twenty-three, the Latina he married after they had two children together. Victor believes that Jacinta "normally babies" their son. He complains that "if I'm being tough with him and she's being soft, he's gonna think I'm being mean . . . and then he's gonna . . . have a feeling of resentment against me . . . when she just supporting him all the time." Jacinta disagrees with his approach:

> He feels he wants him to be tough and not a wimp. . . . And he . . . kind of forced him to play [sports] and to be tough and to be acting like a boy. And if [my son] will be playing with a doll with his sister, he wouldn't like that. And I don't see it as something doing wrong. He's just playing.

Daryl, twenty-six and white, married Michelle when their baby was a toddler. They have had two more kids since then, and Michelle has a seven-year-old son from a previous partner. Daryl complains that Michelle, twenty-four, lets them go to bed later in the summer. "Well, just because the sun is still up doesn't mean I don't have to get up at five o'clock." He complains that he's up late "waiting for the kids all to fall asleep. So I get less sleep because she lets them stay out of the room longer." Michelle says that she doesn't "get to spend enough time usually with the kids . . . coming home at six." Anyhow, she asks, "who wants to go to bed with the sun shining right in [the] window?" Daryl raises his hand. He complains that she doesn't make them eat everything on their plate, mentioning that his stepson will eat food one night and "say he hates it the next just so he can go play. So she'll let him get away with it. And now [my other two kids] are starting to do that." When the interviewer leaves them alone, he suggests to Michelle, "If we take out all the snacks for three days, I bet everyone will eat all their food on their plate." She realizes that she'd be the one to have to enforce this and says, "How

I'm supposed to stop them from eating?" She imitates a child saying, "I'm hungry, I'm hungry." He suggests that she "tell them it's gonna be dinner time soon." She says, "Okay, so just picture me. I get home from work. I'm stressed out because my coworker doesn't do anything ever. So I get home. [Our daughter] is screaming, 'I want candy.' " He is unmoved and says again, "Tell her [it's] dinnertime." She continues, "then I got [my son] crying because he wants his bottle. Then I got [my other son] running somewhere and [the seven-year-old's] yelling because he's fighting with one of his friends. And I'm supposed to say 'It's okay, baby, wait 'til dinner'?" He gets sarcastic and says, "Fine. So do it the way you want to do it." She says, "You see where I come from?" Sarcastically he says, "Yeah, I see where you're coming from because I've never had to deal with that. . . . I've never spent the whole day alone with the kids all by myself. Right?"

In some cases, the fathers wanting things stricter, like Daryl, are step-fathers to the children involved. Another example is Juan, an unmarried Puerto Rican father, who doesn't like that Priscilla lets her two-year-old son with another father hit her. He thinks that the two-year-old should be taught that if he does hit his mother, someone is going to hit him back. He wants Priscilla to at least talk to her son firmly, and, if necessary, hit him. Priscilla concedes that she would "feel bad if he hits me when he's big," but right now she doesn't know what to do, because when she tries to control him "he screams and he start crying." Two years later, when this boy is four, she is living with another man, and he too thinks she is too lax. He says "she's got to be a little bit more rough with the kids."

Kenneth, an unmarried black father, lives most of the time with Ciana, their two children,[17] and Ciana's eighteen-year-old son by another father. Ciana says that her son has dropped out of high school, is unemployed, hangs out with guys that get in a lot of trouble, only comes home to sleep, and has gotten a girl pregnant (she had an abortion). It is other things about her son that bother Kenneth, however:

> Like she really tries to do more for him even though he . . . should contribute to certain things around the house, household chores and stuff, but she don't try to hear the things I'm saying because . . . that's her son. That's her firstborn and she would give . . . him her last. So I really think that's wrong.

When left to discuss the issue alone, he says to Ciana, "What about discipline? . . . You don't discipline." She retorts, "He's too old to be disciplined." He says, "No, he's not too old." She bemoans the fact that "he don't listen to nothing I say." Kenneth says, "If he don't listen to anyone he can find his own house. . . . He don't wanna abide by no rules." Ciana asks if Kenneth means that her son should leave. Kenneth says "Don't that make sense?" Ciana partially concedes, saying, "Yeah, it makes sense," but continues, "I just can't put my kid out. I mean I could, I have done it, but I'm just gonna have to have a long talk with him."

In many of these cases, the man wants the woman to impose more discipline during times when she, rather than he, is in charge of the children, such as when he is at work. He is asking her to do what they both see as "her job" differently. She is the one who would have to deal with the child's protests if she makes the rules stricter. Doing what he wants would make her job more difficult for her, at least in the short run. And, as the parent doing the day to day child rearing, she is often more bonded to the children, and "feels their pain" more, making tightening up even more difficult. Because she would bear the costs of changing to a stricter regime, it is not surprising that she often opts for the more lax status quo, even if she too would like the benefits of a less chaotic household. In these cases, the man would receive the benefits of the change in her strictness without bearing the costs. Thus, the division of labor creates a clear conflict of interest between them.

She Thinks He Is Too Harsh

The other subcategory of cases in which the father wants things stricter is where the mother doesn't like how strict or harsh he is. In these cases, either she complains that he should lighten up, or he complains that she doesn't back him up or let him carry out the discipline he thinks is needed.

LaVera, forty-two, an African American married mother, brings up an example of when Briana, two, was crying. She says her husband, Dave, forty-three and also black, said, "What you crying for? Stop all that crying." But LaVera protests, "She is just a baby, of course she's gonna cry." Dave says,

> Okay, she could be right. I don't mean to come off like that or mean, intimidating, or scary or nothing like that. And maybe 'cause how my voice is, it carries. . . . It's . . . harder with girls 'cause they got these extra needs and extra emotions whereas you tell a boy you know "come in." . . . I just ain't . . . that kind of wuss but I'll try to work on it. I mean I love them to death, but I just got to learn to change my ways.

Yasmine was not married to Paco when they had their daughter that brought them into the study. We talk to the Latino couple four years later, after they have gotten married, when she is twenty-six and he is thirty. Their older daughter, according to Paco, is "hard to raise." Yasmine complains that "he's too hard with her." She concedes that their older daughter's "got an attitude" but says that "he treat the other one better than her." Both are their children together, so this is not a stepfather issue. Yasmine thinks the preferential treatment may be why the older daughter misbehaves. But Paco says, "If I don't be hard with her, she's going to step on me." Yasmine insists that

> she don't feel loved. . . . That's why I think she do all that stuff because she feel that I don't love her and you don't love her. . . . But I think more on you because you give more love to the other ones than her. You talk bad to her. And you gotta calm down and talk slow so she can understand. If you're screaming she's not going to understand.

When the man is a stepfather to the child, he sometimes isn't sure the child's mother will think he has the right to discipline the child. Sean, a thirty-six-year-old married African American father says,

> When you're in a marriage and all the kids aren't yours biologically, it's always an issue and I guess it depends on the partner and how she or he feels. . . . I feel that if I grab [my stepson], just use a threat to try to straighten him up—I may pop him or something. And I just feel that . . . my wife should back me up about it. I feel that she knows that I'm not gonna, you know, beat them or anything like that.

Nubia, his thirty-one-year-old African American wife, says, "I don't see no reason for him to have to get the belt." She suggests that he give them a time out rather than threaten with a belt. She continues, "I even have a problem with, even our daughter, that's his biological child . . . even him popping her . . . it just makes me cringe." Sean clarifies, "I'm not the type of person that's like gonna beat them, put them in the hospital or anything like that" and later says, "I never use the belt." He points out that sometimes Nubia "popped" their two year old, and he claims that "she's grabbed the belt too like she's gonna whoop them" but says that, like him, "she hasn't whooped them with it." Later, Nubia reveals that part of what bothers her is that he didn't wait to bond emotionally with his stepchildren before starting to discipline them:

> It should be more the bonding thing first. You can't discipline a child until you love them and until you bond with that child. . . . If you're not taking them anywhere, if you're not doing anything with them, the only thing that comes out of your mouth is discipline, what is that? . . . There's a lot more about dealing with children other than discipline. . . . No, because you're not interacting, you're not going in their room when . . . they're laying in their bed reading books, you're not taking them to the park, you're not doing anything. You're not . . . taking them to make sure they got tennis shoes, doctor's appointments. Don't come to me with discipline when you're not doing all of these things. . . . Love got to be in there.

When left alone to talk she reiterates that "doing things and bonding has to be up there before you can holler discipline." He says, "Okay, I get you and I know what you're saying. . . . But . . . you ain't always there. I want discipline. It's a respect thing. They need more soul."

Nubia doesn't want Sean, who is stepfather to her children, to be as strict or punitive as he thinks he has a right to be. But we can't tell for sure that she wouldn't have the same disagreement with the biological father if she were still with him. Indeed, though the problem may be exacerbated when he is a stepfather, it seems a more general gender conflict, as many of the mothers think the fathers are being too strict with their joint biological child. The other gendered aspect of the issue is that more men than women believe that it is important for men to be tough with boys.

Conclusion

We have identified and described two common gender conflicts in a sample of low-income couples, some married and some cohabiting. About a third of the couples identified the issue of the father wanting a stricter regime with the kids than the mother. Of equal salience was the issue of mothers wanting more attention from men—wanting them to spend time with them, talk and listen to them, and show affection. Few men had this complaint.

What we did not find is as interesting as what we found. Arguments about money did not trump other topics in this low-income population. Arguments about money were almost as prevalent as the two issues we have focused on—his wanting things stricter and her wanting more attention. There was no clear gender pattern to these money issues, however. The 30 percent who chose money issues were about equally divided: women who found the men irresponsible with money, men who found the women irresponsible, and couples who made no accusation of wastefulness or irresponsibility but had different spending priorities that caused conflict. We suspect that if more separated couples had held couple discussions, we might have found a sharp gender patterning of disagreements, with women critical of men for not providing more child support. In these cohabiting or married couples, however, we found no clear pattern.

What about housework? Sociologists have emphasized the inequitable burden of housework that women bear. In this low-income population, we find that it is an issue, though not as common as mothers wanting more attention or parents disagreeing about how strict one or the other should be with children. About 30 percent of couples chose attention, about 30 percent chose strictness, and approximately 20 percent chose housework.

The common scenario in which the father wants the mother to be more of a "bad cop" was not about who does how many hours of child care labor, but rather about who was in control of the regime. The typical disagreement arose when the mother is in charge of most of the child care, often while the father is at work, and the father doesn't like some consequence of how she does it. He is, in effect, telling her that he wants her to perform her job differently, either for his sake or the children's. If he were to get his way, she would be the one feeling the push back from the children in response to her stricter regime. It is easy for him to suggest a tight ship when he doesn't have to bear the costs of enforcing the new rules but would get some of the benefits of the less chaotic household. In other cases, these disagreements involved fathers themselves wanting to punish more harshly than mothers wanted to allow.

Limitations of our study condition what we can infer. Each partner in a couple was asked to name the most important issue. Both knew that the issues they chose would have to be discussed with their partner. This probably limited the range of things named to those that aren't too destabilizing to the relationship to discuss. For example, we know that many of these couples had experienced sexual infidelity of at least one partner, usually the man, earlier in their relationships (see chapter 5, this volume). Infidelity was on the checklist but almost never chosen as one of the two main issues. This may be because it wasn't much of an issue in the relationships that survived to the third and fourth waves when we did the couple conflict discussion. Joanna Reed shows us in chapter 6 that couples reporting cheating early in the relationship were less likely to stay together. It may also be, however, that many who reveal a partner's infidelity in an individual interview do not feel comfortable bringing it up when the partner is present. In general, couples talked about relatively safe topics. In addition, the checklist may have affected the choice of topics, though the selections included many diffuse items, so it may also have helped broaden the range of issues they drew from.[18]

In sum, we can't say for sure that the two items we have identified are the most important issues determining whether low-income couples stay together. We seriously doubt the issues emphasized here are as destabilizing as sexual infidelity or the rarer issues of drug use, violence, and incarceration for participation in the drug trade. However, we are confident in concluding that mothers wanting more attention and fathers wanting stricter child discipline are big issues in low-income households. Are they more important in low- than middle-income couples? Our sample was small enough and homogeneous enough that we could not pick up significant class differences within the sample. We don't know if a larger, more class-diverse dataset would show significant class differences in important couple conflicts. We can at least say that the longing for greater emotional intimacy by women is not *just* an upper-middle-class issue. Putting other research—such as Lillian Rubin's (1983) and Francesca Cancian's (1987)—together with our findings suggests that this is a big issue up and down the class hierarchy. It may lead to more breakups among middle than working and lower class couples, because more serious problems predominate at lower class levels, but it may nonetheless drag down women's relationship satisfaction across classes and races.

Notes

1. We thank Sue Martin for exceptional transcription and assistance with coding. We also thank the MacArthur Foundation Network on the Family and the Economy and the National Science Foundation for supporting this research.

2. A historical perspective shows that marriage has not always been expected to provide emotional intimacy or fulfillment (Cancian 1987; Swidler 2001; Coontz 2005).

3. The first author was one of the interviewers for the waves with the couple discussion.

4. Every wave contained a couple interview and two individual interviews. Couples who had broken up were asked if they were willing to do a couple interview, but most declined.

5. A few of these couples (6 percent at wave three and 13 percent at wave four) consist of the mother from the original TLC3 sample with her new marital or cohabiting partner (referred to as a social father). Substantive conclusions do not differ if these couples with new partners are excluded. The bulk of the sample is original TLC3 couples who have remained together and did a couple interview and discussion at wave three, four, or both. Though we did not require it for inclusion in our analytic sample, all couples that were still romantically involved by wave three or four were either married or cohabiting at the time of the couple discussion.

6. We assessed this by a series of bivariate chi square tests for association between whether the couple ever—at either wave three or four—identified this as one of their two most important conflicts. We also used logistic regression to predict whether the issue was identified by the couple at either wave from marital status at the time of the discussion, controlling for race, age, mother's and father's educational attainment, whether mother's reported household income was below or above the sample median, and whether each of mother and father had biological children with other partners. Marriage never had a significant effect in either the bivariate or multiple regression analyses. Results are not shown but are available upon request.

7. The mean was $27,000. This was taken from the mother's report. In cases of missing values, we imputed the reported household income from wave two of the Fragile Families Survey.

8. Table 3.1 includes this calculation only for the original TLC3 sample fathers, not the few new social fathers involved in these interviews because we did not collect data on these men's other children.

9. Our protocol for these discussions was developed by Nancy Cohen based on qualitative research with Fragile Family sample members (Cohen 2003a, 2003b) and adapting an instrument developed for married couples by Hooven, Rushe, and Gottman (the general approach is described in Gottman 1994).

10. One purpose of this preparatory discussion is to evoke some of the affect present when the issue comes up. In this way, the ensuing discussion is more similar to a discussion of the issue the couple might have in daily life.

11. Issues were written down in a very brief way; for example, "John's drinking." Watching the videos, we noticed that often one parent would pick up the piece of paper and point to one of the two issues to try to keep the other on task.

12. To assess these associations, we examined cross-tabulations and calculated chi square statistics for the association of whether a couple identified a given issue in either wave three or four couple discussions and selected characteristics. The characteristics included mother's and father's race, whether the couple was married at the time of the interview, mother's and father's educational attainment, whether mother's report of their household income was below or above the sample median, and whether mother or father had biological children with other partners. We took race, marital status at wave three and four couple discussions, and partners' children with other partners from the TLC3 data. Income and educational attainment were taken from the third wave of the Fragile Families study, because this was close in timing to the third wave of TLC3. We also performed logistic regressions predicting each conflict area from the characteristics mentioned. Relationships were never significant except that whites more often reported a conflict in which men wanted stricter parenting.

13. It may be, though, that it is seen as less legitimate to complain about lack of sex in a discussion about couple relationships, an example of what Francesca Cancian (1987) has called the feminized conception of love in our culture.

14. This uses mother's race. If we use father's race, we get very similar figures: 40 percent of blacks, 33 percent of Hispanics, and 10 percent of whites. The discrepancy arises from the few interracial couples.

15. The exception is one couple, Corretta and Jordan, whose child died within a year after birth. Also, for the few interviews with social fathers, the child bringing the mother into the study is not his biological child.

16. This uses mother's race. We obtain similar results—60 percent, 27 percent, and 10 percent for whites, blacks, and Hispanics, respectively—if we classify by father's race. The disparity results from the small number of interracial couples.

17. They have had three children together, but their first child was taken away by child protective services. Ciana had several children by a previous father taken away for neglect at a time she was using drugs. Because of this, when she had a new baby with Kenneth shortly thereafter, it was automatically

taken from her. Her mother still has custody of the first child she had with Kenneth, as well as several of her children from her previous partner.

18.   An example is communication, which many couples checked and chose, but was not a useful coding category because there was usually a specific substantive issue underlying that they had failed to resolve. Undoubtedly, communication skills affect what can be resolved, but we found it more useful to code by the content of the issue.

References

Amato, Paul R., and Denise Previti. 2003. "People's Reasons for Divorcing: Gender, Social Class, the Life Course, and Adjustment." *Journal of Family Issues* 24(5): 602–26.

Amato Paul R., and Stacy J. Rogers. 1997. "A Longitudinal Study of Marital Problems and Subsequent Divorce." *Journal of Marriage and the Family* 59(3): 612–24.

Amato, Paul R., David R. Johnson, Alan Booth, and Stacy J. Rogers. 2003. "Continuity and Change in Marital Quality Between 1980 and 2000." *Journal of Marriage and Family* 65(1): 1–22.

Bloom, Bernard L., Robert L. Niles, and Anna M. Tatcher. 1985. "Sources of Marital Dissatisfaction Among Newly Separated Persons." *Journal of Family Issues*, 6(3): 359–73.

Brines, Julie. 1994. "Economic Dependency, Gender, and the Division of Labor at Home." *American Journal of Sociology* 99(3): 652–88.

Cancian, Francesca. 1987. *Love in America: Gender and Self-Development*. Cambridge, Mass.: Cambridge University Press.

Carlson, Marcia J., and Frank F. Furstenberg, Jr. 2006. "The Prevalence and Correlates of Multi-Partnered Fertility in the United States." *Journal of Marriage and Family* 68(3): 718–32.

Cherlin, Andrew J. 1978. "Remarriage as an Incomplete Institution." *American Journal of Sociology* 84(3): 634–50.

Chodorow, Nancy. 1978. *The Reproduction of Mothering: Psychoanalysis and the Sociology of Gender*. Los Angeles, Calif.: University of California Press.

Clingempeel, W. Glenn. 1981. "Quasi-kin Relationships and Marital Quality in Stepfather Families." *Journal of Personality and Social Psychology* 41: 890–901.

Cohen, Nancy E. 2003a. "Guide to Preparing Couples for the Discussion Task." Unpublished training guide used to train TLC3 interviewers.

———. 2003b. "Unmarried African American Fathers' Involvement with Their Infants: The Role of Couple Relationships." Ph.D. diss., University of California, Berkeley.

Conger, Rand D., Glen H. Elder, Jr., Frederick O. Lorenz, Katherine J. Conger, Ronald L. Simons, Les B. Whitbeck, Shirley Huck, and Janet N. Melby. 1990. "Linking Economic Hardship to Marital Quality and Instability." *Journal of Marriage and the Family* 52(3): 643–56.

Coontz, Stephanie. 2005. *Marriage, a History: From Obedience to Intimacy, or How Love Conquered Marriage*. New York: Viking Press.

Cowan, Carolyn P., and Philip A. Cowan. 1992. *When Partners Become Parents: The Big Life Change for Couples.* New York: Basic Books.

Cowan Carolyn P., Philip A. Cowan, Gertrude Heming, Ellen Garrett, William S. Coysh, Harriet Curtis-Boles, and Abner J. Boles III. 1985. "Transitions to Parenthood: His, Hers, and Theirs." *Journal of Family Issues* 6(4): 451–81.

Edin, Kathryn, and Maria Kefalas. 2005. *Promises I Can Keep: Why Poor Women Put Motherhood Before Marriage.* Berkeley, Calif.: University of California Press.

Ellwood, David T., and Christopher Jencks. 2001. "The Growing Differences in Family Structure: What Do We Know? Where Do We Look for Answers?" Unpublished paper. John F. Kennedy School of Government, Harvard University.

Frisco, Michelle L., and Kristi Williams. 2003. "Perceived Housework Equity, Marital Happiness, and Divorce in Dual-Earner Households." *Journal of Family Issues,* 24(1): 51–73.

Furstenberg, Frank F., Jr., and Graham B. Spanier. 1987. "Remarriage and Reconstituted Families." In *Handbook of Marriage and the Family,* edited by Marvin B. Sussman and Susan K. Steinmetz. New Brunswick, N.J.: Rutgers University Press.

Gottman, John M. 1994. *What Predicts Divorce? The Relationship Between Marital Processes and Marital Outcomes.* Hillsdale, N.J.: Lawrence Erlbaum Associates.

Halle, David. 1984. *America's Working Man: Work, Home, and Politics Among Blue-Collar Property Owners.* Chicago, Ill.: University of Chicago Press.

Hochschild, Arlie, with Anne Machung. 1989. *The Second Shift: Working Parents and the Revolution at Home.* New York: Viking Penguin.

Huber, Joan, and Glenna Spitze. 1980. "Considering Divorce: An Expansion of Becker's Theory of Marital Instability." *American Journal of Sociology* 86(1): 75–89.

Kitson, Gay C. 1992. *Portrait of Divorce: Adjustment to Marital Breakdown.* New York: Guilford Press.

Komarovsky, Mirra. 1964. *Blue-Collar Marriage.* New Haven, Conn.: Yale University Press.

Kurz, Dernie. 1995. *For Richer, For Poorer: Mothers Confront Divorce.* New York: Routledge.

Lareau, Annette. 2003. *Unequal Childhoods: Class, Race, and Family Life.* Berkeley, Calif.: University of California Press.

Levinger, George. 1966. "Sources of Marital Dissatisfaction among Applicants for Divorce." *American Journal of Orthopsychiatry* 36(5): 803–7.

Maccoby, Eleanor E. 1998. *The Two Sexes: Growing Up Apart, Coming Together.* Cambridge, Mass.: Harvard University Press.

Maccoby, Eleanor E., and Carol N. Jacklin. 1974. *The Psychology of Sex Differences.* Stanford, Calif.: Stanford University Press.

MacDonald, William L., and Alfred De Maris. 1995. "Remarriage, Stepchildren, and Marital Conflict: Challenges to the Incomplete Institutionalization Hypothesis." *Journal of Marriage and the Family* 57(2): 387–98.

Mackey, Richard A. and Bernard A. O'Brien. 1998. "Marital Conflict Management: Gender and Ethnic Differences." *Social Work,* 43(2): 128–41.

McLanahan, Sara. 2004. "Diverging Destinies: How Children Are Faring Under the Second Demographic Transition." *Demography* 41(4): 607–27.

Musick, Kelly, Paula England, and Sarah Edgington. 2005. "Education and Class Differences in Planned and Unplanned Fertility." Paper presented at the Annual Meetings of the Population Association of America. Philadelphia, Pa. (March 31–April 2, 2005).

Rainwater, Lee, Richard P. Coleman, and Gerald Handel. 1959. *Workingman's Wife: Her Personality, World and Life Style.* New York: Oceana Publications.

Rubin, Lillian B. 1976. *Worlds of Pain: Life in the Working-Class Family.* New York: Basic Books.

———. 1983. *Intimate Strangers: Men and Women Together.* New York: Harper Colophon Books.

———. 1994. *Families on the Fault Line: America's Working Class Speaks About the Family, the Economy, Race and Ethnicity.* New York: Harper Collins.

Stohs, Joanne Hoven 2000. "Multicultural Women's Experience of Household Labor, Conflicts, and Equity." *Sex Roles* 42(March): 339–61.

Strauss, Anself, and Juliet M. Corbin. 1990. *Basics of Qualitative Research,* 2nd ed. Thousand Oaks, Calif.: Sage Publications.

Swidler, Ann. 2001. *Talk of Love: How Culture Matters.* Chicago, Ill.: University of Chicago Press.

Teachman, Jay D. 2002. "Stability Across Cohorts in Divorce Risk Factors." *Demography* 39(2): 331–51.

Voydanoff, Patricia. 1991. "Economic Distress and Family Relations: Review of the Eighties." In *Contemporary Families: Looking Forward, Looking Back,* edited by Alan Booth. Minneapolis, Minn.: National Council on Family Relations.

Voydanoff, Patricia, and Brenda W. Donnelly. 1999. "Multiple Roles and Psychological Distress: The Intersection of the Paid Worker, Spouse, and Parent Roles with the Role of the Adult Child." *Journal of Marriage and the Family* 61(3): 725–38.

West, Candace, and Don H. Zimmerman. 1987. "Doing Gender." *Gender and Society* 1(2): 125–51.

White, Lynn K., and Alan Booth. 1985. "The Quality and Stability of Remarriages: The Role of Stepchildren." *American Sociological Review* 50(5): 689–98.

Yogev, Sara, and Jeanne Brett. 1985. "Perceptions of the Division of Housework and Childcare and Marital Satisfaction." *Journal of Marriage and the Family* 47(3): 609–18.

Chapter 4

Expectations and the Economic Bar to Marriage Among Low-Income Couples

CHRISTINA M. GIBSON-DAVIS

E MPIRICAL RESEARCH indicates an interesting contradiction regarding marital beliefs and behavior among low-income individuals. Marriage rates among the disadvantaged are lower than those for the general population (Goldstein and Kenney 2001), yet their attitudes, as indicated by survey data, reflect a deep belief in and reverence for marriage (Lichter, Batson, and Brown 2004; Sayer, Wright, and Edin 2004). A series of recent qualitative studies suggest a resolution to this apparent incongruity between values and actions: marriage has been imbued with such a high degree of symbolic significance that it may actually deter people from marrying (Edin 2000; Edin and Kefalas 2005; Smock, Manning, and Porter 2005). It has become a sign of success, a crowning achievement, because it is an indication that a couple has accomplished what is required for marriage (Cherlin 2004). Specifically, previous studies suggest that couples feel they should marry only after they have achieved financial and emotional stability, as indicated by steady employment, savings for a house or a wedding, and guarantees that their relationship will not be sullied by divorce (Edin and Kefalas 2005; Gibson-Davis, Edin, and McLanahan, 2005; Smock, Manning, and Porter 2005). Not surprisingly, couples, particularly those on the lower end of the socioeconomic spectrum, are finding it very difficult to achieve these standards.

These standards of marriage have been found in work with several qualitative studies (Edin and Kefalas 2005; Edin, Kefalas, and Reed 2004; Gibson-Davis, Edin, and McLanahan 2005; Smock, Manning, and Porter

2005). All conclude that cultural attitudes toward the economic requirements of marriage, in combination with low economic resources, play an important role in deterring marriage. The studies report that respondents delayed marriage because they believed their economic circumstances dictated that they were not ready for the institution. If a couple was barely surviving financially, unable to afford a mortgage, or without the funds to celebrate a wedding properly, then the couple had not exceeded the financial threshold for a marriage, and should wait to marry until those things were in place.

The work cited, however, relied on cross-sectional data. As a result, it is unclear how enduring these beliefs are, and if individuals will lessen their economic expectations of marriage if they are making little financial progress. Furthermore, the role of the expectations on marriage decisions is unclear. It is unknown whether meeting these economic expectations will encourage a couple to marry.

I address these questions by using data from the Time, Love and Cash among Couples with Children study, a longitudinal qualitative study of seventy-five low-income parents, to explore how the economic bar to marriage influences marital behavior. This chapter builds on previous work with the TLC3 sample that found that unmarried, new parents had a strong desire to marry, but were hesitant to do so in part because of limited assets and earnings (Gibson-Davis, Edin, and McLanahan 2005). I use longitudinal data from forty-seven TLC3 couples who were unmarried when we first interviewed them, shortly after the focal child's birth, to explore how couples discuss their expectations of marriage, and to see if financial expectations continue to act as a barrier to marriage. Because I find that most of the couples have consistently held that economics pose a barrier to marriage, I then analyze how meeting a limited economic bar is correlated with getting married. Because of the small sample size, the conclusions presented here are preliminary and the findings warrant future replication. However, the qualitative data presented here presents unique insights into how marriage beliefs at the time of a baby's birth might translate into relationship decisions over a four-year period.

Background

The changes in the American family over the past fifty years are well documented. Marriage rates have fallen 12 percentage points since 1960, as only 55 percent of the population over the age of fifteen is married (Popenoe and Whitehead 2004). This is, in part, due to marital delay: the average age of a first wedding is now twenty-five for women and twenty-seven for men, an increase of five years over three decades (Fields 2004). Yet Americans are not necessarily eschewing two-adult households, as the decline in the number of married couples has been offset by the

800 percent increase in the number of cohabiting couples (Bumpass, Sweet, and Cherlin 1991; Bumpass and Lu 2000; Fields 2004).

What is particularly interesting about these changes is how they vary by socioeconomic status. Marriage rates have fallen for all individuals, but have fallen further for those with less education (Goldstein and Kenney 2001). Divorce rates are estimated to be 60 percent for those who drop out of high school and 36 percent for those who graduate from college (Raley and Bumpass 2003). Additionally, all women are generally delaying marriage, but only those with higher educations are likewise delaying childbearing (Ellwood and Jencks 2004a). Finally, cohabitation, though by no means confined to those with fewer resources, is more common among those who are less educated, earn less, and have lower total household incomes (Bumpass and Lu 2000; Carlson, McLanahan, and England 2004; Fields 2004).

This complex interplay between marriage, divorce, cohabitation, and class has stimulated numerous queries into why the American family is changing so rapidly. As reviewed by David Ellwood and Christopher Jencks (2004a), two types of explanations are offered to explain these changes: one stems from traditional economic theories of marriage formation, where marriage is viewed as a mutually beneficial contract between a man and a woman, and the other relies on the profound social and cultural shifts experienced in American society over the last half of the twentieth century.

Broadly speaking, economic theories of marriage formation rest on its fiscal utility: people enter into a marriage contract insofar as it enhances their financial well-being (Becker 1981; see also Wilson and Neckerman 1986). Economic theories predict a strong correlation between marital behavioral and economic conditions. Low employment and wage rates for men should depress marriage, for example, because women are less likely to marry partners with little labor market potential; likewise, high employment and wage rates for females should also discourage marriage, because their economic independence reduces the potential economic gain of a spouse.

Alternatively, sociocultural theories of family formation look to changes in social norms and sexual practices to explain the decline in marriage (Akerlof, Yellen, and Katz 1996; Goldin and Katz 2000). Under this framework, the legalization of abortion and the widespread use of contraception reduced the risk of nonmarital childbearing, increasing the appeal of out-of-wedlock sexual activity. In turn, this reduced the necessity of marriage in that a marriage license was no longer required for cohabitation and sexual intimacy. Couples were also less likely to get married simply because of a pregnancy (the so-called shotgun marriage) because society stopped morally penalizing unmarried parents.

However, though both an economic and sociocultural explanation of marital behavior can partly explain trends in marriage behavior, neither is enough. The empirical evidence for an economic explanation of marriage is decidedly mixed: the labor market participation of men is positively associated with marriage (Brown 2000; Carlson, McLanahan, and England 2004; Clarkberg 1999; Oppenheimer 2003; Sweeney 2002; Xie et al. 2003), but the connection between female employment and marriage is less clear (Fein et al. 2003; Moffitt 2000; Oppenheimer 1997). Additionally, viewing marriage as a contract cannot explain the seeming divorce between marriage and fertility among low-income couples, and does not address the dramatic rise in cohabitation. Furthermore, though there is little doubt that changes in contraceptive practices have had profound implications for social norms and sexual behavior, it is unclear if they can explain the marked class and race differences in family formation. Moreover, changes in sexual and legal practices that occurred in the 1960s and 1970s are less persuasive in explaining continued declines in marriage (Ellwood and Jencks 2004a).

An alternative explanation for marital behavior posits that the delay in marriage is due to a cultural reframing of the requirements of marriage (Edin 2000; Edin and Kefalas 2005). According to a number of qualitative studies, poor, working, and lower middle-class couples believe that marriage requires a certain level of financial stability (Edin, Kefalas, and Reed 2004; Smock, Manning, and Porter 2005). In this view, marriage is a capstone achievement, signaling that a couple has arrived in both a financial and emotional sense (Cherlin 2004; Edin 2000; Edin and Kefalas 2005). Kathryn Edin and Maria Kefalas (2005) argue that the symbolic significance of marriage has grown precisely because the instrumental value of marriage has declined (see also Cherlin 2004). Activities once regarded as the exclusive province of marriage—sexual activity, sharing a household, raising children—are now acceptable outside of marriage. Removed from these more prosaic functions, marriage has taken on greater meaning—it has become a "super relationship" (Whitehead and Popenoe 2001, 7) available to a select few.

Previous work with the TLC3 sample, for example, has shown that couples are hesitant to marry unless they have steady employment, assets or savings, and enough money to pay for a wedding (Gibson-Davis, Edin, and McLanahan 2005). These expectations apply to both men and women, because each member of the couple should be financially stable and well off (Edin and Kefalas 2005). Additionally, couples view marriage as the ultimate relationship and don't want to desecrate what they view as a sacred institution with divorce, so put off marriage until they are certain that their relationship will endure (Edin and Kefalas 2005; Gibson-Davis, Edin, and McLanahan 2005).

The delay and decline in marriage as a function of economic barriers is both consistent with current empirical findings on the role of economics in marriage formation and offers a more plausible way to address the patterns of cohabitation and marriage observed among the lower class. It is also consistent with empirical studies that indicate a strong role for male wages and earnings, and would also suggest that women with low wages do not marry because they view their lack of economic viability as a sign that they are not ready for marriage. It further suggests that couples delay marriage until they reached a certain economic threshold, a finding confirmed in a number of quantitative studies (see Oppenheimer 1997; Thomas 2006).

As for the role of cohabitation, Kathryn Edin, Maria Kefalas, and Joanna Reed (2004) found in their review of three qualitative studies (including TLC3), that couples who live together do so to evaluate the suitability of their relationship to marriage—a demonstration to family and friends that they are considering marriage without having to commit fully to the institution. It is worth noting that this view is not universal (Smock and Manning 2004); studies have shown that couples who do not have a child together or do have more economic advantage may cohabitate without regard for future marriage plans (Manning and Smock 2005). But for low-income parents, who are particularly likely to believe that cohabitation cannot substitute for marriage (Sayer, Wright, and Edin 2004), living together is the first (and necessary) step toward becoming husband and wife.

Limitations to the evidence supporting the economic bar to marriage are significant, however. First, with the exception of previous TLC3 research (Gibson-Davis, Edin, and McLanahan 2005), qualitative studies have relied on data drawn from individuals, not from couples. Data from couples is necessary because an important tenet of the argument is that both members of the couple are financially viable and secure (Edin and Kefalas 2005). Without information from both men and women, then, it is impossible to fully explore this view. Additionally, though quantitative studies on marital behavior are numerous (for a review, see Ellwood and Jencks 2004a, 2004b), none have specifically addressed the substance of the economic bar and so do not contain detailed information about how it is conceived, whether couples feel they have overcome it, and if so, at what point. The qualitative studies that have addressed this issue, as mentioned, are not longitudinal, and therefore provide only limited information on the effect of meeting the bar.

Here I address these limitations by following a sample of romantically involved unmarried couples over a four-year span, and by drawing on conversations and information from each. An additional strength is that, unlike previous analyses (see Edin and Kefalas 2005), it is not limited to low-income single mothers living in high poverty neighborhoods in one city, but includes both mothers and fathers from three cities that represent a broader socioeconomic spectrum than previously considered.

Methods

The primary objectives of this chapter are twofold: to see, first, whether economic requirements continue to act as a barrier to marriage as couples' relationships mature and, second, whether improvements in financial circumstances over time are related to subsequent marriage decisions. I relied on data from the marriage portion of the interview. Respondents were asked to describe their feelings toward marriage, and whether they believed that they would marry their partner. They were also asked under what conditions they might imagine marrying this partner, and what would have to change in their relationship or circumstances for that to happen. Couples who married were asked at the subsequent wave to describe the primary factors contributing to the decision to marry.

For the first part of my analyses, I examined what couples had to say about marriage and what role economic standards were playing in their marital decisions. For this analysis, I relied on data for forty-seven of the forty-nine unmarried TLC3 couples. I omitted two couples who were interviewed during only one round of the study.

For the second part of the analysis, I examined both the baseline economic circumstances of couples and whether they had seen improvements in those economic circumstances and therefore would meet the economic bar to marriage. These data were drawn from interview questions about current employment and sources of income in each wave. For couples who did not marry, I compared their economic circumstances during the first round to the most recent round when they were still a couple. For couples who married, I compared those in the first round to those in the round before their marriage.

This analysis was limited to thirty-six of the forty-seven couples. Seven couples were omitted because they broke up in their child's first year of life. Another four couples married after their baby was born, but before we could complete all of the baseline interviews with them. Thus, we did not have any income data on them as individuals before their marriage. The thirty-six couples do include one mother who had broken up with the father of the focal child, but quickly formed a new relationship, thus allowing us to collect economic data at baseline and onward.

In the context of this study, meeting the economic bar is defined in terms of four dimensions: stable employment, increases in income, reliance on public assistance or friends, and overall perceptions of financial well-being. These criteria were chosen based on textual analysis of the interviews, and strongly correlate with the economic barriers found in earlier analyses of this sample (Gibson-Davis, Edin, and McLanahan 2005). I coded couples as having satisfied the bar if they met all of the following criteria: their total household income increased at least 10 percent between wave one and later waves; both parents were working, going to school, or one stayed home voluntarily while the other worked or went to school; they were not relying on public assistance or family and friends to help them make ends meet; they were able to reliably pay their bills each month; and they did not feel that their economic situation was unstable or shaky.[1] In keeping with the couples' stated beliefs that both members must be economically ready for marriage, the economic bar is defined on a couple, rather than individual, level.

After I determined whether the couple had met the bar, I looked at whether they had married. I then created four categories: those who married and met the economic bar; those who married but did not meet it; those who did not marry but had met it; and those who had neither married nor met the bar. One additional assumption was that couples were beneath the bar when they were first observed, which I made because the vast majority of couples (83 percent) discussed financial barriers during the first round interview. Omitting the couples who did not discuss the bar does not substantively change the results presented here.

There are limitations to this categorization. First, though couples often mentioned how they felt about their financial situation, they were not directly asked to assess their economic well-being. Thus, I cannot be sure that my categorization would align with the couples' self-assessment. Second, other important dimensions of economic well-being, such as home ownership, savings, and other assets were not routinely collected by TLC3 and were therefore not considered, though couples did discuss the importance of these factors at baseline (Gibson-Davis, Edin, and McLanahan 2005). My goal was to construct a measure that met most couples' minimal standards, and that I could apply consistently across all couples. Only a few couples even reached this minimal standard.

The Economic Bar to Marriage

When we asked about views and attitudes toward marriage during the fourth round of interviews, couples not yet married but still romantically involved expressed their belief that marriage requires a certain level of economic stability and emotional preparedness, and said they would not consider marrying until those goals were met. The primary concerns were financial—couples repeatedly talked about the need to "have their money together" or to be "financially stable." In general, this means that the couple must have steady employment and money to pay for a wedding and a reception. They must also be free from debt, and perhaps have accumulated enough assets to be able to buy a house.

These expectations remain strong four years after the birth of a shared couple even if the couple's economic circumstances are rather dire. For example, Claudia, nineteen and Puerto Rican, has been cohabiting with her Hispanic partner, twenty-three-year-old Don, ever since the study began, and they live with their daughter and Claudia's son from a previous relationship. Claudia said that the couple needs to have their own place and be able to afford a wedding before they will marry:

> The situation has to be a lot better financially. . . . I don't want to have to owe any credit cards, I don't want to—I want to have my own place, and just have everything okay financially, completely okay, and say—let's just get married! You know, and have a wedding, you know, a nice wedding if we want to.

Currently, however, the couple is strapped financially because Don is unemployed and their combined credit card debt is significant.

An African American couple, Kenneth and Ciana, thirty-four and thirty-two, respectively, live in a distressed Chicago neighborhood and subsist primarily on Kenneth's $1,000 a month earnings from his job at a nursing home. The couple has a long history together, and share two children, but Kenneth told us that if he were to get married, the couple would have to be "financially stable," and they would first want to acquire "a nice home or something. A nice yard for the kids to play [in], something like that." For both couples, the gap between their current financial circumstances and their economic expectations of marriage is striking. However, their words underscore the important symbolic meaning of marriage: by equating marriage with the accumulation of significant assets (either through a new house or a wedding), couples believe that marriage is not an activity of the lower class, but rather one that is reserved for those who are able to move up the economic ladder (Edin and Kefalas 2005).

What is notable about these economic expectations is that their specific components—the desire for a house, the need to finance a respectable wedding—changed little over the length of the TLC3 project. The economic goals associated with marriage are remarkably durable, and are neither lowered nor altered by the passage of time. For example, when we first interviewed twenty-three-year-old Jason, a Hispanic father of three, he was unemployed, and he and Veronica, his twenty-one-year-old African American partner, were living with relatives. At the time, Jason believed that the couple could not marry until they had enough financial security: "Once I accomplish having a lot of money and being able to afford paying a mortgage and I get to that point in life, then I think I'll look toward marriage again." Four years later, things have improved: both Jason and Veronica are working steady jobs (he at a blood bank, she in a mortgage office), the couple is renting their own apartment, and their monthly income has increased from $1,500 to $2,500 a month. Jason, however, is still waiting for the "financial freedom" that will signify the couple is ready to wed:

> I'm getting ready to take this test so I can be licensed in real estate, and I'm really, really banking on that taking off. But like once that takes off, that's gonna give us the financial freedom that we need to you know, buy a house, kinda have the family life, so you know . . . a [place] we can call home, you know.

In our interview with Veronica, she tells us that Jason is also waiting to save up $10,000 or $15,000 to spend on a wedding—a significant sum given the couple's limited economic means.

Even couples whose incomes had not increased were likely to still be discussing the economic requirements of marriage. Beverly and Andre, an African American couple in their early twenties, were living together and raising three children, one of them shared, and had an income of $1,800 a month. Most of this came from various welfare programs, though Andre did contribute $400 a month from his under-the-table job laying carpet. The couple had said that they were planning to marry, but Andre said that it "don't make no sense" for them to do so unless their economic situation was better. Four years later, the couple's monthly income is still about $1,800, though Beverly is earning $1,000 working at a fast food restaurant (the rest comes from disability and food stamps). Andre is unemployed, having been arrested, and serving out his parole by doing community service. They still have plans to marry, according to Andre, but only if he can find a job and they can make some economic progress:

> We're waiting to get married until we have financial stability. Satisfied with our careers. It would mean that we is on the steps to the right road. We could be in that direction, but I'm not working, so that's the whole big problem.

To Andre, the clear problem with getting married now is that they are not on "the right road," given that they are both not stably employed. His words underscore that marriage is not something that anyone can do; instead, a couple must work toward it (by obtaining employment) and only then can they wed.

Given the way couples discuss the economic bar to marriage, it might appear that all that stands between them and wedded bliss is money. But we also found that couples may use the financial expectations of marriage argument as a way to conceal other, more pressing concerns about marriage. Some couples offer narratives that imply that they may not want to marry even though they claim they are contemplating it. Rather than admitting their feelings readily, they may find it easier to explain the lack of a marital tie to relatives, friends, and researchers by discussing it in terms of their lack of economic stability. Magdalena, an African American woman in her early twenties, has three shared children with DaJuan, a twenty-nine-year-old African American. She said that he was using the fact that they did not have enough money as a reason they could not marry. She explains:

> [He says] "We're not ready yet. Still got a lot of growing to do. We're not stable yet. Money's not right yet." . . . He wants to have this big old wedding, and I don't need a big, old, great wedding. I can go down to City Hall!

Although unusual in her desire to forgo a large wedding, Magdalena implies that DaJuan is dragging his feet and using their poor financial circumstances as a reason why they are not marrying. When we discuss the possibility of marriage with DaJuan, we learn that he is not completely convinced that he wants to marry Magdalena and may have some hesitations about the relationship generally.

Given the seriousness with which these couples take marriage, some feel that they are not ready to undertake the behavioral changes they ascribe to marriage. One such respondent is twenty-five-year-old Antonio, an African American father of four. Antonio at first described for us the economic circumstances under which he would marry someone: "I have to have a job, have my own apartment, be kind of stable financially, before I marry somebody." But when asked if he would get married if his financial situation improved, he indicated that he wouldn't. "I'm not ready to get married," he said. "I'll give it four, four or five more years, maybe. But right now, no. I like women. Not just one. Yeah. And I ain't ready for [settling down] yet." Thus, though part of Antonio's hesitation to marry may be financial, he also believes he is not ready for the monogamous behavior he believes marriage requires.

Other respondents have serious reservations about marriage because of the poor relationship experiences they have had. Frieda, an eighteen-year-old Hispanic mother, had a child with twenty-two-year-old Marco, also Hispanic. That relationship did not survive beyond the first year of the TLC3 project. By the fourth round, Frieda had two children with two other fathers, one of whom Frieda left because of domestic abuse. She is now living with Joey, the father of her youngest child. At first, she says that the couple needs to be able to buy a house before they can get married:

> I tell him I wanna first have our house, where we could buy a house first, and he'd be settled in the house and knowing that when we get married we just go straight to our house, you know with the kids and stuff? And um . . . that's what we're waiting for. That's why we wanna open a bank account because we wanna save up money for that.

As the interview progresses, however, it is clear that Frieda has hesitations about marriage that transcend economics, and because of her relationship history, she isn't quite sure if this relationship can be trusted. She admits to having fears about marriage because of all that she has had to endure in previous relationships:

> I'm living the life that I wanted to be living way back before. This is my dream. And . . . then just suddenly anything can happen and we could break or something. That's what scares me a lot. You know that, that's, that's my point, is that I get scared a lot . . . that I don't know if I should give it my ALL to, you know, or what, what should I do. So it's like I get scared of getting married.

Frieda is typical of a significant portion of our sample—relationships characterized by conflict, infidelity, and mistrust. Economic considerations aside, such relationships may not be stable enough for marriage. Rather than discussing these more difficult and personal concerns, however, respondents may couch their hesitations in financial terms.

Comments from Frieda, Antonio, and others indicate that the economic bar to marriage may not be a true barrier, but instead a socially acceptable way to avoid marriage. These parents may feel social pressure to say that they want to marry once they meet their economic bar, and may be even sincere on some level. Nevertheless, they may have serious reservations about their partner or the institution that would not be addressed by changes in their economic circumstances. If respondents believe that current cultural norms dictate it is acceptable to remain single if they are not financially stable, however, this may serve as the most expedient reason to explain why they are not marrying. If so, then an improved economic situation might not affect their marital decisions, unless their other hesitations about the institution were resolved.

Accounts of Marriage

I next turned to couples who got married over the course of the TLC3 project, and examined the accounts of their decision to wed; I was particularly interested to see if couples referenced improvements in their economic circumstances as a reason they married. Eighteen marriages occur in the sample: fourteen between members of the TLC3 couple (three of these would subsequently separate or divorce) and four for mothers who marry someone other than the focal father (including one mother who married the TLC3 focal father, divorced, and then married someone else). The reasons offered for marriage are diverse, and vary widely from couple to couple. They include family pressure, immigration issues, the desire to make the relationship official, and to ensure that health or death benefits were available to the other partner.

For example, one Hispanic couple in their middle twenties, Paz and Alejandro, married shortly after the birth of their first child largely because of his mother's disapproval of out-of-wedlock childbearing. A black mother, nineteen-year-old Camille, had ended her relationship with her Hispanic partner, twenty-year-old Freddie, within two years after the birth of their first child. By the fourth round, Camille had married a French-African man, Efraim, and indicated that the primary reason they married was to begin to establish her husband's citizenship status. "So if it wasn't for the immigration stuff, we probably would have waited for a while. But that was like, we had to get the ball rolling. Because you see how long [the immigration process] is taking." The father in a Hispanic couple, twenty-four-year-old Victor, shares two children with nineteen-year-old Jacinta, and said that they got married because he wanted to make his relationship "by the book":

> I guess just to make it official, now we're living together, let's just get married, not necessarily because I love you more, or I love you less . . . but I guess, just to make it like official, by the books, I would say, husband and wife, I guess.

Yasmine and Paco, a Hispanic couple in their middle twenties with three shared children, married in part so that Yasmine could have access to Paco's health insurance. An African American couple living in Milwaukee, twenty-eight-year-old Reggie and twenty-one-year-old NaKeisha, had a unique motivation: NaKeisha was going into the army, and according to her, needed to be married to have her children accompany her to basic training.

As indicated by the explanations described, no dominant theme or reason motivated parents to marry. Couples' marital decisions were deliberate. They recognized that getting married was "taking it to the next level," as one respondent put it. There was no sense, however, that these decisions were the result of increases in income or improvements in employment. In fact, except for one father who mentioned not marrying until he had saved enough money for a ring and Yasmine and Paco's concerns about health insurance, there was almost no discussion of a couple's financial well-being.

That couples did not reference specific financial improvements in their stories of marriage does not necessarily mean that those improvements did not happen, or that these improvements did not cause them to wed. The current cultural framing of marriage may be such that couples do not explain their marital decisions in terms of financial achievements, even if that is the primary reason they married. Likewise, couples may use different scripts to describe their marital decisions that may not correlate well with their previous descriptions of barriers to marriage. To see whether economic improvements do influence marriage decisions, I turn to the analysis of the couples' economic trajectories and their marital outcomes.

Table 4.1   Cross-tabs of Meeting Limited Economic Bar versus Getting Married

	Met Bar	Not Meet Bar	Total
Married	7	5	12
Row percentage	58.3	41.7	
Column percentage	77.8	18.5	33.3
Not married	2	22	24
Row percentage	8.3	91.7	
Column percentage	22.2	81.4	66.7
Total	9	27	36
	25.0	75.0	

Source: Author's calculations.
Pearson chi^2(1) = 10.6667; Pr = 0.001

Economic Improvements and Marriage Decisions

Economic theory offers one plausible explanation as to why marriage may be motivated by economic circumstances yet not described in those terms. The concept of revealed preferences (Samuelson 1947) indicates that the choices individuals make are the best indicator of what their desires are. Under this framework, actions trump words. Therefore, as indicated by this theory, even if couples do not reference economic improvements in their explanations of marriage, they may nevertheless wait to marry until they have seen positive financial changes, believing that these are the ideal conditions under which to marry. If this account is true, then meeting a limited economic bar should be highly correlated with those who marry.

An alternative view, mentioned earlier, is that the bar has little explanatory power, but does serve as a socially acceptable excuse for avoiding marriage. People may find it easier to reference poor financial circumstances than to discuss other reservations, such as personal concerns about their partner. If so, then changes in economic circumstances are unlikely to be associated with marital decisions.

To see which of these accounts is more plausible, I again coded couples into one of four groups: married, met limited economic bar; married, did not meet limited economic bar; not married, met bar; and not married, not met bar. The results are presented in table 4.1. If the proposed connections between the economic bar and marriage is correct, then the table should indicate that most cases fall into one of two cells: those who married and met the economic bar, and those who did not marry or meet the economic bar.

The results largely confirm what the economic barrier to marriage thesis would predict. Of the thirty-six couples observed, seven met the bar and married, five did not meet the bar but nonetheless married, two met the bar but did not marry, and twenty-two neither met the bar nor married. Although the relationship is not perfect, it is strong enough to produce a significant ($p < .01$) chi square test even with this small population of thirty-six. The most revealing contrast is that 78 percent of those who met the bar married, but only 19 percent of those who did not meet it did so. Focusing only on those twelve couples who married, at first glance the results are equivocal, since seven met the bar and five did not. If the base rate of not meeting the bar (75 percent) is considered, however, then it becomes clear that those who married were much more likely to meet the bar than the sample as a whole. Of course, because so few met even the limited economic bar operationalized here, it is not surprising that the vast majority of couples (twenty-two of thirty-six) neither met the bar nor got married. Their marital behavior is thus consistent with the idea that the bar is important.

The second most common category was the seven couples who met the limited economic bar and got married. They had seen improvements in their overall household incomes, did not rely on public assistance, and generally showed a positive trajectory in their economic circumstances. For example, LaReina and Richie, a Hispanic couple in their early twenties who married after the first TLC3 round, had their income increase by more than a $1,000 a month when Richie left his job as a chef and started working for the Metropolitan Transit Authority (MTA). Richie also talked excitedly about the prospects of making six figures if he stayed with the MTA long enough. Another young Hispanic couple, Flora and Ramon, both twenty, were living with their respective families when Flora gave birth to their first child. The couple was subsisting on Ramon's earnings from his factory job, WIC, and help from family and friends. Three years later, the couple had married, moved into an apartment on their own, and, thanks to Flora's full-time employment, had seen their household income more than double.

At five, the portion of couples who had not fared as well economically but nevertheless married was slightly smaller. Their labor market participation was sporadic, and some spent time living with friends or family members because they could not live on their own. Alex, twenty-six, and Rochelle, twenty-one, were an African American couple with two shared children living with relatives in a housing project in Chicago when we first met them. Neither had a steady source of income, and they relied primarily on welfare for subsistence. Their total monthly income was $1,020, of which $670 came from food stamps. Four years later, little had changed: they were still living with relatives, neither had found steady employment, and their overall household income had actually decreased somewhat (to $975) because their food stamp benefits had gone down. The couple had, though, tied the knot three years into TLC3.

Also included in this group are two couples who married despite difficult financial times. Lauren, twenty-seven, and Michael, twenty-six, both African American, had just had their first child together. About the time of the birth, Michael started a cleaning business with money that Lauren had inherited from her mother. The business, though, soon folded, taking the couple's finances and credit rating down with it. It was at this point that the couple decided to marry, to "start fresh," as Lauren put it. Unfortunately, the marriage did not last, and Lauren had married another man by the end of our study. A white couple in their early twenties with three children, Michelle and Daryl, had been planning to get married in a couple of years, but then Daryl lost his job as an operations manager at a truck company and had an Internet business fail. The couple knew that if they got married, they would receive money as gifts, and so they got married sooner than intended to accumulate some cash. Daryl explained, "And then I lost my job. My business closed down. So we decided to get married, push up the wedding to help get some money." Both couples married in relatively bleak economic circumstances, rather than waiting until after they had achieved some level of financial stability.

By far the smallest category was the two couples who met the bar but did not marry. For both, the father's earnings had increased dramatically, and neither had to rely on welfare or assistance from friends or family to make ends meet. One white couple, thirty-four-year-old Ted and twenty-seven-year-old Melissa, was also receiving a windfall because Ted is part Native American, and receives large ($17,000) annual payouts from his tribe's gambling profits. The Hispanic father in the other couple, twenty-three-year-old Matt, had seen his monthly earnings from his construction job almost double and reported an additional $4,400 a month from reselling clothes on the streets of New York City. For neither couple, however, does marriage seem likely. Ted's previous marriage had ended in a divorce that left him financially and emotionally scarred, and he said bluntly that he would never marry Melissa. Matt's relationship with Maria, his twenty-two-year-old Hispanic partner, has been rather tempestuous, and he told us during the fourth round interviews that he was planning to leave Maria shortly.

The most common category had no change in their marital status or financial well-being and were one of two types of couples. One group were very economically disadvantaged, lived paycheck to paycheck and needed periodic help to pay their bills from family, friends, or the government. The other group may have been steadily employed but saw no dramatic increase in their monthly income. Calista and Gavin are an example of the second type. They are African American, both thirty-five, had one child together, and lived together throughout the four years we observed them. At year one, Gavin, who stopped work after becoming disabled, did the occasional odd job and Calista was doing data entry for a telemarketing firm, bringing in the bulk of their $1,900 a month income from her salary.[2] Four years later, their monthly income was almost the same because Gavin did not have a reliable source of income and Calista had the same job at approximately the same wage.

Given their sociodemographic profile, it is not surprising that so few couples saw improvements in their economic circumstances. Educational levels for the unmarried TLC3 sample were generally low—35 percent of mothers and 43 percent of fathers did not have high school diplomas—and slightly less than 65 percent of the mothers had received some type of public assistance in the year before TLC3 began. Furthermore, the types of jobs that TLC3 sample members had (cooks, janitors, factory workers) are not those that generally lead to large wage increases. Moreover, the period under study, from 2000 to 2004, did not see economic expansion for the low-wage labor market. Under these circumstances, the lack of economic mobility is to be expected.

Yet this analysis indicates that though improvements in economic conditions were rare, when they did occur, marriage was most likely to follow. In all but two cases, when couples met the limited economic bar, they married soon after. Meeting the economic bar does not guarantee that a couple will marry, however. Other motivations, such as love, family pressure, and expediency, may prove the primary motivator. This finding casts doubt on the thesis that the economic bar is offered simply as a way to fend off social pressures to marry. Instead, it suggests that couples are sensitive to their economic circumstances and may indeed be waiting until things improve financially before they wed.

Conclusion

This study has shown that the economic expectations of marriage, which dictate that marriage requires steady incomes and stable employment, do not fade with the passage of time or with downward adjustments to couples' economic situations. Over the course of a four-year period, couples repeatedly articulated that employment of both partners was a prerequisite for marriage, and that welfare receipt or economic reliance on others were markers that a couple was not yet economically prepared to wed. More generally, couples emphasized the importance of being able to reliably meet their expenses each month and of feeling that they had reached a place of economic stability. As these results have shown, even if couples do not meet these goals or make progress toward them, they continue to believe that the standards must be met before marriage. The durability of this belief could be a comment on concerns as to what would happen if couples married without being economically prepared. Evidence from other qualitative studies indicates that not being financially secure is associated with fears that a marriage will not last (Edin, Kefalas, and Reed

2004). Women in particular do not want to depend on a man financially, would rather have a sound fall-back position in case the relationship should end (Edin and Kefalas 2005).

As for the explanatory power of the economic bar, evidence suggests that meeting it does correlate with marriage. Although when asked why they marry, couples are likely to name other motivations, an analysis of their employment patterns, income changes, and other factors shows that more than 75 percent of those who met the modest economic bar I constructed got married. At the same time, not everyone who married had met the bar; of the twelve couples who married, five did not see positive financial changes. This suggests that meeting this bar is more of a sufficient condition than a necessary one: that is, while it is true that couples usually married when they met the bar, love, family pressures, a military enlistment, and other factors also prompted couples to wed. In any case, these findings imply that couples are sincere when they say they plan to marry, and are not using economic barriers as a convenient excuse.

It is worth noting that the topic of public assistance was largely absent from conversations regarding marriage. Although couples believed that receiving public assistance was an important economic symbol that they were not prepared to marry, they did not discuss the possible loss of public assistance as a reason why they should not wed. Furthermore, none of the couples who did marry discussed how their marriage affected their public assistance status (though one did mention health insurance), or commented on the implications of their marriage for programs such as the Earned Income Tax Credit. Although couples were not asked explicitly about the implications of marriage for their public assistance status, it is striking that in the lengthy and repeated conversations about marriage the topic did not arise.

The desire for economic stability before marrying is not necessarily unique to the lower class. High economic expectations of marriage have also been documented in lower-middle-class samples (Smock, Manning, and Porter 2005; Manning and Smock 2005), and according to nationally representative data, more than two-thirds of Americans ages twenty to twenty-nine now believe that a couple should be "economically set" before they marry (Whitehead and Popenoe 2001, 11). What may differentiate lower class individuals from their counterparts, however, and explain why they are less likely to marry, is that they have a harder time achieving economic stability. There may thus be a disconnect between their motivation to marry and their ability to bring about the conditions necessary for marriage. In sociological terms, low-income couples are high on marital intentionality, but low on marital efficacy (Rainwater 1960; see also chapter 2).

If there is a disconnect that is exacerbated by poor financial circumstances, then policy makers who wish to promote marriage among low-income couples should address the conditions of the low-wage labor market. Currently, however, programs to promote marriage, such as the federal government's Healthy Marriage Initiative, address relationship skills and quality, but do little about a couple's financial situation. Yet, according to the couples interviewed here, a healthy relationship is but one part of the marital equation. Moreover, the TLC3 couples were not looking to boost their incomes through additional public handouts; indeed, their language indicated that participation in traditional welfare programs was a clear sign that a couple was not ready for marriage. Instead, these results suggest that policies and programs that encourage employment while boosting income—increasing the minimum wage, for example, or an expansion of the Earned Income Tax Credit—would be the most effective in promoting marriage.

Notes

1. As half of the couples married between the first and second waves of the study, we have only one round of income data before the couple married, making it difficult to measure changes in their economic circumstances. In these cases, I relied on data collected during the second round that asked about employment, earnings, and income changes over the year prior to their marriage. There were also two other mothers who married after ending their relationship with the focal father. However, their new husbands were interviewed only after the couple had married.

2. Gavin did not indicate whether or not he would lose his disability check if he married, as he never discussed it as an incentive or disincentive to marry.

References

Akerlof, George A., Janet L. Yellen, and Michael L. Katz. 1996. "An Analysis of Out-of-Wedlock Childbearing in the United States." *The Quarterly Journal of Economics* 111(2): 277–317.

Becker, Gary. 1981. *A Treatise on the Family.* Cambridge, Mass.: Harvard University Press.

Brown, Susan L. 2000. "Union Transitions Among Cohabitors: The Significance of Relationship Assessments and Expectations." *Journal of Marriage and the Family* 62(3): 833–46.

Bumpass, Larry L., and Hsien-Hen Lu. 2000. "Trends in Cohabitation and Implications for Children's Family Contexts in the United States." *Population Studies* 54(1): 29–41.

Bumpass, Larry L., James A. Sweet, and Andrew J. Cherlin. 1991. "The Role of Cohabitation in Declining Rates of Marriage." *Journal of Marriage and the Family* 53(4): 913–27.

Carlson, Marcia, Sara McLanahan, and Paula England. 2004. "Union Formation in Fragile Families." *Demography* 41(2): 237–61.

Cherlin, Andrew J. 2004. "The Deinstitutionalization of American Marriage." *Journal of Marriage and Family* 66(4): 848–61.

Clarkberg, Marin. 1999. "The Price of Partnering: The Role of Economic Well-Being in Young Adults' First Union Experiences." *Social Forces* 77(3): 945–68.

Edin, Kathryn. 2000. "What Do Low-Income Single Mothers Say About Marriage?" *Social Problems* 47(1): 112–34.

Edin, Kathryn, and Maria J. Kefalas. 2005. *Promises I Can Keep: Why Poor Women Put Motherhood Before Marriage.* Berkeley, Calif.: University of California Press.

Edin, Kathryn, Maria J. Kefalas, and Joanna M. Reed. 2004. "A Peek Inside the Black Box: What Marriage Means for Poor Unmarried Parents." *Journal of Marriage and Family* 66(4): 1007–14.

Ellwood, David, and Christopher Jencks. 2004a. "The Spread of Single-Parent Families in the United States Since 1960." In *The Future of the Family*, edited by Daniel Patrick Moynihan, Lee Rainwater, and Timothy Smeeding. New York: Russell Sage Foundation.

———. 2004b. "The Uneven Spread of Single Parent Families: What Do We Know? Where Do We Look for Answers?" In *Social Inequality*, edited by Kathryn Neckerman. New York: Russell Sage Foundation.

Fein, David J., Nancy R. Burstein, Greta G. Fein, and Laura D. Lindberg. 2003. "The Determinants of Marriage and Cohabitation Among Disadvantaged Americans: Research Findings and Needs." In *Marriage and Family Formation Data Analysis Project.* Bethesda, Md.: ABT Associates.

Fields, Jason. 2004. "America's Families and Living Arrangements: 2003." In *Current Population Reports*, P20-553. Washington: U.S. Census Bureau.

Gibson-Davis, Christina M., Kathryn Edin, and Sara McLanahan 2005. "High Hopes but Even Higher Expectations: The Retreat from Marriage Among Low-Income Couples." *Journal of Marriage and Family* 67(4): 1301–12.

Goldin, Claudia, and Lawrence F. Katz. 2000. "The Power of the Pill: Oral Contraceptives and Women's Career and Marriage Decisions." NBER Working Paper No. 7527. Cambridge, Mass.: National Bureau of Economic Research.

Goldstein, Joshua R., and Katherine T. Kenney. 2001. "Marriage Delayed or Marriage Forgone? New Cohort Forecasts of First Marriage for U.S. Women." *American Sociological Review* 66(4): 506–19.

Lichter, Daniel T., Christie D. Batson, and J. Brian Brown. 2004. "Welfare Reform and Marriage Promotion: The Marital Expectations and Desires of Single and Cohabiting Mothers." *Social Service Review* 78(1): 2–24.

Manning, Wendy D., and Pamela J. Smock. 2005. "Measuring and Modeling Cohabitation: New Perspectives from Qualitative Data." *Journal of Marriage and Family* 67(4): 989–1002.

Moffitt, Robert. 2000. "Female Wages, Male Wages, and the Economic Model of Marriage: The Basic Evidence." In *The Ties that Bind: Perspectives on Marriage and Cohabitation*, edited by Linda J. Waite. New York: Aldine de Gruyter.

Oppenheimer, Valerie Kincade. 1997. "Women's Employment and the Gain to Marriage." *Annual Review of Sociology* 23: 431–53.

———. 2003. "Cohabiting and Marriage During Young Men's Career Development Process." *Demography* 40(1): 127–49.

Popenoe, David, and Barbara Dafoe Whitehead. 2004. "The State of our Unions 2004." In *The National Marriage Project.* Piscataway, N.J.: Rutgers University.

Rainwater, Lee. 1960. *And the Poor Get Children: Sex, Contraception, and Family Planning in the Working Class.* Chicago, Ill.: University of Chicago Press.

Raley, R. Kelly, and Larry Bumpass. 2003. "The Topography of the Divorce Plateau: Levels and Trends in Union Stability in the United States after 1980." *Demographic Research* 8(8): 245–60.

Samuelson, Paul A. 1947. *Foundations of Economic Analysis.* Cambridge, Mass.: Harvard University Press.

Sayer, L., N. Wright, and Kathryn Edin. 2004. "Class Differences in Family Attitudes." Unpublished manuscript. Northwestern University, Evanston, Ill.

Smock, Pamela J., and Wendy D. Manning. 2004. "Living Together Unmarried in the United States: Demographic Perspectives and Implications for Family Policy." *Law & Policy* 26(1): 87–117.

Smock, Pamela J., Wendy D. Manning, and Meredith Porter. 2005. "'Everything's There Except Money': How Money Shapes Decisions to Marry among Cohabitors." *Journal of Marriage and Family* 67(3): 680–96.

Sweeney, Megan M. 2002. "Two Decades of Family Change: The Shifting Economic Foundations of Marriage." *American Sociological Review* 67(1): 132–48.

Thomas, Adam. 2006. "Crossing the Threshold: Do Low-Skilled Men Face an Economic Barrier to Marriageability?" Unpublished manuscript. Harvard University, Cambridge, Mass.

Whitehead, Barbara Dafoe, and David Popenoe. 2001. "Who Wants to Marry a Soul Mate? The State of our Unions, 2001." In *The National Marriage Project.* Piscataway, N.J.: Rutgers University.

Wilson, William Julius, and Kathryn A. Neckerman. 1986. "Poverty and Family Structure: The Widening Gap Between Evidence and Public Policy Issues." In *Fighting Poverty: What Works, and What Doesn't*, edited by Sheldon H. Danziger and Daniel H. Weinberg. Cambridge, Mass.: Harvard University Press.

Xie, Yu, James M. Raymo, Kimberly Goyette, and Arland Thornton. 2003. "Economic Potential and Entry into Marriage and Cohabitation." *Demography* 40(2): 351–67.

Chapter 5

Steppin' Out: Infidelity and Sexual Jealousy Among Unmarried Parents

HEATHER D. HILL

COMMITTED RELATIONSHIPS—whether married, cohabiting, or dating— are defined largely by the expectation of sexual monogamy and are seriously threatened by violations of that expectation (Christopher and Sprecher 2000; Treas and Giesen 2000). Extramarital sex has been consistently and strongly linked to divorce (Amato and Previti 2003; Amato and Rogers 1997; South and Lloyd 1995) and conflict about sexual jealousy and infidelity is associated with intimate-partner violence (Daly and Wilson 1988; Paik, Laumann, and Haitsma 2004; Puente and Cohen 2003). Despite sharing the normative expectation of monogamy, unmarried couples express less commitment to their relationships than married couples do and are more likely to conflict about sexual jealousy and to be sexually unfaithful (Forste and Tanfer 1996; Paik, Laumann, and Haitsma 2004; Treas and Giesen 2000; Waite and Gallagher 2000). As Philip Blumstein and Pepper Schwartz (1983) note, infidelity is fundamentally an indication that a couple is not committed to a future together.

Despite plentiful research on extramarital sex (for reviews, see Allen et al. 2005; Blow and Hartnett 2005a) and a handful of studies of infidelity that include unmarried couples (Blumstein and Schwartz 1983; Forste and Tanfer 1996; Hansen 1987; Treas and Giesen 2000), we still know very little about how unmarried adult couples define, negotiate, and enforce monogamy. No studies have examined the prevalence, precursors, or effects of infidelity among unmarried couples parenting young children, a group that has increased dramatically in size over the past fifty years and that holds particular current interest among policy makers. What commitments do unmarried couples with children make regarding sexual exclusivity? How common is infidelity in these relationships? When and with whom does cheating occur, and how is it discovered? When an expectation of monogamy is violated, what is the couple's process for coping with a breach of commitment, and what are the consequences of infidelity for the future trajectory of the relationship?

This chapter explores these questions qualitatively using data from couples in the Time, Love, and Cash Among Couples with Children study that were unmarried at the birth of the study's focal child. The participants in this study face a wide gap between what they describe as real and ideal relationships. On one hand, the vast majority of parents subscribe wholeheartedly to the principle of sexual monogamy, not just in the abstract, but in the context of specific relationships. On the other hand, the majority of couples reported at least one incident of infidelity in the course of their relationships. Additionally, many parents in this study hold a deep suspicion and cynicism about the potential for men and women to enjoy platonic relationships, and consequently interpret mundane interactions as precursors to or evidence of infidelity.

For these couples, the prevalence of infidelity has significant implications not just for personal happiness and relationship stability, but also for the quality of parenting and children's long-term well-being. To varying degrees, unmarried parents will share responsibility for child rearing throughout their adult lives, regardless of the longevity of their romantic involvement. My analysis suggests that many of these couples have high expectations for stable, monogamous relationships, but face substantial barriers to achieving those expectations in the form of sexual betrayal and distrust. This is critical information for researchers, policy makers, and service providers working to gauge and improve the potential for the relationships between unmarried parents to be lasting, healthy features of the lives of adults and children.

Background

A recent review of research on infidelity describes the "dearth of well-designed studies," which use diverse samples of appropriate size to examine "real-life" infidelity (Blow and Hartnett 2005a). It is true that many studies of infidelity and sexual jealousy ask hypothetical survey questions (for example, "How would you feel if . . .") of small, nonprobability samples of married couples (often college students). Our understanding of sexual behavior is improving, however, with recent studies of infidelity and polygamous sexual relationships among the unmarried (Forste and Tanfer 1996; Treas and Giesen 2000; Youm and Paik 2004), and analysis of large nationally representative surveys designed specifically to elicit sensitive information about sex, including the General Social Survey (GSS) (for example, Atkins, Baucom, and Jacobson 2001; Smith

1994) and the National Health and Social Life Survey (NHSLS) (for example, Laumann et al. 1994).

Infidelity and Relationship Status

The majority of men and women in committed romantic relationships, married or otherwise, expect sexual exclusivity (Blumstein and Schwartz 1983; Christopher and Sprecher 2000).[1] In this respect, cohabiting and married couples look quite similar: 99 percent of married couples and 94 percent of cohabiting couples expect monogamy (Treas and Giesen 2000). More permissive attitudes about extramarital sex are associated with high education, low religiosity, being male, being African American, and having more permissive attitudes about premarital sex (Glass and Wright 1992; Smith 1994). No study that I know of measures the expectations of monogamy, as opposed to behavior, among adult dating couples, but we would expect more variation in the commitment level of these relationships.[2]

Despite these near universal expectations for monogamy, studies estimate that approximately 25 percent of married men and 15 percent of married women have ever engaged in extramarital sex (Christopher and Sprecher 2000; Laumann et al. 1994; Wiederman 1997).[3] The incidence of infidelity is even higher in less stable or committed forms of relationships. Using NHSLS data, Linda Waite and Maggie Gallagher (2000) estimate that 4 percent of married men, 16 percent of cohabiting men, and 37 percent of men in dating relationships had sex with someone other than their primary partners in the year before the interview. The comparable rates for women are 1, 8, and 17 percent.

A higher rate of infidelity is one of many established differences in the nature of married and cohabiting relationships, which generally predispose cohabiters to less positive relationship outcomes. These outcomes result partially from existing differences in the characteristics of people who do and do not live with a romantic partner before marriage (Axinn and Thornton 1992; Brown and Booth 1996; Smock 2000; Thomson and Colella 1992). Even after controlling for many of these differences, however, relationship type still strongly predicts infidelity. For instance, holding a host of background characteristics constant, married women are five times less likely than cohabiting women to report infidelity, whereas the rates of infidelity among dating and cohabiting women are statistically indistinguishable (Forste and Tanfer 1996).

Studies of both college students and inner-city residents of diverse age suggest that casual sex, which is not accompanied by a commitment to monogamy, has become increasingly common. On college campuses, dating has been at least partially replaced with hooking up, the practice of engaging in short-term physical encounters without expectations of future commitment and not uncommonly with relative strangers or friends (Grello, Welsh, and Harper 2006; Lambert, Kahn, and Apple 2003;

Paul and Hayes 2002; Paul, McManus, and Hayes 2000). Recent findings from the Chicago Health and Social Life Survey (CHSLS) corroborate qualitative evidence (Anderson 1990; Andrinopoulos, Kerrigan, and Ellen 2006) that African American boys and men commonly carry on short- or long-term sexual relationships with multiple partners simultaneously (Youm and Paik 2004). Finding a high rate of multiple sex partners among black youth living in an inner-city community, Elijah Anderson (1990) argues that boys engage in a game of duping girls into casual sex as a way to compete for stature amongst their male peers, and use talk of romance and long-term commitment primarily as a means to that end.

Other Correlates of Infidelity

Why are the high expectations for sexual fidelity reported in surveys not realized by so many couples? The relationship between intentions or expectations and actual behavior is a largely unexplored topic in the study of infidelity. The few studies that examine the decision-making process involved with an eventual extramarital affair indicate that relevant cognitive or psychosocial processes might include: minimization of the risks involved; a focus on short-term rather than long-term consequences; initial rationalization of increased, but nonsexual, involvement with the potential partner; and emotional vulnerability (Allen et al. 2005).

There is also a set of individual and contextual correlates of infidelity. Men are more likely to have permissive attitudes toward extramarital sex and to be sexually unfaithful than women (Glass and Wright 1992; Greeley 1994; Oliver and Hyde 1993; Treas and Giesen 2000; Waite and Gallagher 2000; Wiederman 1997). There is evidence, however, that this gap is narrowing (Oliver and Hyde 1993; Wiederman 1997) and that women are more likely than men to engage in infidelity that involves an emotional connection with the other person (Blumstein and Schwartz 1983; Glass and Wright 1992; Thompson 1984). The incidence of extramarital sex is also higher among nonwhites, those who have remarried, those in the lowest and highest educational categories, urbanites, and the less religious (Choi, Catania, and Dolcini 1994; Christopher and Sprecher 2000; Treas and Giesen 2000). In one study, the odds of ever having had extramarital sex were 79 percent higher for men than women and 106 percent higher for African Americans than other racial groups (Treas and Giesen 2000).

Infidelity also requires opportunities to meet potential sexual partners and to engage in a sexual relationship surreptitiously. The gendered division of labor may offer women fewer opportunities to cheat and partially explain the gender differences in rates of infidelity. Unfortunately, opportunity is both conceptually murky and difficult to operationalize because it may depend on some combination of access to potential sex partners, sexual desirability, involvement in networks that either promote or discourage infidelity, and the material means to arrange for a clandestine sexual encounter (Blow and Hartnett 2005b). Select studies have found associations between proxies for opportunity—such as employment status, income, sexual experience, and religiosity—and the probability of committing infidelity (Atkins, Baucom, and Jacobson 2001; Treas and Giesen 2000), but measurement of this construct has been too varied to draw broader conclusions.

One of the least understood aspects of infidelity is its relationship to relationship quality or satisfaction. Some studies find that higher ratings of marital satisfaction or happiness correlate with lower probabilities of infidelity (Atkins, Baucom, and Jacobson 2001; Treas and Giesen 2000). Others do not (Blumstein and Schwartz 1983). Even if such a relationship exists, it is difficult to determine its directionality: dissatisfaction or unhappiness might lead to infidelity, result from it, or relate to it only through some other variable, such as conflict. Denise Previti and Paul Amato (2004) used structural equation modeling to address this issue and found a statistically significant and bidirectional relationship between marital quality and extramarital sex; divorce proneness (measured using a twenty-seven-item scale of relationship stability) increased the odds of infidelity and vice versa.

Consequences of Infidelity

Because monogamy is the cornerstone of most successful, long-term relationships, infidelity has serious and detrimental consequences for couples. Infidelity precedes as many as 40 percent of divorces (Sweeney and Horwitz 2001), is the most commonly reported cause of divorce by survey respondents (Amato and Previti 2003; Kitson, Babri, and Roach 1985), and consistently predicts divorce in both retrospective surveys of divorcees and longitudinal studies (Amato and Rogers 1997; Previti and Amato 2004; South and Lloyd 1995). Reports of marital problems related to a spouse's extramarital sex increase the odds of divorce in a twelve-year period by 300 percent or more (Amato and Rogers 1997). Infidelity also mediates the psychological aftermath of divorce: the likelihood of depression following a divorce is particularly high for individuals who did not initiate the divorce and whose spouses committed infidelity (Sweeney and Horwitz 2001).

Even if infidelity does not sink a relationship, it may increase sexual jealousy and conflict. Jealousy can be viewed as a response to actual, perceived, or feared infidelity. A recent study of urban sexuality contributed one of the first analyses of jealousy using a large random sample of married, cohabiting, and dating individuals (Paik, Laumann, and Haitsma 2004). The authors find that 28 percent of men and 36 percent of women report conflict at some point in their relationships about sexual jealousy; being black or Hispanic, younger, or unmarried predict higher levels of jealousy. Jealousy has been linked to gender role traditionalism, low self-esteem among women, and fewer perceived marital alternatives (Hansen

1985). One of the most troubling aspects of sexual jealousy is its consistent association with violent conflict in relationships (Daly and Wilson 1988; Puente and Cohen 2003; Raj et al. 1999). Anthony Paik and his colleagues (2004) find that conflict about jealousy is, in fact, more predictive of intimate-partner violence than any other topic, including sex, money, and alcohol or drugs.

The consequences of infidelity are not limited to adults. Infidelity and sexual jealousy may have long-lasting effects on the development of children and the quality of their later adult relationships. Positive parenting behaviors are consistently linked to both children's well-being and parental relationship quality, regardless of the parents' marital status (Boyle et al. 2004; Carlson and McLanahan 2006; Erel and Burman 1995; Kitzmann 2000; Krishnakumar and Buehler 2000). Both divorce and marital conflict have been linked to a variety of poor psychosocial outcomes for children, largely through the weakening of parent-child bonds (Amato and Booth 2001; Amato and DeBoer 2001; Amato, Loomis, and Booth 1995; Amato and Sobolewski 2001). In addition, there is considerable evidence that exposure to family violence has negative implications for children's psychological, physical, and cognitive development (for review, see Margolin and Gordis 2000).

Methods and Data

The TLC3 study lends itself to examining infidelity because interviews elicited rich detail on the current nature and quality of the couple's relationship, their relationship history, and the substance and process of couple conflicts. Interviews conducted with each parent separately facilitated discussion of sensitive topics, such as infidelity or domestic violence. I relied on data from the wave-four individual interviews because they included direct questions about the occurrence and nature of infidelity and sexual jealousy in couples' relationships. Although interviewers could modify wording, the suggested questions were:

> A lot of people have told us that their partner has cheated on them. Has she or he ever cheated on you anytime since you started seeing each other (worded "anytime before you broke up" for couples who are broken up)?

> Have you ever gotten involved with someone else since you started your relationship?

> Tell me about any problems that you have in your relationship with trust or honesty.

Interviewers were instructed to probe for information on the full story of each instance of infidelity, including when it happened and with whom, whether the couple was living together or broken up, whether cheating led to breakup, how the respondent felt about it, and what counts as cheating to the respondent (for example, does it need to be sexual).

Before analysis of the TLC3 data began, project staff coded the interview transcripts into fields that roughly match the topics of the interview protocol. This coding process identified not only direct answers to the questions, but as well any information that the respondent provided throughout the interview related to infidelity and sexual jealousy. In addition to the wave four data, I also used interview data from earlier waves for background and clarification of the relationship histories. Overall, I analyzed more than 400 pages containing relevant portions of interview transcriptions.

Sample

For the purposes of this study, I narrowed the unmarried TLC3 sample (forty-eight couples, ninety-six parents) to the forty couples for whom at least one parent completed a wave four individual interview.[4] In most cases, I had data from both parents.[5] Table 5.1 presents descriptive information for couples included in this analysis. The majority were cohabiting at the time of the focal child's birth, but relationship status was far more heterogeneous four years later. At that time, fourteen of the forty couples (34 percent) were cohabiting and twelve (29 percent) had ended their romantic relationships by breaking up, divorcing, or separating. Eight of the forty (20 percent) married between the baseline and wave four interviews and the remaining four (10 percent) were romantically involved but not living together. The sample is divided almost exactly in thirds by the highest educational grade achieved by either parent: fourteen couples have less than a high school diploma (includes GED), eleven include a partner with a high school diploma, and another thirteen include a partner with postsecondary education, which includes technical training. The majority of mothers and fathers in this sample were black or Hispanic. On average, mothers and fathers were twenty-four and twenty-six years old, respectively, when they entered the study.

Analytic Approach

This chapter presents two related but distinct analyses. I first documented the prevalence of infidelity and problematic sexual jealousy in the study sample by constructing four binary variables based on the qualitative interview data: mother's report of father cheating, mother's report of mother cheating, father's report of mother cheating, and father's report of father cheating. These codes were then collapsed into three binary variables for any report of infidelity, any report of father's infidelity, and any report of mother's infidelity. For the purposes of this analysis, I defined

Table 5.1   Descriptive Statistics of the TLC3 Couples Included in
Analysis (n = 40)[a]

	Number	Mean/Proportion of Sample
Baseline relationship status		
Cohabiting	30	.75
Dating	10	.25
Wave four relationship status		
Married	8	.2
Cohabiting	14	.341
Dating	4	.098
Broken up (never married)	12	.293
Married but separated	1	.024
Divorced	1	.024
Highest educational grade achieved by either partner		
Some high school[b]	14	.341
High school diploma	11	.275
Some college	13	.317
College degree[c]	2	.049
Couple's race		
Black (non-Hispanic)	15	.375
Hispanic	14	.341
White (non-Hispanic)	2	.049
Interracial	9	.22
Mean age of parents (standard deviation in parentheses)		
Mother	—	23.5 (5.0)
Father	—	25.65 (5.0)

Source: Author's calculations.
Note: Based on baseline and wave four TLC3 individual interviews.
[a]All demographic data collected at study entry, except relationship status at wave four interview.
[b]This category includes individuals with a GED.
[c]This category includes one couple in which both partners have graduate degrees.

infidelity as sexual interaction with a person outside the focal relationship during a time when at least one partner in the couple believed they were committed to sexual exclusivity. These criteria included relationships in which sexual intercourse did not occur but the respondent described some sexual contact (for example, "fooling around" or kissing), and infidelity that occurred during short, contested breakups or separations.[6]

Not surprisingly, partners did not always agree on whether infidelity occurred. For instance, one father reported that the focal mother had a sexual relationship with another man, but the focal mother claimed it was only a friendship. In another case, the couple disagreed about whether they were romantically involved or broken up when one of them started a sexual relationship with someone else. For the purposes of measuring the prevalence of infidelity, I did not attempt to reconcile these stories, but instead counted any report of infidelity as valid. This approach could lead to overestimation of the occurrence of infidelity in this sample, although I believe it improves on relying on self-report alone, which is likely to produce underestimates of the prevalence of infidelity.

In the second analysis, I narrowed the sample further to those couples that reported some history of infidelity in their relationships. I analyzed these narratives using methods of analytic induction, a standard approach to leveraging the commonalities and distinctions between individual cases to develop more universal concepts (Ragin 1994). I used an iterative process of coding for increasing levels of specificity and for specific dimensions of infidelity. I dissected each story into common dimensions, including timing and frequency, relationship status, the other woman or man, discovery, and outcome.[7] For each dimension, I identified the full range of possibilities represented in the data—for instance, the outcome of an instance of infidelity might be the relationship ending, the couple recommitting and moving on, or increased suspicion and jealousy. I also coded for commonalities and differences between the couples' cheating narratives, identified contrary or disconfirming cases, and looked for a modal story, if one existed.

In this chapter, I use three cases of specific couples to illustrate types of infidelity; that is, their stories represent both common features and important distinctions of the infidelity narratives in the sample as a whole. For these cases, I also drew on previous waves of data to place the couple's experience with infidelity in the larger context of their relationship trajectory.

Prevalence of Infidelity and Sexual Jealousy

Infidelity is the rule, not the exception, among the couples in this study (table 5.2). Twenty-three of the forty couples (58 percent) report at least one instance of infidelity by either parent during the course of their relationships.[8] Most commonly, the father cheated, but in more than 30 percent of the cases both the mother and the father had been unfaithful, and in another 13 percent the mother alone had been. There is a gradient on the prevalence of infidelity by the relationship status of the couple, with the lowest rate among couples who had married each other by the wave four interview (43 percent) and the highest rate among those who had ended their relationship by that time (71 percent). Cohabiting and dating

Table 5.2   Prevalence of Infidelity Among Unmarried TLC3 Couples

	Total	Infidelity (Percentage)
All couples	40	23 (58%)
Wave four relationship status		
Married	7	3 (43)
Cohabiting or dating	19	10 (53)
Broken up, divorced, or separated	14	10 (71)
Highest educational grade achieved by either partner (at the birth of the focal child)		
Some high school[a]	14	9 (64)
High school diploma	11	7 (64)
Some college	13	6 (46)
College degree[b]	2	1 (50)
Couple's race		
Black (non-Hispanic)	15	9 (60)
Hispanic	14	6 (43)
White (non-Hispanic)	2	1 (50)
Interracial	9	7 (78)

Source: Author's calculations.
Note: Based on combined report of mothers and fathers in TLC3 wave four individual interviews. The associations between reported infidelity and the demographic variables (relationship status, education, and race) are not statistically significant.
[a] This category includes individuals with a GED.
[b] This category includes one couple in which both partners have graduate degrees.

couples fall between the two (53 percent).[9] The lower the combined educational attainment of a couple, the more likely they report some history of infidelity. In addition, black and interracial couples were more likely than Hispanic to report cheating. With only two white couples in the sample, no meaningful white-nonwhite comparison could be made. In addition, the sub-group differences that do exist are not statistically significant and may be the result of response bias rather than real differences.[10]

Sexual jealousy is even more prevalent than infidelity among the unmarried TLC3 parents (table 5.3). Nearly three-fourths of the couples describe sexual distrust or jealousy as a problem in their relationships. Not surprisingly, couples that have a history of infidelity are more likely to report problematic sexual jealousy than those that do not. It is striking, however, that many of the couples with no history of infidelity also report some problem with sexual jealousy (ten of seventeen couples). Unlike infidelity, reports of sexual jealousy varied little by educational attainment or race. The breakdown of who is jealous in the relationship mirrors the statistics on who commits infidelity. That is, men are more likely to

Table 5.3   Prevalence of Problematic Sexual Jealousy Among TLC3 Couples

	Total	Problematic Sexual Jealousy (Percentage)
All couples	40	29 (73%)
History of infidelity		
Yes	23	19 (83)
No	17	10 (59)
Wave four relationship status		
Married	7	4 (57)
Cohabiting or dating	19	16 (84)
Broken up, divorced, or separated	14	9 (64)
Highest educational grade achieved by either partner (at the birth of the focal child)		
Some high school[a]	14	11 (79)
High school diploma	11	9 (82)
Some college	13	8 (62)
College degree[b]	2	1 (50)
Couple's race		
Black (non-Hispanic)	15	11 (73)
Hispanic	14	10 (71)
White (non-Hispanic)	2	1 (50)
Interracial	9	7 (78)

Source: Author's calculations.
Note: Based on combined report of mothers and fathers in TLC3 wave four individual interviews. The associations between reported sexual jealousy and the demographic variables (relationship status, education, and race) are not statistically significant.
[a] This category includes individuals with a GED.
[b] This category includes one couple in which both partners have graduate degrees.

cheat and women are more likely to be jealous. Interestingly, parents report problematic sexual jealousy at high rates regardless of relationship type, although it is most common among cohabiting or dating couples.

The Nature of Infidelity

Taken together, couples' stories offer insight into common dimensions of infidelity: how and when infidelity occurs and is discovered, the degree to which sexual exclusivity was an expectation of the relationship, the couples' process of coping with a breach of commitment, and the consequences of infidelity for relationships. Here we look at detailed case studies of three TLC3 couples, plus supporting evidence from other couples in the sample, to understand these common dimensions.

Marilyn and Damian: "I Was a Steady Cheat"   Damian says he had a crush on Marilyn from the first day he saw her at the law school they were both attending in Wisconsin.[11] Once he "got up enough nerves to call her," they began dating, despite the fact that Marilyn was involved with another man at the time. Just when Damian thought their relationship was becoming serious, Marilyn decided to break it off and go back to her old boyfriend. While she would return to Damian soon enough, this inauspicious beginning foreshadowed the volatility that would characterize their now ended ten-year relationship, which resulted in two children.

Damian admits to being a "steady cheat" throughout the course of his relationship with Marilyn, and indeed his exploits read like pulp fiction. He had sexual relationships with at least ten women, some of which he knew from high school and college, others that he met at church, at his law office, or in court. At times, Damian sounds vaguely contrite, but ultimately does not seem interested in or capable of maintaining a monogamous relationship:

> I don't think it's ever okay to cheat, but I justify my cheating when she's being difficult to get along with, when I feel as though she's unappreciative or she nags a lot, complains a lot. . . . I'm always greedy to the point of I want to keep her, but I still want to keep doing whatever I want. . . . I needed something from different women to feel happy. And I would take this from her, this from her, this from her. And all combined, it was cool. But I can't find one woman that can complete what I need.

Although Damian never committed himself to monogamy with Marilyn, he realizes that her expectations for the relationship were different than his. He says, "Me and Marilyn, no we were not really serious. . . . She thought we were in a monogamous relationship which she thought was going somewhere. So it was pretty serious. To me it wasn't super serious. . . . I just sowed my wild oats and I wasn't ready for a serious, committed relationship."

Unlike Damian, Marilyn did not cheat repeatedly with multiple partners, but she did return to her ex-boyfriend, whom she was dating when she met Damian, several times in the course of her relationship with Damian. After discovering that Damian was cheating with multiple women and rejecting his suggestion that they have an open relationship, Marilyn broke up with Damian and moved to another state for a short period. During this time, both Marilyn and Damian reunited with ex-lovers. When Marilyn returned to Wisconsin six months later, she was engaged to her ex-boyfriend and Damian was engaged to another woman with whom he had had a longstanding on-again, off-again relationship. For some time, Damian and Marilyn dated each other and their fiancées simultaneously. Eventually, Damian says the couple "made the decision to see each other exclusively" and shortly thereafter became pregnant with their first child and then moved in together. Despite this renewed and expanded commitment to each other as partners and parents, Damian continued to pursue sexual relationships with other women.

Four years after the birth of their first child, Damian and Marilyn had broken up, a turn of events they both attribute primarily to Damian's dishonesty and infidelity. Damian still holds out the possibility that he and Marilyn will not only reunite but marry as well. Almost in the same breath, however, he questions the benefit of monogamy or marriage: "I don't know anybody who is happily married. . . . Even people who are engaged or live together just complain about it. . . . If you can have ten women, why pick one?"

Clarity of Commitment   What commitments do unmarried couples with children make regarding sexual exclusivity? Many of the couples in this sample are quite young, so it would not be surprising if they were dating casually without a firm commitment to monogamy, particularly before having a child together. If this were the case, infidelity might not even be the proper terminology to describe their behavior. Instead, these relations might be better described as polygamous sexual relationships, or hooking up.

Damian and Marilyn illustrate how difficult it is to measure a couple's level of commitment. Many of the relationships with chronic infidelity, such as theirs, are characterized by seemingly continuous cycles of dissolution and reconciliation and perpetual uncertainty about the expectations for sexual exclusivity. It is true that both isolated and chronic cheating often occurred at the beginning of a relationship or during volatile periods when the couple's level of commitment to each other was uncertain. Seven couples describe instances of infidelity during a turbulent period in their relationship. In several cases, including Jason and Veronica, couples began dating each other when one or both were still involved in serious relationships with other people and it took time to extricate themselves from those relationships and make a firm commitment to each other. In others, a period of conflict in the relationship led to "taking a break," which left the status of the relationship uncertain.[12]

Myron and Suzanne are a white couple who were twenty-three and twenty-two when they entered the study. At the time that Myron cheated on her, right before the birth of their child, Suzanne says they "were having issues." When Myron went to live with a female friend from work for about a month, he thought that he and Suzanne were "technically" not together. Suzanne, however, says, "I thought we were taking a break from each other and taking time, but I never thought we broke up." A twenty-five-year-old black father's description of his relationship status when he became involved with someone else epitomizes wishy-washy: "It's sort of . . . you know . . . it wasn't like we were together around the time when, you know, I wasn't really dealing with her so . . . it was, you know, trials and tribulations through that time, so it wasn't, you know we were (just) dating in that period of time." However, the confusion about relationship status may not always be innocent. Freddie, a Hispanic man who was twenty when he entered the study, says his former partner, Camille, a nineteen-year-old African American woman, believed it "wasn't cheating because she planned the two-day breakup to go sleep with the guy. And then got back with me after that. Whatever technical term she wants to use . . . I consider it she cheated on me."

Infidelity was not restricted to relationships that were on uncertain ground or going through turbulence, however. Unfortunately, the available data does not allow me to determine each couple's relationship status (for example, married, cohabiting, or visiting) at the time of every instance of infidelity. My best estimate is that nearly half of the couples who report infidelity describe at least one incident that occurred while they were living together. In one case, the couple was married at the time. Furthermore, a few explicitly recount their experiences with infidelity in the context of committed relationships with clear expectations for faithfulness. A twenty-three-year-old black father who admits to cheating says, "we agreed at the time that we were going to be together, yeah. We didn't have one of those relationships where you can see anybody you want to . . ." Another African American father, age twenty-five when he entered the study, says "no, it wasn't no open thing" of his relationship with his child's mother, which involved infidelity on the part of both partners.

Timing and Frequency   Damian and Marilyn had a chronic problem with infidelity, both sporadically pursuing relationships with former partners while still involved with one another. In addition, Damian became sexually involved for short periods of time, often just one night, with a series of women he met in nearly every context of his life. The timing and frequency of Damian's and Marilyn's infidelity may seem extreme, but are in fact the most common form of infidelity in this sample. Fourteen of the twenty-three couples that report some infidelity describe repeated incidents by one or both partners, occurring steadily, or at least repeatedly, during the life of the relationship.

Keisha and Jazz are a young African American couple who were nineteen and twenty-one years old when they entered the study. Keisha says that she and Jazz, who was incarcerated at the time of the wave four interview, have "about five thousand" problems with trust because he "got caught up" (cheated) so many times. She estimates that she has actually discovered his infidelities five or six times, including multiple times while she was pregnant with their three children. All of these incidents occurred while the couple was living together. Paradoxically, his persistent cheating makes him less trusting of *her*. She says "he's always giving me a hard time. He thinks I'm cheating on him. 'Cause he knows he done f'd up so many times." Between his cheating, distrust, and physical abuse, Keisha wavers on whether she wants to stay with Jazz when he returns from jail.

The relationship of Katrice and Tim, another young, African American couple that has been separated for long stretches of time by the father's incarceration, has been marked by volatility and uncertainty about their level of commitment to each other. Katrice says that Tim cheated on her with at least ten women over the course of their relationship, and that she has been unfaithful, "a couple of times" when she was "in the mood" or wanting to get back at her partner for his infidelities. A twenty-three-year-old black father in the sample, Ollie, "lost count" of his former twenty-year-old black partner Adrienne's cheating and has trouble recounting his own, which may contribute to his self-proclaimed reputation for being a "male whore," referring to the number of women he has had sex with, not to prostitution.

Sometimes chronic infidelity does not take the form of casual sexual relationships with numerous partners, but rather ongoing semi-committed relationships with one or two partners (in addition to the focal partner). Marilyn's involvement with the man she dated before Damian exemplifies this type of infidelity. Trevor and Delilah, an African American couple who were twenty and nineteen when first interviewed, broke up shortly after the birth of their first baby when she discovered that he had been steadily seeing two other women at the same time. The couple was not living together at the time, but Trevor frequently spent the night at Delilah's house. Delilah learned of Trevor's indiscretions when one of the other women he was seeing arrived at her doorstep. When Trevor realized what was happening, he jumped in his car and sped off, leaving the two women to become acquainted. Delilah challenged the other woman, "Who are you?" "I'm Trevor's girlfriend," the woman responded matter-of-factly. "Well, welcome to the club, sweetie," Delilah scornfully replied.

In contrast to the chronic cheaters, nine couples recount just one or two isolated incidents of infidelity during their relationships. Isolated cheating appears particularly likely to happen at the beginning of a relationship before the couple had clarified their commitment to one another. For instance, a Hispanic father who was twenty-three years old when first interviewed, Jason, describes sexual involvement that he and his twenty-one-year-old African American partner, Veronica, each had with other people in the early stages of their relationship: "like when we were still just dating she was dating some other guys and I actually went back and did something with my ex wife . . . but . . . it was kinda like a few months apart from each other." Maria and Matt, a Hispanic couple who began dating as adolescents and were first interviewed when they were twenty-two and twenty-three, respectively, were only together for six months when Matt began a sexual relationship with the girlfriend of Maria's uncle, a much older woman. According to Matt, "It was exciting for me you know, you're young, and you got an old girl," but he has not cheated since.

In two cases, an isolated incident of cheating occurred when the couple had been together for much longer. This was true for Daisy and Paulo, a Puerto Rican couple that entered the study at ages twenty-two and twenty-nine, respectively. Seven years into a ten-year abusive relationship with Paulo, Daisy met a man through work who gave her the attention and affection she felt was lacking in her relationship. The two developed a close relationship that was primarily emotional, but did include some kissing and cuddling. Daisy ended the relationship after just a few weeks and her infidelity remains a secret from Paulo.

Flora and Ramon: "Is the Baby Yours?"   Flora and Ramon were eighteen years old when mutual friends insisted on setting them up.[13] Flora says what "was mostly a friendly thing ... suddenly got serious." Five years later, the couple shared a marriage, two children, and a history of violent arguments when Flora learned of Ramon's affair with another woman. She vividly recalls the confrontation:

> I said, "who's the girl, because you're not going to leave me for nobody. You have to have somebody lined up ..." and he was like "I've been talking to somebody on the south side ..." I left him there. I just started driving around. ... I was like, "Oh my God." ... So, I came back and told him to leave." [Talking to is used here as it is by other sample members as slang for having a sexual relationship.]

Flora later learned from acquaintances that the other woman was not much more than a girl, eighteen years old to Ramon's twenty-four, and still in high school. Flora and her friends went to the girl's house and confronted her, but she laughed in Flora's face. When Ramon found out about the confrontation between the two women, he got into a violent argument with Flora in which both of them were hitting each other in the face. She tried to press charges, but the police said they could not arrest Ramon because the violence had been mutual.

Just a few weeks before the wave four TLC3 interview, Flora's hurt and sense of betrayal was multiplied when she learned that Ramon's lover was pregnant and that the baby was very likely Ramon's. The couple separated shortly thereafter and Flora filed for divorce, but Ramon had not agreed that the relationship was over. Ramon was so obsessively tracking her and their children that Flora successfully obtained a restraining order against him. Flora believes that Ramon's intentions are not just to spend time with his children but to woo her back into a relationship with him. As hurtful as she found his infidelity, Flora intimates that she might have been able to forgive him and to consider reconciliation but for the other woman's pregnancy. Now that "there's a baby involved," however, she sees no future with her husband.

Discovery   Flora became suspicious when Ramon repeatedly came home late and her suspicions were confirmed when, in the process of leaving her, Ramon admitted he was involved with another woman. Their story represents one of numerous scenarios for how the "wronged" partner discovers sexual infidelity. Often friends, family members, or acquaintances play a role in revealing the infidelity. In a few cases, including Trevor and Delilah (the African American couple mentioned earlier who were nineteen and twenty when first interviewed), mothers in the study were confronted by the women with whom their partners were cheating. Some cheaters were caught in the act by their significant others, while others gave themselves away by staying out too late or making phone calls to their lovers.

Steven and Dominique are a black couple first interviewed when they were twenty-three and twenty-one. Steven says he discovered his partner's infidelity twice when her ex-boyfriend called on the phone. The second incident occurred shortly after Steven moved into Dominique's apartment and the fight that ensued resulted in her throwing him out of the apartment and ending their relationship. His basis for believing she was cheating was that she acted suspiciously and "covered the mouth part of the phone" when she spoke to her ex. In two cases, disinterest in sex was also taken as adequate proof of infidelity. This evidence may seem slim; on the other hand, three sample members (all women) confronted their partners with no concrete evidence of their infidelity because they "just knew."

Reactions to the discovery of cheating were equally varied, ranging from indifference to violence. Shortly before Marilyn became pregnant with her second child, Damian heard that she had cheated with a guy from his baseball team. Damian and Marilyn were described in the first case study; both African American, they were twenty-four and twenty-nine years old when they entered the study. Damian, chronically unfaithful himself, was "devastated," not by the infidelity itself, he says, but by its circumstances. "God, I was like, if you want to do your dirt, I don't have any problems with that. But just do it with somebody I don't know. And don't let yourself get pregnant by him. It was just messy." The incident brought the paternity of Damian's daughter into question. For a mixed race couple, Tabitha and Howie, age thirty and thirty-five at the beginning of the study, the discovery of infidelity led to an ultimatum. In Tabitha's words:

Oh my God, I was devastated. I was so hurt to the gut of my stomach. I lost fifteen pounds. I was a mess. Finally I said to him, well you know what it was, I was allowing him to do that. I was like . . . "Listen, either you end all ties with the girls or I'll forget about [our relationship], I'm leaving." I think when he realized it came down to that point then he was like alright you know. And then that was it. He stopped seeing the girl and he told me it was just to make me jealous.

In a few cases, the reported infidelity was discovered by the wronged party only after the relationship ended, or remained a secret at the time of the interview. Freddie, for example, did not discover Camille's infidelity until two years after it occurred, by which point the couple was no longer romantically involved. An acquaintance of the couple told Freddie that Camille was unsure who the father of their daughter was when she was born. When Freddie confronted Camille, she denied that she had cheated until Freddie brought up the paternity issue, at which point he says, "She started crying. She asked me who told her. And that was it. . . . That's when I really stopped caring about Camille, when I found that out." Daisy, the twenty-two-year-old Puerto Rican mother mentioned earlier, has concealed her short, primarily emotional relationship with another man from her abusive partner, Paulo, twenty-nine and also Puerto Rican. She fears what will happen if he ever finds out, "God forbid . . . because he will . . . hurt me real bad," but is still tempted at times to admit her cheating to hurt him.

Infidelity-Related Pregnancies   Unlike Damian and Marilyn, Flora and Ramon spent six years in what was, by all accounts, a committed monogamous relationship, culminating in marriage after the birth of their second child. They experienced an isolated incidence of infidelity, but one that precipitated Ramon's leaving Flora and resulted in his getting another woman pregnant. This case exemplifies a troubling dimension of infidelity: in six cases, infidelity led to a pregnancy or the questionable paternity of a child, substantially increasing the consequences of infidelity for the future of the couple's relationship. In two cases, men impregnated multiple women within months of each other. In several others, the paternity of a child remained uncertain because of the mother's infidelity around the time of conception. An African American mother who was twenty when first interviewed, exclaimed in a shocked voice that "[My daughter's] little brother is two weeks younger than her!"

Trevor, who carried on sexual relationships with Delilah and two other women simultaneously, became a father to three children by three different women within several months' time. Trevor recollects his admission of this fact to Delilah: "Actually, she found out because I told her. I took it upon myself to . . . [tell] her about, you know, Brandy being pregnant and Aisha being pregnant. She was okay with it because it wasn't nothing that she could do about it." On further questioning, Trevor admits that Delilah was not really "okay" with his transgressions and modifies his story to: "she was angry, of course. She broke up with me. Because she figured 'well, you've been with me all this time and you got two females pregnant. . . . You had to be spending time with them, too'." In this way, children represent inescapable evidence of promiscuity or infidelity that makes it more difficult for a couple to recover and move on.[14]

Children also increase the stakes of infidelity, transforming the "other (wo)man" into the "other family." Even if a relationship survives infidelity that results in pregnancy, it cannot help but be substantially altered by the responsibilities (however seriously taken) of a parent to his or her children. Consistent with findings presented in other chapters of this volume (Reed, chapter 6 this volume), multiple partner fertility can lead to sexual jealousy of "other baby mamas" (or daddies) and an additional source of conflict for the couple. Although it is very common in this sample for parents to have children outside the focal relationship (see chapter 6), multiple partner fertility still seems to cast a shadow of doubt on a person's virtue. Explaining why his relationship did not work out, and specifically why it did not progress to marriage, a twenty-three-year-old black father says "I just knew she was still sleeping around. . . . I mean I was happy being with her but I just couldn't marry a woman who got basically three kids by three other dudes. You know what I'm saying. I just couldn't marry a woman like that." It is not clear from this data whether this stigma is widely held and whether it applies equally to men and women.

Suzanne and Myron: "We Worked Through It."   Suzanne and Myron met when they were just out of high school and they began hanging out with a group of mutual friends.[15] Just three and half months into dating, Myron began having trouble with his parents and decided to move in with Suzanne and her mother. "He slept out on the sofa," says Suzanne, who "kinda made a little dresser area for him" in her bedroom. Nearly ten years later, the couple remains romantically involved with a four-year-old son and a one-year-old daughter. They describe their relationship in positive terms and have hopes of marrying in the future. Like all couples, however, Suzanne and Myron have had ups and downs, including a period right before the birth of their son during which uncertainty surrounded the future of their relationship and Myron pursued a relationship with a coworker. In describing this clearly very stressful period in their relationships, Suzanne places some of the blame for Myron's infidelity on herself:

> We were just having so many problems because I was letting a lot of family issues get into our relationships more, so he was ending up feeling like he was just around just to be around, not really that I wanted him

around. . . . So we were fighting a lot. . . . So through that whole, I think, four-week period he was staying with a friend that he worked with, at first they were friends, but then they were more.

Despite living with the woman for a month, Myron claims that the relationship never became physical, but Suzanne thinks that though Myron and the other woman never had sexual intercourse, they did "fool around." They both seem unsure of whether to label Myron's behavior as cheating, but agree that the relationship with the other woman was more than just a friendship and that his lying to Suzanne made his behavior more egregious. Although they differ on the details of the events during this time, Suzanne and Myron agree that this episode was isolated and an aspect of their relationship that they have successfully resolved. Suzanne says, "I, of course, was hurt and it took me a while to trust him and every once in a while I would get upset about it or something, but we worked through it." She gives several reasons for why she forgave Myron's betrayal. First, he believed they were broken up at the time, though she did not. Second, "it wasn't like he was looking for someone to cheat with." Third, by both their accounts, the relationship with the other woman was primarily emotional. According to Myron, the couple has so successfully moved past this episode that jealousy is not even a problem in their relationship. He says that Suzanne worries some because he gets "flirted with a lot" at his job, but that she knows he "wouldn't be able to get away with [cheating] even if [he] tried." They seem not only to have moved on from Myron's brief episode of infidelity, but to have come out stronger.

Breaking Up or Reconciling   In the next chapter, Joanna Reed draws attention to the high stakes of infidelity. Her analysis of relationship dissolution among these same couples suggests that infidelity, alone or in combination with other relationship problems, is the most common reported cause of a relationship ending. Similarly, I find that infidelity is a commonly reported cause of break-ups and that men's infidelity is more often associated with the end of a relationship than women's is.

My analysis also suggests that chronic infidelity has more severe consequences for relationships than isolated infidelity. In the first case study, Marilyn and Damian, chronic infidelity was at least partially responsible for the demise of the relationship. Seven of the fourteen couples categorized as chronically unfaithful (either parent had cheated repeatedly) ended their relationships before the wave four interview, and all seven describe cheating or distrust as the biggest problem in their relationship or the reason for their break-up, or both. In contrast, just one of the nine couples that report isolated instances of infidelity broke up by the wave four interview.[16]

Like Suzanne and Myron, several couples' narratives of infidelity end in recovery and recommitment, particularly with isolated episodes of infidelity early in the relationship. Jason and Veronica, a mixed-race cohabiting couple, were able to forge a committed relationship after a turbulent beginning. In Jason's words, "And it was sorta kind of an issue but we were both able to just talk about it and put it behind us and move forward. Because it was like a new beginning stage was us getting, really serious about each other." In fact, these issues rest so far in the past for Veronica that she does not even mention them when asked about relationship problems in her wave four interview.

Several parents attribute improvements in their relationships around the issue of monogamy to maturity and the birth of children. In the words of a twenty-one-year-old black father, he had "been going straight and faithfully;" he says he does not want to cheat on the mother of his children because he loves his family and would rather keep them together than cheat. Tabitha, a thirty-year-old white mother, reflects on changes in her relationship:

> I trust him. Just like, you know, he trusts me. . . . I guess we've grown up. He KNOWS if he cheats on me, if I find out, this relationship is not going to last. And he doesn't want that for his kids. He grew up without a father. He doesn't want that to happen for his kids. To him that's very important. So I know he won't screw up. [emphasis in transcript]

The Nature of Sexual Jealousy

Not all couples have the fortune or capacity to survive infidelity with their faith in each other intact, as Suzanne and Myron did. Sexual jealousy and distrust are common in this sample, and quite extreme in some cases. For example, a Puerto Rican mother and her black partner, Gabriella and Travis, who were twenty-two and twenty-five when they entered the study, rarely participate in social activities together because, according to Travis, Gabriella acts jealous of nearly any woman with whom he comes in contact. He says, "If we went to the mall together and a woman was to walk by [me], she'll hit me in the back of the head, like 'what you looking at?' And I'm like, I didn't do nothing." He says he would be scared to take Gabriella out to dinner because, "If we get a lady waitress, I'm in trouble." He even suggests that she would be uncomfortable with his interaction with the female interviewer.

Gabriella does not deny that she is extremely jealous. She admits, for instance, getting up in the middle of the night to rummage through his dirty clothes checking for pieces of paper with phone numbers on them. She points out that her jealousy stems partially from real life experience and that Travis is extremely distrustful in certain circumstances:

> He say he don't [have trouble trusting me] and I think that the reason is I haven't gave him no reason for him to feel like he [shouldn't]. . . . I haven't

given him no doubts or nothing. . . . But when I do break up with him, all
he does is talk all night. . . . He probably think like she broke up with me . . .
[and] went out today and met somebody and somebody gave her the number. . . . So he just call and call and I just looking at the caller ID like mmhmm
you'd better keep on calling. . . . I ain't answering no phone. It's done, it's
over.

Without being asked directly about jealously-related violence, five of
the couples describe an incident of sexual jealousy leading to violence. In
one case, a Puerto Rican mother who was first interviewed at nineteen
describes a violent episode when she broke up with her child's father
because of his chronic cheating. She states bluntly, "he strangled me. He
was acting strange and then he found out I was going to leave and he just
went crazy." Sometimes the violence was taken out on someone outside
the relationship. Ted, a thirty-four-year-old man of white and Native
American descent, describes his rage when a man flirted with Melissa, the
twenty-seven-year-old white mother of his child.

When we first got together . . . [we] walked in a bar, some guy grabbed her
ass. I dislocated his arm, broke his jaw, and spent three nights in jail. . . .
What's mine is mine, and it better stay mine. If it's mine, don't touch it.
Don't, it's mine.

Interestingly, all of the violently jealous men in this sample admit to
not being monogamous themselves. These men's own transgressions
seem only to increase their distrust of their partners.

Sexual jealousy is quite prevalent even among the couples who do not
have a history of infidelity (table 5.3), although they describe less severe
problems with distrust than do the couples who report infidelity. More
often, distrust about sexual fidelity occurred early in these relationships—
when their commitment to each other was unclear—and did not seem to
fundamentally threaten the stability of the relationship. For instance, none
of these couples describe relationship violence related to sexual jealousy.

Rochelle and Alex, an African American couple twenty-one and
twenty-six years old and cohabiting when the study began, attribute a
year-long break-up during the course of the study to Alex's distrust of
Rochelle. Ultimately, however, the couple reunited and married by the
time the focal child turned four. Several other respondents describe lower
intensity jealousy in their relationships:

I could say one time that only thing he was worried about was [her child's]
father . . . [but] that'd be the last person I'd EVER go back to. The LAST.
[emphasis in transcript]
    Well, there isn't anything I don't trust about my woman. It's not her, it's
some of her friends, like real influence-y friends. "Let's drink, let's smoke,
oh look at that guy, he's so cute!"

One factor contributing to widespread sexual jealousy is a narrow and pessimistic view of platonic male-female relationships. When asked questions about what counts as cheating, the TLC3 couples unanimously agree that sexual intercourse constitutes infidelity, and most extend that definition to include any physical contact of a sexual nature—including kissing, hand holding, and even hugging. However, a majority of parents also include in the definition a host of behaviors that are not themselves physical but suggest some intent to develop a physical relationship with someone. These actions might include getting someone's phone number, calling someone on the phone, and spending significant time together. According to an African American woman who was twenty-seven when she entered the program, "when you are talking to someone and you got their [phone] number, that means you're planning it." Similarly, a Hispanic mother who was first interviewed at eighteen questions why a man would want to spend significant time with another woman: "Why go out there and take some girl to the movies when you could take your own girl to the movies, you know what I'm saying? That's cheating—when you're having another relationship with somebody else." These comments seem to leave little room for the possibility of platonic friendship between men and women.

Discussion

Nationally, 25 percent of men and 15 percent of women report ever having been unfaithful during the course of a marriage (Christopher and Sprecher 2000; Laumann et al. 1994; Wiederman 1997). This study supports previous findings that rates of infidelity are higher among cohabiting and dating adults (Waite and Gallagher 2000). In addition, it uncovers previously undocumented high rates of infidelity among couples who are unmarried, but share children. More than half of the couples in this sample report sexual infidelity by at least one of the partners during the course of their relationship. Consistent with other research on infidelity, fathers are far more likely than mothers to have been unfaithful. However, four cases involved cheating by the mother only, and another eight couples report cheating by both partners at some point in their relationship history.

In chronicling views on infidelity among a sample of poor unmarried mothers in the Philadelphia area, Edin and Kefalas (2005) write: "though some believe a relationship can survive a one night stand, most feel that cheating is seldom a one time event, but rather a habitual pattern rooted in a personality trait that leads a man to repeat behavior over time." The findings of this study lend some support to this perspective, though they obviously cannot speak to the origins of infidelity, whether in a personality trait or otherwise. Among the unmarried parents in the TLC3 study, more than half of those who report some infidelity describe chronic or a habitual pattern of cheating. What is more, the majority of couples who report chronic cheating had ended their relationships four years after the birth of the focal child, but the majority who experienced isolated instances of infidelity had not. This analysis, along with that of chapters 6 and 8 in this volume, also uncovers how pregnancies that result from infidelity can heighten the consequences by creating indisputable evidence of the betrayal and an ongoing connection and responsibility to the other man or woman.

Finally, whereas some couples reconcile after the discovery of cheating, others have substantial, sometimes violent, conflict over sexual jealousy. It is significant that many of the couples in this sample define infidelity in such a way that precludes friendships between men and women, and in fact makes any interaction—at work, on the street, or in a store—suspect. These pessimistic expectations lead to sexual jealousy and distrust, even among couples who have not experienced infidelity, which may threaten and in some cases contribute to the failure of relationships.

It is important to consider the sexual behavior reported here in the context of the parents' age and stage in the life course. On average, the TLC3 couples were in their middle to late twenties at the time that the study began. It is possible then that what I refer to as incidents of infidelity are in many cases simply concurrent but casual sexual encounters, much like those documented among college students of similar ages (Lambert, Kahn, and Apple 2003; Paul and Hayes 2002; Paul, McManus, and Hayes 2000). However, my analysis suggests a more complicated picture. It is true that having multiple partners often occurred at the beginning of a relationship or during periods of volatility, when the exact level of commitment between the two partners was unclear. However, no one refers to their relationship with the other parent as purely casual, and several say explicitly that the infidelity violated a clear commitment. For the most part, the sexual interactions described by these couples appear not to be hook-ups as much as betrayals of committed relationships. Nonetheless, there is a clear connection between events that bring a relationship's future into question, such as the incarceration of one partner or a major disagreement, and incidents of infidelity.

The distance between intentions and behaviors for these couples is not necessarily any greater than for other married and unmarried relationships, most of which are premised on expectations of monogamy, but a substantial minority of which fall short of that ideal (Blumstein and Schwartz 1983; Christopher and Sprecher 2000). Additional qualitative research is needed to better understand the individual process and relationship dynamics leading up to an incident of infidelity.

In policy circles, concern for declining marriage rates and increasing numbers of children born out of wedlock has placed a particularly bright spotlight on the nature and quality of relationships among unmarried parents. Pilot programs under way in several states are offering unmarried parents training in communication and other relationships skills in hopes that these relationships can lead to marriage and offer more stable environments for raising children (for more information, see Dion 2005). This study suggests that concurrent sexual relationships and distrust pose serious barriers to relationship stability and marriage among unmarried parents. Identifying and addressing these issues will be critical to helping unmarried parents decide whether to make a stronger commitment to one another. Given that sexual jealousy has been linked to intimate-partner violence (Paik, Laumann, and Haitsma 2004), a history of infidelity may be a particularly good indicator for parents and program staff that the risks, to both the adults and their children, that are associated with staying together may outweigh the benefits. Even when romantic relationships end, a history of infidelity and sexual jealousy may negatively affect parents' ability to work together to raise their common children. In these cases, families may benefit from programs that offer counseling to parents focused on resolving past relationship problems sufficiently enough to facilitate co-parenting.

Notes

1. This is less true for relationships between gay men, in which having multiple partners is more often expected and deemed acceptable (Blumstein and Schwartz 1983; Laumann et al. 1994).

2. In a nonrandom sample of college students, S. Shirley Feldman and Elizabeth Cauffman (1999) found that late adolescents generally disapproved of sexual betrayal, but thought it was more acceptable if the primary relationship was bad.

3. Because studies of married individuals exclude the divorced, who are likely to have even higher rates of infidelity, these estimates are probably biased downward.

4. This sample overlaps with, but is not identical to, the samples used by Joanna Reed and Lindsay Monte in chapters 6 and 8 of this volume to describe two topics related to infidelity, relationship dissolution and multiple partner fertility. For this reason, our calculations of equivalent measures (for example, the proportion of couples with a history of infidelity) may differ slightly.

5. Four fathers were incarcerated or untraceable at the time of the wave-four interview.

6. In other analyses presented in this chapter, I explore how the TLC3 couples themselves define cheating. Their responses suggest that my definition of infidelity is conservative; all respondents agreed that sexual relationships constitute cheating, but many of them also included nonphysical relationships with members of the opposite sex.

7. I used a similar coding process to analyze sample member views on sexual jealousy and the definition of cheating. All couples, including those who do not report infidelity, are included in these analyses.

8. These statistics are based on both mother and father reports. A couple is classified as having experienced infidelity if either parent reports that he or she or his or her partner had a sexual relationship with someone else.

9. Married TLC3 couples are not the focus of this chapter, but in separate analyses I find a lower rate of infidelity among those couples. Only four of the eighteen couples (22 percent) who remained married from baseline to wave four and who completed a wave four interview reported infidelity by either partner ever in the relationship. This is roughly consistent with the rates reported in surveys for married couples (Laumann et al. 1994; Wiederman 1997).

10. For instance, individuals in ongoing relationships may be less likely to admit to infidelity because they have a lot to lose if their partners were to discover their indiscretions, while individuals in relationships that have ended have nothing to lose from full disclosure.

11. Damian and Marilyn are both African American. At study entry, they were unmarried but living together, and their ages were twenty-nine and twenty-four, respectively. In this sample of predominantly low-educated parents, Damian and Marilyn are unusual for both having professional degrees.

12. In one case, the couple's commitment was temporarily brought into question when one of the parents was incarcerated for a period of time.

13. Flora and Ramon are both Puerto Rican. When they entered the study, they were both twenty years old and dating, but not living together.

14. This is consistent with Reed's finding in chapter 6 (this volume) that though couples who reconciled after a breakup were just as likely to have listed infidelity as a reason for their original breakup as were couples who remained apart, the incidents of cheating were much less likely to have either led to new relationship or a pregnancy.

15. Suzanne and Myron are both white. At study entry, the mother was twenty-two and the father was twenty-three years old, they were living together, and engaged to be married.

16. The design of this study does not allow for any conclusions to be drawn about cheating causing the dissolution of relationships. In addition, the turbulent nature of many of these couples' relationships makes it difficult to know whether relationship status at one point in time is an outcome of the relationship or simply one stage in a longer relationship trajectory. In fact, two couples with histories of chronic infidelity broke up sometime during the study period, but had reconciled by wave four.

References

Allen, Elizabeth S., David C. Atkins, Donald H. Baucom, Douglas K. Snyder, Kristina Coop Gordon, and Shirley P. Glass. 2005. "Intrapersonal, Interpersonal, and Contextual Factors in Engaging in and Responding to Extramarital Involvement." *Clinical Psychology Science and Practice* 12(2): 101–3.

Amato, Paul R., and Alan Booth. 2001. "The Legacy of Parents' Marital Discord: Consequences for Children's Marital Quality." *Journal of Personality and Social Psychology* 81(4): 627–38.

Amato, Paul R., and Danelle D. DeBoer. 2001. "The Transmission of Marital Instability Across Generations: Relationship Skills or Commitment to Marriage?" *Journal of Marriage and the Family* 63(4): 1038–51.

Amato, Paul R., and Denise Previti. 2003. "People's Reasons for Divorcing: Gender, Social Class, the Life Course, and Adjustment." *Journal of Family Issues* 24(5): 602–26.

Amato, Paul R., and Stacy J. Rogers. 1997. "A Longitudinal Study of Marital Problems and Subsequent Divorce." *Journal of Marriage and the Family* 59(3): 612–24.

Amato, Paul R., and Juliana M. Sobolewski. 2001. "The Effects of Divorce and Marital Discord on Adult Children's Psychological Well-Being." *American Sociological Review* 66(6): 900–21.

Amato, Paul R., Laura Spencer Loomis, and Alan Booth. 1995. "Parental Divorce, Marital Conflict, and Offspring Well-Being During Early Adulthood." *Social Forces* 73(3): 895–915.

Anderson, Elijah. 1990. *Street Wise: Race, Class, and Change in an Urban Community.* Chicago, Ill.: The University of Chicago Press.

Andrinopoulos, Katherine, Deanna Kerrigan, and Jonathan M. Ellen. 2006. "Understanding Sex Partner Selection from the Perspective of Inner-City Black Adolescents." *Perspectives on Sexual and Reproductive Health* 38(3): 132–8.

Atkins, David C., Donald H. Baucom, and Neil S. Jacobson. 2001. "Understanding Infidelity: Correlates in a National Random Sample." *Journal of Family Psychology* 15(4): 735–49.

Axinn, William G., and Arland Thornton. 1992. "The Relationship Between Cohabitation and Divorce: Selectivity or Causal Influence?" *Demography* 29(3): 357–74.

Blow, Adrian J., and Kelley Hartnett. 2005a. "Infidelity in Committed Relationships I: A Methodological Review." *Journal of Marital and Family Therapy* 31(2): 183–216.

———. 2005b. "Infidelity in Committed Relationships II: A Substantive Review." *Journal of Marital and Family Therapy* 31(2): 217–33.

Blumstein, Philip, and Pepper Schwartz. 1983. *American Couples: Money, Work, Sex.* New York: William Morrow and Company.

Boyle, Michael H., Jennifer M. Jenkins, Katholiki Georgiades, John Cairney, Eric Duku, and Yvonne Racine. 2004. "Differential-Maternal Parenting Behavior: Estimating Within- and Between-Family Effects on Children." *Child Development* 75(5): 1457–76.

Brown, Susan L., and Alan Booth. 1996. "Cohabitation versus Marriage: A Comparison of Relationship Quality." *Journal of Marriage and the Family* 58(3): 668–78.

Carlson, Marcia J., and Sara S. McLanahan. 2006. "Strengthening Unmarried Families: Could Enhancing Couple Relationships Also Improve Parenting?" *Social Service Review* 80(2): 297–321.

Choi, Kyung-Hee, Joseph A. Catania, and M. Margaret Dolcini. 1994. "Extra-marital Sex and HIV Risk Behavior among US Adults: Results from the National AIDS Behavioral Survey." *American Journal of Public Health* 84(12): 2003–7.

Christopher, F. Scott, and Susan Sprecher. 2000. "Sexuality in Marriage, Dating, and Other Relationships: A Decade Review." *Journal of Marriage and the Family* 62(4): 999–1017.

Daly, Martin, and Margo Wilson. 1988. *Homicide.* Hawthorne, N.Y.: Aldine de Gruyter.

Dion, M. Robin. 2005. "Healthy Marriage Programs: Learning What Works." *Future of Children* 15(2): 139–56.

Erel, Osnat, and Bonnie Burman. 1995. "Interrelatedness of Marital Relations and Parent-Child Relations: A Meta-analytic Review." *Psychological Bulletin* 118(1): 108–32.

Feldman, S. Shirley, and Elizabeth Cauffman. 1999. "Your Cheatin' Heart: Attitudes, Behaviors, and Correlates of Sexual Betrayal in Late Adolescents." *Journal of Research on Adolescence* (93)3: 227–52.

Forste, Renata, and Koray Tanfer. 1996. "Sexual Exclusivity Among Dating, Cohabiting, and Married Women." *Journal of Marriage and the Family* 58(1): 33–47.

Glass, Shirley P. and Thomas Wright. 1992. "Justifications for Extramarital Relationships: The Association Between Attitudes, Behaviors, and Gender." *The Journal of Sex Research* 29(3): 361–87.

Greeley, Andrew. 1994. "Marital Infidelity." *Society* 31(1): 9–13.

Grello, Catherine M., Deborah P. Welsh, and Melinda S. Harper. 2006. "No Strings Attached: The Nature of Casual Sex in College Students." *The Journal of Sex Research* 43(3): 255–67.

Hansen, Gary L. 1985. "Perceived Threats and Marital Jealousy." *Social Psychology Quarterly* 48(2): 262–8.

———. 1987. "Extradyadic Relations During Courtship." *Journal of Sex Research* 23(3): 382–90.

Kitson, Gay C., Karen B. Babri, and Mary J. Roach. 1985. "Who Divorces and Why: A Review." *Journal of Family Issues* 6(3): 255–93.

Kitzmann, Katherine M. 2000. "Effects of Marital Conflict on Subsequent Triadic Family Interactions and Parenting." *Developmental Psychology* 36(1): 3–13.

Krishnakumar, Ambika, and Cheryl Buehler. 2000. "Interparental Conflict and Parenting Practices: A Meta-analysis." *Family Relations* 49(2): 24–44.

Lambert, Tracy A., Arnold S. Kahn, and Kevin J. Apple. 2003. "Pluralistic Ignorance and Hooking Up." *The Journal of Sex Research* 40(1): 129–33.

Laumann, Edward O., John H. Gagnon, Robert T. Michael, and Stuart Michaels. 1994. *The Social Organization of Sexuality: Sexual Practices in the United States.* Chicago, Ill.: University of Chicago Press.

Margolin, Gayla, and Elana B. Gordis. 2000. "The Effects of Family and Community Violence on Children." *Annual Review of Psychology* 51(2): 445–79.

Oliver, Mary Beth, and Janet Shibley Hyde. 1993. "Gender Differences in Sexuality: A Meta-Analysis." *Psychological Bulletin* 114(1): 29–51.

Paik, Anthony, Edward O. Laumann, and Martha Van Haitsma. 2004. "Commitment, Jealousy, and the Quality of Life." In *The Sexual Organization of the City*, edited by E. O. Laumann, S. Ellingson, J. Mahay, A. Paik, and Y. Youm. Chicago, Ill.: The University of Chicago Press.

Paul, Elizabeth L., and Kristen A. Hayes. 2002. "The Casualties of 'Casual' Sex: A Qualitative Exploration of the Phenomenology of College Students' Hookups." *Journal of Social and Personal Relationships* 19(5): 639–61.

Paul, Elizabeth L., Brian McManus, and Allison Hayes. 2000. " 'Hookups': Characteristics and Correlates of College Students' Spontaneous and Anonymous Sexual Experiences." *The Journal of Sex Research* 37(1): 76–88.

Previti, Denise, and Paul R. Amato. 2004. "Is Infidelity a Cause or a Consequence of Poor Marital Quality?" *Journal of Social and Personal Relationships* 21(2): 217–30.

Puente, Sylvia, and Dov Cohen. 2003. "Jealousy and the Meaning (or Nonmeaning) of Violence." *Personality and Social Psychology Bulletin* 29(4): 449–60.

Ragin, Charles C. 1994. *Constructing Social Research*. Thousand Oaks, Calif.: Pine Forge Press.

Raj, Anita, Jay G. Silverman, Gina M. Wingood, and Ralph J. DeClemente. 1999. "Prevalence and Correlates of Relationship Abuse Among a Community-Based Sample of Low-Income African American Women." *Violence Against Women* 5(3): 272–91.

Smith, Tom W. 1994. "Attitudes Toward Sexual Permissiveness: Trends, Correlates, and Behavioral Connections." In *Sexuality Across the Life Course*, edited by A. S. Rossi. Chicago, Ill.: University of Chicago Press.

Smock, Pamela. 2000. "Cohabitation in the United States: An Appraisal of Research Themes, Findings, and Implications." *Annual Review of Sociology* 26(1): 1–20.

South, Scott J., and Kim M. Lloyd. 1995. "Spousal Alternatives and Marital Dissolution." *American Sociological Review* 60(1): 21–35.

Sweeney, Megan M., and Allan V. Horwitz. 2001. "Infidelity, Initiation, and the Emotional Climate of Divorce: Are There Implications for Mental Health?" *Journal of Health and Social Behavior* 42(3): 295–309.

Thompson, Anthony Peter. 1984. "Emotional and Sexual Components of Extramarital Relations." *Journal of Marriage and the Family* 46(1): 35–42.

Thomson, Elizabeth, and Ugo Colella. 1992. "Cohabitation and Marital Stability: Quality or Commitment?" *Journal of Marriage and the Family* 54(2): 259–67.

Treas, Judith, and Deirdre Giesen. 2000. "Sexual Infidelity Among Married and Cohabiting Americans." *Journal of Marriage and the Family* 62(1): 48–60.

Waite, Linda J., and Maggie Gallagher. 2000. *The Case for Marriage: Why Married People Are Happier, Healthier, and Better Off Financially*. New York: Broadway Books.

Wiederman, Michael W. 1997. "Extramarital Sex: Prevalence and Correlates in a National Survey." *Journal of Sex Research* 34(2): 167–75.

Youm, Yoosik, and Anthony Paik. 2004. "The Sex Market and Its Implications for Family Formation." In *The Sexual Organization of the City*, edited by Edward O. Laumann, Stephen Ellingson, Jenna Mahay, Anthony Paik, and Yoosik Youm. Chicago, Ill.: University of Chicago Press.

Chapter 6

Anatomy of the Breakup: How and Why Do Unmarried Couples with Children Break Up?

JOANNA REED

Despite high rates of unwed childbearing in the United States, most children born to unmarried parents are involved with both parents at birth. Eighty percent of unmarried parents are romantically involved when their child is born, and just under 50 percent are cohabiting (McLanahan et al. 2003). However, unwed parents often break up. In the United States, unmarried couples with and without children end their relationships more frequently than married couples do, and their relationships are of shorter duration (Graefe and Lichter 1999; Manning 2001; Wu 1995). This makes their children more likely to grow up without both parents, which is linked to a higher risk of poverty and other negative outcomes. In this paper, I explore how and why unmarried parents break up. I use four years of qualitative interviews from the Time, Love and Cash among Couples with Children study to investigate the reasons behind and the process of ending relationships for unmarried couples who have children together and are romantically involved when their baby is born.

There is little research about the dissolution of unmarried relationships, especially those involving children, though there is a large literature on the causes and effects of divorce, and how divorce affects children. The divorce literature shows that children do better when they live with both biological parents, although questions remain about how much of this relationship is causal. As the link between marriage and parenthood continues to relax and more adults and children experience family life in unmarried relationships, we need to broaden our focus and learn more about what happens when unmarried parents break up, how these patterns are similar or different from divorce, and their effects on children. This paper explores these issues with an in-depth look at what happens when unmarried parents end their relationships, and why they choose to do so.

Background

Research on divorce and cohabitation shows that both economic factors and relationship quality are important in understanding breakups. The vast majority of studies pertain to married couples who divorce, few focus on unmarried couples. Researchers have argued that research about divorce should be pertinent to one type of unmarried couples—cohabitors (Wu 1995), who represent more than 80 percent of the TLC3 sample of unmarried couples at baseline. Several other studies show, however, that cohabiting and married couples differ in significant ways, which suggests that patterns common to divorcing couples may not apply to cohabitors.

Most studies of divorce focus on economic factors and are based on theoretical models of rational choice such as specialization and bargaining theory. Although these models are a place to start an investigation of relationship dissolution among unmarried parents, other research about the nature of their relationships calls certain assumptions of the models into question. One of the most influential models for theorizing marriage and divorce is specialization (Becker 1991), which posits that a primary economic rationale for marriage is spouses specializing in different types of labor. Both spouses will benefit if one specializes in paid work outside the home and the other specializes in unpaid (house and childcare) work, together maximizing efficiency for the family. Dividing labor this way deters divorce, which is likely to increase when social conditions make specialization less likely.

Specialization theory assumes that each spouse forgoes individual goals to pursue what is best for the family as a whole and that financial resources are shared. It is unclear whether these assumptions hold for unmarried couples with children. Most cohabitors with children have not made a definite commitment to each other (Reed 2006; Waite and Gallagher 2000), so it seems reasonable to doubt that they have abandoned individual self interest. In addition, there is a lot of variation in how cohabiting couples manage their financial resources (Waite and Gallagher 2000). Other scholars argue that not specializing encourages similar household and work roles that make couples more likely to stay together because they have more in common (England and Farkas 1986, Goldscheider and Waite 1991).

Another approach to theorizing couple dynamics is exchange or bargaining models. External threat point models posit that power within marriage comes from an individual's ability to control resources that are shared in a marriage, but revert to one spouse if the marriage ends

(England and Farkas 1986, England and Kilbourne 1990, Lundberg and Pollak 1996). In this view, one's external threat point—a partner's situation if the relationship ends—plays a central role in partners' distribution of gains from the marriage and decisions about whether to remain in a relationship. Usually the resource in question is income, though this does not have to be the case.

This theory predicts that each spouse's relative income will increase their bargaining power in the relationship, as well as their motivation to initiate divorce if they don't succeed in getting the bargain they want within the relationship. However, the predictions of bargaining theory for divorce are not clear. A change in relative earnings in favor of one spouse increases his or her motivation to divorce if bargaining doesn't work, but simultaneously reduces the motivation for the other. New mothers are likely to be at a disadvantage in marital bargaining, and this is likely to extend to cohabiting couples. Not only are they likely to have fewer economic resources to draw on than men, especially after a birth, but a major contribution they make to the relationship is caring for children. Most women continue to shoulder most of the child care regardless of what happens to the relationship. A woman's ability to use children as a resource for bargaining depends also on how much a father cares about being involved with or having access to his children.

Empirical studies of how earnings affect divorce bear out predictions of specialization theory. Divorce is more likely when men earn less relative to their partners (Hoffman and Duncan 1995; South and Lloyd 1995) or when their wages decline (Weiss and Willis 1997). The effects of women's earnings on divorce are more ambiguous. Some studies find that they increase the likelihood of divorce (Cherlin 1979; Heckert, Nowak, and Snyder 1998; Hiedemann, Suhomlinova, and O'Rand 1998; Moore and Waite 1981) and that the effect is intensified when men's earnings are low (Heckert, Nowak, and Snyder 1998). Others suggest that women's earnings decrease the probability of divorce (Hoffman and Duncan 1995; Weiss and Willis 1997). Still others find no effect (Sayer and Bianchi 2000; South and Lloyd 1995). Robert Schoen and his colleagues (2002) find that women's employment encourages divorce among those who report substantial unhappiness with their marriage.

Research about the effects of sociodemographic variables on divorce show that being black, childless, having less or more education than one's partner, cohabiting before marriage, marrying at a young age, and not attending church are all associated with greater probabilities of divorce (Amato and Rogers 1997, Bumpass, Martin, and Sweet 1991, Bumpass and Lu 2000). People with low incomes also divorce more often than the more affluent (Sayer, Wright and Edin 2003).

Relationship quality is a key factor in marital stability, and in the relationships of unmarried parents (Carlson, McLanahan and England 2004). Higher quality relationships are associated with marital stability—spouses who report being happy with their marriage, or who would be worse off if the marriage ended, are less likely to divorce (Booth et al. 1985, Sanchez and Gager 2000, Sayer and Bianchi 2000). Assessments of relationship quality and what one's life would be like outside the marriage are greatly affected by relationship problems such as infidelity, substance abuse, and domestic violence (Amato and Rogers 1997; Sanchez and Gager 2000; Sayer and Bianchi 2000). In a qualitative study of divorced women, Demie Kurz (1995) finds that escalation of these problems often lead women to initiate divorce. Relationship quality is also important for unmarried couples. In one of few studies of the relationships of unmarried parents, Marcia Carlson, Sara McLanahan and Paula England (2004) examine the effects of economic and other factors on union formation and breakup. They show that the emotional quality of the relationship is an important factor in determining whether relationships will endure or dissolve. They also show that other noneconomic factors powerfully affect union formation.

Having marriage plans seems to be another indicator of relationship quality and stability among cohabiting couples. Those who report plans to marry experience relationships of a similar quality to married couples, but those without them report levels closer to noncohabiting couples (Brown and Booth 1996). The majority of TLC3 couples have marriage plans at baseline (Gibson-Davis, Edin and McLanahan 2005). Several studies, however, have documented differences between married and cohabiting couples that suggest cohabitors have lower quality relationships. They experience slightly more conflict, less communication (Thomson and Colella 1992), feel less secure in their relationships (Bumpass, Sweet, and Cherlin 1991), see them as less permanent, are less likely to pool resources than married couples (Waite and Gallagher 2000) and experience more infidelity (Forste and Tanfer 1996; Waite and Gallagher 2000).

The presence of children adds to the durability of cohabiting and marital unions (Wu 1995). However, children lower the quality of relationships for both kinds of couples (Wu 1995). Thus, having children may push unmarried couples to stay together and lower the quality of their relationships, which are typically lower than those of married couples to begin with. The first year after having a child is especially implicated in declines in relationship quality (Cowan and Cowan 1992, 1995).

Although often included as a measure of relationship quality, conflict in itself does not appear to predict divorce. John Gottman (1994) finds that couples who argue frequently are no more likely to divorce than other couples. Instead, maintaining a ratio with more positive than negative interactions is more important in predicting divorce than factors such as compatibility or communication style. We might expect unmarried couples to follow the same pattern. In a qualitative study of couples that have divorced or split up, Diane Vaughan (1986) finds that conflict has an ambiguous effect on relationships that may ultimately lead to improvement through better communication.

Vaughan (1986) provides one of the few qualitative accounts of the process of uncoupling—the end of a romantic relationship. She interviewed several married and unmarried couples that experienced a breakup and describes the psychological stages each individual goes through as the process unfolds. Her analysis focuses on the psychological rather than the behavioral dimensions of the process. She argues that partners experience these stages at different times and that the initiator of the breakup has a psychological head start, which makes reconciliation difficult. She does not find major differences between the experiences of married and unmarried couples, but does not explicitly compare them.

Data and Methods

To understand how and why unmarried parents break up, I use individual and couple interviews from a sample of twenty-two TLC3 couples who were unmarried and romantically involved when their child was born, followed over the four years of the study, and broke up at least once during that time. I also include material from additional partners who were added to the sample as a result of respondents finding new partners after a breakup, when appropriate. I also occasionally compare my analytic sample to the overall TLC3 sample of forty-eight unmarried couples.

My analytic sample is similar to the overall sample of TLC3 couples in terms of income and educational background. The primary differences are that, in the analytic sample, mothers are slightly younger on average, twenty-three years old, and that 65 percent of mothers and fathers have children from previous relationships. Close to 80 percent of the unmarried couples are living together at the time of their baseline couple interview.

Comparative case studies and narrative analysis are the primary methods I use to explore how and why unmarried parents' relationships end because they emphasize building hypotheses and theories inductively from the data (Denzin and Lincoln 2000; Strauss and Corbin 1998). Case studies are especially effective with longitudinal data because interviewers can track and assess changes as they occur. For this study, I generated a detailed narrative case study for each couple that split up, using all available couple and individual interviews from each data wave. I paid particular attention to the story of the breakup and the reasons respondents gave for it as well as their situations before and after. I also made a graphic representation of each story, seeking to clarify how previous and new partners played a role in breakups and reconciliations. From these narratives and graphic representations I had enough details for each couple to look for patterns in all the breakups together. In this way, I could discern trends and tendencies among the different couples' stories.

In this paper, I think of breakups in two ways: as a given couple's trajectory over the four years of the study, and as discrete events. The first way of thinking about breakups considers them and evaluates them as a process. The second way thinks of breakups as an outcome and is more akin to the way quantitative researchers have studied divorce. Investigating breakups from both of these angles is important for understanding how and why unmarried parents break up. The TLC3 data offer extremely rich and detailed portraits of the relationships of a sample of unmarried parents, but are limited by the small sample size. I present percentages to preserve a sense of proportion in exploring trends, but encourage the reader to keep in mind that the overall numbers of cases are small.

Results

At the end of the TLC3 study, 33 percent (fifteen couples) of the original unmarried couples[1] were no longer together. Over the course of the study, 45 percent (twenty-two couples) broke up at least once. This second group is the analytic sample for this paper, and all percentages that follow pertain to them. About 27 percent[2] reconciled by the last time we spoke with them. The majority of breakups, around 60 percent, occurred during the baby's first year.

Several couples had on-again, off-again relationships, which I define as breaking up and reconciling at least once during the study. Overall, almost 55 percent of couples in the analytic sample had on-again, off-again relationships. Of these, half of the couples were back together by the fourth wave, while the other half seemed to break up permanently.

Natalie, who is white, and John, who is Mexican American, are both eighteen when their baby is born. They are an example of a couple with an on-again, off-again relationship. At baseline, Natalie recently started a full-time job and John is not working. They live together off and on, and each with their own parents when they are not together. Over the course of the study, they have one child together, break up, and reconcile several times. During the second year of the study, after describing a recent breakup, John says "we will break up [in the future], but not like *break up* [for good]." As to why they got back together, Natalie says,

> Well, we've been through everything and stuck together through it all. I mean he cheated on me, and I always told myself if a guy slept with someone else while we were together I'd never stay with him. But that was two years ago and I blocked it out of my mind for a year and a half. . . . And then the hitting. I told myself I'd never stay with a guy who hit me. It's like . . .

John doesn't believe in soul mates, and I don't know if I do, but I know he's like the person for me.

After another breakup the following year, Natalie is sure they will remain apart this time. She says that "it's just too late. . . . I can't change the [negative] way I feel about him." John, however, is trying to reconcile, and she admits that she doesn't know whether she wants to be with him. By the end of the study, John is in jail for attempted auto theft. Natalie says, "I guess I got sick of it. This isn't the life I want to live. . . . I just fell out of love with him."

Why Do Unmarried Parents Break Up?

Respondents report infidelity, mistrust, fighting and arguing, verbal and physical abuse, lack of love and attention, and substance abuse as primary reasons for their breakup, and often have multiple problems. Among the entire TLC3 sample of unmarried couples, those who break up had more troubled relationships from the start. Couples who break up have a higher rate of problems like infidelity, mistrust, substance abuse and domestic violence. They also report more past breakups with each other than couples who stay together, 75 percent to 26 percent, suggesting that their relationships are more unstable all along.[3]

The twin problems of infidelity and mistrust[4] deserve special attention because of their centrality to breakup and propensity to lead to painful, fraught and complicated situations for couples. Infidelity or suspecting a partner of cheating were features of at least 77 percent of breakups over the course of the study. Actual infidelity occurred for at least 59 percent[5] of these couples. (For details of infidelity among the larger sample of TLC3 couples, see Hill, chapter 5 of this volume.) Respondents who break up are more likely than those who stay together to have children from previous relationships. This likely contributes to high levels of mistrust as some respondents worry about or suspect their partner of continuing sexual involvement with their child's other parent.

Overall, cheating or suspected cheating with a man's "other baby mama" (the mother of a previous child), or in one case, a woman's "other baby daddy," is a principal cause in about 18 percent of breakups. Another 14 percent were due to a variation on this problem—cheating that resulted in a pregnancy (creating another "baby mama problem") that overlapped with the mother's pregnancy with the focal child. These couples broke up in short order when the focal mother found out about the other pregnancy.

Katrice and Tim's story shows why couples might worry. Katrice is nineteen and Tim is twenty-two when their second baby is born. They are both African American. They lived in the same housing complex, and their first child was born when Katrice was sixteen. Tim has three children with another woman by the time their second baby is born, and later has two more children with a third woman. Although both admit they were never an exclusive couple, they break up and reconcile between their first and second children, both claiming that the other was cheating. Katrice admits to cheating with an ex-boyfriend, and Tim with one of his baby mamas. After their second baby is born, they break up again. Again both claim cheating by the other as the main reason for the breakup. Afterward, he claims that his first other baby mama is his primary relationship and that he had been seeing Katrice on the side. He and the other baby mama, who lives in another state, got back together after he was briefly in jail on a drug charge, and he was planning to move in with her. Instead, he was sent to prison in Chicago, and by the third year of the study, Katrice and Tim are together again though he is still incarcerated. The final time we speak with her, she says that she and Tim "get along good now, maybe because we have so much air." She says that their children brought them closer together and that she is trying to get him to "shape up and be responsible" when he gets out of prison.

Other problems make important contributions to a relationship's demise but do not usually have as devastating an effect as infidelity does. Couples seem to weather other problems better: infidelity causes breakups by itself and also serves as the coup de grace of an ailing relationship. Problems are often connected, with suspected infidelity or mistrust leading to verbal or physical fighting, tension, and emotional distress. Perhaps the most important point about the role of relationship problems in breakups, illustrated in table 6.1, is that most couples experience several simultaneously.

Priscilla and Rafael, a Puerto Rican couple from Milwaukee, broke up not because of infidelity, but because of a confluence of other problems. She is nineteen and he is twenty-two when their baby is born. At that time, he already had two children with a woman he had been forced to marry at fifteen when their families found out she was pregnant. He met Priscilla about a month after this relationship ended and they were enjoying "more fun, more partying" together. They wanted to have a baby and were living together before the pregnancy. When we first speak with them, Rafael explains how he arranged his work schedule so they could spend more time together. In their couple interview he says, "we was meant to be."

The following year, they are no longer together. She says that after their baby was born, Rafael stopped spending time with her, and left her at home while he pursued his ambition to be a rapper. One night, she says, they had a confrontation, during which he began throwing things in anger. She claims that he choked her and friends called the police. He tells a different story. He lost his job after the baby was born, he says, and then "wanted to keep on partying and she couldn't." He agrees that this caused

Table 6.1 Respondents' Reports of Problems that Contributed to their Breakup

	Cheating	Financial Stress	Domestic Violence	Verbal Abuse/ argue	No Love	Mistrust	Substance Abuse	Incarceration
C-01	1	0	0	1	1	1	0	0
C-05	1	1	0	0	0	1	0	0
C-07	1	0	1	0	0	0	1	1
C-09	0	0	1	0	1	0	0	0
C-12	1	1	1	1	0	1	0	0
C-18	1	0	0	0	0	1	0	0
C-22	0	0	1	0	0	1	0	0
C-23	0	1	0	0	0	1	0	0
C-24	0	1	1	0	0	1	1	1
M-01	0	0	1	1	1	1	1	0
M-05	1	0	1	1	1	1	1	0
M-14	0	1	0	0	1	1	1	0
M-15	1	0	0	0	0	1	0	0
M-16	1	0	1	0	0	1	1	0
M-17	1	0	1	0	0	1	0	0
M-18	1	0	0	0	0	0	0	0
M-19	1	0	0	0	0	1	0	0
M-21	1	0	0	0	1	0	0	0
M-22	1	0	1	1	1	1	0	0
M-24	1	0	0	0	0	1	1	1
N-02	0	0	0	1	0	1	1	1
N-13	0	0	0	1	1	0	0	0

Source: Author's calculations.
Note: Highlighting helps show which problems are most prevalent. A couple receives a score of 1 if one or both partners report a problem contributing to the breakup. Bold text indicates couples that reconciled by the end of the study, and italic text indicates a couple that reconciled, but whose current status is unknown because both are incarcerated.

Table 6.2   Comparison of Baseline Income and Work for Couples Who Broke Up, Married, or Were Still Together by Wave Four

	Household Income	Mothers Working	Fathers Working
Breakup	$2,061	47%	80%
Marry	$2,092	23	77
Stay together	$1,890	32	74

Source: Author's calculations.
Note: Income is monthly.

tension between them. He says that her brother and family were causing problems between them, accusing him of cheating on Priscilla. He denies choking her and says that he was trying to keep her from hitting him the night of the breakup. He says he was upset about the breakup at first, but then happy to have his freedom.

He then went to Puerto Rico. She got pregnant by an older man she says was possessive and abusive and stole from her. After having the baby, she went to Puerto Rico to escape this baby's father. While she was there, she let Rafael see their son. Rafael says that he tried to get back together with Priscilla then, but she wasn't interested. By the third year of the study, Priscilla has returned to her original city and is living with a third man, Juan, whom she met at work. They are thinking of getting married, but he needs to get a divorce from his ex-wife first. Rafael is also back in the same city by the end of the study, and is living with his current girlfriend, Neva, who is pregnant. He says he is more mature now, and that he and Neva are "taking it slow."

Economic Concerns

Financial and economic issues figure heavily in the divorce literature, yet they do not play a central role in TLC3 couples' accounts of their breakups. Couples who break up also do not appear to be more disadvantaged economically than other TLC3 couples. As shown in table 6.2, couples who experienced a breakup, along with those who broke up permanently, have average household incomes similar to couples who did not break up during the study. In fact, both mothers and fathers who broke up report working more than couples that stayed together. For example, 47 percent of mothers who ended up breaking up report working at least part-time at baseline, compared with 23 percent of mothers who eventually married and 32 percent who were still together at the study's end. There were less striking differences for fathers, with 80 percent of those who broke up reporting having a job at baseline, compared with 77 percent of those who married, and 74 percent of those who stayed together. Fathers' incomes, however, were on average considerably higher than mothers'. For example, at baseline, fathers who experienced a breakup report making $1345 per month, compared with mothers' $843.

The fact that almost half of mothers headed toward breakup were working at baseline—soon after giving birth—suggests they did not depend on their baby's father's income. This may represent a desire for financial independence or that the mother could not depend on her partner to contribute financially. Close to 65 percent of couples who break up report keeping their money separate before the breakup, so it isn't clear how much access mothers have to their partner's higher incomes even when the couple is romantically involved. In addition, only 9 percent of mothers who broke up report relying solely on the father's income at baseline, but 41 percent report that their only source of income is from public assistance or relatives.

His Bad Behaviors

Fathers seem to behave in ways that are destructive to the relationship more often than mothers do. This is especially true of infidelity, although fathers also have higher rates of substance abuse and domestic violence. Although both partners cheat, fathers cheat more often than mothers. When infidelity was part of a breakup story, mothers reported that the father cheated every time. Also, every time a mother cheats, she claims that the father was cheating on her at the same time and that there was a degree of revenge in her behavior. In other words, in 46 percent of infidelity cases, both the mother and father claim the other is unfaithful. In 54 percent of cases, the father alone has been unfaithful. Either way, he is implicated in cheating in all of the cases where infidelity is a problem in the relationship, although there are a few discrepancies in these accounts.

Delilah and Trevor are both African American. She is twenty and he is nineteen when their child is born, and she had another baby from a previous relationship. They break up when a pregnant Delilah learns that Trevor has been cheating on her with Aisha, who is also currently pregnant with his child. Trevor says that he had been seeing Aisha off and on since before he met Delilah, and that he began seeing Delilah during an off period of this relationship. After Trevor and Delilah break up, he gets back together with Aisha. Delilah moves back in with her mother and begins working. Although he denies the cheating and the pregnancy at first, he later says that Aisha was jealous that Delilah was pregnant—she figured "she was supposed to be my first baby's mother." We later learn that there is a third woman, who also gets pregnant around the same time. He says that this relationship is the most serious of the three and that they planned the pregnancy. By the end of the study, he is serving a two-year sentence for dealing drugs and is with Brandy, a fourth partner, who is about to have a baby. Delilah is also with a new partner, with whom she has a baby by the end of the study.

Sahara (twenty) and Myles (twenty-two) are an African American couple living together when their baby, the first child for each of them, is born. At the beginning of the study, they both say they are still together because of the baby, and are more "parents than partners," yet are discussing marriage. Both are working and taking care of the baby with help from their families. What exactly happened at their breakup is difficult to say, because both have different stories that change over time, but both claim cheating by the other as the reason. She tells a dramatic story about her mother catching Myles with another woman in the bathroom of their apartment late at night. He says they had a fight at his workplace where he confronted her about cheating and she told him he had to move out of their apartment. Her new boyfriend, Henry, moves in immediately after Myles moves out. A few years later, she admits that she was with him on and off throughout her entire pregnancy with the focal child. Henry says that they were dating for six or seven months before the pregnancy. By the end of the study, Henry and Sahara are married, and both Henry and Myles claim to be the biological father of the focal child.

How Do Couples Break Up?

Unmarried parents' breakups typically follow a pattern, illustrated in figure 6.1. At the time their baby is born, a couple is already under some stress. They have likely broken up previously, and are experiencing one or more relational problems they deem serious. Despite this, they are living together and want to try and work things out, often because of their shared child. Problems continue to mount, however, until something provokes a crisis. Often, this is an episode of or suspicions of infidelity. In other cases, it is an ongoing problem that becomes the proverbial straw that breaks the camel's back. The crisis usually takes place as a dramatic fight that culminates in the mother telling the father that the relationship is over. Usually, he moves out. A partner's exit from the home is the clearest mark of a breakup; most partners will agree they have broken up when this happens. Women almost always initiate the process.

Frieda and Marco generally follow this pattern. They have experienced many problems at once, but his infidelity provoked the final split. At the beginning of the study, they have two children together and have been living together since she was about thirteen. He is a heroin user and sometimes abusive. She says he has cheated on her in the past. Frieda also reports past use of drugs. During her pregnancy with the focal child, she gave him an ultimatum—drugs or her—and he tried to quit. Then, however, he hit her and she "lost feelings for him" and broke up with him. She later took him back and they moved to Puerto Rico. She reports calling the police several times while they were there because of his drug abuse and domestic violence. Eventually, he slept with another woman, which she

Figure 6.1   Typical Trajectory of a Breakup

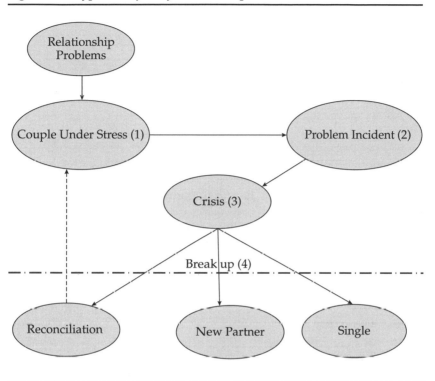

Source: Author's calculations.
Note: Numbers indicate the order of events; dotted line represents the breakup. Relationship problems place a couple under stress. A problem flares up and provokes a crisis, which results in a breakup. Afterwards, partners either remain single, find new partners or the couple reconciles. Couples that reconcile often start the cycle again because stressors that led to the first breakup are usually still present.

said she cannot forgive. After this, she reports that she broke up with him for good. She says, " I just completely left him. I didn't want nothing to do with him. It was over." Shortly after the breakup, she began dating another man who is also involved with drugs. By the second year of the study, she has another baby and is living with this man in another state, and Marco is in jail. By the end of the study, she has another baby with a third man.

What Happens after a Breakup?

After a breakup, partners may start a new relationship, reconcile, or—less commonly—stay single. Because mothers usually stay in the former couple's residence if the couple was cohabiting, fathers usually move back in with their own parents, relatives, or less commonly, friends.

A New Relationship

The clearest indicator that a breakup might be permanent is if one of the partners begins a new relationship. A couple may still reconcile if the mother or father has a casual relationship, but it is unlikely if one of them begins living with a new partner or has a baby with someone else.[6] I consider a new relationship to be one where the respondent is either living with or has had a baby with a partner other than the focal parent.

Respondents often move into new relationships within a few months of the breakup, perhaps reflecting the young age (mostly in their twenties) of sample members. By the end of the study, 73 percent of mothers who had broken up with their original partner had repartnered once, with 20 percent of them going on to a third partner by the end of the study. In contrast, 59 percent of the fathers had repartnered by then. About 30 percent of mothers' new relationships were with someone they knew from the past, either an ex-boyfriend or acquaintance. No mothers went back to the fathers of their other children, however. The majority, about 66 percent, report meeting their new partners after their breakup with the focal father.

Almost 55 percent of the mothers who moved into a new relationship had a baby with the new partner before the end of the study. About 27 percent of these went on to form a third relationship, which also resulted in a pregnancy.[7] Although 45 percent of mothers who repartnered married these men, only one of the moms who had a baby within a new relationship married her baby's father.

Fathers were even more likely to have a baby with a new partner. In slightly over 25 percent of the cases, a father's cheating led to a breakup for an original couple and a pregnancy with another woman. In only one case, however, did the father cohabit or have more than a casual relationship with this new baby's mother. Of the remaining fathers, 80 percent had a child with a new partner in the context of a romantic relationship. At least one of the fathers' new relationships since the breakup is with someone he knew from the past.

Staying Single

Few mothers who break up remain single for long. Of those who broke up with the focal father permanently, about 27 percent are single at the end of the study. In all cases, however, this is likely related to the timing of the breakup. These couples either broke up in the third or final year of the study, or in one case, had an on-again, off-again relationship that appeared to end for good late in wave three. Because most breakups in the study occurred during the focal child's first year, these mothers have not had as much time as the others to find new partners. A little more than 30 percent of fathers who break up permanently are single at the end of the study. Two of the five single fathers are in jail at wave four, which helps explain why they have not found new relationships. Another father broke up with the focal mother late in the study.

Reconciliation

Twenty-seven percent of the couples who broke up during the study got back together by the study's end, and thirty percent of these couples married. In several ways, these couples do not seem to be much different from those who do not reconcile. Their accounts of their breakups are similar, with half reporting an incident of infidelity, and another 33 percent reporting suspicions of infidelity.

Three things stand out for couples who reconciled. They have more children together than those that remain apart—two-thirds of reconciled couples have more than one child with their partner compared to one-third of those who remain apart. In all but one couple, both the mother and father have children by other partners, which is actually more than for the group of couples that remain apart.

Secondly, few became involved in new relationships. Only one respondent who eventually reconciled moved into a new relationship, and no one in this group had a child with someone else. It is interesting to note that either one or both partners is incarcerated for half of the couples who reconciled. Tabitha and Howie got back together by the end of the study. She is white, he is Hispanic. She is thirty and he is thirty-five when their baby is born. They are both in and out of jail for the first two years of the study and are incarcerated at the end of it. He admits to cheating on her, and they broke up after he went to prison the first time. He was out briefly, and during this time, was awarded custody of their daughter. They got back together after her brief stint in jail, and then were both arrested again—he for selling drugs, and she for drug possession and skipping bail on a previous hit and run charge. Although they are both in prison, they consider themselves together and plan a future together when they are released. She has completed a drug treatment program in prison, and he says he is through with the fast life.

The majority of reconciled couples have unstable relationships. The fact that some respondents refer to a partner's incarceration as playing a positive role in keeping them together does not bode well for their future. Indeed, only one couple who reconciled seems to have a strong relationship at the end of the study. They stood out because they seemed genuinely and deeply in love at the beginning of the study and again at the end.

Alex and Rochelle, both African Americans from Chicago, say that it was like fireworks when they met. She was twenty-one and he was twenty-six. He had a child from a previous relationship, and she had three children with a man who had recently been incarcerated. Rochelle and this man have pretty much ended their relationship when she meets Alex—he is in jail and she says he cheated on her. When we speak to them for the first time, Alex is working and in school and Rochelle plans to enroll in a GED program. About a year after their baby was born, Alex and Rochelle lost their apartment because of financial problems. They tried to stay in a shelter together, but that didn't work out, and Rochelle moved in with the family of her other children's father. She and Alex remain together, but things sour after her other children's father gets out of jail and Alex's family tells him that she is cheating on him. Alex then moves to Wisconsin and does not speak to Rochelle for a year. She denies that she and her other child's father were ever back together: "we [she and Alex] just basically fell apart; it wasn't his decision or mine." In the meantime, she moves into a subsidized apartment. They get back together when he comes to Chicago for his birthday and arranges to visit their child. He moves back in with her right away and she becomes pregnant with their second child shortly afterward. At the end of the study, they have recently married in a courthouse ceremony.

Punishing Fathers

Although fathers' behaviors tend to be more responsible than mothers' for the actual breakup, several fathers report that mothers will not allow them to visit their child afterward. Amy Claessens offers an in-depth analysis of mothers' gatekeeping in chapter 9 of this volume. Fathers say mothers act out their anger by not allowing him to see their child, or by agreeing to a visit, and then canceling it at the last minute. A few fathers report their former partners fabricated allegations of domestic violence in order to get a restraining order. Mothers who move into new relationships would sometimes like to forget their child's father altogether. This is especially true when they believe the new relationship is a much better one than theirs with the focal father—like moving "from hell to heaven," as one respondent puts it. They see the new partner as a better father for their child. The central and obvious consequence here is that a breakup between unmarried parents is likely to reduce a father's involvement in his child's life, sometimes involuntarily.

This is exemplified by Camille and Freddie, both Hispanic, who are nineteen and twenty when their baby is born. Freddie has two children from a previous relationship. The focal child is Camille's first. When we first talk with them, they are discussing marriage, but have problems getting along and mistrust one another. Camille works part-time and Freddie full-time when we first meet them. She soon breaks up with him, frustrated that he had lost a job and quit a GED class. He says that "she didn't like it that I would hang out with my friends and get high and drink and smoke. . . . I was hiding it from her for awhile, when I came clean she didn't want to be with me anymore." They got back together and broke up a few more times after this. "It just died out," he explains, "when she met someone else."

By the third year of the study, she is pregnant and engaged to a French African man she met at work. They are married by the end of the study. Freddie complains that after the breakup she would not let him see their daughter and that things got even worse after her engagement. First, he said she did not approve of where he was living with some friends. Then, she would schedule visits and cancel them at the last minute. As a result, Freddie says he hardly ever sees their daughter, despite his frequent attempts. Camille admits that she doesn't make it easy for Freddie, but feels justified. She says that Freddie "chose to be out of [their daughter's] life . . . and I just continued the trend because it's no point in [her] being confused about why the hell [Freddie] don't want to see [her]." She also says that her fiancé doesn't like Freddie, and thinks he is a bad father.

Discussion

A key conclusion from this analysis is that poor relationship quality is primarily responsible for ending the relationships of unmarried parents. The relationships that broke up had many more problems early on than those that persisted through four years of our study. Problems such as infidelity and mistrust, verbal and physical fighting and substance abuse loom large in couples' accounts of their breakups. Infidelity and mistrust particularly play a strong role. Often it is not just one, but several problems at the same time that lead to a breakup.

Unmarried parent breakups follow a general pattern. A couple experiences mounting problems until something provokes a crisis. Often, but not always, infidelity is the tipping point. If the couple is cohabiting, mothers tell fathers to move out of the family residence. At this point, paths diverge—27 percent of couples reconcile, an equal number stay single, and 46 percent break up for good, often finding new partners. Three things stand out for those who reconciled: they had more children together than couples who broke up permanently, partners did not move into a new relationship after a breakup, and, surprisingly, the incarcerations of one or both partners played a positive role in reconciliation for about half of these couples by putting the daily problems of relating on hold, and curtailing problem behaviors, such as infidelity. For those who broke up for good, finding a new partner was a common outcome, especially for mothers.

Fathers tend to engage more frequently than mothers in behaviors that are destructive to relationships. After a breakup, however, mothers may punish fathers by restricting or curtailing access to shared children. Fathers report that this is especially problematic when a mother finds a new partner, especially if she believes the new man is a superior partner and role model. That most mothers repartnered after breaking up with their child's father contributes to the difficulty many fathers report in seeing their children.

The finding that relationship problems are the major force behind unmarried parents' breakups stands in marked contrast to the majority of the divorce literature. Most divorce studies and the theories they are based on focus heavily on economic factors, while they play a minor role here. Despite the fact that most couples in this sample have some financial difficulties, only one mentioned financial problems as directly implicated in their breakup, and in this case it was one of several problems. However, some breakup stories suggest that an economic problem may exacerbate existing problems or lead to more conflict for the couple, both directly and indirectly. For example, in Priscilla and Rafael's case, Rafael mentions losing his job as a factor that led to problems in their relationship. Losing the job means that all of a sudden he has more time to go out with his friends and pursue his dream to be a rapper. It is the latter that upsets Priscilla and leads to conflict and eventually the confrontation that resulted in their breakup. Interestingly, it is not the financial strain of the job loss, but rather Rafael's behavior afterward that is the root of the problem. In a more clear-cut case, losing their apartment together for economic reasons was the first in a chain of events that led to Alex and Rochelle's breakup. Both point to mistrust as the primary reason, but this was directly related to no longer living together and Rochelle's living situation after they lost the apartment. Although we need to learn more about how economic factors influence relationship problems directly and indirectly, they were clearly not the major factor in these breakups.

One reason why economic factors do not play a more direct role may be due to how couples manage their finances. A major assumption of the specialization and bargaining models many quantitative studies are based on—income as a shared couple resource—may not work very well for unmarried parent couples. Both bargaining and specialization assume some degree of income pooling, but income is not a shared couple resource for most of the unmarried parents reported on here. Only about one-third of couples who break up report any sharing of income at baseline, before they have broken up. In most cases, couples report keeping their money separate and have their own systems for working out who contributes to the household and for baby care. Therefore, though mothers do earn less than fathers, it is not clear that they can access a father's higher income as a shared resource. Thus it is not clear that men's income will make women more likely to stay in the relationship, as bargaining theory would suggest.

Most of the couples who break up are not specializing, consistent with the notion that specialization discourages breakup. More mothers who break up work at baseline than those who do not and few report relying solely on the child's father for financial support. That almost half of mothers who broke up are working at baseline is especially striking when we remember that these interviews were conducted within a few months of giving birth. Several respondents, both mothers and fathers, however, report falling back on family members for financial support, and especially a place to live, when a relationship ends. Having a place to go and an alternative support network might make them less likely to stay in a troubled relationship, especially if a couple is experiencing problems that either seem intolerable or could pose potential danger.

Another issue to consider is whether mothers are moving into new relationships after a breakup because of economic need. More than 70 percent of mothers move into new relationships by the end of the study. One-third of them start before or just after the relationship with the father ended, and most are cohabitations. The overlap suggests these relationships are a factor in the decisions the mother makes about whether to break up. A new cohabitation represents an alternative both to staying in the relationship and to relying on family and friends for a place to live or financial support. In only one case, however, did a mother clearly say that she was motivated to move in with a new partner to alleviate economic hardship.

This analysis points to different ways unmarried parents' breakups impact their children. One is that they experience a lot of changes in their lives in a short time, and in family makeup. Another is that they are unlikely to spend much time with their fathers after a breakup. Some researchers argue that the number of family transitions is important for children's well-being, with the fewer the better (Wu 1996). In TLC3, beyond the transition of the breakup, which in most cases involves the father moving out of the child's home, 73 percent of mothers moved into new relationships—most of them cohabitations. Because about half of the mothers that broke up already had children from another partner, the breakup with the focal father is an additional transition for these earlier children.

Another issue worthy of comment is the importance of men's bad behavior in explaining why unmarried parents break up. Why so much infidelity and other destructive behaviors? Do these men intend to behave differently and are somehow unable to, or do they just not care? Are they compensating for their inability to accomplish a traditional masculine provider role? How are values, efficacy, and gender interacting? Are other factors at work?

The idea that performing hypermasculine behaviors such as infidelity and domestic violence is compensatory "doing gender" for not being able to assume a provider role does not seem to be borne out by these data. If we compare couples by relationship status at the end of the study, fathers who broke up worked more than the others at baseline and had household incomes comparable to those of couples who went on to marry. This suggests they were at least as able as those who stayed together to generate some income. Perhaps, rather than compensating for their inability to assume traditional masculine family roles, these fathers are acting out because they do not want to assume the responsibilities expected of them. They are certainly, however, acting out in gendered ways.

Fathers' explanations for their cheating are somewhat illuminating. Some declare it is not in their nature to be with one woman. Others say they can't imagine monogamy, at least not now. Many of their comments are similar to Elijah Anderson's (1999) reports of opportunistic behavior among young urban men. What I believe to be most revealing is that many say they think they are too young to settle down and be in a monogamous relationship, but could imagine it when they are older. These fathers seem to take to heart the idea that they are young and should be "sowing some oats or whatever," rather than living a monogamous and quiet lifestyle they associate with being older.

Other researchers have argued that young people of today experience a period of development called emerging adulthood that extends from the teens through the twenties where they are focused on self-exploration and delay accepting adult responsibilities (Arnett 2004). Although this typically involves delaying having children, perhaps the formation is different among poorer, urban young adults, and this concept could account for some of the "bad behavior" we observe. Whereas more privileged emerging adults may be seen as immature, self-centered, and perhaps a concern to their parents when they delay assuming adult responsibilities, they are not considered a social problem because they usually do not have children who are affected by their actions. Because having children is a traditional marker of adulthood, we tend to view the couples in this study as adults, although they may developmentally be emerging adults. That they have children who are affected by their behavior of course raises the stakes.

Most fathers in TLC3, however do not act this way. In general, as evident in the portraits of couples just described, most have lives marked by relationship and residential instability, financial strain, and often a few young children to care for. But it is important to remember that the couples profiled here are not like most of the unmarried parents in the study. The couples who broke up tend to have the worst relationships of all the unmarried parents in TLC3. In addition, both men and women in the worst situations tend to repeat these patterns as they repartner. Perhaps the chaotic conditions of their lives make it difficult for some to change patterns of behavior that cause problems in a relationship. This seems especially true when a respondent or partner has a history of substance abuse. Maybe the pool of potential partners available to respondents with a lot of problems is limited to others in similar situations, who also have low efficacy, contributing to the cycle repeating itself.

Notes

1. Several respondents who broke up with an original partner went on to form new relationships, and some of these new couples also broke up during the study. These additional break ups are not included in this analysis.

2. An additional couple broke up and reconciled during the study that is not included here. Both are currently incarcerated and have been unavailable for interviews since the second year of TLC3.

3. This figure does not account for the overall length of relationships.

4. See Heather Hill, chapter 5 this volume, for a more detailed analysis of infidelity and mistrust among TLC3 couples.

5. This results in a slightly higher figure than table 6.1 seems to show—the discrepancy is due to rare occasions where a respondent reports infidelity in the relationship, but does not name it as a contributing factor of the breakup.

6. This is true for all original couples in the study, but there are examples of respondents getting back together with a former partner after they themselves have had a child with someone else, namely the focal child. For example, after he and Adrienne broke up, Ollie got back together with his other baby mama, whom he already had two children with, and had another child with her.

7. All mothers who went on to a third partner during the study also had a baby with their second and third partners, three pregnancies during four years of the study.

References

Amato, Paul R., and Stacey J. Rogers. 1997. "A Longitudinal Study of Marital Problems and Subsequent Divorce." *Journal of Marriage and the Family* 59(3): 612–24.

Anderson, Elijah. 1999. *Code of the Street: Decency, Violence and the Moral Life of the Inner City.* New York: W. W. Norton.

Arnett, Jeffrey. 2004. *Emerging Adulthood: The Winding Road From the Late Teens Through the Twenties.* Oxford: Oxford University Press.

Becker, Gary S. 1991. *A Treatise on the Family.* Cambridge, Mass.: Harvard University Press.

Booth Alan, David R. Johnson, Lynn K. White, and John N. Edwards. 1985. "Predicting Divorce and Permanent Separation." *Journal of Family Issues* 6(3): 331–46.

Brown, Susan L., and Alan Booth. 1996. "Cohabitation versus Marriage: A Comparison of Relationship Quality." *Journal of Marriage and the Family* 58(4): 668–78.

Bumpass, Larry L., and Hsien-Hen Lu. 2000. "Trends in Cohabitation and Implications for Children's Family Contexts in the United States." *Population Studies—A Journal of Demography* 54(1): 29–41.

Bumpass, Larry L., Teresa C. Martin, and James A. Sweet. 1991. "The Impact of Family Background and Early Marital Factors on Marital Disruption." *Journal of Family Issues* 12(1): 22–42.

Bumpass, Larry L., James A. Sweet, and Andrew J. Cherlin. 1991. "The Role of Cohabitation in Declining Rates of Marriage." *Journal of Marriage and the Family* 53(4): 913–27.

Carlson, Marcia, Sara McLanahan, and Paula England. 2004. Union Formation in Fragile Families. *Demography* 41(3): 237–61.

Cherlin, Andrew J. 1979. "Work Life and Marital Dissolution." In *Divorce and Separation: Context, Causes, and Consequences,* edited by G. Levinger and O. C. Moles. New York: Basic Books.

Cowan, Carolyn P., and Philip A. Cowan. 1992. *When Partners Become Parents: The Big Life Change for Couples.* New York: Basic Books

———. 1995. "Interventions to Ease the Transition to Parenthood: Why Are They Needed and What Can They Do?" *Family Relations* 44(4): 412–23.

Denzin, Norman K., and Yvonna S. Lincoln. 2000. *Handbook of Qualitative Research,* 2nd edition. Thousand Oaks, Calif.: Sage Publications.

England, Paula, and Gary Farkas. 1986. *Households, Employment and Gender: A Social, Economic and Demographic View.* New York: Aldine de Gruyter.

England, Paula, and Barbara S. Kilbourne. 1990. "Markets, Marriages, and Other Mates: The Problem of Power." In *Beyond the Marketplace: Rethinking Economy and Society,* edited by Roger Friedland and A. F. Robertson. New York: Aldine de Gruyter.

Forste, Renata, and Koray Tanfer. 1996. "Sexual Exclusivity Among Dating, Cohabiting and Married Women." *Journal of Marriage and the Family* 58(1): 33–47.

Gibson-Davis, Christine, Kathryn Edin, and Sara McLanahan. 2005. "High Hopes, but Even Higher Expectations: The Retreat from Marriage Among Low-Income Couples." *Journal of Marriage and Family* 67(3): 1301–12.

Goldscheider, Frances, and Linda J. Waite. 1991. *New Families, No Families: The Transformation of the American Home.* Berkeley, Calif.: University of California Press.

Gottman, John M. 1994. *What Predicts Divorce? The Relationship Between Marital Processes and Marital Outcomes.* Hillsdale, N.J.: Lawrence Erlbaum.

Graefe, Daniel R., and Deborah T. Lichter. 1999. "Life Course Transitions of American Children: Parental Cohabitation, Marriage and Single Motherhood." *Demography* 36(2): 205–17.

Heckert, D. Alex, Thomas C. Nowak, and Kay A. Snyder. 1998. "The Impact of Husbands' and Wives' Relative Earnings on Marital Disruption." *Journal of Marriage and the Family* 60(4): 690–703.

Hiedemann, Bridget, Olga Suhomlinova, and Angela M. O'Rand. 1998. "Economic Independence, Economic Status, and Empty Nest in Midlife Marital Disruption." *Journal of Marriage and the Family* 60(2): 219–31.

Hoffman, Saul D., and Greg J. Duncan. 1995. "The Effect of Incomes, Wages, and AFDC Benefits on Marital Disruption." *The Journal of Human Resources* 30(1): 19–41.

Kurz, Demie. 1995. *For Richer, for Poorer: Mothers Confront Divorce*. New York: Routledge Press.

Lundberg, Shelley, and Robert A. Pollak. 1996. "Bargaining and Distribution in Marriage." *Journal of Economic Perspectives* 10(4): 139–58.

Manning, Wendy D. 2001. "Childbearing in Cohabiting Unions: Racial and Ethnic Differences." *Family Planning Perspectives* 33(5): 217–23.

McLanahan, Sara, Irv Garfinkel, Nancy Reichman, Julien Teitler, Marcia Carlson, and C. N. Audiger. 2003. *The Fragile Families and Child Wellbeing Study: Baseline National Report*. Princeton, N.J.: Center for Research on Child Wellbeing

Moore, Kristin A., and Linda J. Waite. 1981. "Marital Dissolution, Early Motherhood and Early Marriage." *Social Forces* 60(1): 20–40.

Reed, Joanna M. 2006. "Not Crossing the 'Extra Line': How Cohabitors with Children View Their Unions." *Journal of Marriage and Family* 68(5): 1117–31.

Sanchez, Laura, and Constance T. Gager. 2000. "Hard Living, Perceived Entitlement to a Great Marriage, and Marital Dissolution." *Journal of Marriage and the Family* 62(3): 708–22.

Sayer, Liana C., and Suzanne M. Bianchi. 2000. "Women's Economic Independence and the Probability of Divorce: A Review and Reexamination." *Journal of Family Issues* 21(7): 906–43.

Sayer, Liana C., Nathan Wright, and Kathryn Edin. 2003. "Class Differences in Family Attitudes." Paper presented at the Sixty-Eighth Annual Meeting of the Population Association of America. Minneapolis, Minn., May 1–3, 2003.

Schoen, Robert, Nan Marie Astone, Kendra Rothert, Nicola J. Standish, Young J. Kim. 2002. "Women's Employment, Marital Happiness, and Divorce." *Social Forces* 81(4): 643–62.

South, Scott J., and Kim M. Lloyd. 1995. "Spousal Alternatives and Marital Dissolution." *American Sociological Review* 60(1): 21–35.

Strauss, Anselm L. and Juliet M. Corbin. 1998. *Basics of Qualitative Research*, 2nd edition. Thousand Oaks, Calif.: Sage Publications.

Thomson, Elizabeth, and Ugo Colella. 1992. "Cohabitation and Marital Stability: Quality or Commitment?" *Journal of Marriage and the Family* 54(2): 259–67.

Vaughan, Diane. 1986. *Uncoupling: Turning Points in Intimate Relationships*. New York: Oxford University Press.

Waite, Linda J., and Maggie Gallagher. 2000. *The Case for Marriage*. New York: Doubleday.

Weiss, Yoram, and Robert J. Willis. 1997. "Match Quality, New Information and Marital Dissolution." *Journal of Labor Economics* 15(1): S293–332.

Wu, Lawrence L. 1996. "Effects of Family Instability, Income, and Income Instability on the Risk of Premarital Birth." *American Sociological Review* 61(3): 386–406.

Wu, Zheng. 1995. "The Stability of Cohabitation Relationships: The Role of Children." *Journal of Marriage and the Family* 57(1): 231–36.

PART III

PARENTING TOGETHER AND APART

Chapter 7

#1 Father or Fathering 101?: Couple Relationship Quality and Father Involvement When Fathers Live with Their Children

KATHRYN D. LINNENBERG

FATHERHOOD HAS become a hot button issue in the media, politics, and the general public recently. The focus has been on absent fathers, the assumption being that unmarried fathers fall into this category by default. Although there are plenty of examples of absent fathers when studying children from birth to age eighteen, research has now shown that unmarried men are typically present at the beginning of their children's lives. According to the Fragile Families and Child Wellbeing data, 83 percent of unmarried couples are romantically involved at the time of their child's birth—half are cohabiting (McLanahan et al. 2001). In this chapter, I examine differences in father involvement among fathers who are living with a child and the child's mother. How involved are these coresidential fathers with their children? Is that involvement affected by the father's relationship with the mother of his child?

Using qualitative interview data with fifty-seven couples, I look at fathering in the first year after birth to see how fathers in happy and unhappy relationships—some married, others cohabiting—differ in level of father involvement. The data come from the Time, Love and Cash Among Couples with Children study. I use wave one and two interviews to establish portraits of father involvement for married and cohabiting men in happy and stable relationships, happy relationships that have some problems, and those in relationships that are plagued with problems.

159

When children are small, mothers often hold primary responsibility for care work. This means that a father's connection to his child is often mediated by his relationship with the mother of that child. For that reason, I am interested in looking at how relationship status and quality affect father involvement for coresidential couples. Are married fathers more involved than their counterparts? Are fathers in stormy relationships less tied to their children than those in contented unions?

Relationship Quality

Because there is so much variation, considering relationship quality is important as well. According to Carolyn Cowan and Philip Cowan (1992) when couple relationships are happier, parent-child relationships are more positive as well. They argue that ". . . the relationship *between* the parents seems to act as a crucible in which their relationships with their children take shape" (11, emphasis in original). They find this to be particularly true of the fathers. This means that men's involvement with their children is influenced by the quality of their relationship with the mothers. In their study of parent-child play interaction, the Cowans found that low marital satisfaction during the pregnancy or current marital distress leave men more likely to withdraw or be cold with their child. They find that this is especially true of the father-daughter relationship. In effect, any negativity from the marital relationship spills over into the parent-child relationship.

Other researchers have done work that supports the idea of spillover. Osnat Erel and Bonnie Burman (1995) performed a meta-analysis of sixty-eight studies on marital relationships and parent-child relations. They conclude that there is a positive relationship between marital quality and the quality of the relationship between the parent and the child. They claim that the stress from marital disharmony permeates the parent's relationship with the child. Parents are not able to separate their experiences in their role as *partners* from their role as *parents.*

Although Erel and Burman (1995) do not find any significant difference between mother and father's experience of spillover, other researchers do. Spousal relationships influence fathers' relationship with their children, whereas mother-child relationships seem separate from marital quality issues (Lindahl and Malik 1999; Belsky et al. 1991; Barber 1987). Jay Belsky and his colleagues theorize that this gender difference could be because women have a spousal role and a maternal role that are both clearly scripted by social convention. Men, on the other hand, may have a "general pattern of relating—actively involved versus disengaged—[that] is applied to spouse and child alike" (1991: 488).

In a laboratory research project, Katherine Kitzmann (2000) had married couples discuss both a pleasant and a conflictual topic. After each conversation, she brought the couple's six- to eight-year-old sons into the room and measured husbands' and wives' reactions to their sons in a triadic family interaction. She found that many couples who had a demo-cratic parenting style after the pleasant conversation did not maintain it after the conflictual discussion. Instead they demonstrated hostility, com-petitiveness, and a lack of cohesion. Fathers also supported and engaged significantly less with their sons after the conflictual conversation. Relationship quality, then, clearly affects parenting style and quality.

Most research on relationship quality and parenting has focused on married, white, middle-class couples. One exception is Marcia Carlson and Sara McLanahan's 2006 article that uses Fragile Family survey data to broaden the investigation on this topic.[1] Fragile Families focused on sampling nonmarital births with a companion sample of births to married couples. The result was a racially diverse and lower-income sample of married, cohabiting, and romantically involved couples, some of whom do not live together. They find that relationship quality affects parenting similarly across relationship status categories. Specifically, they find that mothers and fathers in more supportive relationships report more posi-tive interaction with their child (for example, greater frequency of play-ing and reading). Carlson and McLanahan's findings extend the spillover theory and show that it holds true for married and unmarried parents. They also broaden previous research that concentrated on emotional spillover and look at how the emotional quality of the parents' relation-ship can spill over to parenting action as well.

It makes sense that emotions from a couple's relationship affect a parent-child relationship not only as emotions, but as action as well. If relationship quality in couples is bad, men may distance themselves from their partners. Because women, on average, do more of the care work and tend to get custody when couples split up, men may distance themselves from the baby as well. This could serve as a sort of defense mechanism. They may be reacting, probably subconsciously: "because I could be sep-arating from this woman soon, and because she will have the baby pri-marily once we are no longer living together, I should begin to disengage from the baby now, and not get too close, so as to avoid the pain of losing an integral part of my life later on."

On the other hand, when relationship quality is good, men may want to spend more time with their partners. Because women and their infants are often a package deal, more or less, the time these men spend with their partners may be family time by default. Babysitters are expensive, so if money is tight and no other easy child care is available, time together as a couple may include the child. Increased exposure to the child may then increase a father's involvement with the care of that child.

Although I am mostly interested in how fathering relates to relation-ship quality, because quality is associated with relationship status, I will also examine the relationship status of couples in different fathering and relationship quality categories. Research has shown that positive and neg-ative aspects of couple relationship infiltrate the parent-child relationship as well. In this chapter, I use TLC3 qualitative interview data to investigate how and why this may be the case. I use respondents' words and stories in discussing their romantic relationships and parenting behavior.

Data and Methods

The data that I use are from the qualitative interview based study Time, Love, and Cash among Couples with Children. The qualitative interviews included many questions that deal with the amount of time and care the father provides for the child and the couple's relationship history.

I limit my analysis to couples who are cohabiting or married because I want to investigate father involvement once the hurdle of coresidence has been met. I focus on the fifty-seven couples who are cohabiting at both wave one and wave two. Eighteen percent of the fathers in my sample are white, 44 percent are black, and 39 percent are Latino. One is part white, part Native American. Of the fathers in this analysis, 49 percent work first-shift jobs and 30 percent work second- or third-shift jobs. Twelve of the men, or 19 percent, were not employed at the time of the individual interviews.

I read the transcripts and found detailed accounts of fathers' interactions with their partners and with their children. I use these stories to create a typology of relationship quality. Then I describe what father involvement looks like, in relation to care work and play, for each category within the typology.

Measuring Relationship Quality

After reading and coding the interview data, I divided the couples into three categories. In determining these, I considered both positive and negative aspects of a relationship. I coded for whether the couple had any serious problems—such as infidelity, drug abuse, or physical abuse—and evaluated whether these were ongoing issues or had occurred in the near or distant past. I also considered less serious problems by examining the things the couples fight about. Finances and distrust over time spent with members of the opposite sex were two that appeared frequently. Not everything that went into my evaluation of couple relationship quality was negative, however. I also looked for examples of love and affection and considered reports of how the couple demonstrates love to each other, if in fact they do. The transcripts are filled with examples of love shown in both vibrant and flashy ways or mundane and everyday ways.

After reading through all of these stories, three categories of relationship quality emerged: happy and stable, happy but problems exist, and plagued with problems. Twenty-three couples fit the happy and stable category. These currently have no serious problems, such as infidelity issues, drug problems, or physical abuse. Only two of the couples report serious issues in the past, and they are in the distant past.[2] Most have never had to deal with these issues. Nineteen (83 percent) were married at baseline, and one couple married between the first and second round of interviews. Members of happy and stable couples can give detailed descriptions of how their partner demonstrates love. They range from hugs and kisses to cooking his favorite meal, from drawing her a bath at the end of a rough day to buying thoughtful presents.

The nineteen happy but problems exist couples tell similar stories about their partner demonstrating love, but also tell stories that are not so positive. Many have money troubles that strain their relationship. More than half have issues of distrust about fidelity that are often grounded in reality and past experience. Drugs and physical abuse, however, are not an issue for these couples. Rather, they fight over time spent with members of the opposite sex—often the parent of a previous child. Nonetheless, these couples have true affection for each other and are working hard to stay together. Six were married when the baby that brought them into our study was born; another three marry within a year. Two others get married about three years after the birth.

The fifteen couples who are plagued with problems tell stories of abuse, drugs, time in prison, and cheating. They often have on-again, off-again relationships. Only one was married when their baby was born, and they had split up two years later. Two couples marry within a year of their baby's birth, but have separated or divorced within two years, one couple gets married about three years after the birth. Although some can tell stories of how they express their love to each other, many talk of how their partner is withdrawn and undemonstrative. These couples often tell stories of extremely volatile relationships.

Now I want to see how father involvement plays out in each group and whether differences exist between groups.[3] Does fatherhood look different for the men in these various types of relationships? Does relationship quality relate to father involvement in some demonstrable way?

Before moving into the detailed descriptions of my typology, I created a cross-tabulation using relationship quality from around the time of the birth to about one year later and father involvement around the birth of the baby (see table 7.1). I divided fathers into three categories based on their level of involvement. Highly involved fathers do much of the care work for their child, engaging in the physical care of the child as well as in play. They avoid no parenthood tasks; they give detailed descriptions of the baby's schedule because they are active participants in it. Involved fathers participate in care work for their child and play. Some specialize in a few child care tasks; others are "mommy's helpers" on all tasks, and do not take the lead in any. Marginally involved fathers spend some time with their child, but the time focuses on play instead of physical care. When they do help, it is more preparatory work than care work. For

Table 7.1   Cross-tabulation of Father Involvement by Relationship Quality

| | Relationship Quality | | | |
	Plagued with Problems	Happy, but Problems	Happy and Stable	Total
Father involvement				
Marginally	8	3	4	15
involved	53.3%	15.8%	17.4%	26.3%
Involved	4	7	11	22
	26.7%	36.8%	47.8%	38.6%
Highly	3	9	8	20
involved	20.0%	47.7%	34.8%	35.1%
Total	15	19	23	57
	100%	100%	100%	100%

Source: Author's calculations.
Note: Father involvement from TLC3 round one data. Relationship quality from TLC3 rounds one and two data.
Chi square = 8.523 (df = 4, p = .074), Somers' d = .183 (p = .129).

example, they make the bottle and then hand it to the mother so that she can feed the baby. Only rarely would a marginally involved father spend time alone with the baby.

Looking at table 7.1, more than half (53.3 percent) of the men from couples who are plagued with problems are only marginally involved with their children. A much smaller percentage of their counterparts—men from happy couples who have problems, and from happy and stable couples—are only marginally involved (15.8 percent and 17.4 percent respectively). This is not unexpected. Surprisingly, though, nearly half of the men from happy couples with problems (47.4 percent) are highly involved fathers, but only about a third (34.8 percent) from happy and stable couples are. The relationship between couple relationship quality and father involvement is statistically significant at the .10 level, which is meaningful given a sample size of only fifty-seven.

Although I have used nuanced qualitative data to describe both the quality of the couple relationship and the level of father involvement, this simple cross-tabulation does not tell the whole story, nor does it answer the question of why father involvement is higher for couples with middling levels of relationship quality. The qualitative analysis I present gets under the surface of these patterns to show that gender ideology, work schedules, and economic distress create some surprising patterns within and between categories that one might not expect.

First, gender ideology guides the actions of most fathers. This prompts a greater level of involvement than may have been typical in earlier generations, but still limits their involvement to the helper and playmate role in most cases, no matter what the state of the relationship. This is not to say that fathers do not offer meaningful help with care work. Indeed, it is clear that most men seek to distance themselves from the traditional role they may have seen their fathers play. They are careful to articulate that they are not the kind of father who holds back, but helping and playing in the shadow of the mother seems to be enough.

The quality of the couple relationship, however, creates nuance within this father as helper and playmate role. Mothers are more likely to trust fathers with helping tasks in the happy and stable couples, whereas those in relationships that are happy with problems tend to supervise fathers in these activities quite closely. Few fathers in relationships plagued with problems even attempt to play any helper role, and only participate in parenting activities that are "fun."

In sum, then, I show that gender ideology circumscribes father involvement in all couples. Two exceptions apply, however. Some fathers in happy and stable couple relationships (35 percent) are spurred to greater involvement by a family-first philosophy, so much so that when both partners are working, they manage to arrange work schedules so that each works a different shift, allowing one parent to be at home with the children at all times. Of course, this also saves on day-care costs, but economics do not seem to be the primary motivation, at least by the parents' accounts. Fathers in happy but problematic relationships, by contrast, are often thrust into full involvement when they are unemployed. These men must care for the child alone when the woman works, in part because the couple is so often financially strapped. Sometimes, though, these fathers also voice a compensatory motivation—that is, they see high levels of father involvement as a way to compensate for poor labor market performance (see also Waller 2002).

The main irony, made clear in the cross-tabulation, is that more of the fully involved fathers are in the second group (happy with problems) than in the first (happy and stable). This seems primarily because of the greater economic struggle these men face and their need to compensate for marginal breadwinning with caregiving. However, I argue that though this might benefit the child in the short term, the larger question is what effect the greater investment in fatherhood has on the stability of the couple relationship over time, especially in light of the economic struggles that result when men are not employed.

Although mothers in relationships with fully engaged fathers are happy with the level of father involvement, they are no more so than those in happy and stable relationships with partners who limit themselves to the helper and playmate role. Furthermore, mothers with partners who are not employed are less happy with the relationship than those whose partner does work (even when the father is fully involved). Thus, though some fathers try to compensate for poor breadwinning performance with higher levels of caregiving, mothers' satisfaction with the couple relationship is more tied to breadwinning than fathering.

Father Involvement in Happy, Stable Couples

Overall, the men in happy and stable couples fall into one of two involvement patterns, which I term fathers as helper and playmate and family-first fathers. The first category includes men in more traditional relationships. These men play with their children, but when they are involved in care work, they tend to do so as the mother's helper. If the couple has older children together, the men may focus on caring for these children while letting the mother take responsibility for the baby. All eleven men from table 7.1 who were involved or marginally involved with their children fall into this category. The family-first fathers are highly involved with their children. They often work a different shift than the mother, if she has returned to the labor force. They have reservations about day care, so their performance of care work is seen as a way to avoid the risks and financial burden. These fathers discuss family activities in great detail as a source of fun and pleasure for them. All eight men from table 7.1 who were highly involved are family-first fathers.

Fathers as Helper and Playmate

Pilar, twenty-one, and Eduardo, twenty-three, are a Puerto Rican couple who have known each other since they were children, growing up on the same street. Eduardo got to know Pilar in part through her cousin, who is his best friend. This couple dated for a year and a half before getting married. They had their first son about a year after they married. Joshua came along two years after that.

This family rents the upstairs apartment in a duplex owned by Eduardo's parents, who live downstairs. Pilar works part-time at a local nonprofit agency and Eduardo is a truck driver who works nights. They are practicing Catholics, and Pilar teaches Sunday School classes each week. This couple has no history of violence, drugs, or infidelity. Pilar states that Eduardo is an affectionate person who is "really good at expressing his love." She talks about how similar the two were from the beginning, saying, "[w]e felt like we were the SAME. . . . We had the same interests, and we had the same type of humor. . . . We just felt a connection. Like he was so much like me, and we just had the same values, and I just felt like he was the one." Eduardo admits that sometimes they have problems, but only small ones, nothing too big. To him these are "just something you deal with everyday. I mean, we're on Earth, what do you expect? We're not in Heaven where it's perfect."

As a father, Eduardo is very interested in his children. He talks about children's developmental levels. He knows Joshua's schedule inside and out, and he talks about his son being a good sleeper and eater. Family time is very important to Eduardo. He works nights, and when he gets home, he sleeps for a few hours. Eduardo then gets up to play with the children and have dinner together as a family. After dinner, he goes back to sleep for a few more hours before heading back to work. His leisure time is also filled with family activities—going on walks, trips to the park or the mall, and picnics.

This happiness with his family does not mean that Eduardo is active in care work. He will watch his sons on his own for an hour or two on Sunday mornings when Pilar goes to church, but this is in part because his family lives downstairs, so he does not have to be in sole charge very often. Instead, Eduardo fills the helper role. He talks about "helping" give the children baths, not bathing them on his own. On diapers he says, "if my wife is busy, and I'm right there, I'll change his diaper. I'm not like one of those guys who just back away. I mean that's my son and I take care of my son." Here he is trying to assert his difference from fathers who refuse to change a diaper, but as he says himself, he will do it *if* his wife is busy *and* he's right there. This is not a regular activity for him.

Pilar is satisfied with Eduardo's level of involvement. She also asserts that the baby has formed a positive connection with his father, saying, "whenever he [the baby] sees him [Eduardo], he just smiles so much." This father-son link is just one more reason Pilar is pleased to be with Eduardo.

Overall, for Pilar and Eduardo, their happiness with each other translates into happiness with spending time as a family. This feeling is common among happy and stable couples. Abigail and Jack, age twenty-five and thirty, respectively, are a white couple who started dating in college when they met through a student group. They are a solidly content couple, together for eight years and married for five when their third child, daughter Rebecca, was born. When asked about ways they show they love each other, both have mundane, unglamorous things on their lists. Jack says that she buys him little things that remind her of him. Abigail mentions that he knows what kinds of candy bars she likes, and that he buys her favorite seltzer water when he goes to the store even though he doesn't like it at all. He also helps with the baby. This involvement with the child, which includes playing games and doing night duty, demonstrates his love for Abigail as well as his involvement as a father. She describes him as "yummy" because he gravitates towards children, and that is one of the things she likes most about him.

Of the twenty-three men in happy and stable relationships, fifteen fit into the category of father as helper and playmate. These men have fairly traditional relationships with their partners. Although Eduardo works nights, most of these fathers work first-shift jobs. Thirteen of the couples are married at the time of the birth—and one of the two cohabiting couples marry over the course of the study. Many of these couples have older children together. Those who do are similar to Eduardo in that they often gravitate towards the older children, rather than the newborn, in a sort of division of child care labor. The men are not avoiding care work altogether, as a strict separate spheres model would suggest. Rather, they specialize in tasks that are easier, fun, and supportive. Overall, the mothers are quite happy with that arrangement.

Family-First Fathers

Roberta and Ryan had been together for sixteen years when their fifth child and first son was born: ten of those years were spent as husband and wife. They are both African American. Roberta is thirty-seven years old, and Ryan is forty. This stable couple even grew up across the street from each other. When asked what could bring about the end of their relationship, Roberta said that only death would break them up. She says, "that's my soul mate. That's what God wanted me to marry. . . . He'll [Ryan] tell you. He said the Lord gave me to him. So why should he mess it up?" She also calls him a perfect husband. Ryan says that he tells Roberta he loves her all the time, and buys her "everything on her Christmas list." They are a joyful couple who emphasize family time. Ryan values their children and being a family: "We do a lot of things that doesn't cost any money. We go to the park, we go swinging, we go swimming . . . we go bike riding. I remember, one time, we was riding . . . and this little girl said, 'I have never seen a whole family go bike riding.' And it's, you know, this is normal for us." He is excited to tell the story of others' reactions to his family outing.

Ryan is also an integral part of the care work for the baby. Because his wife works a first-shift job and he does not go to work until noon, he spends every morning caring for the baby. He revels in being a father to all his children, and says he wants to show them "the positive things in life."

Another couple who follows this pattern is Antoinette and Brian, who are African American and married for three years before the birth of the focal child and together as a couple for seven. Antoinette was twenty-seven when she entered the study, and Brian was twenty-five. They had two other children together before they got married. Brian expresses intense love for his wife in his individual interview. He says, "That was the first person I truly loved. You got these guys that say, 'I love my girl.' But I don't think they really understand. 'Cuz there's nothing that could really ever . . . split us apart." Brian also mentions their similarities. "We have some of the exact same interests and habits, like she doesn't like tomatoes, neither do I. . . . Because I know her and she knows me, because of our ability to have those same interests and everything, it's a lot easier. . . ." He obviously values their similarities, even down to food likes and dislikes. Antoinette and Brian spend a lot of time together as a family, though he does go out with "the boys" on Friday evenings.

Because Brian works days, and Antoinette works nights, he is in charge of their children in the evenings. However, he is so committed to his wife and children that he also comes home from work on his breaks to see them. He reads books about babies, and he wants to learn how to make baby food. Brian also sees part of his job of being a father to his son as serving as a role model for his future relationships with women. He says that "just showing a lot of love to his mother in front of him, that kind of thing . . . show[ing] him how important a female is" are key components of fatherhood.

The family-first fathers make up the minority (35 percent) of the happy and stable couples. All these fathers have different work schedules than their partners—three do not have paying jobs. One is working to begin his own locksmith business; another was recently injured on the job and has to recover from chemical burns before returning to work. Six of these couples are married, like Roberta and Ryan and Antoinette and Brian. The two couples who are cohabiting stay together over the course of the study, but do marry. Previous research does show that when parents work separate shifts, men do more care work than when parents work the same shift (Brayfield 1995; Nock and Kingston 1988; Presser 1988; Presser 1994).

One way these men put family first is by spending leisure time as a family. Although Ryan may give the most eloquent and elaborate description of family activities, most of these men talk about the fact that they enjoy spending time with their partners and children.

Another way these couples put children first, perhaps before the couple relationship, is by working different hours. This cuts down on time that the couple sees each other, but it also reduces the amount of time that the child spends with someone other than a parent. Cutting down on day care is a way to avoid both the costs and the uncertain quality of day care. The large chunks of time alone with the child means that these men go beyond play and helping: they are well versed in all aspects of care work.

Father Involvement in Happy Couples with Problems

In the couples who are happy but have problems, father involvement, on the whole, mirrors father involvement in the happy and stable couples. Many of these fathers have a helper and playmate relationship with their child. The difference between these fathers and the helpers and playmates in the happy, stable couples is that these fathers often get more supervision and guidance from their partners on care work. Others take a more primary role, but for these couples, economic instability within the couple often helps to drive this father-child connection. Because these men are not working for pay, they have much more available time and use it to care for their children. I use the same terms outlined for these two categories of fathers—helper and playmate (63 percent) and the family-first fathers (37 percent)—but the labels mask important differences between groups. First, the helper and playmate fathers in this group place far more emphasis on play than on help, and perform their helping duties under the careful supervision of the mother, who does not fully trust them to perform these tasks on their own. Second, the family-first fathers in this group are often unemployed and thus thrust into the role when their partner works, because they have no financial wherewithal to do otherwise. Men in this group also often feel that they must compensate for not having a job with substantially greater involvement in fathering. In fact, these men shoulder 50 percent of the care work. This breakdown does not coincide completely with the numbers in table 7.1. That is because two of the nine fathers coded as highly involved during round one of TLC3 do not qualify as family-first fathers because their involvement tapered off by the time the baby turned a year old. In addition, even around the time of the baby's birth, their active involvement usually took place alongside the mother.

Helper and Playmate Who Needs Guidance   Myron, twenty-three, and Suzanne, twenty-two, a white couple, were together for four years before their son Johnny was conceived. Suzanne says that they got serious too quickly because Myron moved into her mother's house after dating only three months, when they were just out of high school. Myron had been kicked out of his mother's house. Suzanne's mother invited him to move in with them, and the two slept in separate rooms. Although this couple is cohabiting in their own home at the baseline interviews, they have a history of distrust. Myron says that he was a "compulsive liar," a character flaw he has worked to overcome. They tell of an argument they had when Suzanne found another woman's phone number written on a slip of paper in his dresser drawer. He claimed it was innocent; she was not so certain. This led to an issue of trust that they had to work through. Both have matured, and both clearly state that they intend to stay together. They are still living together four years into our study. Although they discuss marriage, the nuptials have not yet occurred, and they have a second child together.

When they were interviewed shortly after Johnny's birth, they both claim to tell each other they love each other all the time. However, Myron complains that though she "treats me like a king" when he is sick or has a backache, at other times, he wishes she would show more affection. He is quick to say, though, that even if she does not always show it, he knows she cares for him.

With his son, Myron is the playmate more than the caregiver. In one story he tells about feeding the child, it is clear that even baby Johnny knows this. "I feel as though that when she feeds him the jar stuff, he opens his mouth and eats the stuff. And then when I try to feed him— different story. He plays around with the stuff. He's like, 'Oh, I'm with Daddy, it's play time.' "

Part of this concentration on play can be linked to Suzanne's beliefs about Myron as a caregiver. Early on, Suzanne worried about leaving the baby alone with Myron because Myron was such a deep sleeper that he would sleep through Johnny's crying and not respond to the baby's needs. Now that Myron has proven to her that he will wake up by doing so when she is around, Suzanne is willing to leave the baby with him when she runs errands or visits with friends and family. Just as this couple worked to overcome distrust about fidelity, they worked to overcome distrust about his ability to father.

Moises and Antonia, a Hispanic couple age thirty-three and twenty-two, fit this model as well. They had only known each other for three months before Antonia got pregnant. She says that if Moises does not change "his jealousy thing" they will most likely break up, although she admits she has to change as well. Moises says that she is cold but starting to show more affection. Although they tell stories about the weaknesses in their personal relationship, they can also talk about ways they express their love positively. Moises sometimes helps her with the child by changing an occasional diaper or helping feed the baby. But he is tangential enough from the baby's care work that he has no idea what the baby's schedule is. To give him guidance, Antonia posted Donna's schedule in the kitchen so he would have some idea of what to do. Although Moises is a bit unsure of how to care for his child, the family does spend leisure time together. Moises calls this "the gold time."

Of the nineteen couples who fell into the happy with problems group, twelve fathers (63 percent) fit into the helper and playmate who needs watching and guidance category. Five of the couples are married during the study. Three are continuously cohabiting. Four transition from cohabitation to marriage, two within a year and the other two within four years.

Overall, their problems center on distrust. Just like Myron and Moises, they tell stories about past infidelity or flirtations—both real and imagined—or jealousy over previous relationships that lingers between them. These couples are working past their problems, but the specter remains, and it arises in issues of fatherhood. The women express doubts about their partner's ability to parent effectively without supervision. The women often "test" the men before leaving the baby alone with them, just as Suzanne did with Myron. The men have to earn their place as a father just as many had to earn their place as partner after breaking the trust in their relationship.

Thrust into Family-First Fathering

Whereas the problems in the helpers and playmates' relationships tend to center on distrust and jealousy about fidelity that spills over into distrust about the paternal ability to parent, the problems in these family-first fathers' relationships mainly stem from financial stress. These couples make up 37 percent of the happy with problems group. Economic problems dominate, but, on occasion, relational problems are present as well. Only one of the seven is married. Five of the seven are out of work. One works a third-shift job at night and his partner works days—they are the ones who transition to marriage within a year after the birth. Making ends meet is a difficult task for these couples, but they achieve it by having the father step up and actively participate in caring for the baby.

Andre and Beverly, a black couple from Chicago, are both in their early twenties at the beginning of the study. At the time of the pregnancy, they had been together for about a year. Andre has a child with another woman. Beverly has two other children. When they met, both were seeing other people. One month after officially calling it quits with their other partners, Beverly moved her belongings into Andre's apartment. Four years later, they still live together but have not transitioned to marriage, though they say they hope to marry within a year.

At baseline, Andre expresses distrust about Beverly's behavior. "'Cause I stopped trusting . . . she used to go out every day. EVERY DAY. She'd lie to me. 'I gonna go to the store.' Or she say, 'I'm going to my auntie house.' But she won't come back for six, seven hours. I KNOW you not at your auntie's house for six hours. Your auntie live walking distance." Although there is distrust, both also cite dramatic examples of how the other demonstrates love. Beverly says, "He very romantic, you know, just like bubble baths, candles around the table, he makes me dinners and all that. . . . He tucks me in at night. You know, if I'm tired, he massages me, massages my feet." One of Andre's examples was similarly striking. He tells the story of how she braved a snow storm to walk to the grocery and buy him everything he wanted, saying he was touched that "she love me enough to get up and walk in all that snow."

The romantic relationship has its highs and lows, but one big problem they have when their baby is born is that neither has a paying job. Rather than argue constantly about money, Beverly and Andre become complete coparents who "do everything together" and present a "united front." Beverly says that the care work is a fifty-fifty split. Andre discusses the importance of being a family saying, "We a family, we together and we have fun."

Don, twenty-three, and Claudia, nineteen, are a Hispanic couple who knew each other for years before they began dating. A year before she got pregnant, they began dating seriously. Claudia distrusts Don, one of her brother's best friends, at times. She has suspicions of infidelity, so when he gets dressed up, she worries. She asks him, "Why are you putting cologne on?" He answers, "I just feel like dressing up." Don explains, "And she's going, you know, I better not catch you with nobody. . . . And I play around with her head. 'Yeah, I'm going to see my chillas [slang for women].' "

Don is a highly involved father, however. In fact, he is the primary caregiver for their baby. Claudia works a first-shift job and he has a part-time shift from four to eight in the morning. During the day, Don is on baby duty. He can talk about Claudia's schedule in detail and discusses her personality traits. Claudia streamlines his caregiving tasks by doing all the prep work for him when she gets home at night. So she washes the bottles and makes up new ones. She also washes the baby's clothes.

Overall, the relationship troubles that fifty-fifty couples have do not seem to affect the men's fathering in any negative way. In fact, the economic tough times help to *increase* their involvement. Because these men are out of work, they have the time to care for their children. Also, because their partners often do work outside of the home, they need to provide the care because the couple has far too few resources to pay for childcare. Unemployment also creates a compensatory motivation for some, who seek to make up for their lack of employment with increased engagement in fathering. Their unemployment, however, may well prevent the couple's ability to stay together or transition into marriage.

Mothers' satisfaction with the relationship, as opposed to their satisfaction with men's fathering, seems to depend more on men's ability to bring home the bacon than it does on their taking a family-first stance toward fathering. Thus, in happy couples with some problems, family-first fathering may make mothers more satisfied with fathering, but less satisfied with the relationship overall. Christina Gibson-Davis, Kathryn Edin, and Sara McLanahan (2005) and Marcia Carlson, Sara McLanahan, and Paula England (2004) have both shown that relationship quality is a powerful predictor of transition into marriage. In short, it could be that the romantic relationships of fathers who trade fathering for bread-winning, might fare well in the short term, but not over time.

It is also true that such couples are often severely financially constrained. As Gibson-Davis and her colleagues (2005) found using these data, couples with satisfactory relationships do not feel ready for marriage unless they have achieved a certain economic standard—one that requires both to contribute economically. When the man is not working, or is working only a few hours a week, couples fall short of this bar. It is therefore not surprising that the only couple in this group who transitioned to marriage was the one in which the man had a full-time third-shift job.

Father Involvement in Couples Plagued with Problems

The men in couples plagued with problems tend to have lower and more erratic levels of father involvement than their counterparts. Some exhibit immature behavior in their relationships and in their fathering—they want to play with their child and nothing else. If the baby is not fun, they are not interested. Although these fathers also fall into the playful helper category, we might more appropriately call them fun or nothing fathers. For other troubled couples, tumultuous times in their relationship create a breakup-makeup cycle. The volatility of their romance translates into volatility in father involvement, in large part because during some of the breakup periods, the father is out of the house altogether. I call these men rollercoaster relationship fathers. None of the fathers whose relationships are plagued with problems are in the family-first fathering category.

Helper and Playmate: Fun or Nothing Fathers

Paulo and Daisy, a Puerto Rican couple age twenty-one and twenty-two, are cohabiting at baseline even though they have five children together.[4] Previous research has shown that cohabitation is more stable and marriage-like among Puerto Ricans than other groups, though these unions still do not last as long on average as legal marriages (Landale and Fennelly 1992). Paulo and Daisy first got together when she was still a teenager and he was in his mid-twenties. He was engaged to another woman, she had a boyfriend. One night they watched a movie together. When Daisy realized she forgot her keys, she spent the night at Paulo's house—in a separate bed. Daisy's father kicked her out of the house after she failed to come home. Because Paulo felt responsible, he took her in to his family's house even though they objected. Daisy and Paulo spent the next few months shuttling between various family members' homes until they could get an apartment of their own. She then became pregnant with their first child together.

Then, as now, they fought all the time. Paulo has a history of dealing drugs and going to jail, but Daisy claims that has stopped since they got together. She does, however, worry about physical abuse, and he says she has a temper. They are unable to give examples of how the other person demonstrates love to them. Instead, she says, "we've been together six years now. He hasn't gotten me *anything* for my birthday." She also says that "the only time he shows me affection is when he's looking for something else." He says that she insults him, apologizes, and then expects to be "lovey-dovey." When he resists her because he is still upset, she says that when he wants affection, she will not respond to him as payback.

Even Paulo's father thinks these two are a bad match. Paulo tells a story of his father telling him to " 'go get somebody, find somebody new.' But I can't do that 'cuz I already have five kids with this woman. I can't just throw that away to go with somebody else." He cites the children as his reason to stay with Daisy, yet he is only moderately involved. He says he spends an hour a day with them "acting like a clown." When asked if he would like to spend more time with the children he says, "[n]o. I think I've had enough. . . . An hour's enough." Daisy asserts that Paulo does not have enough patience to help with the children. He does talk about wanting to do fun things with them when the children are older, such as go to Coney Island or go fishing.

Matt and Maria are another troubled Hispanic couple, twenty-three and twenty-two when their baby was born. Matt is interested only in the fun part of raising the child. Together off and on since they were fourteen years old, they broke up once when he cheated on her with her uncle's older girlfriend. Matt also spent fifteen months in jail. After he got out, at age fifteen, they wound up back at the same school and reunited. They had their first child together when Maria was eighteen, while she was still living with her grandmother. At about this time, Matt was also wounded by gunfire. By the time their second child was born and they entered our study, the couple had been living together in their own household for three years.

Matt gets very jealous when Maria leaves the house, even when she goes to do the laundry. She now takes their four-year-old son with her "because I know he tells his father everything, so I say I might as well take him. That way he can let his father know that I didn't do anything wrong." This jealousy exists even though Maria has never cheated on Matt and has in fact never even had another boyfriend.

Matt's immaturity in his relationship seems to translate into his fathering as well. When asked about his part in raising baby Nora, he points to the toys. The mother does most of the care work. Maria recounts that Matt will let the baby cry, waiting for her to finish whatever she is doing and then tend to the screaming baby. He concentrates on the pleasant aspects of parenting rather than on the work. He says, "I hug her. I love her. But the fun part hasn't started yet." From Maria's interview four years after the birth, when we talk with her a final time, we can see that he does take part in the fun and play portion of child rearing. When asked who takes care of the children, she responds, "Me, I don't play as much . . . so I'm not the playing type . . . but, that's Matt."

Oscar, a twenty-seven-year-old Latino father, also talks about his baby as being too young to be any fun. His live-in girlfriend Gloria, age thirty-four, complains that Oscar will only spend ten to fifteen minutes with the baby before giving him back to her. This is a couple with significant trust issues. They met because they lived in the same apartment building, and he let her in late one night when she forgot her key. They went up to his apartment starting drinking and wound up having sex. They did not talk again for a month, and she was very embarrassed. Then, when she saw him outside one day, she ran down to see if he would talk to her. He did, and they began dating. About two months later, they found she was pregnant. She, however, is extremely distrustful of his fidelity to her. She recounts the following story: "One time, he came home. It was twelve-thirty at night. And I was standing outside like a nut, with a ball bat. That's how crazy I am. When he came [home] . . . I waited for him, and I said, 'You son of a gun! You BASTARD!' He said, 'I was WORKING! I was WORKING!' I said, 'Swear to God!' He swears. He has to swear to me, and that's bad too." Early on she kicked him out of their apartment because they argued so often, but decided to give him another chance after Princess Diana died. She thought, what if "something happens . . . imagine I don't give him a second chance."

Rollercoaster Relationship Fathers

Couples with rollercoaster relationships have the rockiest father-child bonds. Because their romantic relationships are so volatile, the men are often in and out of these relationships. This means that, at least some of the time, they are not living with their children. Cheating, drugs, abuse, and money problems are all common issues for these mercurial couples, and the overall level and quality of men's fathering is very low.

Marilyn and Damian, both African American, twenty-nine and twenty-four, have an extremely tumultuous relationship. Both are attorneys, which makes them unusual in this predominantly low-income sample with very few college graduates. In the seven years before they conceived their daughter, Trista, they broke up and made up several times. When they discovered that Marilyn was pregnant, they had been about to break up again. This couple has a long history of infidelity. Both had cheated on the other. Marilyn's cheating was limited to reuniting with one ex-boyfriend whenever she and Damian broke up or had a particularly big fight. Damian cheated with multiple partners multiple times, even he admits: "monogamy is a big problem for me." The pregnancy was a complete surprise because they had tried earlier in their relationship to get pregnant and failed.

Marilyn and Damian continue to break up and make up throughout the course of our study. A year after their daughter is born, they have broken up. Four years later, they are again broken up, but only after reuniting long enough to have another child together. They reunited because Damian sued her for joint custody of Trista and won. He had complained to the judge that she was not allowing him visitation, though Marilyn says he saw the baby three to six hours per week. She also says that he has such an intense work schedule that three to six hours was the most he could have seen her anyway. According to Marilyn, he told her he would drop the issue before the placement decision was made if they got back together. Marilyn did not want to be separated from her daughter, and so they did. There was more cheating on Damian's part, but they also conceived the second child. Although Marilyn says she had not been with anyone else, Damian is still considering a paternity test. They fight about money, about work hours, about care work, and about cheating. Damian also has a story about Marilyn striking him during one fight and his pushing her back.

At the time of the focal child's birth, Marilyn and Damian are living together, and he is somewhat involved with the child. He shares in making up the bottles and helps with night duty feedings. One significant source of tension related to care work has to do with caring for the baby in the morning. Damian does the morning tasks in part because Marilyn does not like to get up in the morning. This irritates him. Not only does he think she should get up to care for Trista, he also thinks she needs to get to work earlier to get more billable hours in. Marilyn, on the other hand, asserts that Damian does not do enough for the child. She also complains that when he does care for her, he has to ask Marilyn for directions every few minutes.

Gabriella, Puerto Rican and twenty-two, and Travis, African American and twenty-five, are another on-again, off-again couple. They have economic problems that force them to live with her mother. Their other major source of conflict is his other "baby mama." They fight about her because the baby mama tries to make Gabriella think that Travis is still seeing her. A year after the birth, Gabriella has fled to Puerto Rico with the baby while pregnant with a second child. Gabriella first called the police, accusing Travis of physical abuse. When the police arrested him and took him to jail, she packed and fled the country. Although Travis considers them to be broken up, Gabriella still calls and writes letters saying she will return. He says that at the very least, he would like her to return to the United States so that he can have visitation rights. By the time the child turns two, Gabriella is back and the couple is living together again.

Even at baseline, when they were living together, Travis was not an involved father. He worked a second-shift job and Gabriella went to work early in the morning. Rather than perform any care work in those morning hours, he allowed Gabriella's mother to do it all, a sign of his detachment.

All three of the fathers who qualify as highly involved in table 7.1 are in rollercoaster relationships. For two of these men, at round one, the couple relationship and their level of father involvement were at the top of the hill. As the relationships plummet, the men disappear from the lives of their children. One of them, a nineteen-year-old black father named

Lamar, only gets to see his child when his ex-partner's new boyfriend secretly arranges meetings for him. This is indicative of how tumultuous such father-child relationships can be. Jazz, a twenty-one-year-old black father from Chicago, is the one man in a rollercoaster relationship who maintains a high level of father involvement throughout the study, but none of these men quality as family-first fathers. Interestingly, though his relationship with nineteen-year-old Keisha is filled with stories of his house arrest, suspicions of cheating, actual cheating, and physical abuse, this couple lives together throughout the study. Their relationship is rocky, but it is not characterized by the on-again, off-again nature of the other couples in this category.

Discussion

Overall, we can see that the happy and stable couples and the happy but problems exist couples are more like one another in their father involvement patterns than the couples plagued with problems. Many of the fathers in happy and stable couples, like Eduardo and Jack, are helpers and playmates more than they are take-charge fathers. Fathers who have happy relationships with a few problems thrown in—such as Myron and Moises—are often helpers and playmates as well. The main difference between these two groups is that in couples with problems, the mothers complain about the need to provide more care work guidance. Recall that for Moises, Antonia needed to post the baby's schedule in the kitchen because he had no idea what it was. Also, Myron needed to prove to Suzanne that he would wake up if the baby cried before she would leave Johnny alone with him. This is not unlike their having had to prove themselves as partners. In the happy and stable couples, however, no tension surrounds the helper status. The mothers are happy with the way care work is split and have positive things to say about the contributions their partners make as fathers. A good example is Abigail describing Jack as "yummy," not because he does so much care work, but because he likes to spend time playing with children.

Some of the fathers in both happy and stable couples and happy with problems couples are highly involved with their children. Although the outcome is the same, the process looks somewhat different. Family-first fathers in happy and stable relationships, such as Ryan and Brian, tend to be so because of their strong ideological commitment to the family. They often work different hours than their partners, but have chosen this arrangement to make sure the baby is always with a parent. For the happy couples with economic problems, the men are often pushed into family-first fathering because they are not currently working for pay. They wind up enjoying how the care work is distributed, but it did not originate out of a desire for family time. The bond with the family is an unintended consequence, in part generated by the guilt such men feel for not fulfilling their role as breadwinners.

These findings are in sharp contradiction to some literature based on nationally representative survey samples. In her analysis, Julie Brines finds that the men who are *most* economically dependent on their wives do the *least* housework, as unemployed, underemployed, and low-paid men do almost none. Her interpretation is that they seek to compensate for the damage to their masculinity from their failure to be providers. They therefore "do gender" in another classic way—by refusing to do housework (Brines 1994). This compensatory model does not seem to hold for my sample. Men are compensating, but they are doing so by more fully embracing the fathering role, not by fleeing gender-typed household tasks. Could it be, as Maureen Waller's research with low-income unmarried African American fathers in Trenton, New Jersey, suggests, that at the bottom of the income distribution, where most of our happy with problems couples are, men now define fathering as a worthy masculine endeavor? (2002).

The couples plagued by problems, such as Matt and Maria, fight about care work in addition to everything else. For some of these fathers, the immature behavior that causes problems in their relationship also causes them to neglect all fatherly duties except play. For many, it is just another of the many problems the couple already has. These couples are not just fighting about their relationship, hitting, cheating, and drugs—they also fight about who is doing what for the child. Like Marilyn and Damian's, these relationships often become mired in a repetitive cycle of making up and breaking up. This volatility is not conducive to creating or maintaining a consistent fatherly bond.

Conclusion

Marcia Carlson and Sara McLanahan concluded that "the current initiatives to promote relationship quality and healthy marriage by increasing unmarried parents' relationship skills might yield benefits for parenting behaviors and, hence, for children" (2006, 315). Thus, it behooves us to look at the intersection of relationship quality and father involvement in the nuanced, in-depth manner that these rich, longitudinal, qualitative data allow.

I find that though the worst relationships do coincide with the least father involvement, the fathers most likely to be highly involved in their children's lives—the ones who split the care work equally with their partners—are those in the happy with problems group. These men are usually unemployed, cohabiting fathers. Interestingly, only one of these couples transitions to marriage—the father with the night job and the mother with the day job. It seems that when men do not fulfill their breadwinning rule, it does not matter whether they are highly involved as fathers. For the couple to transition into marriage, the man must be pulling his weight economically. It is not that most mothers expect to rely solely on men's earnings—most believe they should also do their share when possible—but full-time employment seems a necessary prerequisite for long-term relational stability. Recall, for example, that none of the fathers of couples in the happy and stable category were unemployed, though some mothers were. This suggests that, by focusing on relationship skills alone, healthy marriage initiatives will probably not address the key issues that prevent these couples from getting married. Although couples do hold high standards for relationship quality, and will not marry without it, marriage is not considered socially acceptable when finances are marginal.

For the couples who are plagued with problems, the same characteristics that make these men poor partners seem to make them poor fathers, and sometimes poor breadwinners. They are immature and have serious bad habits, such as chronic infidelity and problems with alcohol and drugs, that prevent them from being stable partners and fathers. Because many of these relationships are volatile, they are also on-again, off-again, leaving women solely responsible for the children when the couple is broken up. Based on the narratives, there seems to be less paternal bonding, leading to less involvement with children when the couples reunite. Even when the fathers in these relationships are stably living with their partner and child, however, they seem unwilling to engage in any kind of care work they do not think of as fun—the same attitude that they take with their partner relationship. For the fathers who only want to focus on fun aspects of coupling and fathering, perhaps "healthy marriage" training could be beneficial. For those in truly rocky relationships, ending the couple relationship altogether may, in fact, be most beneficial for the children and the parents, because instability is often harmful to children (Amato 1996; Caspi and Elder 1988).

Causal order is difficult to discern here. In some cases, it seems clear that relationship quality affects level of father involvement. This seems especially true for the weakest relationships. When relationships go bad, the father is often kicked out of the house, at least temporarily, which may diminish his level of involvement when the couple reunites, though it is worth pointing out that few of the fathers who got kicked out were very involved. In other cases, it seems clear that father involvement affects couple relationship quality. For example, some fathers say that they demonstrate love to their partner by taking care of the children and helping out around the house. Some women claim that part of the reason they love their partner is how good he is with the children. My conclusion is that the two are often mutually reinforcing.

Notes

1. Time-use studies that used the Panel Study of Income Dynamics data set do have samples that are representative of the United States (for example, see Sandberg and Hofferth 2001; Yeung et al., 2001).

2. One man reports cheating on his girlfriend early on in the relationship, but he claims to have "grown up" since then. Another man, with a history of alcoholism in his family, was a drinker when the couple first started dating. Phillip actually received a DUI on his way to propose to Kaitlyn after knowing her for only a week. She put her foot down, he changed his behavior. Now, years later, he will have an occasional beer but nothing more. Friends and family comment on the good influence she has been on him.

3. Race of the father does not seem to affect father involvement in any consistently patterned way in the sample used for this paper. Neither does sex of the child. It is true that in the larger TLC3 sample (N = 75), there are a handful of fathers who express resistance to bathing or changing a dirty diaper for a daughter, but not a son. These resistant fathers are disproportionately Latino, but they are also disproportionately in non-coresidential relationships with their children, so most are not included in this analysis.

4. The oldest child is hers from a previous relationship. She had this son at sixteen years of age. Paulo raises him as his own.

References

Amato, Paul R. 1996. "Explaining the Intergenerational Transmission of Divorce." *Journal of Marriage and the Family* 58(4): 628–40.

Barber, Benjamin K. 1987. "Marital Quality, Parental Behaviors and Adolescent Self-Esteem." *Family Perspective* 21(4): 244–68.

Belsky, Jay, Lise Youngblade, Michael Rovine, and Brenda Volling. 1991. "Patterns of Marital Change and Parent-Child Interaction." *Journal of Marriage and the Family* 53(2): 487–98.

Brayfield, April. 1995. "Juggling Jobs and Kids: The Impact of Employment Schedules on Fathers Caring for Children." *Journal of Marriage and the Family* 57(2): 321–32.

Brines, Julie. 1994. "Economic Dependency, Gender, and the Division-of-Labor at Home." *American Journal of Sociology* 100(3): 652–88.

Carlson, Marcia, and Sara McLanahan. 2006. "Strengthening Unmarried Families: Could Enhancing Couple Relationships also Improve Parenting?" *Social Service Review* 80(2): 297–321.

Carlson, Marcia, Sara S. McLanahan, and Paula England. 2004. "Union Formation in Fragile Families." *Demography* 41(2): 237–61.

Caspi, Avshalom, and Glen H. Elder, Jr. 1988. "Emergent Family Patterns: The Intergenerational Construction of Problem Behavior and Relationships" In *Relationships within Families*, edited by Robert A. Hinde and Joan Stevenson-Hinde. New York: Oxford University Press.

Cowan, Carolyn P., and Philip A. Cowan. 1992. *When Partners Become Parents: The Big Life Change for Couples.* New York City: Basic Books.

Erel, Osnat, and Bonnie Burman. 1995. "Interrelatedness of Marital Relations and Parent-Child Relations: A Meta-Analytic Review." *Psychological Bulletin* 118(1): 108–32.

Gibson-Davis, Christina, Kathryn Edin, and Sara McLanahan. 2005. "High Hopes but Even Higher Expectations: A Qualitative and Quantitative Analysis of the Marriage Plans of Unmarried Couples Who are New Parents." *Journal of Marriage and Family* 67(5): 1301–12.

Kitzmann, Katherine M. 2000. "Effects of Marital Conflict on Subsequent Triadic Family Interactions and Parenting." *Developmental Psychology* 36(1): 3–13.

Landale, Nancy S., and Katherine Fennelly. 1992. "Informal Unions among Mainland Puerto Ricans: Cohabitation or an Alternative to Legal Marriage?" *Journal of Marriage and the Family* 54(2): 269–80.

Lindahl, Kristin M., and Neena M. Malik. 1999. "Observations of Marital Conflict and Power: Relations with Parenting in the Triad" *Journal of Marriage and the Family* 61(2): 320–30.

McLanahan, Sara, Irwin Garfinkel, Nancy E. Reichman, Julien Teitler, Marcia Carlson, and Christina N. Audigier. 2001. *The Fragile Families and Child Wellbeing Study Baseline Report.* Princeton, N.J.: Center for Research on Child Wellbeing.

Nock, Stephen L., and Paul W. Kingston. 1988. "Time with Children: The Impact of Couples' Work-Time Commitments." *Social Forces* 67(1): 59–85.

Presser, Harriet B. 1988. "Shift Work and Child Care among Young Dual-Earner American Parents." *Journal of Marriage and the Family* 50(1): 133–48.

———. 1994. "Employment Schedules among Dual-Earner Spouses and the Division of Household Labor by Gender." *American Sociological Review* 59(3): 348–64.

Sandberg, John F., and Sandra L. Hofferth. 2001. "Changes in Children's Time with Parents: United States, 1981–1997" *Demography* 38(4): 423–36.

Waller, Maureen R. 2002. *My Baby's Father: Unmarried Parents and Paternal Responsibility.* Ithaca, N.Y.: Cornell University Press.

Yeung, W. J., John F. Sandberg, Pamela E. Davis-Kean, Sandra L. Hofferth. 2001. "Children's Time with Fathers in Intact Families." *Journal of Marriage and the Family* 63(1): 136–54.

Chapter 8

Blended but Not the Bradys: Navigating Unmarried Multiple Partner Fertility

LINDSAY M. MONTE

I N THE fall of 1969, ABC television launched a new show with a somewhat daring premise for the times: a mother with three daughters who married a widower with three boys. For the next five seasons, the small stories of this large blended family would be a staple of ABC's primetime lineup. That show, of course, was the Brady Bunch, which not only enjoyed the success of its original run, but has also been a hit in syndicated reruns ever since the end of the final season.

The premise was the not new, but still novel, practice of blended families. At the time of that first episode, roughly 10 percent of all American children under eighteen were living in a remarried step-family (Glick 1980), though prior to the divorce boom of the late 1960s and the 1970s, most of these stepfamilies were still formed following the death of a parent (Cherlin 1992). Now the majority are formed following a divorce (Ganong and Coleman 2004), more repartnered couples are electing to live together rather than marry and one-quarter of all cohabitations now include children from a previous union (Coleman, Ganong, and Fine 2000). Further, research has shown that these stepfamilies are often highly unstable (Bumpass, Raley, and Sweet 1995) and confer fewer benefits to children than those formed by marriage following parental death (Manning and Lamb 2003). However, the mechanisms for these effects are unclear. This chapter provides an inductive examination of the family processes in unmarried stepfamilies.

Background

Rising rates of cohabitation (Bumpass, Raley, and Sweet 1995), substantial growth in nonmarital childbearing (Terry-Humen, Manlove, and Moore 2001), and increases in multiple partner fertility (Carlson and Furstenberg 2006) have led to the emergence of a new kind of stepfamily, distinguished both by marital status and by high rates of multiple partner fertility. More than 30 percent of all births are now to unmarried couples (Martin et al. 2006), 60 percent of whom have other children from previous unions (Carlson and Furstenberg 2006). Further, roughly 30 percent of U.S. children will spend at least some time in a remarried or cohabiting stepfamily before reaching adulthood (Coleman, Ganong, and Fine 2000), and unmarried stepfamilies make up 25 percent of all stepfamilies in the United States (Seltzer 2000).

To date, there are few studies which address unmarried couples with at least one shared child and children from previous unions, which I refer to as unmarried stepfamilies (Ganong and Coleman 2004). However, we know that multiple partner fertility is correlated with early childbearing, being African American, having less education, and histories of substance abuse or incarceration, and is three times higher among unmarried than among married parents (Carlson and Furstenberg 2006; Mincy 2002). The hazard of being in an unmarried stepfamily is thus much greater among the otherwise disadvantaged (Blank 1997).

Further, a child born to a mother who has children from another union is more likely to experience parental breakup, though there are no effects on the likelihood that the parents will cohabit or marry. In contrast, in cases where the father has children from past unions, chances of cohabitation and marriage are diminished, but the likelihood of separation is unaffected (Carlson, McLanahan, and England 2004). Additionally, there is evidence that unmarried fathers, like divorced fathers, often withdraw from children after separation from the child's mother (Carlson, McLanahan, and Brooks-Gunn 2005).

The growing prevalence and apparent fragility of unmarried stepfamilies, and the advantages both children and adults glean from being in a stable, two-parent family (see, for example, McLanahan and Sandefur 1994; Waite and Gallager 2000), all mandate a more in-depth understanding of the complex family dynamics of unmarried stepparent families.

The TLC3 Unmarried Stepfamily Sample

The Fragile Families and Child Well-being Study (henceforth Fragile Families) and Time, Love and Cash Among Couples with Children (henceforth TLC3) dataset have many obvious strengths, such as in-depth instruments, a longitudinal design and the inclusion of fathers. However, for this analysis, TLC3 offers an additional benefit—data on a broad range of stepfamily forms, which permit a more complete picture of the lives of these unmarried stepfamilies than traditional research has allowed. That is, the families represented here include both couples where she brings a child into the relationship (similar to the remarried couples who are usually the subject of stepfamily research), as well as both the less well-understood couples in which only the father has other children and couples in which both parents do.

The basic question I address is how the presence of these children, either inside or outside the household, affects couple dynamics. Drawing from rich couple narratives, I explore the ways in which these parents define themselves as parents and stepparents, and the ways they perceive the benefits and challenges of their divided and reconstituted families.

I focus on the twenty-seven TLC3 couples who were unmarried at the birth of their child, in which at least one of the parents has a child or children by a previous partner or partners (regardless of the age or custodial status of these children), and for whom longitudinal data were available.[1] In five cases, only the mother has a child by a previous partner, in eleven, only the father does, and in the remaining eleven, both parents do. In all but three cases, all of the mothers' children live with the couple, and all of the fathers' children live elsewhere (see table 8.1).[2] For two of these families with different residential patterns, both the mother's and the father's children live elsewhere; in the final case, one of the father's other children live with the TLC3 couple.[3]

Although I draw on the widely understood vocabulary of remarried stepfamilies, available terms do not capture the complexity of typical familial relations in this unmarried stepfamily sample. For example, more than one in four of these parents of other children have children with three or more partners, and only four of the thirty-five parents of children by previous partners were ever married to any other parent. However, despite this complexity, in discussing these children and their parents, the TLC3 couples often simply refer to them as his or her "other baby," and the "other baby mama," or "other baby daddy." Therefore, in addition to the terminology of stepfamilies, I also refer to the children that a parent had with someone else not only as stepchildren, but also as "other" children. Similarly, I call the parents of these other children the "other" parents and, occasionally, previous partners, though this last is not always temporally accurate, given that some parents go back and forth between partners (see chapter 5, this volume).

The Analysis: Stepfamily Tensions

What follows is an inductive examination of four waves of qualitative interviews over a four-year span with twenty-seven unmarried couples with both shared children and children by previous partners. It is these children by other partners who set this subsample apart from the rest of the TLC3 parents; virtually all of the TLC3 mothers and fathers say they

Table 8.1   Unmarried Stepfamily Sample

Couple	Other Children Live with Couple	Other Children Live Apart from Couple	Couple Breaks Up	Couple Marries
She has other children, he does not				
Cache & Raheem	M			X
Claudia & Don	M			
Gloria & Oscar	M			
Melissa & Ted	M			
Samantha & Ali	M			
He has other children, she does not				
Calista & Gavin		F		
Camille & Freddie		F	X	
Christina & Justin		F		
Dahlia & Tony		F		
Janell & Leonard		F		X
Katrice & Tim		F		
NaKeisha & Reggie	F	F		X
Priscilla & Rafael		F	X	
Sherise & Anton		F	X	
Tamika & George		F	X	
Veronica & Jason		F		
Both have other children				
Adrienne & Ollie	M	F	X	
Beverly & Andre	M	F		
Ciana & Kenneth		M&F		
Daisy & Paulo	M	F		
Delilah & Trevor	M	F	X	
Gabriella & Travis	M	F		
LaShawnda & Tyrone	M	F		X
Lauren & Michael	M	F	X	X
Michelle & Daryl	M	F		X
Rochelle & Alex	M	F		X
Tabitha & Howie		M&F		

Source: Author's compilation.
Note: M denotes children of the mother, F denotes children of the father.

had had at least one serious romantic relationship prior to the focal partnership, but only 42 percent had children from those unions. Therefore, I limit my analysis to the couples for whom either the mother, the father, or both, have children from previous partnerships. These parents range in age from nineteen to thirty-five, with a mean age of twenty-four for women and twenty-six for men. Roughly 60 percent are African American, some 30 percent are Hispanic (largely Puerto Rican and Mexican American), and about 10 percent are white. Sixteen mothers and twenty-two fathers have children by previous partners. For seven of the couples, the focal child was not the first they had had together.

The couple's relationship history is taken from the baseline couple interview. All other data are drawn from interviews conducted with each partner separately during each interview wave. I focus on those portions of narratives that dealt with the ongoing dynamics of the relationship, especially any conflict or problems the couple was facing, the parenting of children within the household, any information on contact with either children outside the household or previous partners with whom parents have had children.

"It Takes More than Blood To Be a Parent"

The central message these unmarried couples send is that it is investment and time that make a true parent, not shared genetics. Perhaps due to the prevalence of absent or incarcerated fathers, the biological parentage of a child is viewed as less important than fulfilling the role of being a parent, which is evidenced in the amount of time, emotion, and personal and financial support that a partner invests in a child. Cache, who was twenty-four years old when she entered the study, is an African American mother of four children by three fathers. Her current partner is Raheem, the twenty-two-year-old (at the start of the study) African American biological father of her youngest child. However, Raheem also plays the role of father of her two middle children. She says, "Raheem be both of their daddies, 'cause he was with (my daughter) from the time she was born, and he was with my son since he was eight months."[4]

The importance of stepfathers for these families should not be underestimated. In keeping with the general population, most mothers' children by prior partners lived with her, and in more than two-thirds of these cases, these children's fathers were either not involved or only marginally involved with the child. Perhaps because of the absence of so many biological fathers, both the mothers and fathers in our story pointed to the primacy of the social father role.

Ali, an African American father of two biological children, both with his current partner, was twenty-five when he was first interviewed. He told us that he acted as father to all four children in their household, including his two stepchildren, whose father was absent, saying, "my main point is, you know, as far as kids today in this society, it's very important for (them to have a father figure). . . . It don't have to be their father, but an authority figure, you know? Somebody to be around." Similarly, Ted, a white father who was thirty-four when he was first interviewed, says of his relationship with his stepson, "if he ever has a problem, I'll be there for him. I consider that being a father."

The importance of this involvement leads many couples to make a clear distinction between "fathers" and "daddies." That is, in the words of many in this sample, a father may share a genetic link with the children, but the daddy is the one who raises them. Notably, other ethnographies have also found this distinction (Furstenberg, Sherwood, and Sullivan 1992), though in some samples, the meanings of the terms are reversed (Edin forthcoming; Waller 2002).

Beverly and Andre, both African American, were twenty-four and twenty-two when we first interviewed them. The focal child is their first child together, though both have children by previous relationships; Andre has a daughter, and Beverly has two sons by different men. When asked whether her boys had contact with their biological fathers, Beverly replied,

> I think it's really important because a child needs to know their father. . . . They need to know like, "he's my dad and he's the one who had [me with] my mom" and all this and that. Like, my oldest son, he knows who his daddy is just as well as he knows who his father is also. [Interviewer: "And what's the difference there?"] What's the difference? Andre take care of him, his father don't do anything for him, so when somebody says, "what's your daddy's name?" he's gonna tell him, "well, Andre is my daddy, but my real father's name is [so and so]" because he understands.

Further, "daddy" is a title of considerable esteem, and being worthy of the title was deemed an achievement in which a man could take pride. Andre compares himself to the largely absent biological father of Beverly's son this way: "I made it clear to them that they can't choose between me and him. I made it clear to them that I'm your daddy." Andre feels he has worked hard to earn daddy status, and is unwilling to be supplanted just because he did not biologically father the boys.

On the flip side, however, many of the noncoresidential fathers in the TLC3 sample are also adamant that it is not right for their other children's mother to allow another man to replace them. Tony, a Hispanic father who was thirty-one years old when the study began, has three children by three previous partners. When the new husband of one wanted custody of Tony's daughter, Tony said, "as long as I'm breathing, sorry, can't do it." Similarly, Michelle, a white mother who was twenty years old when she was first interviewed, said her son's father would not let her son call her current partner dad. "[His father] said, 'that's not his dad . . . that'll never be until the day I die.' "

That these fathers stake such claims to their paternal identities is particularly noteworthy given how few of them are active in their noncoresidential children's lives. Although some of this father absence is likely due to either maternal gatekeeping or paternal disinterest in the responsibilities of fatherhood (see chapter 9, this volume), it is also important to note that one-quarter of the absent fathers are incarcerated at the time the focal parents are first interviewed, and several more (including several focal fathers) spend time in jail over the course of the study. Their noninvolvement may thus be involuntary and the importance of staking claim to the title of daddy such that it lasts through such separations may therefore be particularly important for these fathers.

No such semantic distinction exists for those mothers whose partners had other children, however; all made sure to make it clear that they were "stepmom," not "mommy." This is probably a reflection of both the residential status of these children (in only one case does his other child live with the couple) as well as the importance and sanctity of the role of mother in those same communities (Edin and Kefalas 2005; Senior 1991).

"They Are Not MY Kids, You Know"

Despite assertions that investment in children outweighs biology, the importance of biological ties is nonetheless still evident in these parental narratives. In all but two cases, parents make clear distinctions between his children and her children, though most are also quick to claim they don't treat his, hers, and our kids differently. When we asked Ted whether his partner received child support from her ex, he said, "she doesn't pursue it because I treat [her son] like he is mine. And I don't slight him in any way. I don't treat him any different."

However, even as parents assert parallel treatment of other kids, there are evident differences depending on whether stepchildren live with the couple, which often results in differences for his and her children by previous partners. That is, children living in the household (usually hers) are more likely to be targeted for emotional and personal investment, and noncoresidential stepchildren (usually his) more often receive financial support. Thus, Ted says of his stepson, who lives with them, " I'll never turn my back on him. Anything he needs and wants in life, I will help him achieve," and Beverly says of her stepdaughter who does not live with them that, "we [spend] the same amount of money as we do on our other kids." Moreover, three other stepmothers of noncoresidential stepchildren claimed they bought clothing or presents for their partner's other children whenever they bought something for their own children. None, though, told stories of more maternal activities such as reading to or cuddling with these children, even though the children often visited on weekends, holidays, and during summer vacation.

Further, fathers' children living elsewhere are often a key source of conflict in these couples, whereas mothers' children in the household are usually not. In fact, stepchildren living in the household seem to be a stabilizing factor and a force of cohesion for many couples, at least when the men embrace the daddy role. In sharp contrast, his other children living elsewhere often destabilize the relationship because they detract from time available to the couple or their shared family.

LaShawnda, an African American mother of two, the oldest by another partner, was twenty-seven at the outset of the study. Her partner Tyrone was twenty-nine, and also had a child from a previous relationship. She says that,

> . . . on [Tyrone's] off day he goes (and) gets his other daughter and she comes over and stay, so . . . we never have any time to ourselves. . . . I think maybe he feel like, since he's not [living] with his other daughter, you know, she probably feeling left out so he wanted [to be with her]. But . . . me and him still needs to spend time together, just the two of us.

LaShawnda says she understands how important it is for Tyrone to be a good father to his other daughter, but she still feels that she and her daughters pay a price.

Mothers are also sometimes jealous of their partner's emotional tie with his other children. Gabriella, a Puerto Rican mother of one who was twenty-two when she was first interviewed, and whose African American partner, Travis, is three years older than her and has two other children, says she feels that Travis dotes more on "his" children than on their shared child; "Sometimes I, I'll see that he love his other kids more than what he do . . . the baby. . . . He say he love 'em all the same, but . . . I think he care more about them than what he do for [the new baby.]" "He [always says] 'I miss my kids,'" she exclaims, but adds, "I think probably cause he live here with me, he sees the baby every day . . . [and] he don't see them like he sees her. . . ."

"The Problem I Have Is the Past"

Noncoresident children by previous partners are also the source of another common tension—conflict with, and jealousy of, the other parent of those children. The colloquial name for this conflict with and over prior partners—baby mama drama—reflects the fact that they are his more often than her previous partners who are the cause of this conflict. Andre explains why his visits to his other children seem to provoke so much tension, saying, "the streets say, 'you got a baby, and your baby's daddy got another girlfriend'—it's the streets that tell you that you got to fight [the other baby's mother]." Other families concur with stories of changed plans, withheld visitation, or even physical confrontations with the other baby mama (and occasionally the other baby daddy) that occur with a frequency that made them seem, as Andre implies, almost obligatory.

Although some of this conflict is likely due to the difficulty of co-parenting across households, there is also often a decidedly sexual element, with many parents saying that the reason the previous partners seek out these fights is jealousy of the new relationship. Andre says that neither he nor his current partner Beverly gets along with his ex-partner because "misery likes company. She don't want you to have what [she] don't have." Further, parents report that other mothers often seek to antagonize current partners by preying on fears of infidelity. Several mothers told stories of fathers' past partners calling them to insinuate they had an ongoing sexual relationship with the father. Even though no one reported that the allegations were true, most mothers reported that it did bother them; LaShawnda says, "the problem I have is the past—(his) baby mama, that's my problem."

This high level of sexual jealousy may seem extreme, but given the history of these relationships, parents' rationale becomes evident. In ten of the twenty-seven couples I analyze here, at least one of the pair was either involved with someone else or very newly "single" when the couple met. In fact, four of the fathers have other children the same age as the focal child, indicating that they were having sex with at least two women at roughly the same time. Where one relationship ends and another begins is thus not always clear, and these blurred boundaries give fears of infidelity with a previous partner an added edge.

Often, the war of baby mama drama is waged using children. Lauren, a black mother of two children by a prior marriage who was twenty-seven when we first interviewed her, says that the biggest problem in her relationship with her twenty-six-year-old partner, Michael, who has three children by a prior marriage, is conflict with his ex. She said, "there was a lot of drama with her. . . . She would keep the kids from him because me and him were together.   It was a big mess . . . baby mama drama." Similarly, Gabriella says of the mother of Travis's other children,

> She'll use her kids . . . 'cause she knows . . . he love his kids, seems like he can't be a whole week without 'em [or] he'll . . . get depressed . . . [and say] "I miss my kids. I haven't seen my kids." And she know that [if] she don't let him see the kids . . . he fittin' to be like sweating her. He fittin' to be on the phone like "can I please see my kids? Lemme see my kids. Why you don't let me see my kids. Let me just see 'em, at least for five minutes." So she'll just hang up and he'll call back. . . . And it's like she loving it, you know. So he'll go to the house and knock. She won't open. . . . So he'll leave and be feeling depressed [and] that's how she'll use the kids like that.

In contrast to baby mama drama, conflict with or over the mother's previous partners is both more explicitly jealous and less likely to be manifest in conflicts over visitation. For example, whereas Beverly and Andre struggle to survive the frequent onslaughts of Andre's previous partner, Andre seems consumed with jealousy over Beverly's only occasional contact with her other baby's father. He says he tells her, "he can't have you all. . . . I want all the love to myself. I want him to get *none*, because he gave up his [girlfriend] and kids. And he had the right to [be daddy, but] he gave that up."

Seven of the fifteen men who acted as stepfathers reported jealousy of their partner's other baby daddy, but these conflicts seldom rise to the level that might earn the designation baby daddy drama, probably largely due to how few of these other fathers are involved in their children's lives. Travis (the partner of Gabriella, introduced earlier) defended his feelings, saying, "I know from experience that the baby daddy can always have his way of coming back. It may not be sexually or mentally, but he's got some kind of involvement in that woman's life, a part that still cares for him." This perception may not be wholly unwarranted, for though only one father used the word "love" to describe his feelings for his ex, several of the mothers referred to their other baby's father as their "first love" or said that they were still in love with him. It is significant, however, that none of the mothers said they had renewed any romantic or sexual involvement with their other children's fathers.

The Frailties and Strengths of Blended Families

Questions of stability loom large for unmarried stepfamilies. Will their relationships succeed or fail? How will their complex family lives affect their ability and willingness to stay together as a family? I find that success for these unmarried stepfamilies takes two forms. Seven of the twenty-seven couples manage to get married by the study's end, about four years after the birth of the focal child.[5] Another fourteen "succeed" simply by making it to their child's fourth birthday without separating. The remaining seven are broken up by the end of the study.[6] To explain these variations, I highlight three couples who exemplify the primary patterns.

Couples Who Separate

Camille and Freddie are young, nineteen and twenty, when their first child together is born just before they were first introduced. Camille is African American and Freddie is Hispanic. They had met and flirted briefly at a mall five years earlier, but were then out of touch for several years before they met again and began dating in earnest, just over a year before the birth. Those intervening years prove important to their story because during that time Freddie had two children with another woman.

Camille's pregnancy with the TLC3 focal child, a girl, was unplanned and unexpected. Both Camille and Freddie say that they wanted to have a child together eventually, but felt unprepared for a child at that time. Camille was especially ambivalent because of Freddie's past and his other family. Freddie said, "Camille wants to be with somebody who doesn't drink, doesn't smoke . . . isn't a drug user . . . somebody who has a good education, good morals, goals, and no kids. . . . I might have only been her guy on looks."

By the time their daughter was born, the couple was living together some of the time, though Freddie went back and forth between her house and his mother's. From the beginning, his other kids and their mother were a common source of conflict. According to Freddie, "when the pregnancy came about . . . we started talking a lot about my kids," and, "her whole issue was, you know, she didn't know if she was going to be able to handle my having kids with somebody else. . . . When [Camille] looks at my kids, she knows that they're a part of me, but they're also a part of somebody else. And I don't think Camille is going to be able to live with the fact that I'm connected to somebody else, another female." His exasperation with her unwillingness to accept his other family is obvious as he reenacts his side of a recurring argument, "Obviously you do not like the fact that I have kids. [So] why did you continue the relationship knowing that I had kids? It's not like the kids are going to one day disappear." Camille, however, points to the hard realities of how Freddie's past will continue to affect her own life, saying, "I never want to have kids with someone who had kids, you know, for all the reasons that goes along with it—this girl [the mother of Freddie's other children] is going to be in my life forever, you know. . . . [we] are always including [his other kids] and [she] is right there. [That's not fair to me because] they're not my kids." Camille and Freddie separate and reunite several times in the months following their daughter's birth, but by the time their child turns two, both claim their relationship is over for good. Although Freddie's other family doesn't seem to be the primary reason for their breakup (she points to his infidelity and his lack of ambition and he points to her constant jealousy), it nonetheless clearly plays at least a secondary role.

The distinction between his and her children seems central to which of these couples' relationships dissolve. In only three of the seven who break up does the mother have any children by a previous partner, but all seven contain fathers with other children, and four of these are explicit about the fact that their problems were, at least in part, caused by his baby mama drama. So the question remains: does the fact that fathers have other children by past partners destabilize these couples' relationships, or does an underlying pattern of problem behavior lead both to the formation of complex families and to breakup?

Like Camille and Freddie, the other couples who break up are plagued with problems from the outset. Three are together only briefly, breaking up during their child's first year of life. Three of the seven have violent fights. One father is a drug addict, and a second is in and out of jail for drug dealing and domestic violence. A third is involved in both drugs and crime and, by his own admission, "can't" be faithful to just one woman (and has five other children by four women when the couple's focal child is born). A fourth couple got together while the father was on a "break" from another partner with whom he has a child, and to whom he returned after his separation from the focal mother.

Obviously, the causal direction is not clear. However, research suggests that an underlying pattern of problem behaviors, including unprotected sex with multiple partners, may in fact be the cause of some of the couples' multiple partner fertility, rather than the result of it (see, for example, Biglan et al. 2004). For this reason, it is perhaps unsurprising that this subset of couples includes those parents with children with the greatest number of other partners. At the birth of the focal child, three of the fourteen parents in this group have children with at least three partners, and another five parents have had children with at least three partners by the end of the study. Further, almost all of the fathers (six of seven) report that at least one of their children was unplanned.

Another feature of these relationships further bolsters this view; these are the couples in which the fathers are least involved with any of the coresidential children. It is possible that their problem behaviors limit their paternal involvement with their coresidential biological children and prohibit them from embracing the daddy role with regard to their stepchildren; this lack of paternal investment may, in turn, make relationships more subject to dissolution. The fact that many of these parents who separate from the other focal parent repartner with someone new by the end of the study lends further credence to the importance mothers place on having father figures for their children and the significance of paternal investment for familial stability. For example, five of the seven mothers go on to date, and three to marry, other men who step in to be daddy to their children, even over the brief four-year window of the TLC3 study. These social fathers, by the mothers' testimony, are filling the void left by the focal fathers and previous partners who seemed unwilling to become involved even when they lived with their children.

Couples Who Marry

LaShawnda and Tyrone, both African American, are twenty-seven and twenty-nine at the beginning of the study. Both have children by previous relationships: LaShawnda has a daughter whose father is incarcerated, and Tyrone has a daughter with whom he is in regular contact. Like Camille and Freddie, they knew each other and dated briefly several years before becoming a serious couple. After an interlude of over a decade, during which both had children with someone else, they ran into each other again on a train platform. They started dating again shortly thereafter, moving in together within a year.

As was true for Camille and Freddie, Tyrone's other child and her mother prove problematic for the couple from the beginning. LaShawnda complained once about the frequent intrusion of his other daughter into their own family time, but his response was not what she had hoped for; "he was trying to say as if, you know, I didn't like his daughter. And I never said anything about [that]. It's kind of messed up with that situation. That's like the biggest problem [we have]—his other daughter and her mother." According to LaShawnda, not only was his other child jealous of their daughter, but the other mother was controlling and treated Tyrone in a degrading manner; LaShawnda was frustrated that he refused to take a stand with her.

As time goes by, Tyrone sees his other daughter less and less and LaShawnda and Tyrone get married. The wedding seems a natural step for the two. As LaShawnda says, "we had a baby and we was living together already, so [we were] in a committed relationship," and Tyrone added, "I just felt like it was the time to ask her to marry [me]." However, the price of this couple's stability seems to be the severing of ties between Tyrone and his other daughter. By the time the focal child is four, Tyrone hasn't seen or talked to the other daughter for at least six months. LaShawnda says the girl's mother is keeping him from his daughter because she's jealous over their wedding, "its like, after we got married, he [wasn't] able to see her. [Our marriage] was a big thing [for the other mom]. You know, before we were married, he could see [his daughter]. He'd get her on his off days. Then once we like said 'I do,' well 'I don't want my daughter over there' and things like that."

Among the couples who marry, involvement with other children versus investment in the new blended family seems to be a zero sum game. In all cases, the new family wins out. In four of the seven couples who marry, both parents have children by other partners, and in the remaining three, one mother and two fathers have other children. However, three important themes emerge that help to explain the trajectories of these couples: all but one have coresidential stepchildren, all but two of the other fathers are largely absent, and all but two of the focal fathers either start off as, or become over the course of the study, absent fathers to their other children outside the home. This presence of a ready-made "inside" family, with minimal "outside" distractions, may be what enables these couples to overcome the challenges of stepfamily life.

The noninvolvement of fathers with their children who do not live with them appears to be a key factor in allowing these families to move into marriage. Thus, though LaShawnda fumes when the mother of Tyrone's daughter no longer allows him to see his child, it is also clear that a source of tension has been removed. Without regular visitation with their other children, these fathers have reduced interaction with former partners, and the baby mama drama that so frequently plagued the couples who break up is a fairly rare event. In fact, the only couple who does report this kind of ongoing tension divorces soon after they marry.

Notably, these couples are almost as likely to include a father with children outside the home (six out of seven) as fathers in couples who break up, though far fewer couples include only a father's noncoresident children (four out of seven versus one out of seven). Thus, all but one of these households contain at least one coresidential stepchild, and the investment of these stepparents in those stepchildren also appears to buffer the families against some of the problems faced by the couples who separate. For example, LaShawnda and Tyrone clearly perceive the intrusion of his other daughter in their lives, though no such problem exists with her other daughter, who lives with them. Although her daughter is not his biological child, the family has grown up around her and her presence is accepted in the same way as their daughter together. Other couples were similarly explicit about the parental roles that stepparents took with stepchildren in the household.

Thus, little or no interaction with outside influences, particularly his other children and their mothers, serves to strengthen (or at least, reduce distractions from) the new family's bond. A key source of sexual jealousy and persistent conflict is gone, and with the additional absence of her children's fathers, any reminder that the stepchildren in the household are not actually shared children is removed. The result is greatly simplified familial interactions, which appears to be part of what enables these couples to marry.

Couples Who Stay Together But Do Not Marry

Gabriella is a twenty-two-year-old Puerto Rican mother of two children—a son by a previous relationship, and a daughter with Travis, the focal father. Travis is black, was twenty-five when he was first interviewed, and had two other children with another woman when his daughter with Gabriella was born. The couple is living together at baseline, along with their daughter and Gabriella's son. Travis's other children live elsewhere, but he is in fairly regular contact with them. Gabriella and Travis met and began dating less than a year before the birth of their child, and though they have had some brief separations, they have basically been together ever since.

From the first interview, the problems of their blended family are evident. Gabriella was jealous of the attention that Travis paid to his other children when they all spent time together, and her jealousy led Travis to be secretive about the visits he makes to see those children at their mother's home. When Gabriella discovered that Travis had taken his other children and their mother to a WIC[7] appointment, she was outraged. His outrage in response matched hers: "I'm not gonna tell you no more when I'm going go over there if you fittin' to keep on getting mad. . . . I'm just gonna go over there, and I'm not even fittin' to let you know when. . . ." However, the problems are not merely a product of Gabriella's imagination. Both agree that the other mother seems set on creating problems for Gabriella and Travis's family, abruptly refusing to grant Travis access to the children or trying to find ways of keeping Travis at her house long enough to make Gabriella worry. In contrast, the father of Gabriella's older child is nowhere to be seen.

One year after the birth of their baby, the couple is still together and Gabriella is pregnant with their second child. Meanwhile, Travis's relationship with his other children and their mother continues to cause turmoil. Gabriella doesn't mind if he sees his children so long as he does so at his own mother's home and not his ex-partner's apartment. Travis explains, saying,

> She care (if) I was over [at the other mother's house] to get them—messing with the mama. Because the other babies' mama plays some games. . . . That's a promise [the other mother] made to me a long time ago. She said she would do anything to have me [and] if she couldn't have me then nobody would have me. . . . She promised me that she would make sure she would interfere with anything.

By their first child's second birthday, this couple says their problems with the other mother continue, though they are alleviated somewhat by the fact that she is now denying him access to his children more frequently. Gabriella says she does so out of jealousy over the apparent success of Travis's new relationship, and so while Travis still pays child support for these children, he is only rarely allowed to see them. However, this jealousy is not one-sided. In the three years they have been together, Gabriella's discovery of Travis's secret visits to see his kids have caused brief breakups, and the other mother's jealousy and game-playing briefly landed Travis in jail after she falsely accused him of beating her, a charge she later recanted.

Problems continued into the fourth year of our study. Travis is back in contact with his other children, but the other mother continues to be antagonistic toward both Travis and Gabriella. Travis's child support payments also cause them some conflict, because Gabriella feels that the outflow of money threatens her own family's financial stability. Gabriella and Travis keep their finances separate as a result, even though they have now been living together for more than five years and have two children together. The couple has discussed the possibility of marriage only once, and though neither thinks the relationship is on the verge of breakup, neither do they say that they think it is necessarily a permanent arrangement.

A common feature in the lives of the couples who remain together outside of marriage is the continued involvement of fathers with all of the parents' children: his children living outside the household, her children living with the couple, and the couple's children together. For example, despite Gabriella's concern at the beginning of our study that Travis might love his other children more than their baby, two years later, she is convinced that he is the "kind of father [who] love [all] his kids." They and the other couples who remain together without marriage are distinct from the couples who break up in that the men are generally invested in both their own children, both inside and outside the home, and in their roles as stepfathers.

Further, treating coresidential stepchildren as one would one's own children is more the rule than the exception among the unmarried success stories. Four of the seven unmarried couples with coresidential step-children[8] are explicit that the father is daddy to her kids, which is indicative of these fathers' investment in these stepchildren. However, unlike fathers in couples who eventually marry, for these couples, investment in children who live elsewhere doesn't dwindle—virtually all of these fathers remained in contact with their other children throughout the course of the study. This allegiance to multiple families may be what prevents these families from making the transition to marriage.

Another common characteristic of this group is that in seven of the nine couples in which the mother has a child by a previous partner, the other fathers are not involved with those children. As with the couples who eventually marry, this may contribute to the ability of these couples to stay together. That is, where previous partners are notably present in the lives of those families that fail and notably absent among the couples who marry, among these unmarried-but-still-together families, the absence of at least the one of the other parents—the other father—may insulate them somewhat from the risks imposed by the complex family they've ended up in.

It is clear from Gabriella and Travis's ongoing story, spelled out in more than a thousand pages of interview narrative over four years, that these two factors have played a significant role in keeping them on their particular trajectory. His continued involvement with his other children, and, more important, the fact that this involvement allows the children's other mother to continue to cause baby mama drama puts continual stress on the relationship. However, Tyrone, like most other fathers in this group, faces no competition from another man in his quest to fulfill the daddy role in the life of Gabriella's oldest son, which is a unique point of simplicity in an otherwise complex family.

Discussion

Like married stepfamilies, unmarried couples with children by multiple partners must navigate the difficult, and often competing, roles of partner, parent, ex and stepparent, frequently all at the same time. However, unlike married stepfamilies, they must do it often without the legal guarantees of marriage or formal visitation arrangements with their former partners. It is also true that, on average, there are simply more children involved in these couples' lives, and by more partners. For these complex families, it is clear that the fact that one or both parents have children by previous partners at the outset plays a key role in the kind of families they become over time.

Investment and involvement appear to be the key factors for both stability and matrimony for these unmarried stepfamilies, though the effects appear to be different for children inside and outside the home. A stepparent's investment in and involvement with coresidential stepchildren seems to cement the family together, whereas a stepparent who maintains emotional distance from a partner's children in the household is more likely to separate from that partner. By contrast, a parent's investment and involvement with children living elsewhere often proves divisive, detracting from time and attention available to the new family, whereas reduced or noninvolvement over time allows the new family to solidify and stabilize.

This is particularly evident for fathers, for whom investment in the new family unit, and freedom from the distraction of the old, are key factors for both staying together and making the transition to marriage. This presents men with a paradox that mothers don't often face; staying involved with children from previous partnerships may be beneficial from the standpoint of those children, but detrimental from the standpoint of the children he has with a new partner. In sum, in the most successful couples, mothers replace other fathers with stepfathers and fathers replace other children with stepchildren, and the cost of their success is that virtually all relationships outside of the nuclear family are severed.[9]

Moreover, though the presence or absence of his and her other children is clearly an important determinant of couple outcomes, it does not appear to have much to do with characteristics of the children in question. There is no evidence in these data that the coresidential stepchildren of the couples who marry are somehow less divisive or easier to parent than those of the couples who separate. Similarly, there is nothing in these data to indicate that the noncoresidential children from whom fathers eventually disengage are somehow more difficult than those with whom the unmarried fathers remain involved. Instead, the primary problem with continued contact with children outside the home is that it draws the new couple into an ongoing relationship with the other baby's mother, and it is the baby mama drama that often appears to be an important impediment to marriage.

Further, though it is likely that some of these fathers do simply choose to disengage from their other children to focus on their new families (though no father I analyzed admitted to doing so), it is also quite clear from these narratives that mothers who encourage all of their children, both shared and unshared, to refer to the new father as daddy are taking steps to shift the allegiances of their children from the other fathers to the TLC3 focal fathers. As Amy Claessens finds in the next chapter, although mothers often report after a breakup that an absent father chose to disengage, the fathers often counter that the mother does not allow them to see their children, thus preventing their involvement. As such, Claessens suggests that father absence may be reached more communally than was previously believed, and these results similarly imply that mothers may actively encourage the father to swap his allegiance from his previous family to the new one. This raises the question of whether the other father loses interest before the new family forms, thus clearing the way for the mother's new partner to embrace the role of daddy unimpeded, or whether it is the new relationship that lowers the biological father's engagement, either because he perceives the new partner as too much competition or because the mother gradually pushes him out in favor of the new stepfather. These data are consistent with both views.

Another unanswered question is the role of money. Most couples in the TLC3 sample are relatively low income, and we know that a couple's financial resources are predictive both of greater stability and of transitions into marriage (Mayer 1997; Carlson et al. 2004). Furthermore, as much as half of the disadvantage that children of single mothers face relative to children who live continuously in a continuous two-parent biological family is due to the fact that single parent families have less money (McLanahan and Sandefur 1994). What role then, do finances play for these unmarried couples in complex families?

Interestingly, a comparison of these couple's financial resources does not help to distinguish between groups. For example, it is clear that to be deemed a successful daddy, a stepfather must offer far more than mere financial support. Roughly half of all parents in all three groups either pool finances or report that they share expenses at the time of the focal child's birth, and there is no clear link between the level of financial support the father has been giving the mother (all of these fathers give some) and the father-daddy distinction. That is, stepfathers don't seem to be earning the title of daddy simply by supporting the mother and her coresidential children financially. This suggests that when parents stress the importance of "being there" as a threshold for daddyhood, they mean it— stepfathers must be physically present, emotionally invested, and personally involved to be daddy.

Child support paid to other children or received from other parents is also neither as pivotal nor as divisive as one might expect. As Katherine Magnuson and Christina Gibson-Davis report in chapter 10 of this volume, both mothers and fathers in the TLC3 sample usually believe that absent parents should pay child support to children they don't live with. However, I find that expectations of payment are tempered by realistic assessments of fathers' ability to pay, so despite the fact that few couples either get or give up much money in child support, most are not unduly upset about it. When these issues do come up among these multiple partner fertility families, such conflicts and concerns are generally only a small part of a larger package of disputes that make up the baby mama drama.

All of this amounts to a portrait of unmarried stepfamilies that is in many ways both familiar and novel. As in married stepfamilies, relationships, both current and former, are complex, though here these complexities are compounded by families' fertility patterns and nonmarital status. Clearly, unmarried stepfamilies have particular challenges and concerns that must be addressed before couples will move into marriage. Further, it is critical that we recognize that though marriage might lead to benefits for the children who live with the couple, it appears to be associated with losses for those who do not. In short, in these circumstances, marriage might well build one family but divide another; thus, these complicated blended families pose additional challenges to policy makers as the positive effects of marriage are clearly not universal in unmarried multiple partner fertility families.

Notes

1. Of the forty-eight couples who were unmarried at the birth of their child, two couples were excluded from the analysis because they dropped out of the study after the first interview, and an additional twelve couples were excluded because neither parent had a child with someone else, either at baseline or over the course of our observations. Of the thirty-four couples who did feature children by prior partners, seven additional couples were excluded for a variety of reasons; two couples were dropped due to insufficient data, one because the paternity of the potential child with another partner was in question, two because the partnership that resulted in the stepfamily was subsequent to the dissolution of the TLC3 focal family and resulted in only one wave of available data for those families, one because all of her other children were killed in a car accident prior to the birth of the TLC3 focal child, and one because the other partner was pregnant but had not yet had the child as of the final interview.

2. It is also important to note that though this sample consists entirely of couples who already had children by other partners at the baseline interview, several of these stepfamilies become even more complex over the course of our observations (for example, the couple separates and a parent finds a new partner), several parents have more children with new partners, and two additional unmarried families who did not have other children at baseline, and who are excluded from this sample due to data limitations, become unmarried stepfamilies over the course of the study.

3. In determining child residence, I rely on the parents' very general descriptions of the primary residence of these children, although it is important to note that few speak in terms of formal or legal custody arrangements, and many children do occasionally stay overnight with their non-coresidential parent.

4. Cache's two children were born eight months apart because the younger was born prematurely.

5. One of the couples (Lauren and Michael) both marry and divorce over the course of the study, and so they are counted among both the married and the separated couples.

6. I define couples as broken up only if the parents say that the romantic relationship between the parents is over for good; given this, I do not count as dissolved those couples who separate briefly over the course of the study but reunite quickly.

7. The Special Supplemental Nutrition Program for Women, Infants, and Children.

8. All of the coresidential children in these seven families are the children of the mother by a previous relationship, but notably two additional mothers have other children who do not live with them.

9. Others have found similar patterns of father involvement, though they find that the strongest predictor of reduced father involvement with noncoresident children is having a new biological child in the father's household (Manning, Stewart and Smock, 2003; Manning and Smock 1999, 2000). Because all of the TLC3 couples feature a new shared child when we first interview them, the patterns I find here can be seen as a further specification of this effect.

References

Biglan, Anthony, Patricia Brennan, Sharon Foster, and Harold Holder. 2004. *Helping Adolescents at Risk: Prevention of Multiple Problem Behaviors.* New York: Guilford Press.

Blank, Rebecca M. 1997. *It Takes a Nation: A New Agenda for Fighting Poverty.* New York: Russell Sage Foundation.

Bumpass, Lawrence L., Raley, R. Kelly, and James A. Sweet. 1995. "The Changing Character of Stepfamilies: Implications of Cohabitation and Nonmarital Childbearing." *Demography* 32(3): 425–36.

Carlson, Marcia J., and Frank F. Furstenberg, Jr. 2006. "The Level and Correlates of Multiple Partner Fertility in the United States." *Journal of Marriage and the Family* 68(3): 718–32.

Carlson, M., Sara McLanahan and Paula England. 2004. "Union Formation in Fragile Families." *Demography* 41(2): 237–62.

Cherlin, Andrew J. 1992. *Marriage, Divorce, Remarriage,* rev. and enlarged edition. Cambridge, Mass.: Harvard University Press.

Coleman, Marilyn, Lawrence Ganong and Mark Fine. 2000. "Reinvestigating Remarriage: Another Decade of Progress." *Journal of Marriage and the Family* 62(4): 1288–307.

Edin, Kathryn. forthcoming. *Marginal Men: Fatherhood in the Lives of Low Income Men.* Unpublished manuscript

Edin, Kathryn, and Marcia Kefalas. 2005. *Promises I Can Keep: Why Poor Women Put Motherhood Before Marriage.* Berkeley, Calif.: University of California Press.

Furstenberg, Frank F., Jr., Kay L. Sherwood, and Mercer Sullivan. 1992. *Caring and Paying: What Fathers and Mothers Say About Child Support.* New York: MDRC.

Ganong, Lawrence H., and Marilyn Coleman. 2004. *Stepfamily Relationships: Development, Dynamics, and Interventions.* New York: Kluwer Academic.

Glick, Paul C. 1980. "Remarriage: Some Recent Changes and Variations." *Journal of Family Issues* 1(4): 455–78.

Manning, Wendy D., and Kathleen A. Lamb. 2003. "Adolescent Well-Being in Cohabiting, Married, and Single-Parent Families." *Journal of Marriage and the Family* 65(4): 876–93.

Manning, Wendy D. and Pamela J. Smock. 1999. "New Families and Nonresident Father-Child Visitation." *Social Forces* 78(1): 87–116.

———. 2000. "Swapping Families: Serial Parenting and Economic Support for Children." *Journal of Marriage and the Family* 62(1): 111–22.

Manning, Wendy D., Susan D. Stewart, and Pamela J. Smock. 2003. "The Complexity of Fathers' Parenting Responsibilities and Involvement with Nonresident Children." *Journal of Family Issues* 24(5): 645–67.

Martin, Joyce A., Brady E. Hamilton, Paul D. Sutton, Stephanie J. Ventura, Faye Menacker, and Sharon Kirmeyer. 2006. *"Births: Final Data for 2004."* National Vital Statistics Reports, vol. 55, number 1. Hyattsville, Md.: National Center for Health Statistics. Accessed at http://www.cdc.gov/nchs/data/nvsr/nvsr55/nvsr55_01.pdf.

Mayer, Susan E. 1997. *What Money Can't Buy: Family Income and Children's Life Chances.* Cambridge, Mass.: Harvard University Press.

McLanahan, Sara and Gary Sandefur. 1994. *Growing Up With a Single Parent: What Hurts, What Helps.* Cambridge, Mass.: Harvard University Press.

Mincy, Ronald. 2002. "Who Should Marry Whom? Multiple Partner Fertility Among New Parents." Fragile Families Working Paper #2002-03-FF.

Seltzer, Judith A. 2000. "Families Formed Outside of Marriage." *Journal of Marriage and the Family* 62(4): 1247–68.

Senior, Olive. 1991. *Working Miracles: Women's Lives in the English-speaking Caribbean.* Bloomington, Ind.: Indiana University Press.

Terry-Humen, Elizabeth, Jennifer Manlove, and Kristin A. Moore. 2001. "Births Outside of Marriage: Perceptions vs. Reality." *Child Trends Research Brief.* Washington: Child Trends, Inc.

Waite, Linda J., and Maggie Gallager. 2000. *The Case for Marriage: Why Married People Are Happier, Healthier and Better Off Financially.* New York: Random House.

Waller, Maureen R. 2002. *My Baby's Father: Unmarried Parents and Paternal Responsibility.* Ithaca, N.Y.: Cornell University Press.

Chapter 9

Gatekeeper Moms and (Un)Involved Dads: What Happens After a Breakup?

AMY CLAESSENS

WHEN ASKED shortly after their child's birth, the vast majority of unmarried fathers say that they want to be involved the child's life. A large proportion of mothers also want them to be. Yet, few fathers who are no longer romantically involved with the mother are visiting their child one year later.[1] Over time, visitation further wanes, and only 58 percent of all twelve- to eighteen-year-olds who were born to unmarried parents have had any contact with their nonresident father in the past year (Koball and Principe 2002). Why, then, despite good intentions, do fathers disappear from the lives of their children? Because one-third of all American children are born outside of marriage, and these relationships break up at higher rates than marriages, understanding why and how fathers disengage after their relationship with the mother ends is clearly relevant.

Media, policy makers and researchers have increasingly focused their attentions on noncustodial fathers, but little is known about these fathers and their involvement with their children. Much of the research on the determinants and consequences of noncustodial father involvement focuses on divorced or separated fathers, usually middle-class, rather than unmarried or low-income fathers (Coley 2001). Studies that do examine father involvement in unmarried couples rely on specific subsamples of fathers, such as teenage parents and welfare mothers. All of these studies provide insight into the determinants of father involvement, such as age, relationship with the mother and familial pressure.

They do not, however, investigate a more diverse and representative group of unmarried and low-income fathers.

Fathers, understandably, are the focus of studies of father involvement, but mothers, as gatekeepers, also play an important role in granting or restricting access to their children. However, the extant research provides little insight into this gatekeeping. In addition, most of the data used in studies of noncustodial father involvement come from maternal rather than paternal reports. Consequently, fathers are not reporting on their own involvement with their children (Coley 2001).

This analysis seeks to describe the roles that both mothers and fathers play in fathers' engagement or disengagement with their children following a breakup. Using in-depth qualitative data, I investigate father visitation and maternal gatekeeping in a diverse sample of fathers who were in a romantic relationship with the mother at the time of the child's birth.

Background

Wide-ranging and multifaceted, father involvement is conceptualized in many ways such as financial support, emotional support, physical presence, and accessibility (Day and Lamb 2004; Hawkins and Dollahite 1997; Lamb et al. 1987; Marsiglio et al. 2000). All of these aspects of father involvement are important. However, focusing on multiple conceptions of fatherhood is beyond the scope of this chapter. Because my focus is maternal gatekeeping and father involvement, father engagement or involvement with his nonresident child or children is limited to father visitation.

A diverse array of factors influence both father involvement and maternal gatekeeping, such as a father's ability to contribute financially,[2] maternal and paternal attitudes toward fathering, parental conflict, maternal gatekeeping, new partners and children, and a father's available time. However, given that maternal gatekeeping is rarely studied, I draw primarily from the noncustodial father involvement literature, focusing on the factors related to father visitation.

Ability to Contribute

Although conceptions of fatherhood have broadened beyond breadwinning, being able to provide for a family is still a central part of the meaning of fatherhood for both men and women (Gerson 1993). A father who cannot contribute financially to the mother and his child might withdraw from his child's life if he feels he cannot fulfill the role of provider. In contrast, a mother might restrict access to the child if the father is not contributing financially to the family.

Research has linked fathers' ability to contribute financially to subsequent visitation, though this research also suggests many potential explanations for the large variation in financial contributions and observed visitation. In a study of young teen mothers, Anu Rangarajan and Phillip Gleason (1998) find that father's earnings have a small positive relationship with visitation. Conversely, Irwin Garfinkel, Sara McLanahan, and Thomas Hanson (1998) find that earnings are positively and significantly associated with child support payments but are much less important in predicting frequency of visitation. In two studies using nationally representative samples, maternal SES is associated with father visitation (Child Trends 2002; Seltzer 1991), suggesting that father economic resources might be related to visitation. However, these studies do not include father characteristics.

In an in-depth qualitative study of low-income mothers, Kathryn Edin and Laura Lein (1997) find that mothers often push out or deny visitation rights to fathers who are unable to provide financial support. Research using survey data supports this finding (Marsiglio and Cohan 2000), suggesting that maternal gatekeeping occurs in response to a father's inability to provide financial support. However, ethnographic work by Elliot Liebow (1967) suggests that fathers who cannot support their children disengage because of feelings of shame or guilt surrounding their inability to provide support.

Role Commitment and Parental Identity

A father's commitment to and attitude toward his role as father might also be associated with his subsequent engagement. A father who places greater importance on the role of fatherhood might be more actively involved with his children regardless of other factors, whereas one who does not might disengage. Marilyn Ihinger-Tallman, Kay Pasley, and Cheryl Buehler (1993, 1995) suggest that the saliency of a father's role identity will predict his involvement following a divorce. Scholars also suggest that maternal views of fatherhood and both parents' conceptions of fatherhood are likely to be important predictors of father involvement (Furstenberg 1995; Marsiglio 1995; Parke 2002; Tamis-LeMonda and Cabrera 1999). The relationship between father role and involvement is a new and emergent area of research (Marsiglio 1995), but evidence supports the hypothesis that paternal role salience is related to father involvement (Juby and LeBourdais 1998; Minton and Pasley 1996; Stone and McKenry 1998), though much of this evidence comes from studies of divorced rather than unmarried parents.

Barriers to Visitation

Several other factors might influence noncustodial father involvement, among them, maternal gatekeeping, characteristics of the child, parental conflict, and mother's and father's new partners and other children. Because children primarily live with their mothers, mothers—as gatekeepers—control access to the child and thus are likely important factors in father visitation. However, most datasets do not typically collect information on maternal gatekeeping. Little is therefore known about it.

Mothers who have good relationships with the fathers might allow them more access and facilitate more involvement, whereas those who have contentious relationships might not. William Marsiglio (1991) suggests that mothers might pressure fathers to be more involved or try to discourage them from visiting. Mothers might allow access to their children because they need child care or other day-to-day help. Conversely, mothers might restrict access to their children for a variety of other reasons, such as protecting their children's physical and emotional well-being. Given that father risky behavior and cheating plays a major role in couple breakup (see chapters 5 and 6 in this volume), maternal gatekeeping might occur in reaction to these risky or bad paternal behaviors. Therefore, understanding maternal gatekeeping independently from paternal behavior is difficult.

A conflicted or strained parental relationship could lead to fathers withdrawing or mothers pushing them away from the children. Evidence has linked parental relationship quality to father involvement (Coley and Chase-Lansdale 1998; Danziger and Radin 1990; Furstenberg 1995; Seltzer 1991). In her interviews with seventy-five primarily middle-class divorced fathers, Terry Arendell (1992, 1995) finds that fathers often withdraw from their children's lives to avoid conflict with their ex-wives. Likewise, qualitative studies of African American fathers find that unmarried fathers' relationships with their children seem to flow through the parental relationship (Hamer 2001; Miller 1994; Nelson, Clampet-Lunquist, and Edin 2002).

In addition, because multiple partner fertility among unmarried parents is common (Carlson and Furstenberg 2004; Mincy 2002), both mother's and father's new romantic partners or new children could also be barriers to visitation. Fathers with new partners or new children might have less time to invest in their nonresident children, and mothers might restrict access to their children out of jealousy or because of conflict over the father's new partner or children. Although the literature in this area is limited, some evidence supports this association. Wendy Manning and Pamela Smock (1999) find that the level of fathers' new familial responsibilities, including the number of new biological children and stepchildren, is associated with decreased visitation.

Additionally, mothers' new partners, referred to here as social fathers, are likely to influence father visitation. Mothers might keep the biological fathers away because they have found another man to fulfill the role of father in their children's lives; however, they might also try to repartner because the biological fathers have withdrawn and been absent from their children's lives. As in the case with a father's new partner, jealousy or conflict over the new relationship might also influence maternal gatekeeping and father involvement. Yet, the direction of the relationship between social father and father involvement is unclear, and there has been little systematic analysis of this issue. Although not focusing on father visitation, studies of child support payment have found that presence of a stepparent is related to less child support payment (Greene and Moore 2000; Fagan 1998; Seltzer, McLanahan, and Hanson 1998; Seltzer 1991), suggesting that the presence of a stepparent or social father might influence father involvement.

Other factors that might influence father involvement are child characteristics such as gender, age, and temperament. Fathers might be more involved with boys than with girls because they might identify more with boys, believe their role in their sons' lives is more important, feel more confident in parenting their boys, or be operating under a set of social expectations that put more emphasis on father involvement with sons. Some studies, though not specifically addressing nonmarital births, suggest that fathers are typically more involved with their sons than with their daughters (Pleck 1997; Marsiglio 1991).

Research does illustrate the characteristics and likely determinants of nonresident father involvement, but we have little understanding of the process by which fathers' involvement is maintained or declines or the role of both mothers and fathers in the process. This study aims to uncover the complexities of father engagement following a breakup, specifically focusing on the roles of both parents.

Finally, a critical issue in research on fathers, especially nonresident, low-income fathers, is that they are often excluded from large national datasets. For example, Irwin Garfinkel and his colleagues (1998) estimate that the 1987 National Survey of Families and Households missed as many as 3.6 million nonresident fathers. This underrepresentation is especially pronounced for low-income fathers (Nelson 2004). Additionally, studies often rely on maternal rather than paternal reports due to the lack of data collected directly from fathers. However, mother and father reports of father involvement often vary dramatically (Coley 2001), with fathers reporting more involvement than mothers. In contrast to much of the previous research on father involvement, this analysis relies on data collected from both mothers and fathers whenever possible.

Data and Methods

The Time, Love, and Cash among Couples with Children study, with its focus on couple dynamics, relationships, parenting, and breakups, provides the opportunity to examine both mothers' and fathers' perspectives on gatekeeping and father involvement after a breakup. Unlike many previous studies, it includes interviews with mothers, fathers, and social fathers, permitting researchers to examine multiple perspectives on and the complexities of father involvement and maternal gatekeeping.

Data

For this analysis, I narrowed the full sample of seventy-five couples to the eighteen who had broken up, and had at least one parent complete an individual interview at the year-four follow-up.[3] Couples were excluded from the final sample of eighteen if, according to either parent's report, the couple was still romantically involved or cohabiting.[4] Additionally, five of the eighteen couples were married at baseline. and are included in the analytic sample because the sample size is small.[5]

From the eighteen couples, I have individual interviews for sixteen mothers, fourteen fathers, and seven social fathers. In sum, I am missing interviews from two mothers and four fathers. Rather than focusing on specific fields in the data, I read complete transcripts of the thirty-seven individual interviews at the year-four follow-up. In addition to these interview transcripts, I also rely on earlier interviews with these couples for background information and clarification when necessary.

Analytic Approach

First, to get a sense of the frequency of both father visitation with the focal child and maternal and paternal reports of gatekeeping, I created four quantitative variables based on the interview data: maternal report of time since father's last visit, paternal report of time since his last visit, maternal report of gatekeeping, and paternal report of maternal gatekeeping. I relied on social father interviews for clarification and confirmation when necessary. These four variables were collapsed into two binary variables of any report of maternal gatekeeping and father contact with child in the past two months.[6] I chose two months as the cutoff because the distribution of time since last visit ranged from the current week to thirty months; however, fathers were clustered into two distinct ranges, between the current week and two months (average time = 2.7 weeks, n = 11), and greater than five months (average time = 14.8 months, n = 7).

For the purposes of this study, I defined gatekeeping as mother or father report of mother controlling access to the focal child. For example, a mother who reported that a father sees his child whenever he wants was not coded as gatekeeping. In contrast, a mother who reported that a father can see his child when specific conditions are met, or a mother who reported that a father cannot see his child at all are coded as gatekeeping. In addition, father reports of being shut out or kept out by the mother were also coded as gatekeeping, but father reports of being able to "see my kid whenever I want" were not.

Not surprisingly, maternal and paternal reports of gatekeeping are not always consistent, but mothers reported it more often than fathers. For this analysis, I counted any report as an instance regardless of the reporter and coded the reason for it. Four distinct reasons emerged: lies-unreliability, poor relationship, safety-lifestyle, and absence.

- Lies-unreliability includes instances in which mothers report that fathers have "lied about coming to visit" or fathers having missed visits as reasons for gatekeeping. Also included are instances in which mothers cite a history of missed visits or lies.

- Poor relationship includes father reports of restraining orders as a reason for not "being allowed" to see their children. Mothers who report that fathers were still pursuing a sexual relationship with them and cited this as a reason for not allowing the father to visit are included in this category. Additionally, mothers who report having a poor relationship with the father and not wanting to see or talk to him as a reason for not allowing visitation are coded as poor relationship.

- Safety-lifestyle includes maternal reports of not allowing children to visit their father due to his unsafe lifestyle. This includes his involvement, or suspected involvement, with drugs or violence. Additionally, this category includes maternal reports of not allowing fathers to visit their children when they are high or reports of fathers living in unsafe situations.

- Absence, cited by mothers, was prolonged father absence. Mothers who report "he been gone so long" or "ain't been here at all" as reasons for not allowing a father to visit are included.

In quantifying gatekeeping, reason for gatekeeping, and father visitation, a clearer picture of the pattern of gatekeeping and father involvement emerges in these couples. Three distinct types of couple gatekeeping-visitation relationships emerge: easy involvement, contested involvement, and gatekeeper mom–uninvolved dad. To provide a better description of the three types of couples, I analyzed the transcripts of each interview and looked for common themes. Using analytic induction, I employ an iterative process of coding the transcripts for the roles that fathers, mothers, and their relationships play in gatekeeping and involvement.

Results

Table 9.1 presents descriptive statistics for the eighteen couples in this analysis. At baseline, five of the couples were married and nine were cohabiting. At the year-four interview, an additional two couples had

Table 9.1   Descriptive Statistics for Analytic Sample

	Number	Proportion of Sample
Baseline characteristics		
Relationship status		
Married	5	0.28
Cohabiting (not married)	9	0.50
Dating (not cohabiting)	4	0.22
Mother's race		
Black (non-Hispanic)	12	0.67
White (non-Hispanic)	1	0.06
Hispanic	5	0.28
Father's race		
Black (non-Hispanic)	11	0.61
White (non-Hispanic)	0	0.00
Hispanic	7	0.39
Wave Four characteristics		
Divorced-separated	7	0.39
Mean age		
Mother	26.89	
Father	28.72	
Mean number of children together	1.29	
Mean total number of children[a]		
Mother	3.75	
Father	4.30	
Father-child contact in past two months	11	0.61
Father report of gatekeeping (n = 14)	7	0.50
Mother report of gatekeeping (n = 16)	12	0.81
Mother resides with new partner	9	0.50

Source: Author's calculations.
n = 18 couples. Some numbers based on total available reports, n = 16 mothers, n = 14 fathers.
[a] This average includes number of children together.

gotten married (and subsequently separated) and half of the mothers were cohabiting with a new partner (social fathers). The couples share on average 1.3 children, and mothers and fathers have a total of about 3.8 and 4.3 children, respectively. The majority of both mothers and fathers are black, and on average mothers and fathers were twenty-three and twenty-five years old, respectively, at the time of the focal child's birth.

Frequency of Visitation and Gatekeeping

Among the eighteen couples, eleven fathers had contact with the focal child in the previous two months based on mother or father report

Table 9.2   Father-Child Contact in Previous Two Months by Maternal Gatekeeping

	Yes	No
Maternal gatekeeping	Contested involvement	Gatekeeper mom, uninvolved dad
Yes	n = 6 (33.3%)	n = 7 (38.9%)
	Easy involvement	
No	n = 5 (27.8%)	0

Source: Author's calculation.

(table 9.1). Maternal gatekeeping is common in this sample, with at least one parent reporting it in 75 percent of the couples. Table 9.2 presents the relationship between gatekeeping and father visitation in the previous two months. This table shows that five couples report no gatekeeping and recent father-child contact, six report gatekeeping and recent father-child contact, and seven report gatekeeping and no recent father-child contact.

Table 9.3 presents the reasons for gatekeeping for the full sample and then by whether the father has recently visited the focal child. In the full sample, poor relationship is the most commonly cited reason for gatekeeping and safety-lifestyle the next most common. However, when the reasons are examined by whether the father had contact with the child in the previous two months, poor relationship and absence are the most common among couples with no recent father-child contact, and safety-lifestyle is the most common among couples with recent father-child contact.

From the initial descriptive analysis, three types of couples emerge: easy involvement, contested involvement, and gatekeeper mom–uninvolved dad (table 9.2). Tables 9.4 through 9.6 present descriptive statistics for the parents by each of the three couple types. Given the small sample sizes, caution should be used in interpreting any differences. Mothers in the easy involvement group are less likely to be repartnered, and both mothers and fathers in this group are slightly older on average than the other couples. Additionally, the gatekeeper mom, uninvolved dad group have broken up more recently, just under two years ago, whereas the other two groups have been broken up for slightly more than two years (not shown). Finally, though not shown in tables 9.4 through 9.6, the same proportion of fathers in each group were formally employed (50 percent), paid formal or informal child support (60 percent), and repartnered. Similarly, the couples reported cheating and problematic jealousy during their relationship at the same frequencies across these groups.[7]

Table 9.3   Reasons for Gatekeeping by Father-child Contact

	Number	Proportion
Full sample (n = 13)		
Reasons for gatekeeping[a]		
Lies-unreliability	3	0.21
Poor relationship	6	0.43
Absence	4	0.29
Safety-lifestyle	5	0.36
Father-child contact in past two months (n = 6)		
Reasons for gatekeeping[a]		
Lies-unreliability	2	0.33
Poor relationship	1	0.17
Absence	0	0.00
Safety-lifestyle	4	0.67
No father-child contact in past two months (n = 7)		
Reasons for gatekeeping[a]		
Lies-unreliability	1	0.13
Poor relationship	5	0.63
Absence	4	0.50
Safety-lifestyle	1	0.13

Source: Author's calculation.

[a] Counts are total number of couples in which reason was cited; couples could cite more than one reason. Proportion based on number of times cited out of number of couples; therefore, total can be greater than 100%

Easy Involvement   Five of the eighteen couples report easy involvement, which I define as no reported gatekeeping and father-child contact within the previous two months. As noted, these parents are slightly older than average, and none of the mothers lives with a new partner. These couples appear to either support each other's roles as parents regardless of their feelings toward each other or need help with the day-to-day child care of their shared child or children.

One example of this type is Marilyn and Damian, both of whom are African American. Damian, who was twenty-four when he entered the study, and Marilyn, who was twenty-nine, have a formal visitation agreement.[8] They have two children together, and though neither lives with a new partner, both are dating other people. They have been to court on several occasions to discuss both visitation and child support, and their current visitation agreement provides for shared custody of the children. The children live primarily with Marilyn, but Damian sees them every other weekend and every Wednesday.

Damian and Marilyn have had a volatile relationship and still have animosity towards each other. However, each says that the other parent

Table 9.4   Descriptive Statistics for Couples, Easy Involvement

	Number	Proportion
No gatekeeping, father-child contact		
n = 4 father interviews, n = 4 mother interviews		
Baseline characteristics		
Relationship status		
Married	2	0.40
Cohabiting (not married)	3	0.60
Dating (not cohabiting)	0	0.00
Mother's race		
Black (non-Hispanic)	4	0.80
White (non-Hispanic)	0	0.00
Hispanic	1	0.20
Father's race		
Black (non-Hispanic)	4	0.80
White (non-Hispanic)	0	0.00
Hispanic	1	0.20
Wave Four characteristics		
Divorced-separated	2	0.50
Mean age		
Mother	31.00	
Father	33.80	
Mean number of children together	1.25	
Mean total number of children[a]		
Mother	3.33	
Father	3.67	
Mother resides with new partner	0	0.00

Source: Author's calculation.
[a] This average includes number of children together.

is important to their children, so they try to make things work. Marilyn wants the children to spend time with Damian because he is their father, but she does not ask them what they do with him when they come home from a visit. She says, "I don't want her to feel guilty, like she can't love him." She says that asking her daughter what she does with her father might make her daughter feel like she must report to her mother about Damian, and Marilyn does not want this.

Marilyn and Damian both indicate that their current relationship is only about the children. Marilyn says, "we only talk about the kids. Nothing else to talk about. I mean, he's a liar, so why else would I talk to him?" Similarly, Damian says, "other than days when it's time to pick them up, I try not to make contact with her." Although they do not seem to get along with each other, they both realize the importance of two parents for their children. Damian says that he respects Marilyn because she

Table 9.5   Descriptive Statistics for Couples, Contested Involvement

	Number	Proportion
Gatekeeping, father-child contact		
n = 4 father interviews, n = 6 mother interviews		
Baseline characteristics		
Relationship status		
Married	1	0.17
Cohabiting (not married)	3	0.50
Dating (not cohabiting)	2	0.33
Mother's race		
Black (non-Hispanic)	2	0.33
White (non-Hispanic)	1	0.17
Hispanic	3	0.50
Father's race		
Black (non-Hispanic)	2	0.33
White (non-Hispanic)	0	0.00
Hispanic	4	0.67
Wave Four characteristics		
Divorced-separated	1	0.17
Mean age		
Mother	24.67	
Father	25.83	
Mean number of children together	1.33	
Mean total number of children[a]		
Mother	4.00	
Father	4.80	
Mother resides with new partner	4	0.67

Source: Author's calculation.
[a] This average includes number of children together.

is his children's mother. Neither couple reports any gatekeeping, but Marilyn might not need to do any because the existing visitation order controls Damian's access to the children.

Unlike Damian and Marilyn, Nubia, a twenty-six-year-old mother, and Sean, a thirty-two-year-old father, both African American and married when they entered the study, do not talk about the importance of the other parent in their child's life. However, they do focus on the need for shared child care. Specifically, Nubia wants Sean's help "raising her [their daughter]." Sean and Nubia are currently separated and, in contrast to Damian and Marilyn, do not have a formal visitation agreement. Sean says that he sees his daughter regularly, including picking her up from school, and he spends a lot of his free

Table 9.6   Descriptive Statistics for Couples, Gatekeeping and No Involvement

	Number	Proportion
Gatekeeping, no father-child contact		
n = 7 father interviews, n = 7 mother interviews		
Baseline characteristics		
Relationship status		
Married	2	0.29
Cohabiting (not married)	4	0.57
Dating (not cohabiting)	1	0.01
Mother's race		
Black (non-Hispanic)	6	0.86
White (non-Hispanic)	0	0.00
Hispanic	1	0.14
Father's race		
Black (non-Hispanic)	5	0.71
White (non-Hispanic)	0	0.00
Hispanic	2	0.29
Wave Four characteristics		
Divorced-separated	4	0.50
Mean age		
Mother	25.86	
Father	27.57	
Mean number of children together	1.29	
Mean total number of children[a]		
Mother	3.71	
Father	4.14	
Mother resides with new partner	5	0.71

Source: Author's calculation.
[a] This average includes number of children together.

time at Nubia's house caring for her. Neither Nubia nor Sean resides with other partners.

Nubia argues that Sean needs to take responsibility for the day-to-day care of their daughter. She says:

> I want him to do everything. Like I told him, and I've been telling him since she was born, "You wanted this child. You need to do it. I did not want her. I didn't want to potty train anyone else. I didn't wanna teach anybody how to spell they name. Stop watchin' soap operas and teach her how to spell her name." That's just my thing. You wanted her, you take care of her.

Nubia does not report any gatekeeping, and since their separation Sean has been in contact with their daughter regularly. Although Nubia indicates that she dislikes Sean, she has not prevented him from seeing their daughter because she really wants his help.

Other couples in this group appear to either respect each other's role as a parent or rely on each other for child care and the day-to-day responsibilities of raising a child. Mothers in this group report that they need fathers to help with child care and other needs of their children. Motivation to gatekeep is therefore absent. The nonresident fathers in these couples appear to have easy access to their children, with the mothers encouraging or supporting their involvement. In addition, some mothers appear to actively encourage father involvement, not necessarily because of the importance of the father's role in the child's life, but because they need this help. Respecting each other's role as a parent or needing assistance appears to relate to both father involvement and an absence of gatekeeping for this group.

Contested Involvement

Six of the eighteen couples fall into the contested involvement category, which I define as maternal gatekeeping with recent father visitation. In this group, the primary reason cited for gatekeeping is safety-lifestyle. Typically, mothers report that the fathers are involved with drugs or violence. Five of the six fathers were recently involved with the criminal justice system. Four of the mothers are living with new partners, and three of the fathers have repartnered, though they are not cohabiting.

Sherise and Antonio are one example. Sherise, an unmarried African American mother who was twenty when she entered the study, and Antonio, a twenty-five-year-old African American father, have two children together. Both have repartnered. Sherise, who is living with her new partner, says that Antonio had not been seeing their children for a while because "I really don't trust [him]." Before his recent arrest, she would not let Antonio visit their children. She says:

> I tell him he couldn't see them [the kids] no more until he got his act together. Now, he's on house arrest, I let them go over there because he's there, he can't go nowhere. He don't have a choice but to watch 'em. . . . He wasn't seeing them before . . . and then suddenly he's stuck.

Sherise kept Antonio away before his arrest because she did not trust him, but now allows the children to spend time with him at his house. She explains that before Antonio was put on house arrest she disapproved of his leaving their children in the care of a relative or a friend when she thought that he should be spending time with them. However, Antonio never mentions not being able to see their children before his house arrest. Instead he speaks about being able to see his kids whenever he wants. He explains that whenever he wants to see his kids, he calls Sherise, and "she bring 'em or I have somebody go get 'em."

Like Sherise, Natalie, an unmarried white mother, who was eighteen when she entered the study, would not allow John, the eighteen-year-old Hispanic father, to take their son Alex to his house because she did not trust his living situation. She says, "I wanted John to be a part of Alex's life and everything, but there's no way I would let Alex go over to their house. Not when his uncle's doing [crack] in the back." Natalie and John had a difficult breakup, during which Natalie says that John was "going psycho." She obtained a restraining order. After some time had passed, Natalie started allowing John back into their son's life. Although Natalie did not think that John was involved in drugs, like his uncle, she did not want their son exposed to the uncle's drug use. Although John is currently in prison, Natalie wants him to be a part of their son's life, but she also wants their son to be safe.

Similarly, Frieda, an unmarried Hispanic mother who was eighteen when she entered the study, would not allow her ex-boyfriend Marco, twenty-two years old and Hispanic, around their two children when he was high. Marco, a heroin addict, is currently in prison. Frieda and her new partner, however, try to help him when he is not. She says that she and Marco are still friends, and that his addiction will not get in the way of their relationship. However, she does say that he cannot see the children if he is getting high. Frieda says, "I told him if he gonna be like that [high], I'm not gonna talk to you, I'm not gonna help you, I'm not gonna give you my kids, 'cause you're in that, in that situation, and he got scared. . . ." She said that when she threatens him like this, he tries to stay clean. Like the other mothers, she does not want to keep her children from their father, but she also wants to protect her children.

Similarly, one mother says that her child came home from a visit with his father, and said, "daddy going to get a gun." She describes her reaction when she heard this: "That's it, he not going with you no more." She said that though she would allow the father to visit at her house, she felt that she could no longer trust him unsupervised with their child.

Given that the majority of these fathers have recently been involved with the criminal justice system for drugs and weapons issues, it is clear that these mothers' concerns about the fathers' lifestyles are real. None of the fathers in this group report feeling as though the mothers are keeping them out of their children's lives. Although the parents have conflicts from time to time, the conflict is typically related to the father's lifestyle and not directly to visitation or the couple's relationship. Mothers report that they want to keep their children safe, but do not want to keep their children's fathers away from them.

Gatekeeper Mom, Uninvolved Dad

Seven of the eighteen couples in this sample fall into the gatekeeper mom–uninvolved dad category. The most commonly cited reason for gatekeeping by both mothers and fathers in this group is a poor couple relationship. Usually the mother already has a restraining order against the father on the basis of a volatile relationship history. In most cases, there is also prolonged father absence. Not surprisingly, couples in this category had the largest discrepancies in their reports of when the most recent father-child contact occurred, and one mother now denies that the father is the biological father.[9] Many of the mothers, as in the other group of gatekeeping mothers, live with new partners. The majority of fathers have also repartnered though they are not living with their new partners.

When the interviewer asked Dominique, an unmarried African American mother who was twenty-one when she entered the study, what she would do if her child's father, Steven, a twenty-three-year-old African American father, wanted to see their child, she responds, "Don't let him see him . . . after all these years." Dominique and Steven have one child together. Dominique is now living with her new partner, and they also have a child together. Dominique says that Steven has not seen their child since "before he even turned one." She explains that Steven has been gone so long that she would not let him back in their child's life. Dominique has a restraining order against Steven. She says that he put himself before his son, and that they broke up because he was not "taking care of her" or their son.

Yet, Steven tells a different story, saying that he has not been able to locate Dominique and his son for quite some time. He "recently found their address." Steven adds, "She did me wrong. She has my address, she could just drop my son off. She has my phone number, [that] hasn't changed. Now, me, on the other hand, I didn't know where she was at."

Steven says that he has not seen his son in more than a year. Dominique puts it at closer to three years. Steven says that Dominique has been the gatekeeper in the past. For example, he recounts a story about trying to visit his son from a year ago, "I came over there to pick up my son, I was two minutes late. [She said,] 'now you can't get him.' " He says that he has to go along with this because she has the restraining order, saying, "She can have me locked up."

Steven also explains that before Dominique moved in with her new partner, his relationship with Dominique was volatile, but she allowed him to see their son. He thinks that Dominique is causing problems for him with her new partner also by telling the partner that Steven wants to rekindle their relationship. Steven asserts, "I only want to see my son."

Adrienne, an unmarried, twenty-four-year-old African American mother, and Ollie, an African American father who was twenty-three when he entered the study, tell a story very similar to Dominique's and Steven's. Although Adrienne and Ollie never married, Adrienne is now married to a new partner. Adrienne describes Ollie as having a "temper problem." She said that since they have broken up "he's still on that I want to be with you trip." She has a restraining order against Ollie and says that she and Ollie have had violent fights in the past. She does not want to be near Ollie, she says. She tells the story of the last time Ollie tried to see their son, and that their son said that he did not want to go with his father. She and the social father therefore no longer make him visit because he does not want to.

In contrast, Ollie says, "I would like to get in touch with my son, but that's a no-win situation." Ollie, who is on probation, does not want to violate those terms. Thus, because of the restraining order, he must keep his distance from both Adrienne and his son. He remembers the incident when his son did not want to see him but says, "that was one time." He does not understand why Adrienne and the social father use this as an excuse to keep him away from their son. Ollie says that things were easier before Adrienne got married because Adrienne allowed him to visit their son. Ollie thinks she is letting social father come between them. However, if the social father is jealous, it might not be unfounded. Ollie explains that the last time he and Adrienne saw each other they did have sex.[10] Ollie recently found Adrienne's phone number, and hopes to reconnect with his son. Adrienne explains that in the past when Ollie has called her, she has had her phone number changed.

According to Camille, an unmarried African American mother who was nineteen when she entered the study, Freddie, a twenty-year-old Hispanic father, made a choice to not be with their daughter. She therefore does not want him in their lives. She says, "he chose to be out of her life for two years. I just continue that." Now married with a new baby, Camille describes what happened with Freddie's involvement with their daughter. "He disappeared. That's how he is." However, Camille says that it is probably better with Freddie out of their daughter's life. She says that Freddie is a terrible father and wants her husband to adopt their daughter. Camille does note that she thinks her new husband is jealous of Freddie. She thinks her husband would prefer to act as though Freddie never existed.

Yet Freddie says, "I'm sick of looking like the bad guy. Because you think I don't want to see my kids?" Currently Freddie is trying to establish formal visitation rights for two children from a relationship before his with Camille. He says he will pursue the same for his daughter with Camille. When asked about how he feels toward Camille, Freddie responds, "I don't care about Camille like that at all. The pain she's put me through by taking my daughter away from me." Freddie explains that both he and Camille moved after their breakup, and that Camille would not allow Freddie to take their daughter to his new house. Camille does not dispute this statement, but says that she does not want Freddie to take their daughter because she felt that he is irresponsible. Freddie, however, feels that because Camille has a new husband and baby, she is trying to keep him away. "I just want my daughter back," he says.

Another mother says that the father's repeated broken promises to their daughter led to her keeping him away. She says,

> I don't even ask him anymore [to come visit]. Because she say mom can you call my daddy? Can he come get me? And I just stopped calling him because you can't, don't lie to her. Don't tell her. He knows where I live, he knows the phone number. She's got [social father] so she's fine.

This mother adds that because she has a new partner, her daughter has a father figure, so her biological father's absence is not important.

In contrast, a father, Jordan, a married African American father who was thirty-one when he entered the study, has not seen his child or ex-wife Coretta, a twenty-six-year-old African American mother, in quite some time. He explains how difficult it is to visit his son, "little" Jordan, because of the restraining order against him. He says, "I can't come within a hundred yards or a city block or something of that nature, [of] her and Jordan. I have to slip and see him, sneak here, sneak there, get somebody else go up there and get him." Jordan says that he and Coretta fought a lot, and she claimed that he hit her. Because of the restraining order and the conflict, he has to find a neutral party to try to go between him and Coretta when it comes to their son.

The mothers in this group of couples gatekeep because they are protecting their children from what they view are irresponsible or volatile fathers. On the other hand, the fathers cite the restraining order and the mothers' new partners as the primary reason for being kept away from their children. They indicate that they would like to be involved with their children, but that the mothers are keeping them out. Meanwhile, the mothers indicate that the fathers are irresponsible and absent and that therefore they would keep the fathers away if they ever tried to visit their children. In these couples, both the parental relationship and the mothers' new partners appear to affect both visitation and gatekeeping.

Discussion

Gatekeeping is widespread among couples in this sample, yet more than half of the fathers have had recent contact with their noncustodial children. The three primary reasons for gatekeeping were safety-lifestyle, prolonged father absence, and poor relationship. When gatekeeping is reported, fathers are more likely to have recently visited their children if the gatekeeping is due to safety or lifestyle reasons rather than absence or poor relationship.

In couples where gatekeeping occurs primarily on the basis of safety or lifestyle, mothers appear to be well intentioned. They do not want their children exposed to the danger inherent in the lives of their fathers, usually some involvement with drugs or violence. In trying to keep their children safe, mothers find other opportunities for the fathers to visit the children, such as at the mother's home, while he is on house arrest, or even taking the children to prison for a visit.

Maternal gatekeeping for safety or lifestyle reasons appears to incorporate clear rules. If fathers follow them, such as staying clean and sober and not putting the children in dangerous situations, mothers will grant access to the children. Mothers also encourage fathers to "get their acts together" so that they can be a part of their children's lives. Although these fathers recently visited their children, it is unclear whether they are seeing their children only because they are forced into a situation that the mothers feel is safe, such as being in prison or on house arrest or are voluntarily following the mothers' rules. Interestingly, none of the fathers in this group discussed gatekeeping or being kept away from their children. In these cases, maternal gatekeeping is inextricably related to bad paternal behavior, including a risky lifestyle. Maternal gatekeeping does not occur independently from paternal behavior, but rather in reaction to it.

Maternal gatekeeping because of prolonged absence or a poor relationship appears to be much more complicated than that for safety or lifestyle reasons. Yet, maternal gatekeeping in these instances again occurs in response to real or perceived poor paternal behavior. As shown in previous studies, the parental relationship is an important determinant of father visitation. In couples characterized by a poor and volatile relationship, fathers typically have not had contact with their children for several months or even years. However, both mothers and fathers interpret the lack of father involvement and the maternal gatekeeping differently. Each story is one-sided, usually blaming the other partner for the problems in the relationship and for the lack of father-child contact.

Additionally, for these couples, restraining orders against the fathers were commonplace. The restraining orders are another indication of a volatile parental relationship, but again the parents' stories differ on the circumstances. Many fathers argue that the orders are not legitimate and that they put fathers in situations that are no-win as far as access to their children is concerned. However, given the history of volatility in these couples, restraining orders might not be unfounded, and the mother might use them to protect the children from their fathers.

Moreover, in these couples with poor relationship and absence as reasons for gatekeeping, social fathers appear to play an important role.

Previous research has found evidence that presence of a stepfather is related to paying child support (Fagan, 1998; Greene and Moore 2000; Seltzer, McLanahan, and Hanson 1998; Seltzer 1991), but few studies have been able to systematically examine the relationship between social fathers and noncustodial visitation. In this analysis, evidence suggests that the mere presence of a social father does not relate to visitation and gatekeeping, because mothers in both the contested involvement and gatekeeper mom—uninvolved dad groups repartner at a similar rate. However, the fathers who had not had recent contact with their children cite the social father as causing tension and as being a catalyst in the mothers keeping the children from the fathers. On the other hand, mothers often note that their children do not need their fathers because of the presence of the social father. Yet the direction of this relationship between social fathers, gatekeeping, and visitation is unclear because a mother might push a father out of their child's life when the she repartners, or a mother might repartner because of a father's prolonged absence.

Although this analysis has uncovered a relationship between gatekeeping and father involvement, it does not allow for directional or causal interpretations about the relationship. Many of the fathers who do not regularly visit their children indicate that their children's mothers are keeping them out even though they would like to be involved. However, though fathers might prefer to be involved, many are not actively pursuing any sort of formal visitation or role in their children's lives. This might be in large part due to their lack of available resources, both financial and social. Without the resources to navigate a volatile relationship with the mother of their children or the court system, these fathers might feel forced to disengage from their children. Similarly, mothers indicate that they would like these fathers to be more involved, but that the fathers' bad behavior and personal choices have forced the mothers to keep them to protect their children.

Noncustodial father involvement among low-income, primarily unmarried men is a complex relationship between the father, mother, and often the mother's new partner. This study shows that gatekeeping does occur in these couples, and that it is an important component of father involvement. The existing literature on father involvement rarely covers the topic of gatekeeping. Research, however, needs to focus on gatekeeping as a critical component in noncustodial father involvement. Researchers should incorporate gatekeeping and reasons for it into studies of broken up and divorced parents to help to further our understanding of noncustodial father involvement.

Finally, future research should continue to investigate the complicated intersection of gatekeeping and father involvement to inform family policy. The two processes are intertwined and developing policies and programs that help couples navigate their complicated relationship could be key to involving more nonresident fathers with their children. In some cases, absent fathers might not want to be involved with their nonresident children, leading mothers to keep or push them away. However, in other instances absent fathers are struggling to navigate a complex and volatile relationship with their children's mother or mothers and new partners, and over time, might give up. Yet a few couples in this study are able to cope with this situation and, in these cases, fathers are actively engaged in their children's lives. Understanding what works for these couples could be critical to helping more fathers and children spend time together.

Notes

1. Author's calculations about involvement and visiting using Fragile Families and Child Wellbeing Study data set.

2. Ability to contribute includes both a father's resources and his willingness to share these resources with his nonresident children.

3. Due to the volatility in couple relationships in this dataset it is difficult to determine if a breakup is permanent or transitory. I focus on year four as it gives me the most information regarding the nature of the breakup.

4. Because of the timing of the interviews, a couple might have been in the process of breaking up at one interview, but still cohabiting, while by the time of the other parent's interview they might no longer be co-residing. These couples are excluded from this sample.

5. In this analysis, couples who were married at the time of the child's birth appear to be no different from the couples who were married around the key analysis areas of gatekeeping or father involvement.

6. In cases in which the mother and father report of his last visit differed, I averaged the two reports so as not to give more credence to either parent. In the five cases with a disagreement about time since last visit, mothers typically reported it being two to three years and fathers reported one to two years.

7. There were also no differences in highest grade completed or income.

8. Damian and Marilyn are unusual in this sample as they both have professional degrees. This in part might be a reason for the formal visitation agreement.

9. She has gone as far as to say that the father never came to the hospital after the focal child's birth; however, this is highly unlikely as recruitment for the sample took place in the hospital soon after the child's birth. Both "fathers" claim to have proof of paternity, though neither produced this proof to the interviewers.

10. Adrienne does not mention this incident, but she does say that she thinks that Ollie is still interested in a sexual relationship with her.

References

Arendell, Terry. 1992. "After Divorce: Investigations into Father Absence." *Gender and Society* 6(4): 562–86.

———. 1995. *Fathers and Divorce.* Thousand Oaks, Calif.: Sage Publications.

Carlson, Marcia J., and Frank F. Furstenberg Jr. 2004. "The Prevalence and Correlates of Multiple Partnered Fertility in the United States." *Journal of Marriage and Family* 68(3): 718–32.

Child Trends. 2002. *Charting Parenthood: A Statistical Portrait of Fathers and Mothers in America.* New York: Child Trends. http://fatherhood.hhs.gov/charting02/ChartingParenthood02.pdf.

Coley, Rebekah L. 2001. "(In)visible Men: Emerging Research on Low-income, Unmarried, and Minority Fathers." *American Psychologist* 56(4): 743–53.

Coley, Rebekah L., and P. Lindsay Chase-Lansdale. 1999. "Stability and Change in Paternal Involvement Among Urban African American Fathers." *Journal of Family Psychology* 13(3): 1–20.

Danziger, Sandra K., and Norma Radin 1990. "Absent Does Not Equal Uninvolved: Predictors of Fathering in Teen Mother Families." *Journal of Marriage and the Family* 52(3): 636–42.

Day, Randal D., and Michael E. Lamb. 2004. *Conceptualizing and Measuring Father Involvement.* Mahwah, N.J.: Lawrence Erlbaum Associates.

Edin, Kathryn, and Laura Lein. 1997. *Making Ends Meet: How Single Mothers Survive Welfare and Low-wage Work.* New York: Russell Sage Foundation.

Fagan, Jay. 1998. "Correlates of Low-income African American and Puerto Rican Fathers' Involvement with their Children." *Journal of Black Psychology* 24(4): 351–67.

Furstenberg, Frank F. 1995. "Fathering in the Inner City: Paternal Participation and Public Policy." In *Fatherhood: Contemporary Theory, Research, and Social Policy,* edited by William Marsiglio. Thousand Oaks, Calif.: Sage Publications.

Garfinkel, Irwin, Sara McLanahan, and Thomas L. Hanson. 1998. "A Patchwork Portrait of Nonresident Fathers." In *Fathers Under Fire: The Revolution in Child Support Enforcement,* edited by Irwin Garfinkel, Sara McLanahan, Daniel R. Meyer, and Judith A. Seltzer. New York: Russell Sage Foundation.

Gerson, Kathleen. 1993. *No Man's Land: Men's Changing Commitments to Family and Work.* New York: Basic Books.

Greene, Angela D., and Kristin A. Moore. 2000. "Nonresident Father Involvement and Child Well-being Among Young Children in Families on Welfare." *Marriage and Family Review* 29(2): 159–80.

Hamer, Jennifer F. 2001. *What it Means to Be a Daddy: Fatherhood for Black Men Living Away from Their Children.* New York: Columbia University Press.

Hawkins, Alan J., and David C. Dollahite. 1997. "Beyond the Role-inadequacy Perspective of Fathering." In *Generative Fathering: Beyond Deficit Perspectives,* edited by Alan J. Hawkins and David C. Dollahite. Thousand Oaks, Calif.: Sage Publications.

Ihinger-Tallman, Marilyn, Kay Pasley, and Cheryl Buehler. 1993. "Developing a Middle-range Theory of Father Involvement Postdivorce." *Journal of Family Issues* 15(4): 550–71.

———. 1995. "Developing a Middle-range Theory of Father Involvement Postdivorce." In *Fatherhood: Contemporary Theory, Research, and Social Policy,* edited by William Marsiglio. Thousand Oaks, Calif.: Sage Publications.

Juby, Heather, and Celine Le Bourdais. 1998. "The Changing Context of Fatherhood in Canada: A Life Course Analysis." *Population Studies* 52(2): 163–75.

Koball, Heather L., and Desiree Principe. 2002. *Do Nonresident Fathers Who Pay Child Support Visit Their Children More?* Washington: Urban Institute Press.

Lamb, Michael E., Joseph Pleck, Eric L. Charnov, and James A. Levine. 1987. "A Biosocial Perspective on Paternal Behavior and Involvement." In *Parenting Across the Life Span: Biosocial Dimensions,* edited by Jane B. Lancaster, Jean Altman, Alice S. Rossi, and Lonnie R. Sherrod. Hawthorne, N.Y.: Aldine Publishing.

Liebow, Elliot. 1967. *Tally's Corner: A Study of Negro Street Corner Men.* Boston, Mass.: Little, Brown.

Manning, Wendy D., and Pamela J. Smock. 1999. "New Families and Nonresident Father-Child Visitation." *Social Forces* 78(1): 87–116.

Marsiglio, William. 1991. "Paternal Engagement Activities with Minor Children." *Journal of Marriage and the Family* 53(4): 973–86.

———. 1995. "Fatherhood Scholarship: An Overview and Agenda for the Future." In *Fatherhood: Contemporary Theory, Research, and Social Policy,* edited by William Marsiglio. Thousand Oaks, Calif.: Sage Publications.

Marsiglio, William, Paul Amato, Randal D. Day, and Michael E. Lamb. 2000. "Scholarship on Fatherhood in the 1990s and Beyond." *Journal of Marriage and the Family* 62(4): 1173–91.

Marsiglio, William, and Mark Cohan. 2000. "Contextualizing Father Involvement and Paternal Influence: Sociological and Qualitative Themes." *Marriage and Family Review* 29(2/3): 75–95.

Miller, David B. 1994. "Influences on Parental Involvement of African-American Adolescent Fathers." *Child and Adolescent Social Work Journal* 11(5): 363–79.

Mincy, Ronald. 2002. "Who Should Marry Whom?: Multiple Partner Fertility Among New Parents." Working Paper 2002-03-FF. Princeton, N.J.: Center for Research on Child Wellbeing.

Minton, Carmelle, and Kay Pasley. 1996. "Fathers' Parenting Role Identity and Father Involvement: A Comparison of Nondivorced and Divorced, Nonresident Fathers." *Journal of Family Issues* 17(1): 26–45.

Nelson, Timothy J. 2004. "Low-income Fathers." *Annual Review of Sociology* 30(4): 427–51.

Nelson, Timothy J., Susan Clampet-Lunquist, and Kathryn Edin. 2002. "Sustaining Fragile Fatherhood: Father Involvement Among Low-income, Noncustodial African-American Fathers in Philadelphia." In *Handbook of Father Involvement Multidisciplinary Perspectives,* edited by Catherine S. Tamis-LeMonda and Natasha Cabrera. Mahwah, N.J.: Lawrence Erlbaum Associates.

Parke, Ross D. 2002. "Fathers and Families." In *Handbook of Parenting, Volume 3. Being and Becoming a Parent,* edited by Marc Bornstein. Mahwah, N.J.: Lawrence Erlbaum Associates.

Pleck, Joseph H. 1997. "Paternal Involvement: Levels, Sources, and Consequences." In *The Role of the Father in Child Development,* edited by Michael E. Lamb. New York: John Wiley & Sons.

Rangarajan, Anu, and Phillip Gleason. 1998. "Young Unwed Fathers of AFDC Children: Do They Provide Support?" *Demography* 35(2): 175–86.

Seltzer, Judith A. 1991. "Relationships Between Fathers and Children Who Live Apart: The Father's Role After Separation." *Journal of Marriage and the Family* 53(1): 79–101.

Seltzer, Judith A., Sara McLanahan, and Thomas L. Hanson. 1998. "Will Child Support Enforcement Increase Father-child Contact and Parental Conflict After Separation?" In *Fathers Under Fire: The Revolution in Child Support Enforcement,* edited by Irwin Garfinkel, Sara McLanahan, Daniel R. Meyer, and Judith A. Seltzer. New York: Russell Sage Foundation.

Stone, Glenn, and Patrick McKenry. 1998. "Nonresidential Father Involvement: A Test of a Mid-range Theory." *Journal of Genetic Psychology* 159(3): 313–36.

Tamis-LeMonda, Catherine S., and Natasha Cabrera. 1999. "Perspectives on Father Involvement: Research and Policy." *Social Policy Report: Society for Research in Child Development* 13(1): 1–32.

Chapter 10

Child Support Among Low-Income Noncustodial Fathers

KATHERINE A. MAGNUSON AND
CHRISTINA M. GIBSON-DAVIS

HIGH POVERTY rates among single mother families and the consequent hardships their children face have focused attention on the role of absent fathers and child support as antipoverty strategy. Nationally, nearly 75 percent of custodial parents receive some kind of financial support from noncustodial parents (Grall 2003), but the percentage of low-income parents, usually fathers, providing for their families is much lower (Sorensen and Zibman 2001). Analysis of welfare populations indicate that only between 20 percent and 30 percent of poor fathers provide cash support to their children, though a slightly higher percentage provide in-kind resources (Miller et al. 2004; Rangarajan and Gleason 1998). Such low levels of support have generated research into why fathers contribute so few resources to their noncustodial children, and whether they have the means to meet child support obligations (Cancian and Meyer 2004; Sorensen and Oliver 2002).

The child support picture becomes complicated when multiple partner fertility is considered. Multiple partner fertility is a term coined by scholars to describe families in which at least one partner has a child by someone else (Furstenberg and King 1999 cited in Carlson and Furstenberg 2006; Mincy 2002). It is particularly common among low-income families. A recent study found that at least 30 percent of welfare recipients in Wisconsin had children with two or more fathers, and 50 percent of mothers and fathers had children with more than one partner (Meyer, Cancian, and Cook 2005). Research with unmarried parents in urban areas—The Fragile Families and Child Wellbeing study—has found similarly high rates of multiple partner fertility (Carlson and Furstenberg 2006).

Currently little is known about how low-income fathers divide their time and money across complex parenting arrangements, and why many provide few resources to households that are home to their noncustodial children (Miller et al. 2004). One possible explanation is that many fathers have low earnings and the demands on their resources are so great that the amount provided to any one child is insignificant (Manning, Stewart, and Smock 2003; Sorensen and Oliver 2002). A father owing child support to children in multiple households will be court ordered to pay a much higher proportion of his income than one whose noncustodial children live in the same household. An alternative explanation is that after the birth of a child, a father channels economic resources to his new family in an effort to demonstrate commitment, and greatly reduces or ends his support for other children (Furstenberg and Cherlin 1991).

We consider influences on fathers' support for their noncustodial children. Data come from the Time, Love, and Cash Among Couples with Children study. To take advantage of the longitudinal nature of TLC3, we explore the cash and material goods that fathers provide for two sets of noncustodial children. First, we describe the child support given for children resulting from unmarried fathers' and mothers' previous relationships. Second, we analyze unmarried TLC3 fathers' financial contributions to their noncustodial children once their relationship with the TLC3 mother ends. We find that fathers with the means to support their children are generally doing so. Fathers point to low earnings and incarceration to explain their lack of support, and to what little they can do as a sign of their ability to "care" for their children. In contrast, many mothers report that they have learned that noncustodial fathers can't be counted on to provide support for children even if promised, and voice frustration that they are unreliable.

Background

State child support enforcement agencies assist in establishing paternity and locating noncustodial fathers. Formal orders are established and modified by administrative hearing or family court. According to federal regulations, custodial parents who receive federal means-tested public assistance (including cash benefits, food stamps, and child care subsidies) are required to sign child support rights over to the state. In recent years, the computerization of records, including the federal new hire notification system, has greatly increased the capability of child support agencies to establish and collect formal child support. With few exceptions, child support orders require payments to be made by wage withholding, which is now the most common form of collection. Thus, once orders are established, fathers who are regularly employed have little discretion over their payments.

In an effort to standardize orders, state agencies provide guidelines for payments, which are typically expressed as a proportion of the noncustodial parents' income after taxes and other mandatory contributions. Court orders are set at one point in time, and adjusted every three years. Thus, unless the father petitions the court in the interim, these orders are not sensitive to short term fluctuations in income. When noncustodial parents are underemployed, orders may be based on a father's previous earnings or expected earnings based on labor market conditions. Those who are not regularly employed must pay through the courts.

Currently, New York and Wisconsin share a similar set of guidelines for a father paying support to a custodial mother: 17 percent for one child, 25 percent for two children, and up to about 34 percent for five or more children. Illinois guidelines are somewhat higher, with rates starting at 20 percent for one child and increasing to 45 percent for five children (Office of Child Support Enforcement 2002). For fathers with children in multiple households, the total amount of support owed is higher as these rates apply for each custodial mother, although child support payments to another household are often deducted in calculating a father's income when a subsequent order is set. For example, a father with two children in one household will owe 25 percent of his income, whereas a father with two children with different mothers will owe about 31 percent.[1]

Mothers may not receive child support for several reasons. First, fathers may not be formally employed, though some states mandate a minimum monthly payment even when a father is not employed. Second, mothers may decide not to pursue a formal child support order, though in most cases welfare recipients are required to do so, either because the parents have an amicable informal arrangement or because she does not want the support. Third, the state agency might not be effective in enforcing orders even when they exist. Currently, states vary widely in their enforcement efforts and the penalties they impose on nonpaying fathers. Most states use a variety of strategies to enforce payment, for example, including suspending driver licenses and seizing tax refunds or property. Some states also allow the courts to impose more severe penalties. Wisconsin, for example, has the most severe policies for nonpayment, which may include finding the nonpayee in contempt of court, which may in turn result in incarceration.

Our research sites vary in child support enforcement, though differences in administrative reporting across states make these comparisons difficult. In 2002, Illinois reported that they had established formal orders for 41 percent of the child support cases, but only 24 percent had any collections. The corresponding rates in New York and Wisconsin were much higher, 73 percent and 79 percent respectively had formal orders and 50 percent and 65 percent had some collections (Office of Child Support Enforcement 2002). In 2000, Illinois ranked among the least effective child support regimes nationwide, whereas New York and Wisconsin were much more effective.

Increased complexity in family structure has piqued interest in how multiple partner fertility and competing parental responsibilities affect child support payments. About 40 to 50 percent of fathers who enter into new relationships enter households with children, and most of these children are not theirs biologically. Indeed, nearly 40 percent of noncustodial fathers live in households with "new" nonbiological children (Sorensen and Zibman 2001; Manning and Smock 2000). In addition, many of these new relationships subsequently produce new biological children.

Multiple partner fertility is more common among low-income and unmarried populations (Meyer, Cancian, and Cook 2005). Frank Furstenberg and Rosalind Berkowitz King (1999, cited in Carlson and Furstenberg 2006) found that nearly 50 percent of a sample of disadvantaged women in Baltimore had births by more than one father. Using the Fragile Families and Child Wellbeing sample, Carlson and Furstenberg (2006) found that 40 percent of married couples and 60 percent of unmarried couples have at least one partner with a child from a previous relationship. Multiple partner fertility is also more common among non Hispanic black mothers, mothers who give birth in their teen years, and fathers with lower levels of education and a history of incarceration (Carlson and Furstenberg 2006).

Early child support research concentrated on sociodemographic factors, and found that fathers who remarry and have higher incomes and educational attainment are more likely to pay support and visit with their noncustodial children. However, this research overlooked the fact that many fathers have children by more than one mother, including children with new partners (Manning, Stewart, and Smock 2003). More recently, evidence has suggested that fathers with children by multiple mothers pay less support overall (Manning and Smock 2000; Cooksey and Craig 1998). Wendy Manning and her colleagues (2003) found that fathers with the most complex family arrangements paid the least support overall, even after household characteristics were taken into account. Similarly, among welfare recipients in Wisconsin, Daniel Meyer, Maria Cancian, and Steven Cook (2005) find that fathers with children by multiple mothers are less likely to make formal child support payments. These studies, however, provide little explanation for why such fathers pay less than other fathers.

As noted, it is possible that in situations of multiple partner fertility, fathers may preferentially direct resources to their new biological children. Frank Furstenberg and Andrew Cherlin (1991) argue that in an effort to show commitment to their new families, remarried fathers may provide less support to their nonresidential children, and essentially "swap families." Unfortunately, the studies that analyze how fathers allocate their resources over multiple families are quite sparse. Some show that child support payments decline as time after the divorce increases, as the "swapping family" hypothesis would predict (Seltzer 1991; Teachman 1991). However, that others find no association between living with another child and levels of child support payments casts serious doubt on this argument (Smock and Manning 1997; Veum 1993). Wendy Manning and Pamela Smock (2000) were the first to offer direct evidence that divorced fathers swap families, but that they do so only when they have new biological children, not when they are living in households with children they did not father.

If men who father children with multiple women are likely to be more disadvantaged, it might explain their lower child support payments. Paying even a little child support may be difficult for fathers with low-wage jobs or irregular employment, who struggle to meet their own basic needs (Sullivan 1989). Although Wendy Manning, Susan Stewart, and Pamela Smock (2003) found that nonresident fathers living with other biological children were less likely to pay formal support and give informal support for their noncustodial children, these differences were largely explained by fathers' characteristics, particularly their earnings. It may be that this association is causal, such that lower earnings constrain father's ability to support their children. This association may also reflect the fact that characteristics that lead men to partner with multiple women may also lead them to have difficulty in the labor market.

Qualitative studies have deepened our understanding of child support dynamics among low-income populations, but have yet to tackle questions related to multiple partner fertility. Fathers in these studies report that they do what they can to provide for their children, and for many fathers, this may mean an informal child support arrangement, whereby they provide under-the-table cash payments or in-kind goods directly to the mother (Edin 1995; Pate 2002; Waller and Plotnick 2001; Roy 1999). Low-income fathers' informal support, however, may be more important as a symbol of their commitment to the child than as a source of financial support (Rainwater 1970). Both Carol Stack (1974) and Kathryn Edin (1995) find that low-income parents expect low-income mothers to shoulder the day-to-day costs of rearing children, whereas economically disadvantaged fathers should simply help out when they can, often providing no more than "pampers" on a regular basis.

Given the correlation between multiple partner fertility and economic disadvantage, we use four rounds of rich, qualitative data to better understand both why noncustodial fathers are not contributing more to their children, and the role that multiple partner fertility may play in explaining patterns of support. The popular discourse often assumes that such men are "deadbeat dads," not willing to take responsibility for the children they've fathered but no longer live with. But another explanation is that they cannot pay child support without impoverishing the children in their own households.

Data

We first consider the extent to which unmarried TLC3 parents either provided (in the case of the fathers) or received (in the case of the mothers) child support. Eighteen mothers who had children with men other than the TLC3 fathers were eligible to be included in this analysis, as were twenty-two TLC3 fathers who had children by women other than TLC3 mothers (37 percent of unmarried mothers and 45 percent of unmarried fathers). One mother and one father were excluded because of insufficient data. Three other fathers and two mothers were excluded because their biological children were not being cared for by the child's biological mother.[2] In sum, we analyzed interviews with fifteen mothers and eighteen fathers, who represented about fifty-seven children. Longitudinal data are available through the fourth wave of individual interviews for all but four of these fathers.[3]

Next, we focus on those couples who were unmarried at the time of the focal child's birth and whose relationship ended over the course of our study. There are fifteen such couples (30 percent of all couples), but two who broke up were excluded from the analysis because the split was so recent that parents had not yet made child support arrangements.[4] Of the thirteen unmarried couples we analyzed, seven were not living together at baseline, and three broke up shortly after the child's birth.

Table 10.1 provides some basic demographic information about the mothers, fathers, and, for the second analysis, couples in our sample.[5] All data are drawn from the individual interviews, primarily the first and fourth waves, though some data were taken from second and third waves of data, particularly when a first or fourth wave interview had not been completed. Where possible, we used both fathers' and mothers' reports of support given (or received), and, as will be evident, parents' perceptions of support sometimes differed (for a discussion of measurement issues, see Nelson 2004). Fathers were asked about their current contributions to all of their children, as well as how those contributions had fluctuated over the last year. We used these data to estimate an annual figure.

Fathers' Children by Previous Partners

The first set of analyses examines the extent to which eighteen unmarried TLC3 fathers provided support to their noncustodial children. More than 70 percent reported providing at least some kind of assistance, either cash or in-kind goods. Seven were paying through the formal

Table 10.1   Descriptive Characteristics of TLC3 Analytic Samples

	Wave One Samples[a]		Wave Four Sample[b]
	Noncustodial Fathers	Mothers	Couples
Cohabitating with TLC3 partner (wave one)	12	13	7
White	0	2	1M/0F
Black	13	9	9M/8F
Hispanic	5	4	3M/5F
Mothers' age	~	24	22
Fathers' age	26	~	23
High school degree or higher	7	10	8M/6F
Chicago	8	6	4
New York	3	3	0
Milwaukee	7	6	9
Average household income[c]	$ 24,719	$ 17,500	$ 26,081
Sample size	18	15	13

Source: Authors' calculations.
[a] These TLC3 parents have children from previous relationships; analyses of this sample focus on transfers to these older children.
[b] These TLC3 couples were no longer in a romantic relationship by the fourth wave of data collection; analyses of this sample focus on transfers to TLC3 focal child.
[c] For couples this is the mothers' household income.

child support system by wage withholding. Six were providing informal support, that is, in-kind goods or cash paid directly to the mother, not through the state system. This leaves five fathers who offered their children little or no support.

On average, fathers' contributions to their noncustodial children were modest. We estimated that these eighteen fathers on average contributed $1,404 per year in formal and informal cash support to their noncustodial children, amounting to about 10 percent of their average yearly earnings ($13,619). However, this average masks considerable heterogeneity. For the thirteen who paid anything, the figure was $2,303. As expected, contributing fathers also had higher average earnings ($20,834).

Formal Child Support Payments

The fathers making the largest contributions to their noncustodial children were those who had had the strongest ties to the labor market and higher levels of earnings as well as formal child support orders (see table 10.2). Tyrone, an African American twenty-nine-year-old father of two, explained that he does not mind that some of his wages are withheld for child support. Having just started a full-time job, he was

Table 10.2   Child Support Among Unmarried Fathers with Noncustodial Children During Wave One

	Formally Employed	Not Formally Employed	Total
No support	1	4	5
Informal support	2	4	6
Formal support	7	0	7
Total	10	8	18

Source: Authors' calculations.

working more than forty hours a week as a bus driver, earning about $34,000 a year after taxes. He estimated that, given his current job, about $3,600 would be withheld from his wages over the next year. Although the order was set when he was working mandatory overtime and his hours had since been reduced, he did not try to get the payments lowered. He explained, "you know it's going to my daughter, it's not really a big issue . . . it's like extra." Four years later, Tyrone, was still driving a bus and both his salary and his child support payments had increased, with pre-tax earnings of about $60,000, he was paying about $5,532 a year in child support.

Fathers with the means to pay support to their noncustodial children were likely to do so, though few had earnings as high as Tyrone did. Most explained that though it was important to contribute to their noncustodial children, they often found paying financially difficult. Gavin, an African American father of two noncustodial children, explained. "They expect you to pay the impossible. Barely make enough and they want to charge you an arm and a leg."

The experience of Freddie, a twenty-year-old Hispanic father of three, illustrates how fathers' employment was linked with meeting formal child support obligations. When first interviewed, Freddie was paying $400 a month for two children from a previous partner. He earned just over $1,000 from his factory job and was living with his mother. He described how paying child support affected his economic situation. "And even though I might not buy little extra things for them, you know, but still, it's a big chunk out of what I make. So, basically I work for my kids. When you think about it, I really don't have much spending money for me."

Over the four years we knew him, Freddie had difficulty keeping a job. By the end of the study, he was working as a sketch artist in a mall. He explained that he was not an employee, but an independent contractor, and thus was paid a portion of the proceeds he earned. He usually brought home about $350 a week, though last month he only made about a quarter of that amount because business was slow. He was making few, if any, child support payments and owed $600 a month. "I can't pay it. How is it going to get paid, you know? I'd have to literally live in a cardboard box to pay that amount of child support. That's like rent and groceries . . . right there alone. . . . So the judge told me to get a better job, and that's what I am doing." Freddie was still hoping to find a job that would provide him with enough income to both pay child support and meet his own expenses.

Fathers who had to pay arrears in addition to regular monthly support felt particularly burdened, because these arrearages often accrued during periods of unemployment. When we first met Tony, the thirty-five-year-old Puerto Rican father with three noncustodial daughters, he worked as a maintenance engineer in a large retail store. He paid about $300 of his $900 per month in salary to child support. Four years later, his daughters had grown up, but he was still paying down child support arrears. He felt the debt had set him back. "Financially, it hurt me. I'm thirty-five years old. I'm supposed to have a house, a car, money in the bank and it's like by the time I hit forty, I'm going to be just now trying to get everything." He says that the arrears ". . . crippled me. I've been busting my ass, excuse my language, since 1995. I have not stopped working. If I lose a job [and don't pay], they'd suspend my license and take every[thing]."

Informal Child Support Payments

Fathers who earned very little in the formal economy and mostly worked off the books were more likely to make informal arrangements. Informal support was also the choice of fathers involved in illegal activities (table 10.2). Informal cash payments were generally smaller than formal payments, in part because earnings were lower. More than half of the informal arrangements were relatively consistent, with cash payments ranging from $75 to $200 a month, according to fathers' accounting.

The timing of informal contributions varied greatly. Some fathers provided money or goods every two weeks; others didn't pay regularly, but gave on an as-needed basis, at least when they happened to have the money. For example, Leonard, a twenty-year-old African American father of three young children, worked in a nursing home, earned about $10,500 a year, and lived with his mother. He had just stopped attending a community college when we first met him because he needed to earn more money. Leonard had a young son from a previous relationship he supported by buying items whenever his child's mother asked for it. "Yeah, I just buy for him. She'll call. 'He needs this.' I'll get it for him. Or I'll be at the mall shopping for myself and I'll see something [and] I'll just get it." He estimated that he spent as much as $200 per month on his son, and by his account this arrangement was satisfactory to all involved.

Travis, a twenty-five-year-old African American father of two, had a work history filled with part-time and low-wage jobs. Yet in the final interview, he disclosed that he had been selling drugs for several years and during a good week would make an additional $500 to $700. His involvement in the drug trade had fluctuated over the years, and at its height he claimed to be making as much as $1,300 a day. Travis said that he had consistently taken care of his noncustodial children, by providing each of their mothers with both informal cash ($75 per week) and in-kind goods. He explained that he provided much more to them than they would receive from a formal child support arrangement, because so little of his income was on the books. "They didn't want child support at that time so it's just support from me so they could keep food in the house, get the diapers if they need it. Most of the time that money was spent on something else and I still had to go buy diapers. I still had to go buy food."

Fathers providing only in-kind support contributed more sporadically than other fathers. These contributions were largely symbolic and did not provide mothers with much assistance. Nevertheless, this support served to substantiate their claims of being connected to and of taking care of their children. For example, Tim, a twenty-two-year-old African American father of five, was unemployed when we first interviewed him and subsequently went to jail for a drug-related offense. He told us he did not give any cash to the mother of his four other children, who lived in Minneapolis. Tim supported his children only when they were staying with him. "When they here, that's when I pick up. That's when I gotta take care of them."

In contrast to fathers paying through the formal system, fathers providing cash or in-kind goods informally could alter their contributions as their financial circumstances changed. For example, Jason had just been laid off from his job as a courier when he was first interviewed. Since then, the twenty-three-year-old Hispanic father of three, had not been able to provide much support for his two noncustodial children from a previous relationship. Jason's current partner, Veronica, the African American twenty-one-year-old mother of his youngest son, said that his ex-wife had understood his financial difficulties because he had regularly provided support in the past. Before being laid off, he was providing close to $400 a month, but since then Veronica had been paying $100 a month from her earnings. She explains, "I guess now she understands that he's not working so she doesn't really hassle him for it. But he knows what he has to do."

No Child Support

The five fathers who were not providing any support to their children were either not earning any money or were incarcerated. They had little or no resources to provide, even though two of the fathers had formal child support orders. For example, Gavin, a thirty-five-year-old African American father, had been unable to work since sustaining an injury and his worker's compensation had run out. He had two teenage noncustodial children for whom he had been paying child support through the formal system for years, though he now only owed support for his daughter. Because he was not working, the child support bill was accumulating. "But it just keep addin' up. Every month. I get a little flak from her mother, but ain't nothin' I can do about it. . . . She ask me, callin' me, ask me do I have any money. Sometime I have it. Sometime I don't. Like when I was getting workman's comp. I'd give her a little something." By the fourth interview, Gavin was still not working; he was staying home and taking care of his youngest child. Meanwhile, his partner, Calista, who worked in a factory, gave $160 of her earnings each month to pay the child support order.

For the four years we knew him, Antonio, a twenty-nine-year-old African American father, did not provide any support for his three noncustodial children from two previous relationships. He also gave only small amounts of informal support to the mother of the focal child to support their two children. Living with his grandmother and never having a formal job, he declined to explain to the interviewers exactly how he earned money, though he intimated illegal activity, "I'd rather not say where it come from. But I do what I gotta do to take care of my kids." His most recent partner, the mother of his two youngest children, claimed that he was addicted to illegal drugs. "It [his habit] was too serious. It got to the point where he was doing anything to get what he wanted." During the last interview, he was on house arrest awaiting a trial, though he still saw four of his five noncustodial children regularly.

Providing support, even irregular or informal support, seemed to affirm and validate a father's connection to his child, and sometimes this connection may have interfered with a mother's new family (see also chapter 9, this volume). Paulo, a twenty-nine-year-old Puerto Rican father of six, had his first daughter at age seventeen. After his daughter's mother got a new boyfriend, however, she disappeared, not telling him where she had gone. "Her man didn't want me involved because he says that he's the father. You know and she didn't want me there either. She told me that she didn't need me there. That my daughter didn't need me there. . . . You know, she told me never to set foot back over there again, and that's what I do." Yet Paulo's economic situation is such that even if he were able to see his daughter, it's unlikely he could provide much support. During the first round of interviews, Paulo had been laid off and was expecting unemployment insurance payments, but had not yet received any. The mother of his five younger children, with whom he lived, was receiving public assistance, and they were struggling to pay their rent and bills.

Changes in Support

Shortly after the birth of the focal child, most fathers claimed they were making some contributions to their other noncustodial children, though they often noted that it created financial strain. By the time these children had reached their fourth birthdays, there was an increase in the number of formal child support orders set and paid. All but three of the fathers interviewed had formal support orders in place by this time.

Michael, a twenty-six-year-old African American father of two noncus-todial children, had just started a job when our study began, after a spell of unemployment that followed the bankruptcy of his cleaning business. At that time, he was not paying his ex-wife any support. Four years later, he had five noncustodial children with three mothers, and was paying formal support for all of them, totaling $700—nearly 50 percent of what he earned from his main job each month. Michael took a second job so that he would have enough money to afford his rent and car payments. He was also providing informal support to the mother of his youngest two children, because of the way child support is assessed when fathers owe for children in multiple households, she was getting a lower percentage of his earnings. "I still buy them pampers because she gets less than the others. . . . They start the percentage high and then it tapers, so I'll just give her a little something extra."

Interestingly, two of three fathers who continued to provide only informal support had been to court and did not have child support orders rendered. Each claimed he was able to convince the judge that they had been, and were continuing, to support their children. As Travis described, the mothers of his children had told the judges that they do not want a formal order. "Well, we've been to court, neither one of them wants it, 'cuz, I mean, I do what I'm supposed to do. If I wasn't doing my job then it would be a different story. . . . I always make sure I try to give more than what the . . . than the government would try to do." However, it is also worth noting that most of Travis's income came from his drug dealing, so the mothers had little to gain from formal orders.

Reductions in child support appear to have resulted from changes in fathers' employment status or incarceration. Although Ollie, a twenty-three-year-old African American father with two noncustodial children, had been working at a factory while under house arrest around the time of the focal child's birth. This job lasted for only a few months—until he was jailed for a parole violation. Since then, Ollie had been unemployed or incarcerated for drug offenses, and thus unable to pay child support. At his last interview, he told the interviewer that he had been looking for work for three months. He admitted that he had spent the past ten years dealing drugs, and but claimed he would like to get a regular job. He said he had been a "wreck . . . getting kinda depressed, can't find a job." He was putting in "ten applications a day" anywhere that might be hiring, but he knew his "bad" work and criminal record did not make him attractive to employers, and he worried that accruing child support arrears and continued nonpayment might land him back in jail.

Ollie was not the only one worried about accumulating arrears. Some mothers were also concerned about the penalties for nonpayment in the formal child support system, particularly jail time. DaJuan, a twenty-nine-year-old African American father of eleven, was incarcerated at the time of the first waves of individual interviews. Magdalena, the twenty-two-year-old African American mother of five of his children noted, "Putting them away, that's still not going to . . . that's still not giving money to the child. . . . And when they get out what? You still don't do it, so you put them back in, so what? You're really not accomplishing much; you're just keeping him away from the kids."

Concerns About Child Support

Fathers and mothers were both concerned about how much money fathers should pay to help support their noncustodial children.[6] Both believed that noncustodial fathers should provide some support. Gavin's partner Calista claimed, "That's his kids, and I know he needs to support them." Tamika, a twenty-nine-year-old African American mother, was frustrated that George, her thirty-year-old African American partner, was reluctant to pay formal support for his noncustodial daughter by another mother. She felt George, who had earnings of about $24,000 a year, should "take care" of his daughter. She told him as she drove him to his court appointment, "You go in there and take the money out [of your wallet]. What in the world is wrong with you? I'm gonna help you pay the bills." Similarly, Dahlia, a twenty-nine-year-old Puerto Rican mother whose partner paid formal child support, shared her perspective, "Kids have to eat and go to school. They need clothes. Yeah, that's his responsibility."

Some parents' comments, however, indicated both uncertainty about how much support custodial mothers should be given and concerns that custodial mothers might try to take advantage of fathers. LaShawnda, a twenty-seven-year-old African American mother, was concerned that Tyrone, the twenty-nine-year-old African American described earlier, was being asked by his former partner to provide too much. She felt that he should not continue to make informal contributions to his child's mother in addition to making formal child support payments. "He's paying like $300 something a month. And the child she doesn't even need that much a month. So I totally disagree and then again for her to ask him to do something out of his pocket. . . . I told him like I wouldn't give her a cent, I don't care what the child needs. . . . That is what child support is for."

Camille, a nineteen-year-old African American involved with Freddie, the Hispanic father of three discussed earlier, explained how the mother of Freddie's older children tried to take advantage of him. "She just makes stuff up too. . . . She'll call and say, 'oh, I didn't get a check this week' or whatever." Camille's description reflects a common sentiment among new partners. Although mothers are entitled to support for their children from noncustodial fathers, fathers need to be careful that they are not being exploited.

Mothers' Children by Previous Partners

In contrast to the relatively high number of unmarried TLC3 fathers who described providing at least some support for their noncustodial children, during the first round of baseline interviews very few unmarried TLC3 mothers reported receiving any assistance for children from previous relationships. All of the mothers in our sample had at least joint custody of their children. Most had full custody. Of the fifteen mothers who reported having children with someone other than the focal child's father, only three reported receiving financial assistance regularly—one formally and two informally.

When asked why they were not receiving support, these mothers uniformly claimed it was because their former partners could not provide it, either because of unemployment or incarceration. At least 40 percent said that their partner's involvement in the criminal justice system was the reason for their lack of support. Rochelle, a twenty-one-year-old African American mother of three, told the interviewer that she tried to get support from the child's father through the state system, but "never received anything . . . because he's in and out of jail. He's never working." The last time she checked on the amount she was owed, it was approximately $24,000. Similarly, when asked why she was not getting child support for her older daughter, LaShawnda responded, "Well he can't do anything. He's incarcerated." The majority of TLC3 mothers had sought formal support from their ex-partners at one time, but with little payoff.

Fathers' Financial Contributions

We next considered how unmarried fathers' patterns of support for their children changed over time by analyzing contributions to their noncustodial focal children after their relationships to these children's mothers ended. We compare the financial support these fathers provided shortly after the child's birth to that about the time of the child's fourth birthday (our fourth round of interviews).

How much financial support did they provide when the focal children were born? Two to three months after the birth of the child, when we interviewed each father one on one, 85 percent said they were providing formal or informal financial support for the child. This is not surprising, given that six of the thirteen fathers lived with the child and earned on average $22,000 a year. The five noncustodial fathers were providing about $3,000 a year to TLC3 mothers, if their current levels of support were maintained. The contributions, however, were not always regular or consistent. Only two were not providing any support.

Four years later, things had changed dramatically. Half of the fathers had little to no contact with their child, and a handful more saw the child only sporadically. In all cases, the child lived with the mother. Although nearly 70 percent were providing some type of support, only 38 percent (five of the thirteen) were providing regular child support through the formal system. Payments ranged from a low of $1,440 a year to a high of $8,976 a year (a father paying support for several children). Again, the father's employment was a key determinant of whether he was meeting his obligations (see table 10.3). Fathers employed in the formal economy were most likely to be paying regular support through the formal system. Those with weak ties to the labor market were paying little, if anything.

The five fathers who were providing only informal support to their children had difficulty maintaining a job. For example, Marco, a twenty-two-year-old Puerto Rican father of two, struggled with drug addiction and was periodically incarcerated. Nevertheless, he did manage to give a small amount of money to Frieda, the eighteen-year-old Hispanic mother of his two children, whenever he was out of jail and had work. "He would give me twenty or forty dollars for the kids . . . like that every time he would go to work, 'cause he was working, in the beginning he was working. So, he would, he would pay his rent or whatever he has to do, buy his food, and whatever was left he would give to his kids. Or he would take his kids out to Chucky Cheese or whatever."

At times, finding work was a problem even for fathers who had no history with the criminal justice system. For example, George moved to St. Louis when his daughter was about two years old. Tamika said that George bought their daughter shoes or clothes occasionally, but that it had been more than a year since he had given her money. Consequently, Tamika went to the state agency for assistance in setting a formal award and collecting child support. However, George's papers were sent to his former Chicago address, Tamika's mother's home, so she knew there was little chance that she would receive formal support.

A few months later, George said that he was sending Tamika a check for $186, half of the cost of their daughter's day care, each month, though he admitted it sometime took him a few days to get the check mailed. He was earning about $1,200 a month working full time for a pharmaceutical

Table 10.3   Child Support for the TLC3 Focal Child Among Unmarried Fathers During Wave Four

	Formally Employed	Not Formally Employed	Total
No support	1	2	3
Informal support	1	4	5
Formal support	5	0	5
Total	7	6	13

Source: Authors' calculations.

packaging company, and had a part-time sales job on the weekends to make an additional $300 a month. He explained that he had not been providing support before because he had been out of work, "I was struggling, trying to get a job, but after that, you know, I started getting [visiting] my daughter, right now, for at least the last year on a consistent basis, I started sending her money and she doesn't take into account I buy my daughter stuff too as well."

Here too, fathers who provided only in-kind support portrayed their contributions in a positive light. By buying clothes and other necessities, fathers felt they were demonstrating commitment, ensuring that their children had all that they needed. Complying with mothers' requests for assistance, if only intermittently, gave fathers the ability to claim they were fulfilling their obligations as fathers. A twenty-five-year-old African American father of five, Antonio cared for his two daughters by the focal child's mother on the weekends after being sentenced to house arrest. He also provided cash when their mother, Sherise, needed to get something for their children. "She asks me, you know, buy 'em shoes, or buy 'em this, whatever—I get them what they need." However, when asked if Sherise was satisfied with his contributions, he said, "basically . . . she ain't never too satisfied."

By the final round of interviews, only three fathers were failing to provide any type of support. Again, incarceration and low earnings were key explanations for why these fathers were not providing even occasional informal support for their children. John, an eighteen-year-old Hispanic, for example, was incarcerated during the study for stealing car stereos. John and Natalie, the white eighteen-year-old mother of the focal child, had a tumultuous relationship, breaking up and reconciling several times before splitting for good. John had several low-wage jobs during the four years of our study, each followed by several months of unemployment. By the time their son was three years old, John had been incarcerated for several months. When Natalie was last interviewed, John had finished serving his first sentence but was back in jail again, this time for a parole violation.

A paternity dispute was at the center of one father's lack of payments. Ironically, Myles, a twenty-two-year-old African-American father, had a steady job and was eager to pay child support. He filed papers hoping to get both a formal order and visitation rights established. However, the child's mother, Sahara, a twenty-year-old African American, and her new husband claimed that Myles was not the biological father of the child, and did not want the support or for him to have any contact with the child.

Mothers' View of Support

Whereas many noncustodial TLC3 fathers indicated that their support for their children was constrained by their unemployment and incarceration, the mothers who received only informal support felt that fathers were ignoring their responsibilities and they were frustrated by fathers' unreliable assistance. According to these mothers, the fathers' unemployment and criminal activity, particularly drug use, were evidence of their irresponsible behavior, not of their inability to pay. Many mothers had not expected to bear the full cost of raising their children after ending their relationships. Instead, they had anticipated receiving substantial support from their ex-partners, but some mothers learned the fathers' contributions could not be counted on. Sherise was African American and had two daughters with Antonio. She explained,

> He'll agree and he'll wind up not doing it and I'll wind up doing myself. Like they got a layaway in the store now and I owe them like $72 but I had asked him when it was time for me to make the payment, like last week. I had asked him to give me the money, he said he was gone give it to me. I had the money, I just wanted to see if he was gon' give it to me. He was like, yeah, I'm gone give it to you. Never heard from him.

Natalie was combining her earnings from a series of low-level retail jobs, child care assistance from the state, and financial support from her family to make ends meet. She described what happened when she asked John for help in paying for their son's day care:

> I didn't think it was much to ask so it's not like he's done anything for the past year and a half. But he said he'd love to help me with money, this is his chance to prove himself to me. But he could never come up with the money. He bought himself a car. Like, thanks for the money for day care. I'm glad you got yourself a car when you don't have a license.

Like Sherise and Natalie, many other mothers said that their children's fathers promised help and support, but rarely provided it. After being misled repeatedly, they no longer expected support regardless of fathers' expressed intentions.

After repeated disappointments with Freddie, Camille, the nineteen-year-old African American mother discussed earlier, became resigned to the fact that she would have to care for her daughter by herself. When her daughter was born, Camille was living with her parents, attending college, and working part-time. After graduating from college, she was earning just over $25,000 a year as a program coordinator for a medical study, but resented the ease with which Freddie had avoided his financial responsibility, "I don't have the option of saying 'oh, I'm not going to buy this for my daughter because Freddie would get it.' I have to get it because I KNOW he won't get it. . . . So I just think it's too easy for them."

Other Sources of Support

Given the relatively low levels of support from biological fathers, how were these mothers, most of whom worked at fairly low-wage jobs, managing to provide for their children? For many mothers, a new romantic partner was providing support for her children. Ten of the thirteen mothers were involved in new relationships, and three had married. Seven had given birth to a child with a new partner by the study's end. New partners were particularly prevalent among mothers receiving little support from the focal child's father. Indeed, seven of the nine mothers getting only informal support or no support at all were involved with new men—five of them living with their new partner. In contrast, only two of the four receiving regular support through the formal system had entered into a new romantic relationship and both lived with this partner.

For these mothers, the presence of a new relationship meant a partner who was able to help them take care of their children, particularly financially. The new romantic partners were providing either direct or indirect support for the focal child. Whereas once the child's cohabiting fathers were contributing to the support of the focal child, four years later none contributed more than a few thousand dollars, and most contributed less than a few hundred. In contrast, the new romantic partners cohabiting with mothers were contributing about $15,000 on average. Even new partners who were not yet cohabiting with mothers were also providing cash or in-kind goods specifically intended for the focal child.

Mothers found these new partners' willingness to care for their children appealing. As Adrienne, a twenty-year-old African American mother of four, explained, her new fiancé had helped her provide for her sons early on in their relationship. "Right when we met he was like, he didn't even move in with us yet and he bought the kids shoes. He just realizes that people need stuff, and he knows he can give it."

A nineteen-year-old Puerto Rican mother, Priscilla, said that she wanted nothing from her former partner Rafael, a twenty-two-year-old Puerto Rican. Their relationship ended about a year after the birth of their daughter. A few years later, Priscilla was living with her new partner Juan. When we last spoke with her, Rafael's weekly child support payment was nearly a month late because he had been laid off from his job. However, Priscilla was quite adamant that she could take care of the child, with Juan's help, and that the child support ($125 per month) was not necessary, "I don't want shit from [Rafael] never, ever in his life. [My child] got everything he needs. And everything, all of this, me and Juan." For some mothers, their new partners had taken on the role of father so completely that the focal child called him "daddy."

Conclusion

This chapter focused on the reasons that many low-income fathers provide so little support to their noncustodial children (Miller et al. 2004). One of the factors that could contribute to this lack of support might be the high incidence of multiple partner fertility. We outlined two possible reasons that having children with multiple partners might lower financial contributions. First, fathers may prefer to support the children they live with—the "swapping families" hypothesis. Alternatively, it may be that the characteristics that prompt some men to father children by several partners may also lead to low levels of employment and earnings, which in turn limits their ability to make financial contributions to the mothers of their noncustodial children (Sorensen and Zibman 2001).

Among this sample, the most common reason for a lack of paternal support is not that the father has withdrawn allegiance from the former family in favor of the new family; indeed both mothers and fathers strongly affirm the importance of making contributions to the households of prior children, even when the payments put strain on the budgets of the new family. Instead, incarceration and weak ties to the labor market seem to be the primary culprits. Without regular jobs, these fathers' formal support orders went unpaid. This was true regardless of whether fathers had noncustodial children with one mother or with more.

Fathers with intermittent and informal employment, however, were likely to be providing at least some informal or as needed in-kind support. These small contributions gave fathers a sense of connection to their children and reassured them that they were taking care of their children. Following a breakup, fathers' informal contributions to the focal child, particularly when provided irregularly or only during visits, were often of little instrumental assistance to mothers, who shouldered the bulk of the costs of caring for a child.

Because many noncustodial fathers had so little money to offer, few mothers received regular support and their efforts to pursue formal child support were more often than not fruitless. They attributed the lack of support to the fathers' unemployment, incarceration, and economic disadvantage, and did not expect future support to be forthcoming. Mothers learned, through a series of repeated disappointments, not to count on fathers' financial support. They came to expect little assistance from the fathers, whom they regarded as unreliable, and were discouraged from seeking additional assistance given the low probability of pay-out. Although mothers recognized that the fathers were facing financial hardship, many were not sympathetic to their financial difficulties. Rather, they viewed unemployment and criminal activity as evidence that fathers were irresponsible.

These comments raise an important issue about the extent to which employment is driving fathers' payment of support, rather than fathers' desire (or lack of desire) to pay support driving their employment. Clearly, the fact that fathers paid support when they were formally employed indicates that wage withholding is usually an effective collection strategy. However, if a large proportion of fathers' earnings are garnished to pay child support, they may respond to this disincentive to seek and maintain formal employment by reducing formal employment. Informal work may be more appealing because they can keep all of their wages. However, during the course of the study, rates of unemployment for racial and ethnic minority males were relatively high in the central cities of New York, Chicago, and Milwaukee, which suggests that employment may have been hard to find. In addition, most fathers expressed a desire to find formal employment and were concerned that avoiding current obligations led to arrears and possible incarceration. Nevertheless, associations between child support obligations on one hand and unemployment, informal work, and illegal activities on the other hand are complex.

These data suggested little association between fathers' multiple partner fertility and meeting child support obligations. Whether fathers provided support to their noncustodial children had little to do with the arrival of a new child. Fathers who had strong attachments to the labor market were providing at least some support to their noncustodial children, although these children received just a fraction of what custodial children received. This finding parallels Manning and Smock's (2000) conclusion that some fathers may reduce their payments to noncustodial children following the birth of a new child, but most continue to provide some financial support.

How, then, did mothers provide for their children? Most worked in low-wage jobs, and for many a new partner provided key economic resources. These new men in their lives shared the costs of raising their children and contributed regular financial support. Mothers' perceptions of their new partners' generosity differed from their descriptions of the TLC3 fathers' irregular contributions. In addition, a few parents hinted that some mothers no longer want noncustodial fathers' involvement once they have found new partners (see chapter 8, this volume). Future research should consider whether women's multiple partner fertility may be more important to understanding patterns of child support than men's multiple partner fertility.

One area of possible important influence on fathers' contributions to their children that we did not explore is the quality of the parents' relationship. Previous research has pointed to the quality of mother-father relationships as an important influence on the amount fathers contribute to their children (Bloomer, Sipe, and Ruedt 2002; also see Nelson 2004 for a review). In our study, broken-up couples with the most strained relationships were those in which the fathers were providing low levels of support and the least likely to be involved with their child. However, it was difficult to disentangle whether the poor relationship predicted lower levels of support, or whether lower levels of support further worsened already tenuous relationships. This is an interesting and important avenue for future research.

Only about 20 percent of the mothers in our study said they received financial support for children from previous partners, but 70 percent of the fathers of the focal children said that they provided support to their children's mothers, at least in period immediately following the breakup. Why might the rates of support have been lower for mothers who had children from previous relationships compared with mothers who had more recently ended their relationships? First, it is possible that fathers may overstate and mothers may underreport support (see Nelson 2004). Second, the study's design might be part of the explanation, in that all mothers were selected into the sample because they were still involved romantically with the father of the focal child at the time of the child's birth. If mothers who receive little or no support from noncustodial fathers are more likely than other mothers to repartner, it might explain the lower levels of support mothers received from ex-partners in the first wave of interviews. Third, that mothers' children from previous relationships were older and their parents' relationship had ended longer ago might also account for differences in support (Rangarajan and Gleason 1998).

We also found that mothers with children from previous relationships seemed to be more resigned to the fact that the children's noncustodial fathers were not providing support, most often pointing to fathers' lack of resources as an explanation. However, mothers who broke up with the father of their child during the course of the study seemed, in comparison, more frustrated by the lack of support, even though they were more likely to receive some support. It is unclear what accounts for this difference. The TLC3 mothers point to the TLC3 fathers' expressed intention to provide support as a part of their frustration, with the demise of their relationships being relatively more recently, several were in the process of learning when and if fathers could be counted on to provide support. In contrast, mothers with children from previous relationships had a much longer time to come to terms with the amount and type of support they would (or would not) receive from their children's fathers. In addition, by definition, these mothers had all repartnered with the father of the focal child, thus they might have no longer wanted or sought child support, which might in turn have reduced their feelings of frustration.

Some limitations should be noted. The sample, though similar in many respects to the larger Fragile Families sample, is small and represents the experiences of a select group of parents with young children in three U.S. cities. Caution should therefore be exercised in generalizing to the experiences of all low-income parents. In particular, it is unclear how support may change as the child ages beyond the preschool years. Some literature indicates that fathers are less likely to provide support to older children (Rangarajan and Gleason 1998).

In conclusion, all of the analyses suggest that fathers were contributing something to the support of their noncustodial children if they had the means to do so. There is little evidence of "deadbeat dads"—fathers who can support their children but choose not to pay anything. Incarceration, unemployment, and low pay were the primary explanations given by both mothers and fathers for low levels of support. However, noncustodial fathers providing low levels of support often portrayed their informal and irregular contributions in a positive light and asserted that they took care of their children. In contrast, mothers described fathers' irregular informal contributions as of little help and were frustrated by not being able to count on them for financial assistance. No longer expecting or seeking their help, four years after the birth of the focal child, many mothers relied on a new partner to help provide for their families. Overall, the picture this analysis yields is one of irregularly employed fathers who pay little and more stably employed fathers who make regular payments, most often by having their wages garnished by the state.

Notes

1. One child's order will be set at 17 percent of the father's income, and the next order set will be based on his income net of the first child support order, thus amounting to about 14 percent of his total income.

2. One father had terminated his parental rights and it was unclear who had custody of the child, one father had his mother caring for the child, and one couple had children involved in the foster care system.

3. For five of these fathers, we did not have an individual interview completed during the first wave of data collection. However, these fathers are included in our analysis because the TLC3 mother and later interviews provide a clear portrait of their child support during this time. Longitudinal data are available through the fourth wave of individual interviews for all but four of these fathers. One father in our study died, two were incarcerated, and one was not located.

4. Two of these fathers are incarcerated during the fourth round of individual interviews, and so we rely on mothers' descriptions of child support.

5. There is some overlap among the couples in each analysis. For example, both a father might have had children from a previous relationship and also broken up with the TLC3 mother. Taking this into account we analyzed the data of at least one partner in twenty-nine of the TLC3 couples.

6. Interviewers asked how the TLC3 mothers felt about child support in general, but did not ask about how they felt more specifically about their partners' contributions. Nevertheless, the mothers sometimes commented directly on their partners' situation.

References

Bloomer, Stacey R., Theresa A. Sipe, and Danielle E. Ruedt. 2002. "Child Support Payment and Child Visitation: Perspectives from Non-Resident Fathers and Resident Mothers." *Journal of Sociology and Social Welfare* 29(2): 77–91.

Cancian, Maria., and Daniel Meyer. 2004. "Fathers of Children Receiving Welfare: Can They Provide More Support?" *Social Service Review* 78(2): 179–206.

Carlson, Marcia J., and Frank F. Furstenberg, Jr. 2006. "The Prevalence and Correlates of Multi-Partnered Fertility in the United States." *Journal of Marriage and Family* 68(3): 718–32.

Cooksey, Elizabeth C., and Patricia Craig. 1998. "Parenting from a Distance: The Effects of Paternal Characteristics on Contact Between Nonresident Fathers and Their Children." *Demography* 35(2): 187–200.

Edin, Kathryn. 1995. "Single Mothers and Child Support: The Possibilities and Limits of Child Support Policy." *Children and Youth Services Review* 17(1/2): 203–30.

Furstenberg, Frank F., and Andrew J. Cherlin. 1991. *Divided Families: What Happens to Children When Parents Part.* Cambridge, Mass.: Harvard University Press.

Furstenberg, Frank F., and Rosalind Berkowitz King. 1999. "Multipartnered Fertility Sequences: Documenting an Alternative Family Form." Paper presented at the Population Association of America Meetings, Chicago, Ill.

Grall, Timothy S. 2003. "Custodial Mothers and Fathers and Their Child Support: 2001." *Current Population Reports,* P60-225. Washington: U.S. Government Printing Office for U.S. Bureau of the Census.

Manning, Wendy D., and Pamela J. Smock. 2000. " 'Swapping' Families: Serial Parenting and Economic Support for Children." *Journal of Marriage and the Family* 62(1): 111–22.

Manning, Wendy D., Susan D. Stewart, and Pamela J. Smock. 2003. "The Complexity of Fathers' Parenting Responsibilities and Involvement with Nonresident Children." *Journal of Family Issues* 24(5): 645–67.

Meyer, Daniel R., Maria R. Cancian, and Steven Cook. 2005. "Multiple Partner Fertility: Incidence and Implications for Child Support Policy." *Social Science Review* 79(4): 577–601.

Miller, Cynthia, Mary Farrell, Maria Cancian, and Daniel Meyer. 2004. *The Intersection of Child Support and TANF: Evidence from Samples of Current and Former Welfare Recipients.* New York: MDRC.

Mincy, Ronald. 2002. "Who Should Marry Whom? Multiple Partner Fertility Among New Parents." *Fragile Families* Working Paper #2002-03-FF. Princeton, N.J.: Bendheim-Thoman Center for Research on Child Wellbeing.

Nelson, Timothy J. 2004. "Low-Income Fathers." *Annual Review of Sociology* 30(4): 427–51.

Office of Child Support Enforcement. 2002. *Annual Statistical Report.* Washington: Administration for Children and Families, U.S. Department of Health and Human Services.

Pate, David J. 2002. "An Ethnographic Inquiry into the Life Experiences of African American Fathers with Children on W-2." In *Nonexperimental Analyses of the Full Disregard and Pass-Through,* vol. 2, edited by Daniel R. Meyer and Maria Cancian. Madison, Wisc.: Institute for Research on Poverty.

Rainwater, Lee. 1970. *Behind Ghetto Walls: Black Families in a Federal Slum.* Hawthorne, N.Y.: Aldine de Gruyter.

Rangarajan, Anu, and Philip Gleason. 1998. "Young Unwed Fathers of AFDC Children: Do They Provide Support?" *Demography* 35(2): 175–86.

Roy, Kevin. 1999. "Low-Income Single Fathers in an African American Community and the Requirements of Welfare Reform." *Journal of Family Issues* 20(4): 432–57.

Seltzer, Judith A. 1991. "Relationships Between Fathers and Children Who Live Apart: The Father's Role after Separation." *Journal of Marriage and the Family* 53(1): 79–101.

Smock, Pamela J., and Wendy D. Manning. 1997. "Nonresident Parents' Characteristics and Child Support." *Journal of Marriage and the Family* 59(4): 798–808.

Sorensen, Elaine, and Helen Oliver. 2002. *Policy Reforms are Needed to Increase Child Support from Poor Fathers.* Washington: Urban Institute Press.

Sorensen, Elaine, and Chava Zibman. 2001. "Getting to Know Poor Fathers Who Do Not Pay Child Support." *Social Service Review* 75(3): 420–34.

Stack, Carol B. 1974. *All Our Kin: Strategies for Survival in a Black Community.* New York: Harper and Row.

Sullivan, Mercer. 1989. *Getting Paid: Youth Crime and Work in the Inner City.* Ithaca, N.Y.: Cornell University Press.

Teachman, Jay D. 1991. "Who Pays? Receipt of Child Support in the United States." *Journal of Marriage and the Family* 53(3): 759–72.

Veum, Jonathan R. 1993. "The Relationship Between Child Support and Visitation: Evidence from Longitudinal Data." *Social Science Research* 22(3): 229–44.

Waller, Maureen R., and Robert Plotnick. 2001. "Effective Child Support Policy for Low-Income Families: Evidence from Street Level Research." *Journal of Policy Analysis and Management* 20(1): 89–110.

PART IV

MIXING QUALITATIVE AND QUANTITATIVE METHODS AND DATA

Chapter 11

Mixing Methods: Reliability and Validity Across Quantitative and Qualitative Measures of Relationship Quality

SCHOLARS IN the social sciences have debated the merits of mixed methods research for several decades. Yet, relatively little is known about whether multiple methods provide complementary data or an opportunity for additional insight. In this chapter, I explore two primary questions. First, what value is added to conclusions that can be drawn from mixed methods research as opposed to traditional, strictly qualitative or quantitative designs? And, second, to what extent do qualitative interviews and quantitative survey items that tap similar constructs yield similar results?

I use the Fragile Families and Child Wellbeing Study and Time, Love, and Cash among Couples with Children; the latter is a qualitative study of a subsample embedded in the larger quantitative survey.[1] This design offers the opportunity to explore the extent to which different methods yield comparable results. This chapter compares measures that tap similar constructs across the TLC3 and the Fragile Family Survey. Because the entire TLC3 qualitative subsample is also part of the Fragile Family Survey sample, individuals' responses to questions meant to measure similar constructs within each study can be compared. This comparison allows me to explore the following:

- How does information provided during in-depth qualitative interviews help to expand or explain brief survey responses? Also, do qualitative methods (in-depth interviews) appear to result in greater disclosure about sensitive subjects than quantitative surveys?

- To what extent do responses appear to be reliable across the qualitative and quantitative studies (or, how similar are individuals' responses across data sources)?

- Are there some subjects that people report on more reliably than others? For example, are individuals more reliable across studies when discussing topics that are not stigmatizing (perhaps reporting about affection in the relationship would be easier for respondents than reporting on relationship problems)?

- Are there differences in reliability by gender or by educational attainment?

- How do similar measures from the Fragile Family Survey and TLC3 relate to outcomes? Specifically, is either data source more or less predictive of whether couples break up?

Comparing Data Sources

In general, quantitative methods such as those used in the Fragile Family Survey and qualitative methods such as those used for the in-depth interviews of TLC3 provide different types of information. Quantitative research is suited to describing and examining patterns of variation and covariation across a large number of cases, whereas qualitative interviews are more often focused on providing in-depth information (Ragin 1994). The Fragile Family Surveys and TLC3 interviews reflect these different methodological approaches. The Fragile Family Surveys took from twenty to forty-five minutes (typically about thirty) to administer. TLC3 interviews lasted from two to three hours. The Fragile Family Surveys collect brief, factual information about a number of domains including children, relationships, and income. TLC3 interviews were semistructured and often evolved into open-ended conversations. The dialogue for those administering the Fragile Family Surveys was scripted. Interviewers were expected to ask questions verbatim and could not provide encouragement to respondents, as it could be considered to be leading. This resulted in data that were uniform across cases, allowing for the synthesis of information that is often the goal of large-scale survey research.

TLC3 interviewers, on the other hand, were trained to word questions and structure conversations to maximize rapport and encourage participants to share a detailed narrative whenever possible. The TLC3 interviews were useful for collecting data that was best shared in narrative form (that is, process data such as an in-depth description of a couple's relationship history), and the participants often guided the direction of the interviews. Other topics that tap people's emotional experiences such as feelings about partners and children are also captured well using in-depth interviews. TLC3 interviews were designed to collect process data that are nuanced and detailed, providing access to a person's reasoning and interpretation.

Interviewers who collected and analyzed data from both TLC3 and the Fragile Family Survey note that the open-ended and participant guided nature of TLC3 interviews resulted in data that were more rich and complex but also more difficult to work with.[2] One interviewer who collected data for both studies provided an example, saying that in a Fragile Family Survey, a respondent would simply be asked to provide an answer, on a Likert scale, about the extent to which there was violence in his or her romantic relationship. She explained: "In TLC3, on the other hand, [when discussing relationship problems and violence] someone might say, 'No, we don't have a violent relationship, he only hits me when I go after him.' Thus, there is their interpretation, and our interpretation is overlaid on theirs."

Differences across methods indicate that we should expect variation in the types of information provided by the two data sets. However, little research exists on what can be gained from mixed methods studies. Christina Gibson and Greg Duncan (2005) describe the benefits of mixed methods employed in the evaluation of the New Hope program, writing that they "used the qualitative data to understand some of the 'black-box' program impacts emerging from the quantitative data . . ." (284). For example, when quantitative analysis of experimental data found more positive program effects for boys than girls, they used ethnographic data to generate a hypothesis about why—that mothers were more worried about their sons getting in trouble and devoted more time and resources to them as a result of their concerns.

Thus, I expect that on subjects where the Fragile Family Survey and TLC3 interviews overlap, TLC3 data will help us further understand the meaning of a simple survey response. The extent to which the Fragile Family Survey and TLC3 data will yield similar answers to basic questions, however, is an open question.

Variables

I compare constructs that tap information about couples' perceptions of their relationships. These constructs measure both positive and negative aspects of the relationship, such as reports on conflict and on love-affection. As would be expected in two data sets created using very different methods, the questions asked and constructs measured are never identical (see table 11.1). In fact, it is important to note that the qualitative interviewers working on the TLC3 study were specifically instructed

Table 11.1   Questions and Fragile Family Survey from TLC3
Semi-Structured Interview

Fragile Family Survey	TLC3
Year 1	
Thinking about your relationship with (baby's other parent), how often would you say that s/he expressed affection or love for you?	Response to question(s) on how well and how respondent's partner demonstrates love, care and/or affection in the couple's relationship.
Thinking about your relationship with (baby's other parent), how often would you say that she or he encouraged or helped you to do things that were important to you?	Response to question(s) on how well respondent feels partner understands respondent.
How often, if at all, in the last month have you and (baby's other parent) had disagreements about money?	Response to question(s) on how couples managed their money and whether they disagreed about money
Thinking about your relationship with (baby's other parent), how often would you say that she or he hit or slapped you when s/he was angry?	Response to question(s) about whether there are serious problems in the relationship such as drug use or domestic violence.
How often, if at all, in the last month have you and (baby's other parent) had disagreements about drinking or drug use?	Response to question(s) about whether there are serious problems in the relationship such as drug use or domestic violence.
Year 2	
For each statement I read, please tell me how often (other parent) behaves this way: She or he expresses affection or love for you . . .	Response to question(s) on how well and how respondent's partner demonstrates love, care and/or affection in the couple's relationship.
For each statement I read, please tell me how often (other parent) behaves this way: She or he really understands your hurts and joys . . .	Response to question(s) on how well respondent feels partner understands respondent.
In general, would you say that your relationship with (baby's other parent) is excellent, very good, good, fair, or poor?	Response to question(s) about the current relationship from the respondent's standpoint.

Source: Author's calculations.

not to read questions verbatim to participants. Rather, they were trained to determine how and when to ask questions so that they flowed naturally in the conversation to build rapport and maximize the amount of information respondents provided. The following are examples of ways that interviewers asked participants about whether and how their partner displayed love and affection to them. In some cases, this particular question was asked very directly with little variation across interviews. The interviewer simply said, "How does (your partner) show you that he (or she) cares about you?" However, even for a relatively straightforward question like this one, there was still variation in how the question was asked. Taken from verbatim transcripts of the baseline interviews, here are examples of what interviewers said:

> We talked about the problems that you guys, or issues, which are pretty big issues, but I also wanted to get a sense of maybe some things that you like in your relationship. Do you feel like he's affectionate enough for you?

> Do you think he's pretty good about meeting your needs, emotionally? I mean, do you feel like he shows you enough love and affection?

> All couples have different ways of showing each other that they care about them and stuff so . . . and some people have, I guess, more trouble outwardly showing that type of thing. How about you and Coretta, do you have certain ways of . . . like you bought her flowers on Mother's Day . . . are there other ways that you kind of think about showing her your feelings about her?

Thus, administration of TLC3 interviews varied more than Fragile Family Surveys. Although this sometimes results in less consistency in the information available in the TLC3, it also results in richly detailed qualitative data. Despite these differences in administration, a number of questions are similar enough across the data sets to allow for direct comparison. The sample for the analyses conducted here is always the 150 individuals (seventy-five couples) who make up the TLC3 sample.

I created five variables tapping aspects of relationship quality from the TLC3. Table 11.1 presents a complete list of the Fragile Family Survey and TLC3 items I compared. Unless otherwise noted, answer categories are often, sometimes, never. For both the baseline and the wave two follow-up, I compare the Fragile Family Survey responses to a question about how often the respondent felt that his or her partner expressed love or affection with a variable from TLC3 I constructed from responses to questions such as "how does he show you that he cares for you or loves you?" I also compared the Fragile Family Survey question "thinking about your relationship with (baby's other parent), how often would you say that she or he encourages or helps you to do things that are important to you?" with a variable constructed from TLC3 responses to the question "how well would you say she or he understands you?"[3]

I constructed the TLC3 variables to have the same answer categories as the Fragile Family Survey variables. In doing so, I pulled representative quotes for each of the categories to examine whether they provide a better understanding of what individuals might mean when they respond to Fragile Family Survey items. I also constructed a variable about relationship quality from TLC3 questions asking participants about their feelings about their relationship. The five response categories—excellent, good, very good, fair, poor—made it comparable to a Fragile Family Survey item asking respondents to rate their relationship quality.

Both the Fragile Family Survey and TLC3 include baseline information about reported financial disagreements. Using the TLC3 baseline interview, quantitative variables were created indicating whether the mother or father reported that the couple had financial disagreements. Interviewers asked couples how they managed their money and whether they had disagreements about money. After these sections of the transcripts were read, a dichotomous variable (yes-no) was created indicating whether there were financial disagreements of any kind.[4]

The questions I compared about violence were the mother-father report from the baseline Fragile Family Survey data of how often the other parent hits-slaps him or her with a yes-no variable from TLC3 indicating whether the mother-father reports that the other parent is or has been physically abusive in the relationship.[5]

The Fragile Family baseline survey included an item that was the mother-father report of how often the couple had disagreed about drugs or alcohol in the last month. In this case, the TLC3 variable constructed for comparison indicates whether the mother or father reported that either parent had drug or alcohol problems. If any problems with drugs or alcohol were indicated, the variable, "any report," is a 1 for yes, 0 for no.

In addition to the described variables, I created a dummy variable for each of the eight Fragile Family Survey and TLC3 measure pairs indicating whether an individual was reliable across data sources. I summed the dummy variables to create an overall measure of reliability for each individual, as well as separate reliability measures for baseline and wave two variables.

Qualitative Methods and Results

I conducted qualitative analyses using interviews that were transcribed verbatim and then sorted topically into broad categories (see chapter 1 for more information about the TLC3 sample and data coding process). These transcripts included information on financial disagreements, problems with violence and substance abuse, how couples express love and affection, and the extent to which individuals felt understood by their partners.

The following sections provide examples of quotes from TLC3 sample members for two variables, illustrating how I sorted those quotes into the categories often, sometimes and never.[6]

Expressing Affection, Baseline

I coded 51 percent of mothers' responses as indicating that their partner expressed affection often, 41 percent were coded as sometimes, and 9 percent were coded as never. For fathers, only 31 percent were coded as reporting that their partner expressed love often, whereas 61 percent were coded as sometimes, and 8 percent were coded as never. I was missing data for six mothers and eleven fathers for this field.

In most cases, it was not difficult to assign one of the three codes based on the subject's response. Individuals coded as often tended to say that their partner expressed affection everyday, always, constantly, or all the time. The following quotes typify responses in this category:

> FI: Do you guys feel like you are a pretty loving, affectionate couple?
> She: Yeah. . . . We always all over each other. Always holding, hugging each other. He always talking sweet to me.
> FI: So how do you know [he] loves you?
> She: He always tells me. . . . He always tells me every day. (Priscilla, nineteen, Puerto Rican)

> FI: How do you show that to each other, like how does he show you that he cares?
> She: Oh, he still comes over, he still kisses me, hugs me, he tells me he loves me all the time and vice-versa, you know. Very affectionate towards each other, you know, we always tell each other we love each other too, on the phone "love you too, bye" things like that. Play around with each other, play fight, talk, hang out, watch movies together, we sit on the couch and I'll lay on his lap or I'll lay on him and he'll play with my hair, just very affectionate towards each other. (Gloria, twenty-four, Puerto Rican)

> FI: And how about her? Does she express love and affection for you?
> He: Yeah, every day. [Laughter]
> FI: What does she do?
> He: Oh, she tells me that she loves me, and she comes and hugs me, and kisses me all nice. Yeah. (Don, twenty-three, Hispanic)

I coded individuals as reporting that their partner expressed affection sometimes if he or she explicitly stated that the expressions were infrequent or that he or she would prefer more affection, as well as in cases where it was clear that the partner did express affection in some way, but there was no indication that it was expressed frequently. When it was particularly difficult to choose between often and sometimes, I defaulted to sometimes. The following are examples of individuals coded as sometimes.

FI: Is he affectionate? Is he warm?

She: Yeah. He is affectionate. Not in public. Just at home. He lets me know that he loves me.

FI: By telling or by?

She: By his emotions. He'll just walk up to me and give me a hug or a kiss. Sometimes.

FI: Are there other times when you wish he was more affectionate?

She: Sometimes. (Alison, forty, white)

FI: And what about just like you can tell when she's mad or frustrated cause she'll tell you, how does she show you love and care, that she cares for you?

He: [laughs] I don't know, I guess she cooks me dinner once in a while.

FI: That's a nice one!

He: Yeah, usually just cooks, she'll cook, like let's say she really wants to show affection, she'll cook me something real nice, that's about it. (Wesley, twenty-seven, Puerto Rican)

He: I'm usually the one to show more affection than she does. There are times that she shows more than me. Most of the times—than her.

FI: Does it ever, that isn't hard for you, isn't hard for her then to show you that she cares, does that not—

He: Sometimes she does show me. Like there's a couple of times, she usually she's very a quiet person, she don't like me to show or kiss or anything outside. But there's a couple of times we went out, like one day we were only married like a year, year and a half . . . we had got a little tipsy at the time and all of a sudden she started acting like another person, getting wild with me. (Larry, twenty-six, white)

The final category includes individuals who reported that their partner never showed affection. This occurred in 8 percent of cases. The following quotes exemplify this category.

FI: Does she, how does she show you that she cares about you or that she loves you? Can you give me an example of something that she's done?

He: [Long pause] Not right off hand, no I can't.

FI: No, you can't?

He: Nope. (Anton, twenty-five, black)

FI: How does, how does she show you that she loves and cares for you?

He: Hmmm . . . [She's] not an affectionate person. I learned that from her friends, so that's just not her. . . . I mean, she will let me hold her hand at times, but most of the time, she's not, I'm—. So that's just the way she is. I mean, she'll buy me stuff.

FI: When she buys things, does, is that a way of her showing affection?

He: I don't know. [Laughter] (George, thirty, black)

FI: Okay. So, how does he show that he cares for you?

She: That's, that's what we was talking about last night. I told him "You don't even show me that you care for me." He's like "Yes, I do. I show a lot of ways". . . . I was like "which ways you show me?" He said "Well, when I said 'which one—' I put my hand around you." I was like that ain't got to do nothing . . . with showing nothing. That just putting your hand around me. (Gabriella, twenty-two, Puerto Rican).

Understanding, Baseline

About one-third of fathers reported that their partners understood them often, about 62 percent said they were understood sometimes, and only 6 percent said they never felt understood. Among mothers, 37 percent reported that they often felt understood, 55 percent reported sometimes, and 8 percent reported never. It is important to note that substantial data are missing for this variable. Twenty-three fathers and thirteen mothers had no responses in this field. In about four cases, individual's responses did not answer the actual question. These responses were also coded as missing.

My initial hope was that the responses in the TLC3 field asking about understanding would be similar to the Fragile Family Survey question asking how often "she or he encouraged or helped you to do things that were important to you?" After I read the field, however, I found that the subject's response occasionally tapped this construct. More frequently, though, responses tapped the extent to which the subject felt his or her partner understood how she or he felt or what she or he meant. I decided to code the field using the always, sometimes, never categories because it seemed that these two concepts may still be correlated (how well people feel understood versus the extent to which they feel supported and encouraged).

I coded individuals as often feeling understood if they said things such as their partner understood them almost completely, 100 percent, that she or he knew them better than they knew themselves, or that there was virtually nothing that their partner didn't understand about them. The following are examples from this category.

FI: What about, how well do you feel like he understands you?
She: He understands me, sometimes he understands me better than I do myself.
FI: That's kind of good. Is there anything about you he doesn't understand?
She: Just like, like, how, sometimes my ways, he knows my ways, all my ways to the T but he probably doesn't understand cause I be nice to people sometimes that be mean to me. (Beverly, twenty-four, black)

FI: And so what about in terms of understanding? How well would you say that he understands you?
She: He understands me well. If I have a problem, I can go to him and talk it out with him first. He's real sensitive towards that.

FI: And what area would you say that he doesn't really seem to get it? In terms of how you're thinking or feeling?
She: He gets it.
FI: And you'd say all areas.
She: All areas. (Tamika, twenty-nine, black)

FI: So how do you know that she understands you, like how does that . . . ?
He: Cuz actually a lot of things that we think about. . . . I would say, "I was just thinking that same thing." And if she was thinking, I said, "Well, let's go get some fish." She said, "I was just thinking about that." You know. I mean, this is constantly. This is not every now and then, this is constantly.
FI: You're on the same wavelength kind of thing, sometimes?
He: Well, that makes it so much easier—. And thinking alike, I think it just comes from being together so long. (Ryan, forty, black)

If individuals reported that their partners understood them partially they were coded as feeling understood sometimes. Examples include sometimes, in some things yes, in some no, they provided examples of things that were understood and areas that were not, or gave a split like 50-50 or 70-30. The following are examples of individuals who fit this category.

FI: So what about in terms of understanding? How well would you say that she understands you?
He: She understands me about 70 percent. Thirty percent she doesn't seem to understand. (Jazz, twenty-one, black)

FI: And so what about you in terms of feeling understood?
She: Sometimes. Sometimes I feel he understands me. Sometimes I don't.
FI: What's sometimes when you feel like he really gets it or he's on it.
She: Like when sometimes when I get frustrated and then he'll go and he'll talk to the kids and he'll tell 'em, you know, "Help you mother." And sometimes he doesn't. (LaVera, thirty-eight, black)

FI: Do you think she has a good understanding of you? And your feelings?
He: No, she kind of . . . she . . . you know.
FI: How, well do you think it's a high, medium, or low understanding?
He: Medium understanding. (Don, twenty-three, Hispanic)

Finally, in a small number of cases individuals reported that they did not feel that their partners understood them at all or they were barely understood. The following are examples.

FI: How well do you think he understands you?
She: I don't think he do.
FI: No?
She: He's a psycho. (Calista, twenty, black)

FI: Do you think he understands you?
She: He thinks he does, but he doesn't.
FI: How so?
She: I'm a lot more fragile than he thinks I am. (Marilyn, twenty-nine, black)

FI: Do you feel like he ever understands you?
She: No.
FI: Ever?
She: I don't think he understands me. A lot of times, when we get into arguments and stuff, a lot of bad things go through my head to do to myself. (Daisy, twenty-two, Puerto Rican)

As these examples illustrate, qualitative interviews can lead to rich detail that enhances our understanding of, for example, how a respondent conceives of love and affection in her relationship. It certainly does so for what might be behind an individual's response of sometimes to a survey question on how often her partner expresses love and affection. When a respondent provides a detailed narrative response, we are able to better understand exactly how she thinks about a particular issue and also to understand why she feels the way she does.

Comparison and Methods

To compare Fragile Family Survey and TLC3 variables, I ran an overall cross tabulation for each pair of items, then separate analyses for two groups. First I compared men and women and then people with less than a high school education or a high school education or more. The tabulations and associated statistics show how similar responses across the two data sets are. In all cases, the sample size for cross-tabulations is less than 150 for the overall sample, seventy-five when men and women are analyzed separately. This is due to missing data for either the Fragile Family Survey or the TLC3 variable. In particular, missing data for the three variables taken from the TLC3 wave two follow-up interview are substantial.

For each cross-tabulation, I computed a percent consistent statistic that indicates people who were consistent in their responses across the two data sets for a pair of items. For the responses with three answer categories—often, sometimes, never—in both the Fragile Family Survey and in TLC3 to be coded as consistent across data sets, an individual could answer or be coded often and often, often and sometimes, sometimes and sometimes, or never and never. For a question that had three answer categories in the Fragile Family Survey and two in TLC3, to be coded as consistent the answers had to be often and yes, sometimes and yes, or never and no. For the five category—excellent, very good, good, fair, poor—Fragile Family Survey and TLC3 items about relationship quality, individuals were coded as consistent if they answered or were coded as excellent, very good, or good to both the Fragile Family Survey and TLC3 items or fair or poor to both items. All other responses were coded as inconsistent.

For each cross-tabulation, I computed a chi square statistic and a gamma coefficient. The chi square provides a significance test of whether there is a relationship between the two variables. Because the variables are all ordinal, the gamma statistic shows the strength and sign of the relationship. We would anticipate a positive relationship for similar items across the two data sets. The gamma statistic can be interpreted like a correlation coefficient in that it has a range from negative one to positive one, with zero indicating no relationship and positive one a perfect positive relationship.

To further investigate the relationship between reliability on these measures and both gender and education, I ran bivariate OLS and Poisson regressions using first gender and then education to predict the overall reliability scores that I created. I also ran logistic regressions using dummy variables indicating whether individuals were consistent for individual pairs of measures as a dependent variable, again using first gender and then education as predictors.

Finally, to examine the extent to which the Fragile Family Survey and TLC3 measures relate to outcomes, I ran a series of logistic regressions predicting relationship status (broken up or together) using the Fragile Family Survey and TLC3 variables included in my previous analyses. I ran separate regressions for Fragile Family Survey and TLC3 variables and for men and women, predicting relationship status at the one-year, two-year, and three-year follow-up time points.

Results

Results for overall consistency, gamma coefficients, and chi squares show that individual responses to similar items across the Fragile Family Survey and TLC3 data sets are correlated. Overall, consistency ranged from a high of 95 percent for love and affection, wave two, to a low of 63 percent for financial conflict (see table 11.2 for overall and subgroup results for all variables). Chi square results were statistically significant ($p < .05$) in overall comparisons for five of the eight variables compared. Gamma coefficients always indicated a positive relationship between variables and tended to be around .4 or .5, ranging from a high of .63 for physical violence to a low of .13 for support, wave 2. The gamma coefficients were statistically significant ($p < .05$) for seven of the eight variables. Variation by item pairs was substantial in the extent to which people were consistent across data sets. For example, individuals were consistent in

Table 11.2   Summary of Results for Measure Comparisons Across FF and TLC3 (Baseline Variables Unless Indicated)

Variable	Sample	Percent Consistent	Significant Chi Square (p<.05)	Gamma Coefficient*
Love and affection				
Women	66	92	yes	0.59*
Men	64	92	no	0.58*
Less than HS diploma	33	88	yes	0.58*
At least HS diploma	97	93	no	0.58*
Overall	130	92	yes	0.59*
Love and affection (wave two)				
Women	39	92	no	0.51*
Men	47	98	yes	0.31
Less than HS diploma	23	91	yes	0.29
At least HS diploma	63	97	no	0.36
Overall	86	95	yes	0.42*
Support				
Women	60	92	no	0.64*
Men	52	92	no	0.46
Less than HS diploma	27	93	yes	1*
At least HS diploma	85	92	no	0.33
Overall	112	92	yes	0.57*
Support (wave two)				
Women	33	79	no	0.17
Men	44	77	no	0.02
Less than HS diploma	23	57	no	0.16
At least HS diploma	54	87	no	0.11
Overall	77	78	no	0.13
Relationship evaluation (wave two)				
Women	39	64	no	0.56*
Men	45	78	no	0.18
Less than HS diploma	23	48	no	0.04
At least HS diploma	61	80	yes	0.51*
Overall	84	67	no	0.43*
Financial conflict				
Women	60	70	yes	0.67*
Men	57	56	no	0.23
Less than HS diploma	31	58	no	0.28
At least HS diploma	86	65	yes	0.51*
Overall	117	63	yes	0.44*

(continued)

Table 11.2   Summary of Results for Measure Comparisons Across FF and TLC3 (Baseline Variables Unless Indicated) (Continued)

Variable	Sample	Percent Consistent	Significant Chi Square (p<.05)	Gamma Coefficient*
Physical violence				
Women	56	93	yes	0.85*
Men	52	83	no	0.5
Less than HS diploma	31	81	no	1*
At least HS diploma	77	91	yes	0.86*
Overall	108	88	no	0.63*
Drugs-alcohol				
Women	56	77	yes	0.52
Men	59	76	no	0.38
Less than HS diploma	35	71	no	0.69*
At least HS diploma	80	88	yes	0.01
Overall	115	77	yes	0.46*

Source: Author's calculations.
Note: Percent consistent is the percentage of questions across data sets that individuals' responses were consistent on: often and often, often and sometimes, sometimes and sometimes, never and never.
*p<.05

their reports on love and affection more than 90 percent of the time for both the baseline and wave two comparisons. They were consistent only 67 percent of the time, however, when reporting on overall relationship quality.

I also conducted subgroup analyses by gender and by educational attainment, comparing those with at least a high school diploma to those without. For four of the eight variables, women were more consistent than men. For two variables, there was no difference in consistency and for two others, men were more consistent. Gamma coefficients were larger for women than men for all eight variables analyzed, and were statistically significant ($p < .05$) for women on six of the eight variables, but for men on only one variable. Finally, women had significant chi square results for four of the eight variables, whereas male results were significant for only one. Overall, the evidence suggests that women were more consistent respondents across Fragile Family Survey and TLC3 questions than their male counterparts.

Results by educational attainment indicate that individuals with more education (at least a high school diploma) seem more consistent across data sets than their counterparts. Individuals with more education were more consistent in their responses for seven of the eight variables. For example, in the comparison of the overall relationship quality variables,

Table 11.3   Fragile Family Survey and TLC3 Variables and Consistency Scores

Variable	Time	Percentage of Time Consistent
Love and affection	No	92, 95
Support	No	92, 78
Physical violence	No	88
Relationship Eval.	No	67
Drugs-alcohol	last month	77
Financial conflict	last month	63

Source: Author's calculations.

individuals with at least a high school education were consistent 80 percent of the time, versus only 48 percent for those with less than a high school education. Gamma coefficients were statistically significant on four variables for both those with and without a high school diploma. Chi square results were significant for those with at least a high school diploma on four variables, compared to three variables for those with fewer years of education. However, gamma coefficients were larger for only three of the eight variables for those with more education.

In addition to results for individual variable pairs, I used the overall reliability variables to look at the extent to which individuals who were reliable reporters in one wave were also more reliable in the following wave (baseline and wave two), and at whether gender and education predict overall reliability. These variables were created by summing dummy variables for each of the eight Fragile Family Survey and TLC3 measure pairs that indicated whether an individual was reliable across data sources. I created a variable that included all eight individual variable pairs, one for the five baseline variables, and another for the three variables created using data from wave two. I find that the baseline and wave two reliability measures have a correlation coefficient of .28. Coefficients were similar for men and women (.30 and .31 respectively). Thus, individuals' reliability on the items analyzed here is modestly correlated across waves of data collection.

To further investigate the relationship between reliability on these measures and both gender and education, I ran bivariate regressions using first gender and then education to predict overall reliability scores. I found neither gender nor education to be significant predictors of reliability.[7] To see whether gender or education would significantly predict reliability, I also ran logistic regressions using dummy variables indicating whether individuals were consistent for individual pairs of measures as a dependent variable, again using gender and then education as predictors. The results (not shown) also indicated little to no relationship. Thus, though the results from cross-tabulations and the related gamma coefficients indicated that women and, to some extent, individuals with more education seem to be more consistent reporters, regressions indicate that the differences are not large enough to be statistically significant.

I did not find that particular topics resulted in more or less reliable reporting across data sets. It does appear, however, that the wording of the questions makes a difference. Table 11.3 shows percent consistent scores and indicates whether a time frame was referenced in the Fragile Family Survey question. For six of the eight item pairs, no time frame was referenced. However, for substance abuse and financial conflict, the Fragile Family Survey question asked whether disagreements had occurred in the previous month. These questions have lower percent consistent scores (77 and 63, respectively) than five of the six other item pairs. It makes sense that general questions would be more comparable across the data sets, and the lower consistency for items that reference a time frame in the Fragile Family Survey seems to support this notion.

I had wondered whether respondents might report more reliably about items worded positively, such as love and affection, than about items tapping socially stigmatizing concepts such as drug and alcohol use or violence. What I found instead is that the relationship between variables across the Fragile Family Survey and TLC3 seems stronger when concepts were well defined and when interviewers asked for more details during TLC3 interviews. I found greater consistency, for example, for love and affection than for understanding.

Finally, to examine the extent to which the Fragile Family Survey and TLC3 measures relate to outcomes, I ran a set of logistic regressions predicting relationship status using the Fragile Family Survey and TLC3 variables included in my previous analyses. I ran separate regressions for Fragile Family Survey and TLC3 variables, and for men and women, predicting breakup at the one-year, two-year, and three-year follow-ups. I also ran separate regressions including interaction terms for gender (male) and the measure of interest to test whether measures were more predictive for men or women.[8] Table 11.4 displays these results.

We can see that in some cases Fragile Family Survey coefficients are larger than TLC3 coefficients, but in other cases the opposite occurs. Similarly, statistically significant results appear as often for Fragile Family Survey as for TLC3 variables. For example, men who report more frequent expressions of love and affection from their partners at the baseline TLC3 interviews are less likely to be broken up at wave four, though this is not true for women. On the other hand, women, but not men, who report feeling more understood by their partners at the wave two Fragile Family Survey interview are less likely to be broken up by wave four. I also find that whereas results differ on individual variables for men and women, there is no pattern indicating that measures for either men or women are more predictive of relationship status in general. Thus, in this

Table 11.4 Regression Using Individual Measures to Predict Relationship Status

| | Broken Up | | | | | |
| | Wave Two | | | Wave Four | | |
Independent Variable	Women	Men	Sig. Gender Interaction	Women	Men	Sig. Gender Interaction
Baseline						
Violence TLC3	1.179	0.773		1.762	0.857	
	(1.053)	(1.279)		(1.193)	(1.450)	
Violence FF	0.460	0.074		-0.014	0.880	
	(0.961)	(0.860)		(0.962)	(0.695)	
Financial disagreements TLC3	0.647	0.034		1.061	-0.483	
	(0.844)	(0.775)		(0.717)	(0.614)	
Financial disagreements FF	-0.253	0.037		0.384	0.399	
	(0.424)	(0.405)		(0.359)	(0.357)	
Substance abuse problems TLC3	1.176	1.176		-0.036	-0.036	
	(0.712)	(0.712)		(0.702)	(0.702)	
Substance abuse problems FF	0.879	0.846		-0.099	0.746	
	(0.488)	(0.607)		(0.505)	(0.605)	
Understanding TLC3	-0.993	-0.066		-1.811**	-1.047	
	(0.557)	(0.737)		(0.631)	(0.686)	
Support FF	-1.455*	-0.017		-0.595	-0.821	
	(0.699)	(0.624)		(0.673)	(0.549)	
Love-affection TLC3	-1.665**	-1.707*		-0.610	-2.075**	*
	(0.561)	(0.728)		(0.418)	(0.764)	
Love-affection FF	-1.114	-0.849		-0.595	-1.343*	
	(0.724)	(0.574)		(0.673)	(0.568)	

(continued)

Table 11.4 Regression Using Individual Measures to Predict Relationship Status (*Continued*)

| | Broken Up | | | | | | | |
| | Wave Two | | | Wave Four | | | |
Independent Variable	Women	Men	Sig. Gender Interaction	Women	Men	Sig. Gender Interaction
Wave Two						
Relationship evaluation TLC3				-0.889*	-0.190	
				(0.418)	(0.347)	
Relationship evaluation FF				-0.664**	-0.487*	
				(0.230)	(0.237)	
Understanding TLC3				-0.188	-0.685	
				(0.741)	(0.528)	
Understanding FF				-1.514**	-0.010	**
				(0.499)	(0.398)	
Love-affection TLC3				-0.344	-0.862	
				(0.681)	(0.845)	
Love-affection FF				-0.622	-0.935*	
				(0.395)	(0.472)	

Source: Author's calculations.
Note: Average sample size for these regressions is fifty-nine. Sample size varies from thirty-two to seventy-one.
Standard errors in parentheses.
*significant at 5%; **significant at 1%

case, I find that both qualitative and quantitative measures about couples' relationships relate to whether couples later broke up.

Discussion

In reading TLC3 qualitative interviews with the goal of exploring how detailed narratives can enhance our understanding of brief survey responses, I found that, as we would expect, much more information is provided when conversations are open-ended and detailed descriptions are encouraged. A brief answer of "often" to a question about the frequency of a partner's expressions of love and affection offers no explanation, background, or deeper understanding of what often means to that individual. A response to TLC3 coded as "often," on the other hand, can illuminate what that response might mean for an individual. We might see, for example, that this is an issue that the couple struggled with in the past, but that things have improved, so relative to the past, the response is "often." Thus, qualitative interviews do shed light on brief survey responses. It seems as if the best way to use mixed methods to maximize the trade-off between the efficiency of surveys and the depth provided by open-ended conversations is to identify areas where more information or process data is likely to enhance our understanding of an issue. Using surveys and qualitative interviews in tandem allows researchers to both get basic answers to a large number of questions for a large sample as well as gain insight into processes and a deeper understanding of complex issues better unraveled in narrative form.

Comparisons of Fragile Family Survey and TLC3 interview items reveal that there is substantial consistency in similar items across the two data sets. In general, individuals were at least somewhat, and often very, consistent in their responses to questions across data sets. Consistency ranged from a high of 95 percent for reports on love and affection in the first year follow-ups to a low of 63 percent on the baseline financial conflict variables. Of course, responses are never perfectly consistent for several reasons. It is very likely that inconsistent responses across data sets result, at least in part, from the fact that the questions asked across the data sets, though similar, are never identical. At times, the more detailed and open-ended questions asked during TLC3 interviews would be expected to glean more information simply due to the wording of the question. For example, during TLC3 interviews, respondents were asked general questions about money management and financial disagreements in their relationship. The Fragile Family Survey question, on the other hand, asked respondents how often in the last month they had had financial disagreements with their partner. Thus, we would expect to see a higher frequency of reports of financial disagreements in TLC3 data than in the Fragile Family Survey, and we do.

A number of possible explanations account for the greater inconsistency I find for some variables. First, substantial missing data for the TLC3 wave two follow-up variables may be skewing the results. Also, some variables were difficult to code in particular ranges. For example, I coded the relationship quality variable so that it would have five categories identical to the Fragile Family Survey item—excellent, very good, good, fair, or poor. Although it was pretty clear when a relationship was poor or fair, it was harder to discern between excellent, very good, and good relationships. The multiple categories for a positive relationship on the Fragile Family Survey were difficult to replicate in the qualitative data. Although the qualitative data was rich, it was hard to determine which of the codes would be the best fit in a number of cases. In contrast, variables with simple answer categories and a more limited range of likely responses were easier to code in the qualitative data. Also, questions that were asked more consistently and probed more carefully during qualitative interviews were easier to code as well.

Timing is another likely explanation for individuals' inconsistency across data sets. Varying amounts of time elapsed between when the Fragile Family Survey and TLC3 interviews were administered at each wave of data collection. Timing can certainly play a part in how individuals respond to survey and interview questions. For example, if the Fragile Family Survey were administered during a stressful time in a couple's relationship, and six months later some of that stress has abated when the TLC3 interview occurs, differences across data sets would reflect reality accurately.[9]

Finally, there were differences in reliability across subgroups in cross tabulations by gender and educational groups. For several variables, women were more consistent in their responses across the two data sets than men. It is possible that this difference is domain specific, and that women are likely to be more reliable reporters than men on issues related to the couple's relationship, a domain that may be construed as traditionally female. It is also possible that women are simply better subjects, and that they are more engaged respondents than men.

Individuals with more education were more consistent reporters on a number of the variables. Perhaps the additional years of schooling make it more likely that individuals will be aware of their own consistency across interviews, making them less likely to contradict themselves. It is important to note that though gender and educational differences were apparent in the cross-tabulations and using gamma coefficients, additional analyses using OLS, Poisson, and logistic regression did not indicate statistically significant differences in consistency between subgroups. Further work with larger sample sizes and additional questions might help clarify whether these differences in reliability exist and were simply not detectible in these data, or whether there are actually no differences.

Overall, I find that though answers to similar questions across qualitative and quantitative data sets are correlated, they are never identical. The relationship between variables across data sets is likely to vary according to how much the actual questions differed, as well as by how respondents understood and answered them. I also find that when we have both surveys and detailed interviews, the in-depth nature of the qualitative data provides a deeper understanding of what respondents think and feel about a subject than brief survey responses.

Finally, I find that in the case of the variables analyzed here, qualitative and quantitative measures seem equally predictive of couples' relationship outcomes. This finding is somewhat surprising. Many researchers may have anticipated that the extensive information and additional details that in-depth interviews provide would have lent more predictive power to the TLC3 responses. This does not appear to be the case, suggesting that qualitative and quantitative measures can be used with equal confidence in predicting relevant outcomes. Future work should try to replicate this finding using different data sets, because it is valuable to know whether one data collection method provides information that is more predictive of outcomes, or whether different methods are, as this study indicates, similar in their predictive value.

Notes

1. Other recent examples of mixed methods research include The Three-City Study and The New Hope evaluation.

2. I conducted phone interviews with Professors Katherine Magnuson and Christina Gibson-Davis about their experiences in collecting and working with both Fragile Family Survey and TLC3 data.

3. In the wave two follow-up Fragile Family Survey data, a different question was asked. "For each statement I read, please tell me how often (other parent) behaves this way: She or he really understands your hurts and joys." This wording seems as if it is more similar to the question asked in the qualitative TLC3 interviews.

4. This TLC3 variable was coded by Paula England.

5. Variables for substance abuse and violence were coded by Kate Linnenberg.

6. All names have been changed to protect participant confidentiality.

7. I ran both OLS and Poisson models. Because results were not significant and coefficients were very small, results are not shown here.

8. I ran these regressions both with no controls, as well as with controls for race and education. I found that results were similar with and without controls. Due to small sample sizes I present only bivariate results. Also, I ran these models predicting breakup at waves two, three, and four. As results

did not differ substantively across waves, I show results for waves two and four only.

9. In the three cities where the TLC3 sample resided, the baseline Fragile Family Surveys were administered between February and November of 2000. The baseline TLC3 interviews were conducted, in most cases, a couple of months after the Fragile Family Surveys were administered. The wave one Fragile Family Surveys began in March of 2001 and were completed in February of 2002 in the three TLC3 cities. Wave one data collection for the TLC3 occurred during the summer of 2001.

References

Gibson, Christina, and Greg J. Duncan. 2005. "Qualitative/Quantitative Synergies in a Random-Assignment Program Evaluation." In *Discovering Successful Pathways In Children's Development: New Methods In The Study Of Childhood And Family Life,* edited by Thomas S. Weisner. Chicago, Ill.: University of Chicago Press.

Ragin, Charles C. 1994. *Constructing Social Research. The Unity and Diversity of Method.* Thousand Oaks, Calif.: Pine Forge Press.

Chapter 12

Data from the TLC3

EMILY FITZGIBBONS SHAFER

T HE TIME, Love and Care in Couples with Children data are unique for several reasons.[1] First, they are embedded in a large national quantitative data set, The Fragile Families and Child Wellbeing Survey (FFCWS), which gives researchers a plethora of information for each TLC3 respondent. Second, participants were chosen based on a stratified, random sampling scheme; probability sampling is unusual in qualitative studies. Finally, the data are extremely rich—both mothers and fathers participated in unstructured interviews both individually and as a couple in each of the four waves.

The TLC3 data are linked to a large quantitative data set, The Fragile Families and Child Wellbeing Survey (FFCWS), which is representative of non-marital births in cities with populations greater than 200,000. From the FFCWS participant pool, individuals for the TLC3 study were chosen, using a stratified random sampling scheme in three of the FFCWS cities. The three cities, Chicago, New York, and Milwaukee, were chosen purposefully to capture a range of racial and ethnic diversity and differences in economic and policy climates. In Chicago, the included hospital serves a majority African American population, in New York a mostly Hispanic clientele, and in Milwaukee an economically and ethnically diverse population. In each city, FFCWS couples were eligible to participate in the TLC3 study only if they were romantically involved at the time of the birth, if the mother's household income did not exceed $75,000, if both mother and father lived in an accessible geographical area (to be accessible to interviewers), if the father was not in jail, if the child was living with at least one of the biological parents, and if both parents spoke English. As in the FFCWS, TLC3 oversampled unmarried couples: approximately one-third of the seventy-five were married and were included solely for comparison. Our main focus was on unmarried couples and some of the papers in this volume used only these couples.

Once participants were stratified according to the outlined criteria, ninety-seven couples were randomly selected and then approached to participate in TLC3. In the end, seventy-five were successfully enrolled in the study—twenty-five in Milwaukee, twenty-five in Chicago, and twenty-five in New York City. Table 12.1 provides response rates for parents across all four waves, by interview type, and the number of social fathers who were interviewed. We use this term to refer to men who became one of the focal TLC3 mothers' cohabiting partner after wave one when the mother had broken up with the focal father. Although every attempt was made to interview the biological fathers of the focal children even after a breakup, when the mother had started living with a new man, social fathers were also solicited for interviews. Such data are important to understanding the processes families undergo when mothers and fathers repartner—such as parenting children who are not biologically one's own, negotiating with the biological parents who are no longer partners, and the impact this has on the relationship of the new partnership.

Whenever possible, participants were interviewed both as a couple and individually. In waves two through four, if couples had broken up and were willing to be interviewed together about coparenting issues, interviewers did couple as well as individual interviews. If the mother had a new partner, interviewers attempted a couple interview with the new couple. The interviewers followed a structured interview guide so that they would address all areas of interest, but were allowed to vary the order of the questions, to probe, and to encourage open-ended responses. This allowed for a conversation-like flow between interviewees and interviewers. Rapport was generally high, and, whenever possible, the same interviewers were sent to the same couple or individual over waves. Interviews typically lasted between two and three hours and were audiotaped; in the third and fourth wave only they were also video recorded. From these recordings, a team of transcribers coded each interview verbatim, producing approximately two thousand pages for each couple across the four waves. A team of researchers, typically undergraduates, then coded each transcript using paper transcripts and then electronically sorted sections of text into topics. Coders placed all text from the transcribed interviews that pertained to the coding schema into the given category. Researchers developed some of the topics for coding directly from the interview guide prior to coding. However, there was also an inductive aspect to the coding; some topics appeared as important as coding progressed, and a decision was made to create a field for the topic. This transcription and coding process produced an extensive TLC3 database for researchers to use and analyze by topical category. Examples of the schema or category include: attitudes about marriage, how the couple handles their money, and how the couple divides the household labor. After transcription and coding the data were organized in Microsoft Access for management.

Table 12.1 TLC3 Response Rates of Original Interviewees

Wave		Interview Type		Within Individual	
		Couple	Individual	Mothers	Fathers
1	Percent of original sample interviewed	100%	91%	96%	85%
	Number of original sample	75	136	72	64
	Number plus number of social fathers[a]	75	136	72	64
2	Percent of original sample interviewed	75%	81%	81%	81%
	Number of original sample	56	122	61	61
	Number plus number of social fathers	56	123	61	62
3	Percent of original sample interviewed	69%	85%	87%	85%
	Number of original sample	52	128	65	64
	Number plus number of social fathers	56	132	65	69
4	Percent of original sample interviewed	61%	81%	84%	77%
	Number of original sample	46	121	63	58
	Number plus number of social fathers	53	128	63	65

Source: Author's calculations.

[a] A social father is a new partner of a mother, not the biological father of the focal child, and therefore not in the original sample.
For a mother's new partner to qualify as a social father, he had to be living with mother at least some of the time.

TLC3 and FFCWS Comparison

Here I compare the TLC3 parents to parents in the FFCWS sample who met the criteria[2] for the TLC3 sample on a number of items in the FFCWS survey; the sample is referred to as TLC3-eligible participants.[3] The most important eligibility criterion was that the couple still be romantically involved at the baby's birth. The tables include information on the full FFCWS sample as well. To the extent that the TLC3 sample does not differ significantly from the TLC3-eligible sample, we can conclude that it is representative of the portion of fragile families we intended to study—mainly unmarried parents still romantically involved at the birth, whether cohabiting or not, and, for some purposes, married parents using the same hospitals.

Table 12.2 presents characteristics of the FFCWS participants, TLC3-eligible participants, and the TLC3 participants. The samples are racially-ethnically diverse; of the eligible TLC3 sample, approximately 50 percent of both mothers and fathers are black, and there are a significant number of Hispanics (19 percent of mothers and 20 percent of fathers) and Whites (26 percent to 23 percent). The TLC3 sample differs from the TLC3-eligible sample in that it has a larger percentage of Hispanics (33 percent of mothers and 36 percent of fathers), due to the selection of New York City as one of the sample cities and the selection of a hospital in New York City with mainly Puerto Rican and Dominican clientele. Nearly every New York TLC3 parent identifies as Hispanic. Immigrant status is higher in the TLC3 data than in the eligible sample, again because of the clientele in the New York City hospital; this difference is not statistically significant, however. Mean ages for mothers and fathers and educational attainment are relatively consistent across the TLC3-eligible sample and TLC3.

Relationship status at both baseline and wave two, when the baby was about a year old, is also shown in table 12.1.[4] The TLC3 sampling plan sought to obtain a sample that was about one third married, while a lower quota was set for the FFCWS; thus we see a larger percentage of married couples in the TLC3 sample than in the TLC3-eligible sample. We are not sure why the TLC3 sample has a higher proportion of cohabitors relative to visitors than the FFCWS, but the difference is not statistically significant and may simply be sampling error. It may also flow from the higher cohabitation rates of Puerto Rican and Dominican couples that made up the majority of the New York TLC3 sample.

Table 12.3 provides information on household income,[5] work status, and earnings[6] for mothers and fathers at both baseline and wave two by baseline relationship status (married, cohabiting, or romantically involved but not cohabiting). Median values of earnings and household income are provided in thousands of dollars. To determine whether the

Table 12.2   Demographic Characteristics of Mothers and Fathers

Variables	Full FFCWS	TLC3 Eligible	TLC3
Mother's race			
Black	49%	51%	47%
Hispanic	26	19	33**
White	21	26	20
other	4	4	0
Father's race			
Black	49	54	49
Hispanic	26	20	36***
White	20	23	13
other	4	4	1
Immigrant status			
Mother is first-generation immigrant	17	7	9
Father is first-generation immigrant	18	9	13
Mother's age at baseline			
14– <22	34	32	31
22– <27	34	36	41
27+	32	32	28
mean	25	25	25
Father's age at baseline			
15– <24	33	32	33
24– <30	31	32	33
30+	37	36	33
mean	28	28	27
Mother's education at baseline			
No high school diploma	36	27	26
High school diploma	31	35	36
Post-high school education	33	38	38
Father's education at baseline			
No high school diploma	33	27	29
High school diploma	32	37	36
Post–high school education	34	35	35
Relationship status baseline			
Married	24	27	35
Cohabiting	36	47	49
Romantically involved, but not cohabiting	26	25	16
Not romantically involved	13	0	0
Relationship status year one			
Married	30	35	44
Cohabiting	27	34	32
Romantically involved, but not cohabiting	10	10	7
Not romantically involved	33	22	17

Source: Author's calculations.
Note: Significance tests performed between TLC3 and TLC3 eligible samples.
**$p < .01$, ***$p < .001$

Table 12.3 Household Income and Earnings (in 1000s of Dollars) of Participants

	Couples		Full Sample	TLC3-Eligible	TLC3
Baseline household income	All		22.5	22.5	30.0
	Married		42.5	42.5	42.5
	Cohabiting		17.5	22.5	22.5
	Noncohabiting	Mothers	12.5	12.5	17.5
		Fathers	22.5	22.5	17.5
Baseline earnings of all individuals	All	Women	2.0	3.5	3.5
		Men	17.5	17.5	22.5
	Married	Women	6.5	11.3	12.5
		Men	30.0	30.0	30.0
	Cohabiting	Women	2.0	3.5	3.5
		Men	12.5	17.5	17.5
	Noncohabiting	Mothers	0.5	2.0	0.5
		Fathers	12.5	12.5	12.5
Baseline percentage reporting no earnings		Mothers	43	32	28
		Fathers	5	4	6

Year one household income					
All			30.0	30.0	34.5
Married			50.0	50.0	42.5
Cohabiting			25.0	25.0	30.0
Noncohabiting	Mothers		17.0	20.0	33.0
	Fathers		30.0	30.0	43.0
Year one earnings of all individuals					
All		Women	4.7	6.5	2.9
		Men	22.4	23.4	22.1
	Married	Women	4.7	6.8	1.5
		Men	37.5	35.5	36.4
	Cohabiting	Women	5.0	6.7	3.6
		Men	20.6	20.8	12.9
	Noncohabiting	Mothers	4.3	6.1	7.8
		Fathers	15.1	17.4	23.1
Year one percentage reporting no earnings	Mothers		28	24	40**
	Fathers		8	5	8

Source: Author's calculations.
Note: Significance tests performed between TLC3 and TLC3-eligible samp_es.
**p < .01

differences in medians were significant between the TLC3 sample and TLC3-eligible sample, chi square statistics for equality of medians were calculated. From table 12.3, we see that there are no significant differences in medians for household income or earnings variables between the TLC3 sample and TLC3-eligible sample.

Also presented in table 12.3 are percentages of men and women who report having no earnings in the previous year at both waves. At wave two, only 24 percent of mothers in the TLC3-eligible sample report no earnings, whereas 40 percent of mothers in the TLC3 sample report no earnings at that time. This difference between samples is large and significant. Such high percentages are not very surprising—women in both samples are at a point in the life course when they are most likely to drop out of the labor force because at wave two they are reporting earnings from the year in which they were mothers of a newborn. What is surprising is that TLC3 has a significantly higher number of women not working for pay that year than the TLC3-eligible sample. The percentage of fathers who report no earnings at baseline is roughly equivalent (no significant differences) in the TLC3 and TLC3-eligible samples, 6 percent and 4 percent respectively. The percentages for fathers at wave two are 8 percent and 5 percent.

Table 12.4 presents the distributions for a variety of questions for parents in the FFCWS sample, the TLC3-eligible sample, and the TLC3 sample. At baseline, the questions are whether the father's name will be on the baby's birth certificate, whether the baby will have the father's last name, and whether the father visited his baby's mother in the hospital. The questions shown from wave two are whether the child has physical disabilities, the number of times the child has been to the emergency room for an accident or injury, the number of times the child has been to a doctor for a well visit, whether the mother has legal or informal child support arrangements with the father, whether the mother has children with a man other than the baby's father, whether the father has children who live outside of his household and whether the father is currently in jail, working, or in school. There are no significant differences between the TLC3 and TLC3-eligible sample across these variables.

Attrition

Table 12.1 presents the response rates of the original TLC3 participants across all four waves and across interview type. The TLC3 interview team was able to maintain a relatively high response rate; the lowest for mothers' individual interviews is 81 percent (second wave), and the lowest for fathers' is 77 percent (fourth wave). The lowest couple interview response rate is 61 percent (fourth wave). Because many couples who were no longer romantically involved at the time of our later interviews declined

Table 12.4 Multiple Child Well-Being and Parental Relationship Quality Variables

	Full Sample	Possible TLC3	TLC3
Baseline (Wave One)			
Father's name on the birth certificate (asked only of unmarried respondents)	88%	96%	98%
Baby has father's last name (asked only of unmarried respondents)	80	91	93
Father visited mother in the hospital	81	94	96
Year one (Wave Two)			
Child has physical disabilities	3	3	1
Child has never been to the emergency room for accident or injury	85	85	80
Number of times child to doctor for well visit 0	0	0	0
1–3	7	6	4
4+	93	94	96
Mother and father have legal child support agreement (not asked if parents were married and living together)	16	15	11
Mother and father have informal child support agreement (asked if mother and father are not married and not living together for "all or most of the time")	43	51	50
Mother has children with someone other than other focal parent	36	38	33
Father has other biological children not living with him	29	31	41
Father currently			
Working	75	78	75
Unemployed	16	15	22
In jail	5	3	0
In school	2	2	1
School and work	2	3	1

Source: Author's calculations.
Note: There are no significant differences between the TLC3 and TLC3-eligible sample.

our invitation to be interviewed together, the lower response rate relative to the individual interviews is expected.

Tables 12.5 and 12.6 present descriptive statistics on the mothers and fathers who were not interviewed individually or as a couple in each particular wave. The descriptive statistics provided are race, age, education, relationship status, earnings and household income; all are taken from the baseline data. Tests for equality of means and medians were performed. The following significant differences between mothers missing in a particular individual interview and those who are not missing for that interview were found: mothers missing in the first two waves are on average older, mothers missing in the second wave were less likely to be romantically involved but not cohabiting at baseline, and mothers missing in the third wave are less likely to have only a high school diploma. Tests for equality of medians between mothers' total household income for those missing in the third and fourth wave versus those included show significant differences. The finding suggests that mothers missing individual interviews in the third and fourth wave may have been less well off financially at baseline than included mothers.

Table 12.6[7] reports descriptive statistics on fathers missing at each interview. At wave one, the proportion of fathers who are high school dropouts is significantly higher for those missing an individual interview than for those included. Also at wave one, missing fathers are significantly less likely to be married and are significantly more likely to be cohabiting. At wave two, missing fathers are again significantly more likely to be cohabiting and are also significantly less likely to be romantically involved but not cohabiting than fathers who completed an individual interview. Tests for equality of medians reveal significant differences between the missing and nonmissing fathers at waves three and four in their reported baseline earnings and household income. Implied is that those missing had less earnings and household income at baseline than fathers not missing at waves three and four.

As with the analysis of those missing from the individual interviews, the characteristics of mothers and fathers missing a couple interview reveal that those missing may have lower SES than those who completed a couple interview. Of those not represented in a couple interview at wave two, mothers were less likely on average to have post–high school education than mothers in the couples who completed interviews. Those missing couple interviews at wave four were also more likely to be romantically involved but not cohabiting at baseline. Tests for median differences in earnings and household income between fathers missing couple interviews and those not missing them reveal significant differences across all three later waves. All couples completed the couple interview at wave one.

Table 12.5 Characteristics of Mothers at Each Wave

	Missing Individual				Missing Couple		
	1	2	3	4	2	3	4
Race							
Black	0.67	0.57	0.40	0.50	0.58	0.58	0.50
Hispanic	0.00	0.21	0.40	0.52	0.26	0.26	0.27
White	0.33	0.21	0.20	0.08	0.16	0.16	0.23
Age	31.33*	29.07**	24.90	25.00	25.21	24.58	24.23
Education							
No high school diploma	0.33	0.14	0.30	0.17	0.32	0.32	0.27
High school diploma	0.33	0.50	0.10+	0.25	0.42	0.26	0.23
Post–high school education	0.33	0.36	0.60	0.58	0.21+	0.37	0.50
Relationship							
Married	0.33	0.36	0.20	0.33	0.21	0.26	0.27
Cohabiting	0.67	0.64	0.70	0.50	0.68	0.47	0.41
Romantically involved, not cohabiting	0.00	0.00+	0.10	0.17	0.11	0.26	0.32*
Median earned in past year (in $1,000s)	2.00	12.50	4.50	2.75	3.50	3.50	2.00
Median total household income in past year (in $1,000s)	42.50	30.00	30.00+	26.25*	22.50	30.00	26.25

Source: Author's calculations.

Note: Significance tests for equality of means were performed for age and all racial, education and relationship status categories. K-sample tests for equality of medians were performed for median earnirgs and median total household income.

**p < .10, *p < .05, + p < .10

Table 12.6 Characteristics of Fathers at Each Wave

	Individual				Couple		
	1	2	3	4	2	3	4
Race							
Black	0.64	0.50	0.64	0.59	0.63	0.58	0.64
Hispanic	0.27	0.43	0.36	0.35	0.32	0.37	0.27
White	0.09	0.07	0.00	0.06	0.05	0.05	0.09
Age	26.45	28.36	25.18	25.41	23.74	27.16	26.27
Education							
No high school diploma	0.64**	0.29	0.36	0.29	0.32	0.37	0.32
High school diploma	0.18	0.36	0.27	0.35	0.42	0.32	0.27
Post–high school education	0.18	0.36	0.36	0.35	0.26	0.32	0.41
Relationship							
Married	0.09+	0.29	0.18	0.29			
Cohabiting	0.73+	0.72+	0.55	0.47			
Romantically involved, not cohabiting	0.18	0.00+	0.27	0.24			
Median earned in past year (in $1,000s)	2.50	17.50	7.50+	7.50*	12.50+	12.50	12.50*
Median total household income in past year (in $1,000s)	17.50	30.00	21.25*	30.00*	23.75	30.00+	26.25**

Source: Author's calculations.
Note: Significance tests for equality of means were performed for age and all racial, education and relationship status categories.
K-sample tests for equality of medians were performed for median earnings and median total household income.
**$p < .10$, *$p < .05$, +$p < .10$

Overall, there appears to be a pattern in the differences between those who were not interviewed and those who were. If significantly different, those who were not interviewed were worse off at baseline, whether economically or in terms of educational attainment. Such a finding could be troublesome; for example, the data may not represent those who are most economically disadvantaged, thereby skewing generalizations made from the TLC3 data. However, the pattern is not consistent and most differences are not large. It simply reminds us that, if anything, our portrait understates the disadvantage of unmarried parents.

Conclusion

The TLC3 data are unique and exciting for a variety of reasons, including the innovative qualitative sampling design, the rich qualitative interview data, the longitudinal data, and the link to the quantitative Fragile Families and Child Wellbeing Survey. This chapter has shown that though some differences exist between TLC3 sample and the broader FFCWS study, TLC3's sampling design make us fairly confident that the couples in the qualitative sample are representative of romantically involved unmarried new parents in large cities throughout the country. Overall, the TLC3 data are an invaluable contribution to the study of the growing number of "fragile" families today.

Notes

1. I thank Paula England and Sara McLanahan for their thoughtful comments on this paper.

2. Important to note is that for comparison purposes the sample TLC3-eligible participants includes FFCWS participants from every city sampled for FFCWS. In other words, it is not limited to those from the three TLC3 cities, but all twenty.

3. The TLC3-eligible participants are those in the FFCWS study meeting five criteria: romantically involved or married at baseline, mother's household income did not exceed $75,000, father's interview not conducted in jail, neither interview conducted in Spanish, and with custody of the child.

4. One couple told the FFCWS interviewers that they were unmarried at the time of the baby's birth, but revealed later that they had been secretly married, though not living together. In analyses in this chapter, they are counted as unmarried. However, all our qualitative analyses in other chapters treat them as married at baseline because we are certain that they were.

5. At baseline, respondents were asked to identify a household income category, not a specific amount. At baseline for household income, respondents were asked their total household income before taxes in the previous twelve months.

They were then given a choice of categories: less than $5,000, $5,000 to $9,999, $10,000 to $14,999, $15,000 to $19,999, $20,000 to $24,999, $25,000 to $34,999, $35,000 to $49,999, $50,000 to $74,999, and more than $75,000. To report median household income, I assigned each individual the median income of the category that he or she identified. For those who identified the top category, I assigned an income value of 1.6 times the lowest income of that range, which approximates assuming the Pareto distribution for the right tail. At wave two, however, individuals were first asked a specific amount and only asked to identify an income category if they replied that they did not know or refused to give a specific amount. At wave two, if respondents could not or would not give a specific amount for their total household income, they were asked to identify a household income range. The range (different from baseline) was: less than $5,000, $5,001 to $10,000, $10,001 to $15,000, $15,001 to $20,000, $20,001 to $25,000, $25,001 to $30,000, $30,001 to $40,000, $40,001 to $60,000, or more than $60,000. Because at baseline respondents can have an income only as high as $120,000, the household income range at wave two is much greater.

6. At baseline, the total earnings of individuals are based on having the participant identify a range of possible earnings. Mothers were asked how much money they had received from earnings in the previous twelve months and given the following categories from which to choose: less than $1,000, $1,000 to $1,999, $2,000 to $2,999, $3,000 to $3,999, $4,000 to $4,999, $5,000 to $5,999, $6,000 to $6,999, $7,000 to $7,999, $8,000 to $8,999, $9,000 to $9,999, $10,000 to $12,499, $12,500 to $14,999, $15,000 to $17,999, 17,500 to $19,999, $20,000 to $25,000, and more than $25,000. Fathers were asked about how much they had earned from all of their regular jobs in the last twelve months. They were told to not count earnings from any off-the-books or under-the-table jobs and were given the following categories from which to choose: less than $5,000, $5,000 to $9,999, $10,000 to $14,999, $15,000 to $19,999, $20,000 to $24,999, $25,000 to $34,999, $35,000 to $49,999, $50,000 to $74,999, and more than $75,000. The response categories, it is important to note, differ slightly by gender of respondent. Here I assign mothers and fathers the median value of the category they identify. Those who identify the highest category for earnings (for mothers, more than $25,000, and for fathers, more than $75,000), I assign 1.6 times the bottom of the category, that is, $40,000 for mothers and $120,000 for fathers. At wave two, earnings are calculated quite differently. Mothers and fathers were asked an open-ended question about how much they usually earn before taxes and deductions for their main job. Responses varied from an amount per hour, per day, week, and so on. To transform this figure into yearly earnings, I use the individual's responses to questions about when he or she began the job, how many hours normally worked per week and per day. If mothers or fathers reported earnings greater than $150,000, they were recoded to $150,000. Separately, mothers and fathers were asked to identify their yearly earnings if they worked more than one job. Approximately 19 percent of fathers and 11 percent of mothers responded that they had done so in the previous twelve months. If they could not give an exact amount, they were given a range of earned incomes from

which to choose. I replaced their values for earned income with the median value of the category identified only if they were missing on the original exact-amount earnings variable.

7. No statistics are provided for relationship status and missing couple interviews in table 12.6. This is because the information is already provided in table 12.5. Relationship status is the only variable of the table in which the man and woman in a couple have equal scores by definition.

Index